Indefensible Space

Indefensible

The Architecture of the National Insecurity State

Space

Edited by MICHAEL SORKIN

Routledge
Taylor & Francis Group
New York   London

Routledge
Taylor & Francis Group
270 Madison Avenue
New York, NY 10016

Routledge
Taylor & Francis Group
2 Park Square
Milton Park, Abingdon
Oxon OX14 4RN

© 2008 by Michael Sorkin
Routledge is an imprint of Taylor & Francis Group, an Informa business

Printed in the United States of America on acid-free paper
10 9 8 7 6 5 4 3 2 1

International Standard Book Number-13: 978-0-415-95368-9 (Softcover) 978-0-415-95367-2 (Hardcover)

Library of Congress Cataloging-in-Publication Data

Sorkin, Michael, 1948-
    Indefensible space : the architecture of the national insecurity state / by Michael
Sorkin.
        p. cm.
    Includes bibliographical references.
    ISBN-13: 978-0-415-95368-9 (pbk.)
    ISBN-13: 978-0-415-95367-2 (cloth)
    1. Terrorism--United States--Prevention. 2. National security--United
States. 3. Civil defense--United States. 4. War on Terrorism, 2001- 5. United
States--Defenses--Public opinion. 6. Fear--Social aspects--United States. 7.
Paranoia--Social aspects--United States. I. Title.

HV6432.S695 2007
363.325'170973--dc22   2007009500

Visit the Taylor & Francis Web site at
http://www.taylorandfrancis.com

and the Routledge Web site at
http://www.routledge.com

Contents

Introduction
The Fear Factor

MICHAEL SORKIN

Across the street from the building where I have my studio is a massive, block-square federal building with separate entrances for the Passport Agency, Veterans Administration, Labor Department centers, and a post office. Although they have no identity on the street, a number of other agencies are also housed in the building and there are rumors of secret facilities, including a branch detention facility for terrorist suspects. Since 9/11, the building has been progressively fortified. Access to the Passport Agency requires an airport-style walk through a metal detector—shoes, belt, briefcase on the X-ray belt, proof of identity, and an appointment, guards everywhere. The building perimeter has been secured by a wall of bollards and massive concrete "planters." Exterior walls are festooned with CCTV cameras and a walk around the neighborhood reveals dozens more, inscrutably—but certainly—networked, and plans have recently been announced by the city to add additional thousands. Uniformed police are ubiquitous: New York City cops sit in a parked cruiser opposite the building, Port Authority officers constantly cruise by, federal police of various stripes man the entrances, and the cars and troopers of the new "Homeland Security" police lurk everywhere.

This scene increasingly repeats itself around the city, around the country, and around the world, part of an accelerating transformation of the built and political environments: for every bomb that falls on Iraq, it seems

20 bollards (generally with little actual defensive value) are added in front of yet another high value target at home—status symbols. America is in the grips of war fever, a delirium of suspicion and fear. A new Fortress America is being built but its bulwarks are not simply directed—like those bomb-proof planters—at a threat that can be physically externalized. The barrier turns inward as well, making each of us simultaneously soldier and suspect, enmeshed inextricably in the permanent warfare of all against us.

The number of American dead in Iraq has now passed the number killed on 9/11, with no end in sight. This melancholy marker signals both the militarization of the event for us and its radical civilianization for the people of Iraq, where as many as 100,000 have now died, victims of the chaos unleashed by our invasion or "collateral" damage from our violence. Back home, the "war" on terror with its opaque objectives and sinister rhetoric has also been transformative and the country takes on more and more aspects of a garrison state, defended by a labyrinth of intrusions that, relying on the constantly stoked paranoia over an invisible, shape-shifting, enemy, makes suspicion universal. The bugaboo is no longer "Reds under the beds" but illegal aliens, terrorists, perverts, Muslims, who legitimate the swelling Orwellian apparatus that pervades our national life.

9/11 was accelerant for processes long underway, a boon for the fear-mongering state and for our own al-Qa'eda, the "network" of global corporations that profits so handsomely from anti-terror operations. Constantly evoked as an unanswerable claim on our compliance, 9/11 has provided justification for a range of measures that have radically altered the character of daily life. The intrusion into bank records and phone calls. The biometric screening of international arrivals at airports. The mandatory DNA tests. The call for tamper-proof ID cards for aliens or their massive expulsion and the construction of a wall—and the deployment of troops—along the Mexican border to keep them from coming back. The appointment of a general to head the "civilian" CIA. The suspension of the right to trial and the growth of a global gulag for the incarceration of terror suspects, often "rendered" to states with less delicacy in matters of torture. The reconstruction of the cityscape with blast barriers, check-points, and other defensive architectures. The cameras. The sniffer dogs. The random searches. The robot drones circling soundlessly overhead.

And this is just the beginning. Owners have, for years, been able to obtain implants for their pets and livestock, subcutaneous microchips that—via GPS—locate roving dogs and cows within feet anywhere on the planet. Human implants of such radio frequency identity chips are underway, with the nominally benign initial "household" purpose of allowing keyless access to cars, computers, or medical records. Parents equip their kids with GPS cell-phones that allow their movements to be tracked at all times, a response to a general sense of danger, the threat posed by a variety of threatening others that lurk in the shadowland of our anxieties, bombers, kidnappers, molesters, gangs. Schools are guarded against Columbine-style terror attacks, giving children an early introduction to metal detectors and police oversight, to random searches of their bags and lockers, to the care they must take to avoid the telling remark or the foolish hyperbole that might appear to conceal an actual threat.

Following the arrest of an alleged terror "cell" in the spring of 2006, accused of plotting to blow up the Sears Tower in Chicago—America's current tallest building—Attorney General Gonzalez described the motley plan as "more aspirational than operational." The buffoonish group at the heart of the conspiracy had been aggressively manipulated by an FBI informant who organized their slap-stick recitation of an al-Qa'eda "pledge of allegiance" and took their shoe sizes to purchase the fashionable combat boots required to undertake the mission. Recent arrests of members of a group discussing the possibility of blowing up a tunnel under the Hudson River and flooding lower Manhattan was also preemptive: although this group seemed comprised of marginally more competent individuals than those accused of trying to bring down Sears, they, too, were just at the "talking stage." Like free speech, conspiracy is a usefully elastic concept.

Freedom of speech—the articulation, hence politicization, of freedom of thought—depends on the protection both of its contents and its sites: speech has no meaning unless it is heard. In the physical environment, democracy expresses itself in freedom of assembly, association, and movement, in what Henri Lefebvre has called "the right to the city." The steady ratcheting-up of constraints on this right marks the insinuation of a militarized network of command and control that constantly tests the limits of its authority. At one scale, the Department of Homeland Security's "National Asset Data Base" is an anticipatory (or aspirational) target list, a compilation of 77,000 sites that might figure in terrorist desires. The list appears ridiculous, including—among the bridges and power plants—the Amish Country Popcorn Factory, the Sweetwater Flea Market, and the Columbia Tennessee Mule Day Parade, and finding twice as many sites at risk in Indiana than in California. However, by publicizing the probabilistic absurdity of these places, a geography of paranoia is extended to embrace the most marginal and remote sites, drafting virtually any assembly into the regime of anxiety. A subsidiary benefit is to portray Homeland Security as Keystone-Copsish, an obvious far cry from anyone's Gestapo or KGB, taking the sting out of the existence of their lists.

Make no mistake, though: there are plenty who wish America ill, plenty ready to try to deliver, plenty angry at unexpected places: who could anticipate anthrax in the mail room of the *Star,* the shootings at Columbine, or the bodies under John Wayne Gacy's floorboards. This volume is not intended to debate our own responsibility in creating this animus—whether in the psychopathology of individuals or in the victimization of groups—rather to investigate what "we," and others, are doing in response to it and what those responses mean for us. Although "terrorism" has a long history and invariably exists in a context of grievance, this book seeks to avoid unanswerable questions of cause and "equivalence," weighing superior wrongs, original sin. The doomed outcome of such discussions is nowhere better exhibited than in the clogged conflict between Israel and Palestine in which attempts to assign differential responsibility—historically, ethically, metaphysically—are invariably manipulated to serve the purposes of intransigence. That situation is discussed in this book (which is mainly focused on U.S. examples and models) precisely because it is so exemplary, a field of experiment for advanced strategies of terror and control, filled with revelatory asymmetries. As the pious and arcane discussion of origins twists through its endless involutions, the technologies of repression do their dirty jobs and the web of hatred grows.

Political violence always seeks to justify itself, and the violence produced by the war on terror is no exception. The questions pursued here are primarily about the nature of that violence, the web of institutions and practices it produces, and the striking and coercive transformations in our physical and mental landscapes that are so profoundly coercive. There is a well-cultivated climate of fear in America and it registers at every level of our national life. This fear has its origins in both events and interests and the purpose of this collection is not to delve into this history in detail, rather to unpack some of its effects. These essays examine this mainly from the perspective of space, the kinds of rearrangements of the physical environment that mark an ongoing transition to a new set of conditions and constraints that have deep implications both for our habitat and our freedoms. In order to understand these physical shifts, it is also important to understand transformations in the enabling discourse of the environment, structures that march in the streets to produce arrangements observable on the ground. These include, among other things, a new theoretical intercourse between urban and military theory, a shift in seeing that remakes both our own cities and those of our "adversaries" according to the values of war, rather than community, and a growing *newspeak* lexicon to insulate us from the real meaning of events.

There are a number of classic texts that anticipate the paranoid, militarized, character of this contemporary space. A dystopian literary tradition—from George Orwell's *1984* to Philip K. Dick's *Minority Report*—has portrayed the physical and mental media of totalitarian control with scary prescience. Cinematic science fiction—from *Metropolis* to *Blade Runner* to

Star Wars to *The Truman Show,* the most telling medium for the projective imagination of city life—has, for years, given us almost nothing but nightmares, irresistible portraits of a creepy future, of pervasive mind control, dangerous and alienating spaces, concentrated power, endless violence, and cultural flatness against which the only recourse is death. The images surely dance in the stunted imaginations of Bush and Bin Laden both, two rich men decked out as warriors—flyboy or jihadist—with the semiotic panache of an Edith Head. In a world of total media, image is prophecy.

Michel Foucault has founded what is perhaps the central metaphor for contemporary dystopian space (one that hovers over many of these essays): the Panopticon, Jeremy Bentham's proposal for a model prison built as a ring of cells supervised by an unseen jailor in a guard box at the center of the circle. The Panopticon is both a resonant symbol of the systems of surveillance that leave no corner of the earth unseen and of the mental life that they produce. The genius of the panoptic scheme lay less in its efficient supervisory geometry than in invisibility of the eyes at its center. Once the prisoners had been inculcated with the idea of their perpetual exposure, the prison could function even when the guard was absent. Persuaded that there was no escape from the gaze of authority, prisoners internalized the means of their own repression and behaved *as if* they were being watched, even without any concrete evidence that they were.

The idea of spatial arrangements as tools of control has a long history. The practices of architecture and urbanism—like that of so many human practices—are an endless dialectic of both physical and representational effects, invariably political in the concreteness with which they diagram social relations. Spaces of freedom—from the Athenian *polis,* to the cities of the Hanseatic League, to the barricaded streets of the Paris Commune, to Woodstock—offer empowered, if contested, images of constructed environments. Modernism, spawn of the Enlightenment, was—and is— suffused with narcissistic rationality and its rhetoric rang with reform. Building was to be a means of radical redistribution, providing access not simply to sunny, safe, and sanitary dwellings in a world in which everyone worked, and happily, but the crucible from which the "New Man"—the universal subject—was to emerge.

The urban project of modernism had, as its stimulating antagonist, the vision of the industrial city of the nineteenth century, with it darkness and filth, its enslavement of the working class to the machinery of production and the horrible circumstances of daily life under Mammon's foot. Modernism's relationship to the parallel emergence of the bourgeois city was a shade more ambivalent. Here was a place of sumptuary inequality at once entrancing and fraught, simultaneously dedicated to private consumption and filled with spaces of public life. The boulevards and cafes, the department stores and electric light, the crowds and the movement, required new subjects, new behaviors, new analysis, new politics. Captivated and distressed, its great observers—Poe, Dreiser, Simmel, Beaudelaire, Wharton, Benjamin, Marx, Flaubert—understood the rapidity with which new sites for both freedom and constraint were being produced by it. The model citizens of the city—the detective, the *flanneur,* the clerk, the bohemian, the shopper—peopled a discourse in which space and behavior were both entangled and autonomous.

These complex antinomies of degradation and pleasure, liberation and control, openness and defense, form the imaginative substrate for the formal study of the city and for the emergence of modern urban planning that took place during the nineteenth and twentieth centuries. Successively codified and inflected in the field, these practices assumed both that the city could be understood—demographically, economically, sociologically, ecologically, politically, morphologically—and, by extension, that it could be designed to achieve these effects. Although issues of control of both internal and external disorder and contamination have been part of the history of cities from the first and have registered physically in the form of walls, castles, passages, turnstiles, cathedrals, plazas, aqueducts, coliseums, dungeons, and the rest of the infrastructure of urban construction, the combination of the totalizing style of rationalism, the appearance of a population of modern urban subjects, the dramatic increase in the scale of urbanization, the availability of new technologies of movement, communication, and hygiene, and the rise of bureaucratic systems of urban governance and management, engendered a radical shift in ideas about what the city could be and what it could do.

As many will have recognized, the title of this volume evokes Oscar Newman's *Defensible Space* of 1973. Subtitled "Crime Prevention through Urban Design," Newman's book was part of a broader critique of the public housing projects of postwar urban renewal, increasingly seen as vertical ghettoes and—like the environments they were meant to "cure"—more and more ravaged by crime. Like Jane Jacobs, who argued in her 1961 *Death and Life of Great American Cities* that a vital neighborhood ecology required the constant presence of the benign "eyes on the street" provided by shopkeepers, pedestrians, and intimate scale, Newman believed that the key to a safe environment lay in a sense of its tractability and control. His prescriptions for "defensible" places were about physical means of establishing a sense of proprietorship for individuals via articulate hierarchies of public and private, careful modulations of visibility, and clarity of intended use.

Although Newman's analysis originated in a liberal perspective, and while many of his prescriptions made sense—particularly in their desire to promote architectures that would affirm individual identity and control—the book has a disquietingly behaviorist aura, raises many problematic questions about the relationship of community and privacy (and of medium and message), and—by emphasizing the physical—mislocates larger issues. He praises, for example, the architecture of a middle-class urban renewal scheme on the South Side of Chicago (much reviled by Jacobs) while ignoring the context of the removal of a poor population previously on site. He proposes a system of "natural surveillance through electronic devices" for a New York City housing project but suggests it be monitored by "tenant patrols." The fallacy lies in the imagined eternity of good intentions, in the notion of technology's neutrality, in the idea that, treated properly, Big Brother can be a helpful guy.

While Newman's work may have been well intended, his project carried on the larger idea of an instrumental architecture, able to conduce forms of good behavior, a project embodied in the founding rationality of the same failed housing projects Newman sought to reform, not to mention the Panopticon itself. Although the line between empowerment and manipulation can be fine, design culture today is again shot through with a sense of the preventive dimension of its practices and—especially since 9/11—virtually every aspect is being reimagined from the perspective of threat, whether of terrorism, criminal intrusion, environmental decay, or giant hurricanes. Articulated as completely comparable to measures to assure fire safety or structural integrity in buildings, this threat resistance is naturalized by association with these unarguable operations, as if there were a universal equivalence in risk between earthquakes and machine gun attacks.

One of the more sinister locutions of the effort to co-opt planning and design for national security purposes is the "deputizing" of ordinary objects to do double duty as barriers. The proliferation of blast-proof planters, bollard phalanxes, and beefed-up street lamps represents the same instrumental mentality that helped inform Newman's work, now dramatically modified by a very different threat and a very different set of objectives. In both practices, though, the presumption of danger becomes the defining criterion for planning: a high level of risk is always assumed and everything that follows is simply tactical. It is part of the astute manipulation by the operatives of the Insecurity State that the discussion of its methods always seems to engage the very risks they pose to our liberties as a way of forestalling any question of their larger necessity. I have just gotten off the phone with a reporter from *USA Today* who has called for my opinion about the *design* of bollards, about whether their unsightliness might be mitigated by greater use of the more inconspicuous CCTV. I have told her that this is like asking whether the cells at Guantánamo should be wallpapered or carpeted, that the problem with the prison is not the design but the fact. And so we are left answering questions about how the medium of security should present itself, the visible cameras versus the hidden ones, the uniformed cop versus the one in plain clothes, the obvious barrier versus the more behavioral one, how *much* freedom to give up for the sake of "security." Proportionality is an issue that arises only *after* the surrender to fear.

The struggle over the roll-out of the National Insecurity State must engage whether it is really necessary–defensible—and the question of to whom its benefits are actually addressed. Halliburton stock is doing nicely. The Department of Homeland Security is hemorrhaging personnel to the go-go private security sector, to creepy corporations founded on lucrative anxiety like Fortress America, Civitas Group, Roam Secure, Good Harbor Consulting, Shifting Culture, ChoicePoint, Global Secure, Cross Match Technology, as well as to historic defense heavies such as Lockheed Martin, GE, or Unisys. The lacuna in national purpose opened by the end of the Cold War is being filled by a recontoured military-security-industrial-infotainment complex, even as Kim Jong Il—as if on signal—lofts his dud missiles to rejuvenate the languishing Star Wars program. The intelligence "community" sees its resources and possibilities expanding exponentially. Hundreds of billions of dollars are pumped down this pipeline, diverting attention and resources from other risks—disease, environmental degradation, mass starvation, automobile accidents, killers on a scale that makes the aggregate effects of terrorism microscopic, however focusing they may be for collective anxiety.

Although the threat of "terror" is surely real, this volume questions its location and weighs the relationship between its plausible danger and the nature of our response. The "homeland" has not been attacked since 9/11 but it is not clear whether this is the product of increased vigilance (signaled by periodic announcements of the interception of some unspecified threat or the presentation of "aspirational" conspirators nipped in the bud) or simply *post hoc ergo propter hoc*. In either case, the credibility of the threat barometer depends on persuasive evidence of the imminence of mass destruction. Absent any at home, the administration and the media rely on a pathetic displacement. Images of the horrific carnage in Iraq, of the daily car bombs, IEDs, suicide attacks, and mass murders, are leveraged by a fallacious logic to suggest that if it weren't happening there, it would be here. And what if we were to leave Iraq and bombs failed to go off on Broadway?

Cultures produce the threats they need and the "war on terror" is part of a larger project of fear-fed manipulations that is a profound danger to our rights and possibilities. This book is conceived in alarm and, looking at the spaces around us, it seeks to focus attention on the rapid institutionalization of a series of protocols and arrangements that—in the guise of offering us "comfort"—narrow the terms of our freedom of association, interaction, and choice. We are being trained to be phobic, to be constantly on guard, to stay at home, to be wary of difference. Gated communities and the homogeneities of gentrification provide "safe" communities via radical resegregation. American houses grow exponentially larger, laced with security and communications devices, demanding a protective indolence and estranging us from neighborliness. Architectures of vague nostalgia reassure us of the vitality and relevance of family values and less dangerous times and call other forms of expression—sexual, artistic, political—into question. Surveillance is everywhere.

Scare tactics are nothing new. My own first exposure to the architecture of state-sponsored terror came during the Cold War days. After the repeated duck-and-cover training that began in grammar school, after the school visit to the neighborhood Nike missile site, after an afternoon of frantically trying to dig a fallout shelter in the backyard, I had been thoroughly introduced to a style of paranoia, the well-named dread specific to the day. That complex of fears—much like today's—had enormous consequences for the investment of the national wealth, the definition of a population of irredeemable others who viewed us with pure, unreasoned, malevolence, and the deepening suspicion of the presence of an invisible seam of traitors that could only be detected through police-state scrutiny and a manly disdain for civil liberties, privacy, and freedom from fear of the Big Other. It had also, in part, dictated the pattern of the suburbs where I lived. Encouraged by national subsidy for highways and mortgages, the suburbs were, *inter alia,* a settlement pattern created to promote a protective dispersion of population, to vitiate the effects of the A-bomb.

Paul Virilio has written about the relationship of warfare and the scopic—the weapon and the eye—the cinematic view from above that has universalized the planet as a target. One is amazed and appalled by assassinations carried out by American and Israeli robot planes, firing missiles through the windows of cars or apartments, but quickly understands that this is the contemporary projection of panoptic power: to be seen is to be dead. In the words of former U.S. Defense Secretary William Perry, "once you can see the target, you can expect to destroy it." The willing surrender of our privacy because of the blandishments of an illusory fear makes us all targets, of suspicion, of attack. Because of new technologies of intrusion, architecture is rapidly losing its primal role as a barrier to seeing.

Hellfire missiles are just part of the threat. The symmetries between our networks of consumption and surveillance, between A. J. Nielsen and the NSA, are not simply technological coincidences. A legion of spooks is trying to corner Osama with the same cookies that flood my computer with Spam. Bin Laden's star power—the clarity of his brand—makes the whole thing go, works for both sides with equal effect. This is the meaning of "brandscape": the environment is becoming a field of choices controlled from the top, in which the power of the image is everything. As neoliberal economics reorganizes the planet into a unitary field of consumption, our choices become at once limitless and nil. Terrorism usefully inspires acquiescence in the rules and regs, the disciplines that come with living under siege. To escape the bombers, the child molesters, the alien hordes, the pathogenic atmosphere, the implacable misery of a world of inexplicable, raging, irrational, uncivilized others, we rip off our clothes for Panopticon, the price we pay for being safe. The terror and the violence, in its very randomness, also reassures us that accidents can still happen, that Big Brother (how dangerous could that idiot Bush be?) is not really in control, that we still have room.

The surfeit of physicality of bombing and warfare, directed at the destruction of living flesh, lives in balance with the disembodied world of virtual and conceptual space. This fundamentally new condition informs the so-called revolution in military affairs, a fantasy tenaciously installed by the Rumsfeld Pentagon, in which warfare, conducted by remote control, is to have no effect on our own human "assets," only on the enemy other, still living in his or her own skin. But, because of a disturbing symmetry in asymmetrical warfare, the enemy flashes through the Web, self-organizing digital agency with an "improvised" explosion at the end. And so we must also police communications and ideas in their ethereal, disembodied, transactions—any one of which might be suspect—justified by the risk they pose to our bodies, ourselves. Are we surprised that the spectral Osama remains "uncaught" while simultaneously appearing everywhere? Because he is loose in hyperspace, we have reason to extend our domination—put our boots on the ground and our ears to the ether—to the ends of the earth and the spectrum. We sanction his free expression (despite occasional tepid cavils about Al Jazeera) in order to more effectively repress our own. Every tape that slips from his cave adds another layer to the form and meaning of the Insecurity State.

A recently passed Florida law forbids sex offenders from living within 1000 feet of a school bus stop, effectively excluding them from almost every community in the state. It's classic zoning, red-lining the landscape with territories of exclusion. We have long segregated Native Americans, African Americans, Asian Americans, poor Americans with the authoritative rigor of "planning," protecting privilege by the construction of reservations, ghettos, internment camps, prisons, and gated communities. We have segregated female Americans in inviolate homes where many have endured the special terrorism of domestic violence. We have skillfully demonized recognizable groups—Irish, Blacks, Jews, immigrants—for their criminal potential, placing them under discriminatory scrutiny. Our tactics of selective repression are so well developed, they simply appear to be part of the landscape.

What makes the new war on terror more singular—more sinister—is that the convergence of unsettling fear, shadowy demonized foe, hyper-technology of ubiquitous reach, and the communal power of the corporate state, has truly globalized the condition of fear. If every space is susceptible to attack and every person a potential attacker, then the only recourse is to watch everyone and fortify everyplace. If every communication is potentially a fragment of conspiracy, then all must be recorded. Walking the streets nowadays, with troops at the subway entrance, barricades around buildings, cameras staring from lamp-posts, metal detectors and card-swipes at the office door, cops profuse, newsstands billboarding alerts from every cover, involuntary anxiety at the sight of handbags and kerchiefs, it feels—more and more—like the battle for freedom is being lost. This book seeks to be part of the defense.

Cities and the 'War on Terror'

STEPHEN GRAHAM

Introduction

Programs of organized, political violence have always been legitimized and sustained through complex imaginative geographies. This term—following Foucault (1970), Said (1978) and Gregory (1995)—denotes the ways in which imperialist societies tend to be constructed through normalizing, binary judgments about both foreign and colonized territories and the home spaces which sit at the heart of empire. Edward Said (1978, 2003), for example, argues that imaginative geographies were crucial in sustaining Orientalist treatments of the Arab world as Other among Western colonial powers. Such imaginative geographies, as Derek Gregory (2004: 18) puts it, work by "fold[ing] distance into difference through a series of spatializa-tions." They operate "by multiplying partitions and enclosures that serve to demarcate 'the same' from 'the other.'" And, as "imaginations given substance," or "architectures of emnity," they do geopolitical work by des-ignating the familiar space inhabited by a putative 'us,' and opposing it to unfamiliar geographies inhabited by the putative Other—the 'them' who become the target for military or colonial power (ibid.).

Imaginative geographies thus tend to be characterized by stark binaries of place attachment. These tend to be particularly powerful and uncom-promising during times of war. As Ken Hewitt (1983: 258) has argued, "War [...] mobilizes the highly charged and dangerous dialectic of place attachment: the perceived antithesis of 'our' places or homeland and 'theirs.'" Very often, such polarizations are manufactured and recycled

1

discursively through racist and imperial discourses and propaganda which emanate from both formal state and other media sources. These work to produce "an unbridled sentimentalizing of one's own while dehumanizing the enemy's people and land" (ibid.). To Hewitt, such binaried constructions "seem an essential step in cultivating readiness to destroy the latter" (1983: 258).

The purpose of this chapter is to demonstrate that the Bush administration's war on terror rests fundamentally on such two-sided constructions of (particularly urban) place. The essay argues that the discursive construction of the 'war on terror' since September 11, 2001, has been deeply marked by attempts to rework imaginative geographies separating the urban places of the U.S. homeland and those Arab cities purported to be the sources of 'terrorist' threats against U.S. national interests. Such reworkings of popular and political imaginative geographies have worked by projecting places, and particularly cities, into two mutually exclusive, mutually constitutive, classifications: those, in Bush's famous phrase, who are either "with us" or "against us" [*sic*] (see Graham, 2004).

In a world of intensifying transnational migration, transport, capital, and media flows, however, such attempts at constructing a mutually exclusive binary—a securitized inside enclosing the urban places of the U.S. Empire's homeland, and an urbanizing outside where U.S. military power can preemptively attack places deemed sources of terrorist threats—are inevitably ambivalent. They are also full of internal contradictions. Binaried portrayals suggesting an absolute separateness between 'homeland' cities and the Arab cities of the target Other rest alongside the ratcheting up of state surveillance and repression against Others targeted *within* U.S. cities and society. They are paralleled, as we shall see later in this chapter, by military strategies which increasingly treat the inside spaces within the United States and the foreign ones in the rest of the world as an integrated battlespace prone to the rapid movements of terrorist threats into the geographical and urban heartlands of U.S. power at any instant. They obscure the geographies that tie predatory postwar reconstruction contracts in Iraq and homeland security contracts in U.S. cities to the same cartel of Bush-friendly private military corporations. And they are contradicted by neoconservative geopolitical ideologies that, ironically, stress the importance of deeply connecting of countries deemed to be hotbeds of threats to U.S. interests into processes of neoliberal globalization (see Barnett, 2004; Roberts et al., 2003).

Although dramatic, the imaginative geographies underpinning the war on terror are far from original. In fact they revivify long-established colonial and Orientalist tropes to represent Middle Eastern culture as intrinsically barbaric, infantile, backward or threatening from the point of view of Western colonial powers (Gregory, 2004a). Arab cities, moreover, have long been represented by Western powers as dark, exotic, labyrinthine, and structureless places that need to be 'unveiled' for the production of order through the superior scientific, planning and military technologies of the occupying West. By burying "disturbing similarities between 'us' and 'them' in a discourse that systematically produces the Third World as Other," such Orientalism deploys considerable symbolic violence (Guster-son, 1999). This is done, crucially, in order to produce both "the Third World" and "the West" (ibid.).

The Bush administration's language of moral absolutism is, in particular, deeply Orientalist. It works by separating the civilized world—the home-land cities which must be defended—from the "dark forces," the "axis of evil," and the "terrorists nests" of Arab cities, which allegedly sustain the evildoers who threaten the health, prosperity, and democracy of the whole of the free world (Tuastad, 2003). The result of such imaginative geogra-phies is an historical, essentialized, and deeply Orientalist projection of Arab civilization that is very easily worked to "recycle the same unverifi-able fictions and vast generalizations to stir up 'America' against the for-eign devil" (Said, 2003: vi). The Orientalist notions of racial worth that helped to shape the real and imagined geographies of Western colonial-ism are particularly important foundations for the war on terror (Gregory, 2004a). As Paul Gilroy suggests, these:

> old, modern notions of racial difference appear once again to be active within the calculus [of the 'war on terror'] that tacitly assigns differential value to lives lost according to their locations and sup-posed racial origins or considers that some human bodies are more easily and appropriately humiliated, imprisoned, shackled, starved and destroyed than others. (2003: 263)

Discourses of 'terrorism' are crucially important in sustaining such dif-ferential values and binaried notions of human worth (Collins and Glover, 2002). Central here is the principle of the absolute eternality of the 'terror-ist'—the inviolable inhumanity and shadowy, monster-like status of those deemed to be actual or dormant 'terrorists' or those sympathetic to them (Puar & Rai, 2002). The unbound diffusion of terrorist labeling within the rhetoric of the 'war on terror,' moreover, works to allow virtually any polit-ical opposition to the sovereign power of the United States and its allies to be condemned as 'terrorist' or addressed through emergency antiterror-ist legislation. Protagonists of such opposition are thus easily dehuman-ized, demonized, and, above all, delegitimized. "Without defined shape, or determinate roots," Derek Gregory writes, the mantle of terrorism can now be "be cast over *any* form of resistance to sovereign power" (2003: 219, original emphasis).

In such a context, this chapter traces in detail the ways in which the deep-rooted dialectics of place attachment, and the imaginative geographies of cities that fuel them, are at the very heart of the war on terror. To achieve this, the chapter addresses three particularly important aspects of what we might call the *urban* imaginative geographies which sustain the war on terror. These are: the reworking of imaginative geographies of U.S. cities as homeland cities that must be reengineered to address supposed imperatives of national security; the intensified imaginative construction of Arab cities as little more than terrorist nest targets to soak up U.S. military firepower; and the increasingly integrated treatment of both homeland and target cities within contemporary U.S. military doctrine and techno-science.

Reimagining 'Homeland' Cities as National Security Spaces

> "Everything and everywhere is perceived as a border from which a potentially threatening Other can leap" (Hage, 2003: 86)

The first key element in the imaginative geographies of the 'war on terror' is an appeal by the Bush administration to securitize the everyday urban spaces and technics of a newly "rebordered" U.S. homeland (Lutz, 2002). Here, discourses of 'security,' emphasizing endless threats from an almost infinite range of people, places and technologies, are being used to justify a massive process of state building. Widespread efforts are being made by U.S. political, military, and media elites in order to "spread [...] generalized promiscuous anxiety through the American populace, a sense of imminent but inexact catastrophe" lurking just beneath the surface of normal, technologized, (sub)urbanized, everyday life in the United States (Raban, 2004: 7). Despite the unavoidable and continuing interconnections between U.S. cities and more or less distant elsewheres, "the rhetoric of 'insides' needing protection from external threats in the form of international organizations is pervasive" (Dalby, 2000: 5). This reimagining of homeland cities involves at least four simultaneous processes.

The Domestic Front in the War on Terror

First, the Homeland Security drive is being organized as a purported attempt to protect those "insides"—the bodies and everyday spaces of valued, nonthreatening, legitimate U.S. citizens—from demonized Others apparently lurking, armed with a wide range of threatening technologies and pathogens, both within and outside U.S. national space. Fuelled by the larger mobilization of terrorist discourses discussed earlier, and the blurring of the boundary separating law enforcement from state military activity (Kraska, 2001), this process has "activate[d] a policing of points of vulnerability against an enemy who inheres within the space of the U.S." (Passavant & Dean, 2002, cited in Gregory, 2003). The enemy here is constructed as dormant terrorists and their sympathizers, a rhetoric that easily translates—in the context of the wider portrayals of the homeland at war against secretive and unknowable Others—into an overall crackdown on criticism and dissent, or those simply deemed to be insufficiently patriotic. As a result, to put it mildly, "cosmopolitan estrangement and democracy-enriching dissent are not being prized as civic assets" in the United States (or the United Kingdom) in the early twenty-first century (Gilroy, 2003: 266).

A domestic front has thus been drawn in Bush's war on terror. Sally Howell and Andrew Shryock (2003) call this a "cracking down on diaspora." This process involves deepening state surveillance and violence against those seen to harbor 'terrorist threats,' combined with radically increased efforts to ensure the effective filtering power of national and infrastructural borders. After decades during which the business press and politicians endlessly celebrated the supposed collapse of boundaries (at least for mobile capital) through neoliberal globalization, "in both political debates and policy practice, borders are very much back in style" (Andreas, 2003: 1). Once again, Western nations—and the securitized cities now seen once again to sit hierarchically within their dominant territorial patronage—are being normatively imagined as bounded, organized spaces with closely controlled, and filtered, relationships with the supposed terrors ready to destroy them at any instant from the outside world. In the United States, for example, national immigration, border control, transportation, and social policy strategies have been remodeled since 9/11 in an:

> attempt to reconstitute the [United States] as a bounded area that can be fortified against outsiders and other global influences. In this imagining of nation, the U.S. ceases to be a constellation of local, national, international, and global relations, experiences, and meanings that coalesce in places like New York City and Washington DC; rather, it is increasingly defined by a 'security perimeter' and the strict surveillance of borders. (Hyndman, 2003: 2)

Securitizing Everyday Spaces and Systems

As well as further militarizing national territorial borders, the U.S. homeland security drive is also attempting to reengineer the basic everyday systems and spaces of U.S. urban life—even if this is sometimes a stealthy and largely invisible process. As a result, urban public life is being saturated by intelligent surveillance systems, checkpoints, defensive urban design and planning strategies, and intensifying security (Johnson, 2002; Williams, 2003). In the wake of 9/11, and the Homeland Security drive, the design of buildings and streets, the management of traffic, the physical planning of cities, building zoning, migration and refugee policy, transportation policing, the design of social policies for ethnically diverse cities and neighborhoods, even the lending policies of neighborhood libraries, are being brought within the widening umbrella of U.S. homeland security.

In cities such as Washington, DC, new (and tellingly titled) "urban design and security plans" have been brought in. These emphasize that one of the most important objectives of public urban planning in such strategic centers is now the hardening of all possible terrorist targets. Once again, it seems, geopolitical and strategic concerns are directly shaping the day-to-day practices of U.S. urban professionals. Jonathan Raban, writing of everyday life in post–9/11 Seattle, captures the palpable effects of this militarization on urban everyday life and landscape:

> To live in America now, at least to live in a port city like Seattle—is to be surrounded by the machinery and rhetoric of covert war, in which everyone must be treated as a potential enemy until they can prove themselves a friend. Surveillance and security devices are everywhere: the spreading epidemic of razor wire, the warnings in public libraries that the FBI can demand to know that books you're borrowing, the Humvee laden with troops in combat fatigues, the Coast Guard gun boats patrolling the bay, the pat-down searches and X-ray machines, the nondescript grey boxes equipped with radar antennae, that are meant to sniff pathogens in the air. (2004: 6)

U.S. Cities Within Anti-Cosmopolitan Constructions of "Homeland"

This attempted reconstruction of national boundaries, as well as being sustained by material and technological investments in and around strategic urban spaces, relies on considerable linguistic work (Kaplan, 2003: 85). For example, during his tenure, Tom Ridge, the first U.S. Secretary of Homeland Security (2003–2005), widely invoked metaphors linking soil, turf or territoriality with some essentialized, idealized, and implicitly homogeneous notion of a national U.S. community. On one occasion, he pronounced that "the only turf is the turf we stand on" (cited in Kaplan, 2003: 85). This rebordered discourse constructs an imaginary, domesticated, singular, and spatially fixed imagined community of U.S. nationhood (Andreas & Biersteker, 2003). Such an imagined community—tied intrinsically to some purported, familial, turf—centers on valorizing an exclusive, separated, and privileged population. It therefore contrasts starkly with previous U.S. state rhetoric that centered on notions of boundless mobility, assimilation, and the national 'melting pot' identity (Kaplan, 2003: 86).

Such discourses are central to reimagining the actual and normative geographies of what contemporary U.S. urban life actually consists of or what it might become. Amy Kaplan, in analyzing the languages of Homeland Security, detects a "decidedly antiurban and anticosmopolitan ring" to this upsurge of nationalism after 9/11 (2003: 88). Paul Gilroy goes further and suggests that the widespread invocation by the Bush administration, following Huntington (1993), of the idea of a clash of civilizations, necessarily *requires* that cosmopolitan consciousness is ridiculed" in the pronouncements of the U.S. state and the mainstream media (2003: 266, emphasis added). Post–9/11, he diagnoses a pervasive "inability to conceptualize multicultural and postcolonial relations as anything other than ontological risk and ethnic jeopardy" (ibid.: 261).

The very term *homeland security*, in fact, serves to rework the imaginative geographies of contemporary U.S. urbanism in important ways. It shifts the emphasis away from complex and mobile diasporic social formations, sustaining large metropolitan areas through complex transnational connections, toward a much clearer mapping that demarcates clear, essentialized geographies of entitlement and threat. At many scales—from neighborhoods, through cities and nations to the international—this separation works to define those citizens who are deemed to warrant value and the full protection of citizenship, and those deemed threatening as real or potential sources of terrorism: the targets for the blossoming national security state.

As Amy Kaplan suggests (2003: 84), even the very word *homeland* itself suggests some "inexorable connection to a place deeply rooted in the past." It necessarily problematizes the inherently diverse and mobile fabric of the diasporas that actually constitutes the social fabric of U.S. urbanism. Such language offers a "folksy rural quality, which combines a German romantic notion of the folk with the heartland of America to resurrect the rural myth of American identity" (ibid.: 88). At the same time, she argues that it precludes "an urban vision of America as multiple turfs with contested points of view and conflicting grounds upon which to stand" (ibid.: 88).

Such a discourse is particularly problematic in global cities such as New York, constituted as they are by massive and unknowably complex constellations of diasporic social groups. "In what sense," asks Kaplan (2003: 84), "would New Yorkers refer to their city as the homeland? Home, yes, but homeland. Not likely." Ironically, even the grim casualty lists of 9/11 revealed the impossibility of separating some purportedly pure, inside, or homeland city from the wider international flows and connections that now constitute cities like New York—even with massive state surveillance and violence. Forty-four nationalities were represented on that list—many of whom were 'illegal' residents in New York City. "If it existed, any comfortable distinction between domestic and international, here and there, us and them, ceased to have meaning after that day" (Hyndman, 2003: 1). As Tim Watson writes:

> global labor migration patterns have [...] brought the world to lower Manhattan to service the corporate office blocks: the dishwashers, messengers, coffee-cart vendors, and office cleaners were Mexican, Bangladeshi, Jamaican and Palestinian. One of the tragedies of September 11th 2001 was that it took such an extraordinary event to reveal the everyday reality of life at the heart of the global city. (2003: 109)

Posthumously, however, mainstream U.S. media have overwhelmingly suggested that the dead from 9/11 were a relatively homogeneous body of patriotic U.S. nationals. The cosmopolitanism of the dead have, increasingly, been obscured amid the shrill, nationalist discourses of war. The complex ethnic geographies of a preeminently global city—as revealed in this grizzly snapshot—have thus faded from view since Hyndman and Watson wrote those words. The deep social and cultural connections between U.S. cities and the cities in the Middle East that quickly emerged as the prime targets for U.S. military and surveillance power after 9/11, have, similarly, been rendered largely invisible. In short, New York's "transnational urbanism" (Smith, 2001), revealed so starkly by the bodies of the dead after 9/11, seems to have submerged beneath the overwhelming power of nationally oriented state, military and media discourses.

Homeland security policies also have been associated with a considerable growth in state and nonstate violence against immigrant and Arab American groups. Indeed, "the notion of the homeland itself contributes to making the life of immigrants terribly insecure" (Kaplan, 2003: 87). Here the treatment of individual Arab Americans is quickly conflated to the wider representation of whole urban districts and neighborhoods as zones that undermine the simple binaries of the dominant imaginative geographies of us and them, and so necessitate particularly intense mobilizations of state power. Systematic state repression and mass incarceration have thus been brought to bear on Arab-American neighborhoods such as Dearbon in Detroit—the first place to have its own, local, office of Homeland Security (Howell & Shryock, 2003). Such Arab-American neighborhoods are now overwhelmingly portrayed in the U.S. national media as "zones of threat." Arab Americans are widely represented as "clearly being in" their local cities and "with us," but the point is almost always stressed, as Howell and Shryock (2002: 444) put it, that "their hearts might still be over there, 'with them.'" Thousands of U.S. citizens also have effectively been stripped of any notion of value, to be thrown into extra- or intraterritorial camps as suspect terrorists for potentially indefinite periods of time, without trial. Such people face the constant threat of torture or "rendition" in a covert CIA plane to a covert U.S. base in a friendly state where torture is common-place. More than ever, then, the discourses and practices of the war on ter-ror work to make "'Arab' and 'American' all but antithetical adjectives" (Watson, 2003). As we shall see shortly, this situation is immutably bound up with the widespread demonization of Middle Eastern and Arab cities, and their inhabitants, more generally within war on terror discourses.

Everyday Sites and Spaces as Sources of (Terrorist) Fear

The final element of the homeland security drive is the production of per-manent anxiety around everyday urban spaces, systems, and events that previously tended to be banalized, taken for granted or ignored in U.S. urban everyday life (Luke, 2004). With streams of vague warnings, omni-present color-coded alerts, and saturation media coverage of purported threats to U.S. urban life, everyday events, malfunctions or acts of violence in the city—which would previously have been seen as the results of local social problems, individual pathologies, bureaucratic failings, or simple accidents—are now widely assumed be the results of terrorist action. The homeland is thus cast in terms of a constant state of emergency (Armitage, 2002). In this the only things that can be guaranteed are new sources of fear, calls for further intensifications of extralegal domestic scrutiny and surveil-lance, and oscillations on the Department of Homeland Security's color-coded threat monitor. In the process, parked vans, delayed trains, envelopes with white powder, people with packages, Arab-looking people, colds and flu, low-flying aircraft, electricity outages, stacks of shipping containers, computer glitches, IT viruses, and subway derailments are now sources of mass anxiety. Homeland security, thus, depends, ironically, on a radical and perpetual sense of *in*security. This fuels acceptance that the everyday sites and spaces of daily life within the continental U.S. must now be viewed as battlegrounds—the key sites within a new, permanent, and boundless war.

Cindi Katz (2004) notes a palpable "routinization of terror talk and the increasing ordinariness of its physical markers" within U.S. cities since 9/11. She argues that such processes generate a radical ontologi-cal insecurity because they create pervasive feelings of vulnerability and threat through the material assemblages which necessarily underpin, and saturate, everyday urban life. In the process, such terror talk helps to define reimagined communities of nationhood as well as normative imaginative geographies of homeland and target cities. As Giroux (2003: ix) suggests, "notions of community [in the United States] are now organized not only around flag-waving displays of patriotism, but also around collective fears and ongoing militarization of visual culture and public space."

Ironically, however, as the Katrina disaster in New Orleans demonstrated so starkly, the endless fetishization of the need to "securitize" everyday urban sites in U.S. cities from terrorist risk has been paralleled by a growing exposure of U.S. urban citizens to nonterrorist risks such as floods, earthquakes, fires, and hurricanes. Funding programs addressing such natural hazards have been cut to fund counterterrorist strategies. Expertise has dwindled as emergency management personnel have become disillusioned with their new place subsumed within a terrorist-oriented Department of Homeland Security (DHS) behemoth. And leadership capabilities have collapsed as Bush has appointed inexperienced cronies to key DHS posts (see Graham, 2006a).

Terror Cities: Orientalist Constructions of Arab Urban Places as Military Targets

This leads us to the second focus of our discussion: an analysis of the way in which (selected) Arab cities are being overwhelmingly constructed within 'war on terror' discourses as targets for U.S. military firepower. Far from being isolated from the securitization of U.S. cities, this process is inseparable from it. As Edward Said (2003: xxiii) stressed just before his death, from the point of view of the discursive foundations of both U.S. foreign policy and dominant portrayals of Arabs in the U.S. media, the devaluation and dehumanization of people in the target cities of the Arab world cannot be separated from the securitization of the (re)imagined communities in homeland ones. As the Iraq invasion was prepared, Said wrote that "without a well-organized sense that these people over there were not like 'us' and didn't appreciate 'our' values—the very core of the Orientalist dogma—there would have been no war" in Iraq. Thus, crucially, a powerful relation exists:

> between securing the homeland against encroachment of foreign terrorists and enforcing [U.S.] national power abroad. The homeland may contract borders around a fixed space of the nation and nativity, but it simultaneously also expands the capacity of the United States to move unilaterally across the borders of other nations. (Kaplan, 2003: 87)

The discursive construction of selected Arab cities as targets for U.S. military firepower occurs in at least four interrelated ways.

Vertical Representations of Arab Cities as Collections of Military Targets

The voyeuristic consumption by Western publics of the U.S. urban bombing campaigns that have been such a dominant feature of the 'war on terror' is itself based on mediated representations where cities are actually constructed as little more than physical spaces for receiving murderous ordnance. Verticalized Web and newspaper maps, for example, have routinely displayed Iraqi cities as little more than impact points where GPS-targeted bombs and missiles are either envisaged to land or have landed, and are grouped along flat, cartographic surfaces (Gregory, 2004a). *USA Today,* for example, offered an "interactive map of Downtown Baghdad" on the Web between 2003 and 2004 where viewers could click on bombing targets and view detailed satellite images of urban sites both before and after their destruction.

Meanwhile, the weapons' actual impacts on the everyday life for the ordinary Iraqis or Afghanis, who are caught up in the bombing, as "collateral damage," have been both marginalized and violently repressed by the U.S. military. This has happened as part of their elaborate doctrine of psychological operations and information warfare campaigns. In April 2003, such doctrine led U.S. forces to bomb Al-Jazeera's Baghdad offices because the TV station regularly transmitted street-level images of the dead civilians that resulted from the U.S. aerial attacks on Iraqi cities. Through reducing the transnational diffusion of images of Iraqi civilian casualties—a process already limited by the decisions of an overwhelming majority of Western media editors not to display such material—such campaigns operated to further back up the dominant visual message within the verticalized, satellite-based coverage that dominated the mainstream Western media's treatment of the war, especially during its earlier, bombing dominated, phases. Such coverage combined to propagate a series of powerful and interrelated myths: that Iraqi cities existed as asocial, physical domains, which could be understood from the God-like perspective of remotely sensed or cartographic imagery; that such cities were, at the same time, somehow devoid of their populations of civilians; and that it was not inevitable that Iraqi civilians would therefore be killed and maimed in large numbers when their cities were subjected to large-scale aerial bombardment—even when this targeting was deemed precise through the dominant, verticalized, mediated gaze of Western onlookers. In this imaginative geography, which is strongly linked to the wider history of colonial bombing and repression by Western powers, Arab cities were thus reduced to the:

> places and people you are about to bomb, to targets, to letters on a map or co-ordinates on a visual display. Then, missiles rain down on K-A-B-U-L, on 34.51861N, 69.15222E, but not on the eviscerated city

of Kabul, its buildings already devastated and its population already terrorized by years of grinding war. (Gregory 2004b)

Strikingly, U.S.–U.K. forces invading Iraq have failed to even *count* the civilian deaths that have resulted from the war's bombing campaigns, urban battles, and increasingly savage suicide bombings. By February 2006, the Web site http://www.iraqbodycount.net estimated, using confirmed media reporting, that between 28,400 and 32,300 Iraqi civilians had died in the war. Rigorous sampling methodologies resulted in much higher estimations of over 100,000 by 2004 alone (Roberts et al., 2004). The discursive work done to construct Iraqi cities as asocial, purely physical receiving spaces for ordnance thus was a crucial part of a much broader, philosophical casting out of Iraqi civilians as what Georgio Agamben (1998) has called "bare life"—mere zoological humanity warranting no legal status or discursive or visual presence (Gregory, 2004b).

Constructing Iraqi Cities as Terrorist Nests

As in all wars, violence against the far-off places of the purported enemy has been legitimized in the war on terror through repeated emphases on the supposed security this has brought to the increasingly securitized homeland cities of the U.S. discussed earlier. Backed by pronouncements from leading members of the Bush administration, and supportive right-wing media such as *Fox News,* such a discourse gained enormous power even though not a single piece of serious evidence has yet emerged linking Saddam Hussein's regime to al-Qa'eda. Examples of such rhetoric are difficult to avoid, but two will suffice here. General Sanchez, the first U.S. commander in Iraq, stressed in early 2004 as the insurgency raged across Iraqi cities that "every American needs to believe this; that if we fail here in this [Iraqi] environment, the next battlefield will be the streets of America." Paul Bremer, the first head of American civilian command in Iraq, meanwhile reiterated that he "would rather be fighting [the terrorists] here [in Iraq] than in New York" (both cited in Pieterse, 2004: 122).

In particular, significant discursive and material work has been done by both the U.S. military and the mainstream U.S. media to construct particular, highly symbolic, Iraqi cities as dehumanized 'terror cities'—nestlike environments the very geography of which undermines the high-tech, orbital, mastery of U.S. forces. For example, as a major battle raged there in April 2004 in which over 600 Iraqi civilians died, General Richard Myers, Chair of the U.S. Joint Chiefs of Staff, labeled the whole of Fallujah a dehumanized "rat's nest" or "hornet's nest" of "terrorist resistance" against U.S. occupation that needed to be "dealt with" (quoted in News24.com, 2004; see Graham, 2005).

Such disclosures have been backed up by widespread popular geopolitical representations of Iraqi cities. Derek Gregory (2004b: 202), for example, analyzes how, in their pre-invasion discussions about the threat of 'urban warfare' facing invading U.S. forces in the highly urbanized nation of Iraq, mainstream news media such as *Time Magazine* repeatedly depicted intrinsically devious Orientalized streets where "nothing was what it seemed, where deceit and danger threatened at every turn" and where the U.S. forces' high-tech weapons and surveillance gear were the key to "reveal the traps" and "lift" the Orientalized veil obscuring Iraqi urban places (ibid.).

A group of professional 'urban warfare' commentators, meanwhile, writing regular columns in U.S. newspapers, have routinely backed up such popular geopolitical representations of Iraqi cities. The most important of these has been Ralph Peters, an influential columnist for the *New York Post*. To Peters, cities such as Fallujah and Najaf are little more than killing zones that challenge the U.S. military's ability to harness its techno-scientific might to sustain hegemony. This must be done, he argues, by killing 'terrorists' in such cities as rapidly and efficiently—and with as few U.S. casualties—as possible. During the battle of Fallujah, Peters (2004a) labeled the entire city a "terror-city" in his column. Praising the U.S. Marines "for hammering the terrorists into the dirt" in the battle, he nevertheless castigated the cease-fire negotiations that, he argued, had allowed those terrorists left alive to melt back into the civilian population (2004a).

In a later article, Peters (2004b) concluded that a military, technological solution was available to U.S. forces to the problems of anti-insurgency operations in Arab cities that would enable them to "win" such battles more conclusively in the future: killing faster, before any international media coverage is possible. "This is the new reality of combat," he wrote. "Not only in Iraq. But in every broken country, plague pit and terrorist refuge to which our troops have to go in the future" (Peters, 2004b). Arguing that the presence of "global media" meant that "a bonanza of terrorists and insurgents" were allowed to "escape" U.S. forces in Fallujah, U.S. forces, he argued "have to speed the kill" (2004b). By "accelerating urban combat" to "fight within the 'media cycle' before journalists sympathetic to terrorists and murderers can twist the facts and portray us as the villains," new technologies were needed, Peters suggested. This was so that "our enemies are overwhelmed and destroyed before hostile cameras can defeat us. If we do not learn to kill very, very swiftly, we will continue to lose slowly" (Peters, 2004b).

Although an extreme and individual example, Peters' projections have been indicative of a large output of popular geopolitical depictions of Iraqi and Arab cities within mainstream U.S. media of the challenges of urban warfare in a post–Cold War context. Within this, the overwhelming emphasis has been on the ways in which the purported physical geographies of Iraqi cities interrupt the network-centric doctrine preferred by the U.S. military, force U.S. personnel to resort to low-tech solutions and corporeally occupy urban spaces, and so expose them to the risks of ambush. As we shall see, the dominant military solution proffered by this body of popular geopolitical commentators is to construct new surveillance and targeting systems that are designed specifically to expose the fine-grained geographies of Arab cities to overwhelming force from a distance that renders U.S. personnel safe once again (Graham, 2006b).

Othering by Simulation I: Urban Warfare Video Games

In a world being torn apart by international conflict, one thing is on everyone's mind as they finish watching the nightly news: 'Man, this would make a great game!' (Jenkins, 2003: 18)

The construction of Arab cities as targets for U.S. military firepower now sustains a large industry of computer gaming and simulation. Video games such as *America's Army* (http://www.americasarmy.com) and the U.S. Marines' equivalent *Full Spectrum Warrior* (http://www.fullspectrumwarrior.com) have been developed by their respective forces, with help from the corporate entertainment industries, as training aids, recruitment aids, and powerful public relations exercises. Both games—which were among the world's most popular video game franchises in 2005—center overwhelmingly on the military challenges allegedly involved in occupying and pacifying Arab cities. Their immersive simulations "propel the player into the world of the gaming industry's latest fetish: modern urban warfare" (DelPiano, 2004). Andrew Deck (2004) argues that the proliferation of urban warfare games based on actual, ongoing, U.S. military interventions in Arab cities, works to "call forth a cult of ultra-patriotic xenophobes whose greatest joy is to destroy, regardless of how racist, imperialistic, and flimsy the rationale" for the simulated battle.

Such games work powerfully to further reinforce imaginary geographies equating Arab cities with 'terrorism' and the need for U.S. military intervention. They also serve to further blur the boundaries separating war from entertainment. Worse still, they demonstrate that "the entertainment industry has assumed a posture of co-operation towards a culture of permanent war" (Deck, 2004). Within such games, as with the satellite images and maps discussed earlier, Arab cities are represented merely as "collections of objects not congeries of people" (Gregory, 2004b: 201). When people *are* represented, every single one emerges as the shadowy, subhuman, racialized Arab figure of absolutely external terrorists—figures to be annihilated repeatedly in sanitized action as entertainment, or military training, or both. *America's Army* simulates 'counterterror' warfare in densely packed Arab cities in a fictional country of Zekistan. "The mission" of the game, writes Steve O'Hagan (2004):

> is to slaughter evildoers, with something about 'liberty' [...] going on in the back ground [...]. These games may be ultra-realistic down to the caliber of the weapons, but when bullets hit flesh people just crumple serenely into a heap. No blood. No exit wounds. No screams.

Here, once again, the only role for the everyday sites and spaces of the Arab city in urban warfare video games is as environments for military engagement. The militarization of the everyday sites, artifacts, and spaces of the simulated city is total. "Cars are used as bombs, bystanders become victims [although they die without spilling blood], houses become headquarters, apartments become lookout points, and anything to be strewn in the street becomes suitable cover" (DelPiano, 2004). Indeed, there is some evidence that the actual pysical geographies of Arab cities are being digitized to provide the three-dimensional battlespace for each game. One games developer boasts that "we've built a portion of the downtown area of a large Middle Eastern capital city where we have a significant presence today" (cited in Deck, 2004).

In essentializing Arab cities as intrinsically devious labyrinths necessitating high-tech U.S. military assaults to cleanse them of terrorists, this range of urban warfare video games resonates strongly with the popular geopolitical pronouncements of military urban warfare specialists discussed earlier. Importantly, however, as part of what James Der Derian (2001) has termed the emerging U.S. military–industrial–entertainment complex, they also blur with increasing seamlessness into news reports about the actual Iraq war. Kuma Reality Games, for example, which has sponsored the Fox News coverage of the war on terror in the United States, uses this link to promote urban combat games based on actual military engagements in U.S. cities. In their words, one of these centers on U.S. Marines fighting "militant followers of radical Shiite cleric Muqtaqa al-Sadr in the filthy urban slum that is Sadr city" (quoted in Deck, 2004).

Othering by Simulation II: Urban Warfare Training Sites

Finally, to parallel such virtual, voyeuristic, Othering, U.S. and Western military forces have constructed their own simulations of Arab cities as targets—this time in physical space. The U.S. Army alone is planning to build a chain of 61 urban warfare training complexes across the world between 2005 and 2010, to hone the skills of its forces in fighting and killing in urbanized terrain (Warner, 2005). Leading examples include Fort Carson, Colorado (which has three different "Iraqi villages"), Fort Polk,

Louisiana, and Fort Richardson, Alaska. Such constructions are the latest in a long line of military construction projects, based on building simulations of the urban places of target nations. In World War II, for example, the composition and design of U.S. and British incendiary bombs were honed through the repeated burning and reconstruction of extremely accurate German-style tenement blocks and Japanese-style wood and rice paper houses at Dugway proving grounds in Utah (Davis, 2002, 65–84).

Taking up to 18 months to construct, the simulated emerging chain of Arab "cities" currently under construction is then endlessly destroyed and remade in practice assaults that hone the U.S. forces for the real thing in sieges such as those in Fallujah. Replete with mosques, minarets, pyrotechnic systems, loop-tapes with calls to prayer, slum districts, donkeys, hired civilians in Islamic dress wandering through narrow streets, and olfactory machines to create the smell of rotting corpses, this shadow urban system simulates not the complex cultural, social or physical realities of real Middle Eastern urbanism, but the imaginative geographies of the military and theme park designers that are brought in to design and construct it.

It is also clear that the physical urban simulations emerging here are being carefully co-constructed with the electronic ones, just discussed, emerging through video games and training virtual reality packages. In *America's Army,* for example, participants develop urban warfare skills in an electronic simulation of the McKenna military operations in urban terrain training complex at Fort Benning in Georgia—which its builders purport to be a physical simulation of an Arab city. Meanwhile, the University of Southern California's Institute for Creative Technologies (ICT)—which has had a major input into the development of *Full Spectrum Warrior*—now offers so-called augmented reality urban training programs to the U.S. military. One such project, known as the Urban Terrain Module, based at Fort Sill, Oklahoma, blurs the latest electronic simulation technologies seamlessly into physically staged dioramas of Arab urban environments. Built with the help of Hollywood stagecraft professionals, and including electronically simulated virtual humans, the project's designers argue that the electronic simulations are so convincing that the borders between the virtualized and physical elements are increasingly indistinguishable (Strand, 2003).

Constructing Homeland and Target Cities Within U.S. Military Technoscience

> The [U.S.] Air Force wants to be able to strike mobile and emerging targets in fewer than 10 minutes so that such targets will have no sanctuary from U.S. air power. (Adam Hebert, 2003)

All of which leads neatly to the third and final focus in our discussion of the imaginative urban geographies underpinning the war on terror: an exploration of the dialectical production of homeland and target cities within U.S. military strategy. Here, strikingly, our emphasis shifts from discussions of disconnection and separation to those of integration and connection. For the huge research and development program now going on to sustain the war on terror, U.S. military doctrine emphasizes the use of the nation's unassailable advantages in military technoscience to address, and construct, both homeland cities and the targeted, Arab cities as key geographical domains within a completely integrated, transnational, battlespace. Both sites are being integrated through the U.S. military's advances in speed-of-light surveillance, communication and orbital, air and space-based targeting capabilities (the result of what is widely termed the "Revolution in Military Affairs" or network-centric warfare—see Dillon, 2002 and Duffield, 2002, respectively, as well as Boyer in this volume). Post–9/11, this integration also has been marked by the creation of a strategic military command—NORTHCOM—to cover the continental United States (previously, the only part of the globe not to be so covered), and by a marked increase in the deployment and exercising of U.S. military forces to cover key sites and installations in and around U.S. cities.

Crucially, however, this very integration of geographically distanced urban sites through military technoscience is being done in a manner that actually inscribes highly divisive judgments of people's right to life within the war on terror into hard, military systems of control, targeting and, sometimes, (attempted) killing. These systems, very literally, enable, reinforce, and "wire" the geopolitical, biopolitical, and urban architectures of U.S. Empire, with their stark judgments of the value—or lack of value—of the urban subjects, and human lives, under scrutiny. The emerging transglobal surveillance and targeting systems of the U.S. military continually work to try and expose all subjects, in both 'homeland' and 'target' domains, to scrutiny. In the target cities where those subjects are deemed to warrant no rights or protections, this exposure is combined with potentially instant, continuous, violence and death.

How Technology Will Defeat Terrorism

By way of demonstrating this argument, let me start by drawing on one particularly clear example of how dialectical imaginative geographies of cities, and the military technoscience of U.S. Empire, are being produced, and imagined, together, by those helping to shape the direction of U.S. military technoscience. This comes from an article titled "How Technology Will Defeat Terrorism," produced in 2002 by Peter Huber and Mark

Mills—two leading U.S. defense analysts closely involved, through their defense company Digital Power Capital, in the war on terror.

Huber and Mills's (2002: 25) starting point is that the United States now has "sensing technologies that bring to the battlefield abroad, and to the vast arena of civilian defense here at home, the same wizardry that transformed the mainframe computer into the Palm Pilot, the television tower into the cell phone." From the point of view of 'homeland' cities and systems of cities within U.S. national borders, Huber and Mills argue that this advantage in electronic sensing capabilities means that, "step by step, cities like New York must now learn to watch and track everything that moves" (ibid.: 27). This must happen, they argued, as sophisticated, software-based surveillance systems that use algorithms to automatically surveill massive quantities of data to preemptively sniff out signs of terrorist activity, are woven into the complex everyday technics that constitute urban America. "In the post-September 11 world," they write, 'smart' computerized systems need to be rolled out to all the infrastructural systems of urban America so that U.S. Homeland Security agencies can "see the plastic explosives in the truck before they detonate, the anthrax before it's dispersed, the sarin nerve gas before it gets into the air-conditioning duct" (ibid.: 28).

In the target cities and spaces of the Middle East, by contrast, Huber and Mills stress that similar, automated systems of sensing and surveillance must also be seamlessly integrated into the high-tech U.S. military machine. Rather than pinpointing and reducing threats, however, the purpose of these systems, this time, is to continuously project death and destruction to pinpointed locations in the cities and spaces that have discursively been constructed as targets for U.S. military power in the war on terror. "We really *do* want an Orwellian future not in Manhattan, but in Kabul," they argue. Their prognosis is stark and dualistic:

> Terrorist wars will continue, in one form or another, for as long as we live. […] We are destined to fight a never-ending succession of micro-scale battles, which will require us to spread military resources across vast expanses of empty land and penetrate deep into the shadows of lives lived at the margins of human existence. Their conscripts dwell in those expanses and shadows. Our soldiers don't, and can't for any extended period of time. What we have instead is micro-scale technology that is both smarter and more expendable than their fanatics, that is more easily concealed and more mobile, that requires no food and sleep, and that can endure even harsher conditions. (ibid.: 29)

Saturating adversary cities and territories with millions of loitering surveillance and targeting devices, intimately linked into global surveillance and targeting systems, thus becomes the invisible and unreported shadow of the high-profile, technologically similar, Homeland Security systems erected within and between the cities of the U.S. mainland. To Huber and Mills, the U.S. "longer-term objective must be to infiltrate their homelands electronically, to the point where we can listen to and track anything that moves," where the "their" refers to the terrorists inhabiting the targeted cities (ibid. 30). Then, when purported 'targets' are detected, U.S. forces:

> can then project destructive power precisely, judiciously, and from a safe distance week after week, year after year, for as long as may be necessary. [...] Properly deployed at home, as they can be, these tech-nologies of freedom will guarantee the physical security on which all our civil liberties ultimately depend. Properly deployed abroad, they will destroy privacy everywhere we need to destroy it. [...] At home and abroad, it will end up as their sons against our silicon. Our sili-con will win. (ibid.: 31–34)

Technophiliac Unveilings of 'Homeland' and Target Cities

Strikingly, in Huber and Mills's scenario, political judgments about the (lack of) value of human life in the demonized cities and spaces that have been so powerfully (re)constructed in war on terror discourses are actu-ally maintained and policed through automated surveillance and killing systems. For here the disposability of life in such target cities is main-tained continuously by the ongoing presence of Unmanned Combat Aerial Vehicles (or UCAVs) armed with "hellfire" missiles. These weapons can be launched at short notice, sometimes from operators sited at transoceanic distances, once the surveillance webs that saturate the 'target' cities detect some notional target.

Far from being some fanciful military futurology from Huber and Mills's technophiliac fantasies, then, these principles are actually directly shaping the design of new U.S. military systems that are already under development or even deployment. Thus, on the one hand, as already men-tioned, the cities and urban corridors within U.S. national borders are being wired up with a large range of automated sensors that are designed to detect and locate a whole spectrum of potentially terrorist threats. By contrast, the Pentagon's Research and Development outfit, DARPA (the Defense Applications Research and Projects Agency) is now developing the sorts of large-scale, loitering surveillance grids to try and unveil the sup-posedly impenetrable and labyrinthine landscapes of closely built Middle Eastern cities. In a new program tellingly titled "Combat Zones That See" (or CTS), DARPA (2003) is developing systems of micro-cameras and sen-sors that can be scattered discretely across both circling UCAVs and built urban landscapes that automatically scan millions of vehicles and human faces for known targets and record any event deemed to be unusual. "The ability to track vehicles across extended distances is the key to providing actionable intelligence for military operations in urban terrain," the brief for the Program argues. "Combat Zones that See will advance the state of the art for multiple-camera video tracking to the point where expected tracking length reaches city-sized distances" (DARPA, 2003).

Befitting the definition of Middle Eastern target cities within U.S. military doctrine as zones where human life warrants little protection or ornamentation, actionable here is most likely to be translated in practice—Israeli style—as automated or near-automated aerial attempts at killing the targeted person(s). Because urban density in target cities is seen "to render stand-off sensing from airborne and space-borne platforms ineffective" (DARPA, 2003), CTS's main role will be to hold even targets within densely urbanized spaces at risk from near-instant targeting and destruction from GPS-guided weapons. In U.S. military jargon this is termed *compressing the kill chain*—a process that "closes the time delay between sensor and shooter" to an extent that brings "persistent area dominance" (or PAD) even over and within dense megacities such as Baghdad (Hebert, 2003).

Since 2002, for the first time, fleets of apparently identical U.S. unmanned aerial vehicles (UAVs) have indeed patrolled both the increasingly militarized border of the southern United States and the cities and frontier lands of the war zones of the Middle East. Identical, that is, except in one crucial respect. Tellingly, in the former case, however, worries have been expressed about the dangers of accidental crashes from *unarmed* drones flying over the U.S. civilian population by federal aviation safety officers. "How UAVs could be integrated into civilian airspace within the United States is a fundamental question that would need to be addressed by the Federal Aviation Administration," reported a committee to Congress on the issue in 2005 (Bolkcom, 2005). "Integrating UAVs into civilian airspace so that they could operate safely would require not only the creation of regulatory guidelines by the Federal Aviation Administration but also technical developments" (ibid.).

In the latter case, meanwhile, these unmanned aircraft have been armed for the first time with missiles and have undertaken, by remote control, at least 80 assassination raids targeting alleged terrorists (and those unlucky enough to be close by) in Yemen, Afghanistan, Pakistan, and Iraq. On one occasion, in early January 2006, a CIA-piloted Predator drone, ostensibly targeting Ayman al Zawahiri, the deputy leader of al-Qa'eda, in Pakistan, killed 22 innocent civilians and sparked mass protests across Pakistan's cities.

As a further demonstration of how the transnational connections underpinning U.S. military technology contrast starkly with the war on terror's imaginative geographies, some Predator pilots actually operate from virtual reality caves in a Florida air base 8,000 or 10,000 miles away from the drones' target zones. For the U.S. military personnel doing the piloting, this virtual work is almost indistinguishable from a shoot-'em-up video game (except that the people who die are real). "At the end of the work day," one Predator operator reflected in 2003, "you walk back into the rest of life in America" (quoted in Newman, 2003).

The "success" of these aerial and long-distance assassinations has fueled much broader investments in the development of aerial vehicles and munitions that will combine with CTS-type systems to provide the military holy grail of what U.S. military strategists now term *persistent area dominance*. Large-scale efforts are already underway to develop such a capability. These specifically address urban target areas through what is being termed, in the jargon, *total urban dominance layered system* (or TUDLS) (Plenge, 2004). This program, which builds on CTS, is designed to deliver what the weapons designers call "a family of integrated and complementary vehicles layered over an urban area to provide persistent dominance" (ibid.). In the euphemistic geek-speak of the U.S. military, TUDLS will encompass "long hover and loiter propulsions systems, multi-discriminant sensors and seekers, mini- and micro-air vehicles, mini-lethal and non-lethal warheads, autonomous and man-in-the-loop control algorithms, and a strong interface with the battlespace information network" (Plenge, 2004).

For those unused to the euphemisms here, it must be stressed that autonomous control algorithms actually means that the developers of these systems envisage that the flying vehicles, and the computer systems that control them, will, eventually, be designed to take the decisions to kill purported targets without any human intervention whatsoever. Entirely robotic attack aircraft or dominators are already under development by the U.S. Air Force (Tirpak, 2001). As the blurb from one manufacturer puts it, "these dominators will be capable of completing the entire kill chain with minimal human involvement" (Plenge, 2004).

Conclusions

> The ultimate expression of sovereignty resides [...] in the power and capacity to dictate who may live and who must die. (Mbembe, 2003: 11)

This chapter has demonstrated some of the ways in which the political, discursive, material, and geographical dimensions of the Bush administration's war on terror rest fundamentally on dialectical constructions of urban place. Such constructions, essentially, invoke both political and public reworkings of long-standing imaginative geographies. These are shaped and legitimized to do geopolitical work. Moreover, it has been shown that the dialectical constructions of urban place which underlie the 'war on terror' can only really be understood if analysis stretches to cover the *mutually constitutive* representation of both homeland and target cities. Such a perspective demonstrates the vulnerability of both U.S. and targeted Arab cities, and their inhabitants, to an increasingly militarized U.S. national security state mobilizing rhetorics of global, neoliberal transformation based on ideologies of permanent, technologized war. It points to a stark but simple conclusion: that the civilians of both sets of cities are the ultimate victims of the war on terror. And it demonstrates some of the fundamental contradictions that run through the new imaginative geographies underpinning the war on terror.

The emphasis on the mutually constitutive roles of the portrayals of both U.S. and Arab cities within the war on terror within this chapter allows us to close by emphasizing three key conclusions. First, and crucially, it is clear that extremely strong resonances exist between the dialectical constructions of urban places in official U.S. war on terror pronouncements and those in the popular geopolitical domains of news media, novels, Internet chat rooms, films and, most notable of all, video games. This points to the increasing integration of the prosecution, representation, imagination, and, perhaps most important, *consumption* of asymmetric urban warfare in the early 21st century. The growth of the "military–industrial–media–entertainment network" (Der Derian, 2001) that sustains this blurring is occurring as reporters become 'embedded' in urban combat (with the language of "they're moving out" becoming a language of "we're moving out"); theme park designers construct mock Arab cities for U.S. urban combat training; voyeuristic media ratchet-up both fear about attacks in the urban homeland and legitimize preemptive war in target cities; private military corporations soak up huge contracts for both homeland security and overseas military aggression; and the military themselves construct Orientalist and racist video games where virtualized Arab cities are experienced as mere environments for the killing of terrorists as entertainment for U.S. suburbanites in the homeland. Importantly, then, this complex of discourses and representations—themselves the product of increasingly militarized popular and political cultures—works, on the one hand, to problematize urban cosmopolitanism in homeland cities and, on the other, to essentialize and reify the social ecologies of target cities in profoundly racist ways. From such symbolic violence real violence only too easily follows.

Second, this essay has demonstrated that the production of this highly charged dialectic—the forging of exclusionary, nationalist, imagined communities and the Othering of whole swathes of our urbanizing planet—has been a fundamental prerequisite for the legitimization of the entire war on terror. Worryingly, and with dark irony, such fundamentalist and racist constructions of urban place have their almost exact shadow in the charged dialectics of urban place routinely disseminated by al-Qa'eda itself. Here, however, the targets are the infidel, Christian, or Zionist cities of the West or Israel. The sentimentalized spaces of the Islamic homeland, meanwhile, are to be violently purified of Western presence in order to create a transnational Islamic space or *umma*, which systematically excludes all diversity and Otherness through continuous, murderous force.

The real tragedy of the war on terror, then, is that it has closely paralleled al-Qa'eda in invoking homogeneous and profoundly exclusionary notions of 'community' as a way of legitimizing massive violence against innocent civilians. Strikingly, the strategies and discourses of both the Bush administration and al-Qa'eda have been based on charged, and mutually reinforcing, dialectics and imaginative geographies of place construction. Both have relied heavily on: promulgating hypermasculine notions of (asymmetric) war; invocations of absolute theological mandate; and absolutist notions of violence to finally exterminate the enemy without limits in space or time. Finally, both have relied on the use of transnational media systems to repeatedly project good versus evil rhetorics of victimhood, dehumanization, and revenge (Gilroy, 2003).

In so doing, the 'war on terror' has worked to construct a self-reinforcing cycle of terrorist atrocity and counterterrorist atrocity. Once set in train, as we see in both the proliferation of terrorist and counterterrorist outrages against civilians within the Iraq insurgency, and the long-standing cycle of atrocity in Israel-Palestine, such cycles are extraordinarily difficult to unravel or reverse. Ultimately, then, the real tragedy of Bush's war on terror, as Zulaika (2003, 198) suggests:

> is that such a categorically ill-defined, perpetually deferred, simple minded Good-versus-Evil war ['against terror'] echoes and recreates the very absolutist mentality and exceptionalist tactics of the insurgent terrorists. By formally adopting the terrorists' own game—one that by definition lacks rules of engagement, definite endings, clear alignments between enemies and friends, or formal arrangements of any sort, military, political, legal, or ethical—the inevitable danger lies in reproducing it endlessly.

Finally, the reliance of the 'war on terror's' imaginative geographies on projections of absolute difference, distance and disconnection are overlaid by, and potentially usurped through, the manifold flows and connections that link urban life in Arab cities intimately to urban life in the cosmopolitan urban centers of the United States. The binaried urban and global imaginative geographies underpinning the 'war on terror' are inevitably undermined by such contradictions as rapidly as they are projected.

Thus, a revivified Orientalism is used to remake imaginative geographies of inside and outside just as a wide range of processes demonstrates how redundant such binaries now are. On the one hand, the construction of homeland cities as endlessly vulnerable spaces open without warning to an almost infinite range of threats actually works to *underline* the integration of such spaces into the manifold flows and processes of globalization. Similarly, the attempt to discursively demarcate the everyday urban life of U.S. citizens from Arab ones denies the transnational and increasingly globalized circuits of media flow, migration, mobility, resource geopolitics, social repression and incarceration, neoconservative geopolitical ideologies, and the predatory capital flows surrounding neoliberal reconstruction that, paradoxically, are serving to connect U.S. cities ever-more closely with Arab cities. Thus, especially in the more cosmopolitan cities of the United States, the representations and discourses stressing disconnection and difference analyzed in this chapter are continuously contradicted by the proliferation of moments and processes involving connection, linkage and similarity.

Two key problems emerge here. The first is that many such moments and processes—as with the posthumous Americanization of the cosmopolitan dead after 9/11—are themselves often denied and hidden to fit in with dominant representations and imaginative geographies promulgated by politicians, mainstream media, and wider popular geopolitical scripts. It is therefore to the challenge of exposing these increasingly cosmopolitan geographies—through which U.S. cities become mutually constituted with those cities that are so powerfully demonized, dehumanized and Othered as the prime targets within war on terror discourses—that critical research and activism must turn as it attempts to expose the war on terror's fundamental contradictions.

The second problem derives from this chapter's third focus: the treatment of U.S. and Arab cities within emerging U.S. military technology. Here, of course, we see another apparently contradictory coexistence of distancing and division with connection and integration. Certainly, it is true that the technoscientific systems that actually allow U.S. military forces to undertake transglobal military operations as part of the 'war on terror' increasingly treat home and target domains as a single, transnational, and increasingly urban battlespace. However, as we have seen, the ultimate constructions of division and separation lurk within this apparent, technologized (albeit militarized) unity. For the ways in which judgments about the value of the human subjects are being embedded into the high-tech war-fighting, surveillance, and software systems now being developed to expose urban citizens to scrutiny in both U.S. and Arab cities could not be more different.

In homeland cities, to be sure, there is a radical ratcheting-up of surveillance and (attempted) social control, the endless terror talk, highly problematic clampdowns, the hardening of urban targets, and potentially indefinite incarcerations for those people deemed to display the signifiers of real or dormant terrorists. In the targeted urban spaces of the Arab world, meanwhile, clear evidence suggests that weapons systems are currently being designed which might very possibly emerge as systems of automated, continuous (attempted) assassination.

Here, chillingly, software code is being invested with the sovereign power to kill. This trend is backed by neoconservative ideologies suggesting that continuous, overseas U.S. military aggression against sources of terrorism defines what Dick Cheney has called "the new normalcy." It is also being fuelled by the great temptation for the U.S. state and military to deploy autonomous and robotized U.S. weapons against purported, all-too-human, enemies (Graham, 2006b). "The enemy, are they going to give up blood and guts to kill machines? I'm guessing not," suggested Gordon Johnson, head of a U.S. army robot weapons team, in 2003 (cited in Lawlor, 2004: 3).

The grave danger here is that these systems will be deployed stealth-ily by the U.S. state to 'loiter' more or less permanently above and within Arab cities and regions deemed to be the war on terror's main targets. They might then produce realms of automated, stealthy, and continuous violence let loose from both the spaces or times, and the legalities, of war as traditionally understood (in its declared and demarcated guises). A more hopeful scenario is that such fantasies of robotized, colonial war, will wither against the on-going catastrophe in Iraq. For it is on the streets of Iraq that the mythologizing behind rhetoric of clean, robotized war, removing U.S. personnel from risk, has been undermined most powerfully. And now many in the U.S. military themselves—especially in the U.S. Army—are deeply sceptical of any military silver bullets emerging from the think tanks, research complexes, and weapons manufacturers of the U.S. military industrial complex, which purport to guarantee a quick and total demise to anyone who is deemed an adversary within the war on terror's contradictory imaginative geographies.

This chapter is a revised version of a paper that first appeared in the *International Journal of Urban and Regional Research* (2006), 30(2), 255–276.

References

Agamben, G. (1998) *Homo sacer. Sovereign power and bare life,* Stanford, CA: Stanford University Press.

Andreas, P. (2003) A tale of two borders: The U.S.-Canada and U.S.-Mexico lines after 9–11. In *The rebordering of North America,* edited by P. Andreas & T. Biersteker, New York: Routledge.

Andreas, P., & Biersteker, T. (2003) *The rebordering of North America.* New York: Routledge.

Armitage, J. (2002) State of emergency. *Theory, Culture and Society* 19: 27–38.

Barnett, T. (2004), *The Pentagon's new map.* New York: Putnam.

Bolkcom, C. (2005), *Homeland security: Unmanned aerial vehicles and border surveillance.* CRS Report for Congress, February 7, Code RS21698, accessed February 2006, at http://www.fas.org/sgp/crs/homesec/RS21698.pdf.

Collins, J., & Glover, R. (2002), *Collateral language: A user's guide to America's new war.* New York: New York University Press.

Dalby, S. (2000) A critical geopolitics of global governance. International Studies Association, accessed February 2006, at http://www.ciaonet.org/isa/das01/.

Defense Advanced Research Projects Agency. (2003) *Proposer information pamphlet for Combat Zones That See (CTS) Programme.* Washington, DC: Department of Defense.

David, M. (2002) *Dead cities, and other tales.* New York: New Press.

Davis, M. (2004) The Pentagon as global slum lord, accessed February 2006, at http://www.tomdispatch.com/ (Feb 2006).

Deck, A. (2004) Demilitarizing the playground. *No quarter,* accessed February 2006, at http://artcontext.net/crit/essays/noQuarter/.

DelPiano, S. (2004) Review of Full Spectrum Warrior. *Games First,* accessed February 2006, at http://www.gamesfirst.com/reviews/07.10.04/FullSpectrumRev/fullspectrumreview.htm.

Der Derian, J. (2001) *Virtuous war: Mapping the military-industrial-media-entertainment complex.* Boulder, CO: Westview.

Dillon, M. (2002) Network society, network-centric warfare and the state of emergency. *Theory, Culture and Society,* 19: 71–79.

Duffield, M. (2002) War as a network enterprise: The new security terrain and its implications. *Cultural Values.* 6: 153–165.

Foucault, M. (1970) *The order of things.* London: Tavistock.

Gaudiosi, J. (2004) Army sets up video-game studio. *Wired,* June: 23.

Gilroy, P. (2003) 'Where ignorant armies clash by night': Homogeneous community and the planetary aspect. *International Journal of Cultural Studies,* 6: 261–276.

Giroux, H. (2003) *Public spaces, private lives: Democracy beyond 9/11.* Oxford: Rowman and Littlefield.

Graham, S. (2004) Postmortem city: Towards an urban geopolitics. *City,* 8(2): 166–193.

Graham, S. (2005) Remember Fallujah: Demonising place, constructing atrocity. *Environment and Planning D: Society and Space,* 23: 1–10.

Graham, S. (2006a) "Homeland" insecurities? Katrina and the politics of 'security' in metropolitan America. *Space and Culture,* 9(1): 63–67.

Graham, S. (2006b) Surveillance, urbanization, and the U.S. 'Revolution in Military Affairs.' In D. Lyon (Ed.), *Theorizing Surveillance*. London: Willan (forthcoming).

Gregory, D. (1995) Imaginative geographies. *Progress in Human Geography* 19: 447–485.

Gregory, D. (2003) Defiled cities. *Singapore Journal of Tropical Geography*. 24: 307–326.

Gregory, D. (2004a) *The colonial present*. Blackwell: Oxford.

Gregory, D. (2004b) Who's responsible? Dangerous geography. *ZNet*, accessed May 2006, at http://www.znet.org.

Gusterson, H. (1999) Nuclear weapons and the Other in the Western imagination. *Cultural Anthropology* 14: 111–143.

Hage, G. (2003) 'Comes a time we are enthusiasm': Understanding Palestinian suicide bombers in times of Exigophobia. *Public Culture,* 15: 65–89.

Hebert, A. (2003) Compressing the kill chain. *Air Force Magazine,* March: 34–42.

Hewitt K. (1983) Place annihilation: Area bombing and the fate of urban places. *Annals of the Association of American Geographers,* 73: 257–284.

Howell, S., & Shryock, A. (2003) Cracking down on dispaora : Arab Detroit and America's War on Terror. *Anthropological Quarterly,* 76: 443–462.

Huber, P., & Mills, M. (2002) How technology will defeat terrorism. *City Journal,* 12: 24–34.

Huntington, S. (1993) *The clash of civilizations and the remaking of world order.* New York: Simon and Schuster.

Hyndman, J. (2003) Beyond either/or: A feminist analysis of September 11th. *ACME : An International E-Journal for Critical Geographies,* accessed February 2006, at http://www.acme-journal.org.

Institute for Policy Studies and Foreign Policy (IPSFP). (2004) *The sorrows of empire,* accessed February 2006, at http://www.presentdanger.org/papers/sorrows2003.html.

Jenkins, H. (2003) A war of words over Iraqi video games. *The Guardian,* 13 November: 18.

Johnson, J. (2002) Immigration reform, homeland defense and metropolitan economies in the post 9–11 environment. *Urban Geography,* 23: 201–212.

Kaplan, A. (2003), Homeland insecurities: Reflections on language and space. *Radical History Review.* 85: 82–93.

Katz, C. (2004) Banal terrorism. Paper available from the author ckatz@gc.cuny.edu.

Kraska, P. (2000). *Militarizing the American Criminal Justice System: The Changing Roles of the Armed Forces and the Police.* Boston: Northeastern University Press.

Lawlor, M. (2004) Robotic concepts take shape, *Signal Magazine,* accessed February 2005 at http://www.afcea.org/signal/.

Luke, T. (2004) Everyday techniques as extraordinary threats: Urban technostructures and nonplaces in terrorist actions. In S. Graham (ed.), *Cities, war and terrorism: Towards an urban geopolitics.* Oxford: Blackwell.

Lutz, C. (2002) Making war at home in the United States: Militarization and the current crisis. *American Anthropologist,* 104: 733–735.

Mbembe, A. (2003) Necropolitics, *Public Culture,* 15(1), 11–40.

Newman, R. (2003) The joystick war *U.S. News*, 19 May, accessed June 2003, at http://www.usnews.com.

News24.com. (2004) Fallujah a 'rat's nest,' accessed February 2006, at http://www.news24.com/News24/World/Iraq/0,,2-10-1460_1515215,00.html.

O'Hagan, S. (2004) Recruitment hard drive. *Guardian Guide*. June 19–25: 12–13.

Passavant, P. & Dean, J. (2002) Representation and the event. *Theory and Event*, 5(4). accessed, at http:/muse.jhu.edu/journals/theory_and_event/v005/5.4passavant.html.

Patai, R. (1983) *The Arab mind*. New York: Macmillan.

Peters, R. (2004a) He who hesitates. *New York Post*. April 27, accessed, at http://www.nypost.com.

Peters, R. (2004b) Kill faster! *New York Post*, accessed, at, http://www.nypost.com.

Pieterse, J. (2004) "Neoliberal empire," *Theory, Culture and Society*, 21(3): 119–140.

Plenge, B. (2004) Area dominance: Area dominance with air-delivered loitering munitions aids the warfighter. *AFLR Briefs*, accessed February 2006, at www.afrlhorizons.com/Briefs/Apr04/MN0308.html.

Puar, J., & Rai, A. (2002) Monster, terrorist, fag: The war on terrorism and the production of docile patriots. *Social Text*, 20: 117–148.

Raban, J. (2004) Running scared. *The Guardian*, 21 July: 3–7.

Rayment, S. (2004) British commanders condemn U.S. military tactics. *Daily Telegraph*, April 12: 4.

Roberts, S., Secor, A., & Sparke, M. (2003) Neoliberal geopolitics. *Antipode*, 35 (5), 887–897.

Roberts, L., Lafta, R., Garfield, R., Khudhairi, J., & Burnham, G. (2004) Mortality before and after the 2003 invasion of Iraq: Cluster sample survey. *The Lancet*, October 29: 1–8.

Said, E. (1978) *Orientalism*. London: Routledge and Kegan Paul.

Said, E. (2003) *Orientalism*. London: Penguin.

Smith, M. P. (2001) *Transnational Urbanism*. London: Sage.

Strand, L. (2003) ICT demonstrates training for 'universal observer.' *Selective Focus: A Newsletter of Activities at the Institute for Creative Technologies*, University of Southern California 2, issue 5, 1–2.

Tuastad, D. (2003) Neo-Orientalism and the new barbarism thesis: Aspects of symbolic violence in the Middle East conflict(s). *Third World Quarterly*, 24: 591–588.

Warner, J. (2005) Fort Carsondad. *Boulder Weekly*, accessed February 2006, at http://www.boulderweekly.com/archive/061605/coverstory.html.

Watson T. (2003) Introduction: Critical infrastructures after 9/11. *Postcolonial Studies*, 6: 109–111.

Wilkins, D. (2003) Tough new tactics by U.S. Tighten grip on Iraq towns. *New York Times*, accessed February 2006, at http://www.nytimes.com.

Williams, R. (2003) Terrorism, anti-terrorism and the normative boundaries of the U.S. polity: The partiality of politics after 11 September 2001. *Space and Polity*, 7: 273–292.

Zulaika, J. (2003) The self-fulfilling prophecies of counterterrorism. *Radical History Review*, 85: 191–199.

Empire of the Insensate

STEVEN FLUSTY

Figure 1 Caesar's angels.

July 1999: They Who Would Give Up an Essential Liberty for Temporary Security

We were somewhere around Custer, South Dakota, at the edge of the Black Hills when my Nordic colleague got this wicked glint in his eyes. I remember him saying something like, "They're all-day passes, let's go back and check out the monument lighting ceremony ..." And suddenly the rental car had swung around through the scorching heat and soaking humidity, and was hurtling back toward Mount Rushmore (n.b. Thompson, 1998). From Sergio Leone's taciturn gunslingers to Maurice 'Morris' de Bevere's *Lucky Luke* and Jean 'Moebius' Giraud's *Blueberry*, the peoples of the European subcontinent have a strong penchant for playing Cowboys-and-Indians. In my colleague's case, this penchant was tempered by a gleefully morbid engagement with the regalia of the federal government that rigorously ensured those cowboys came out the winners every time. Nor was he alone in this. During a stopover at the monument to the 1890 massacre at Wounded Knee just a few days earlier, the only languages we heard in the cemetery were French and German.

For me, however, engagement with this federal government was anything but gleeful. *Patriotism* is entirely too close for my liking to *patriarchy, paternalism* and *patronizing*, bringing to mind adolescent fears of being sent on compulsory excursions to Grenada, Libya, or El Salvador from which I might have returned in a plastic bag. So being dragged to visit Mount Rushmore twice in one day (and with the ghosts of Wounded Knee still dancing at my heels) felt akin to Gutzon Borglum, after smashing his manquettes of General Lee and hightailing it from Stone Mountain, making a U-turn and rushing into the arms of the pursuing Georgian troopers and the Ku Klux Klan (institutions that, at the time, would not have been all that distinct from one another).

Of course, Borglum did nothing of the sort. Instead, he took up long-term (and unextraditable) refuge in the Dakotas where, presented with the task of carving the likenesses of frontier celebrities into the geology of his choice, he went one better (or, at least, bigger). Borglum was one for working large, thematically as well as geologically. So why spend one's life pecking out gigantic Buffalo Bills or George Armstrong Custers when there's a *nation* to megalithicize (Taliaferro, 2002; also Boime, 1998)?

Not that monumental bas reliefs are all there is to be found at Mount Rushmore. The inscribed mountain is merely the jewel in a filigreed setting designed to inscribe the nation deep into the visitor's soul. An Avenue of Flags provides a pharaonic processional axis, framing the mountain with banners that represent each of the 50 states. A forecourt is inscribed in perpetuity with the names of those who spent years, even decades, serving

Figure 2 Freedom fire.

their country on the mountain's face. Concession stands mix affordable, instantly antiqued simulations of the nation's foundational documents with four-score-and-twenty-berries ice cream. It is as if every manifestation of *banal nationalism* (Billig, 1995)—every schoolroom pledge of allegiance, every pregame performance of the national anthem, every Presidents' Day barbecue and every automobile-mounted U.S. flag ever peddled from off a street corner—has been brought to this one place and refined into an impenetrable concentrate. But all of this is, like the enormous mound of stone tailings beneath the carvings themselves, just the residue of the foundational six-story-high portraits of George Washington, Thomas Jefferson, Abraham Lincoln, and Theodore Roosevelt.

Transiting through the age of mechanical reproduction, there is a tendency to collapse these likenesses into a single deified figure, a four-headed American Brahma from whence issues the United States of America itself. As with any such godhead(s), though, many avatars reside within this mysterious one-who-is-four. Washington we have been made to know as the nation's progenitor, Jefferson as its guide, Lincoln as its unifier, and Roosevelt as its champion. Conversely, however, we also can understand this deity as constituting an imperial circle of sorts: Washington as the warrior-hero who refuses the crown; Jefferson as the philosopher-king bearing the light of ancient Athens and Rome; Lincoln as the reluctant hero who sacrifices himself to conquer internal weakness and division; and finally Roosevelt as the ultimate outcome—the full-fledged warrior-king who begat the Pax Americana to bring the world to heel.

Although some more-or-less simplified version of the latter, *triumphallist* reading was evidently fecund in our heads the day of our (re)visit, it was the former we were avidly encouraged to carry home alongside our replica Declarations of Independence. And it was to this end that the monument lighting ceremony was performed. This ceremony was a complex aggregate of semiscripted multimediation, designed to inscribe in *us* a particular, preferred sense of who we are. And we, in turn, were expected to cognitively inscribe that sense back into the literal inscriptions on the mountain.

The ceremony commenced in daylight, well before anything could be effectively lit up at all. It took an increasingly popular American form of which my own redaction of events is itself not innocent: the personal confession. On a large projection screen in front of an open air amphitheater carefully oriented toward the altar of the mountain, the image of a ginormous Stars and Stripes appeared. Out in front of this stepped a scrub-faced youth in a National Park Service uniform (jarring for a moment, I realized I had subconsciously expected something more akin to George C. Scott as Patton). Gazing up at the flag, our hostess took a microphone and launched into a folksy story of what the flag and, by synecdoche, America meant to her—how as a child her father had her mow the lawn in exchange for her allowance. How this, in turn, taught her to appreciate America as a place of opportunity where honest work yields virtuous citizens free to enjoy the material fruits of their labors.

My accompanying Nord flinched a bit. We had both come for banalized national mythologizing, but public confessions of the personal are neither common nor particularly appreciated in Fennoscandian cultural contexts.

Her testimony complete, the hostess carried the microphone into the audience and, in the style to which we have become accustomed from habitual viewings of Montel Williams and Jerry Springer, invited us to testify to what the Stars and Stripes meant to us. The microphone moved about the amphitheater, with what I now perceived as national parishioners interpreting the hermeneutics of the flag as everything from generosity and self-sacrifice to affluence and videogame consoles.

The Nord's flinching gradually became squirming.

And then, unexpectedly, the microphone passed into a heretical pair of hands. A guttural accent rang out through the loudspeakers: "I am originally

from South Africa, and flags remind me of how national symbols are so easily used to make us feel okay about doing horrible things to other people."

Now the entire amphitheater squirmed. Most were shifting about in
glaringly angry attempts to locate the traitor. For the Nord and me, it was
more about sudden concern for the continued physical well-being of the
speaker and, vicariously, for our own. I rifled through my head for a follow-
up response should the microphone migrate my way. I would answer, I
concluded, that the U.S. flag makes me think of the Fifth Amendment
to the Constitution—the guarantee of freedom from self-incrimination.
There was no need for concern, however, as the microphone was promptly
returned to the head of the congregation. Now the climax of the ceremony
began. A medley of patriotic words, songs, and images swelled from the
speakers and from the screen up front, while slowly, majestically, banks of
spotlights gradually illuminated the mountain from below.

By now, the Nord's morbid engagement had turned into a rapt obsession.
He scrutinized montage after montage of waving flags, soaring eagles, and
purple mountains' majesties. Visions of *heimatslands* marching through
his head, he muttered something to the effect that "this is no different than
the fascism Europeans are so familiar with … this looks like the sorts of
empires Europe used to run."

I, however, noticed something that salved and settled me for the first
time since our arrival, and pointed it out. Running along the lower corner
of the projection screen was what had evidently been a massive rip, now
haphazardly repaired and nastily puckered by long jagged strips of duct
tape. "There is what's different" I said. And I sat back to envision a slapdash
empire of horseshoes and hand-grenades, exercising a hegemony barely
held together with duct tape that nobody could even bother to conceal.

December 2001: To Be Secure in Our Persons

Whether or not duct tape can hold together an empire, for a time a strong
new sentiment emerged that it constituted an essential guarantor of our
own continued personal well-being. With copious quantities of duct tape
conjoined to plastic sheeting, we could weather the ill—and allegedly
anthrax-laden—winds suddenly blowing back on us. Far from being
concealed, those thick roles of silvered adhesive tape became prominent
fixtures on news broadcasts and store shelves. They took up residence in
every ordinary household as a talisman for warding off the diffuse evil of a
Them, a They who is not Us, that abruptly suffused the interstices of everyday life. Nor was *heimatsland* any longer a mere vision marching through
some foreign head. It had, as we were endlessly and explicitly reminded,
become *the* homeland, our homeland, complete with its own namesake

Figure 3 Terror coin.

departments and offices to secure both this land and us within it. And in our never-faltering readiness to wield our duct tape, we would each be doing our part to hold ourselves and the homeland together. All in one.

Tape securely in place, we could sally forth fearless but vigilant to do the things we would have done anyway. After all, were we to do otherwise, They would win. So knowing where my own tape was (I had, after all, had the same roll stored in the same place for years), I felt fully prepared and protected to go out and see a movie. But there, on the screen in the darkened auditorium of the movie theater, I came face to face with Them.

By and large, though, They were not so much a Them as they were an It—a mass of undifferentiated black bodies, not a collection of individuated persons, but a swarm that existed in only two states of activity. The first was one of directionless lethargy, milling about the streets in search of either basic sustenance (even to the extreme of stripping corpses) or of nothing determinable at all. The second state was one of hostile excitation. Herein, they took the form of a fleet-footed mob bent on wiping out anything within reach that was not Them, by means of machine guns and rocket propelled grenades or even just bare hands. On the rare occasions where a figure stood out from this swarm, it took the form of a sly warlord. His expressions ranged from the savage grin to the angry grimace and his actions were confined to barking orders for the destruction of his foes.

And We were his foes, in the form of sorely outnumbered and over-whelmingly white-bodied U.S. Army Special Forces and Delta Force troopers. Unlike Them, We were permitted ample screen time to express histories, biographies, hopes, feelings, and ambivalencies. We had entered the theater of combat for Their own good, to moderate Their savage urges and the lumpen anarchy it had spawned. But in Their benightedness, They did not want Us there, and responded violently. When They killed Us it was on a one-by-one basis. It hurt. When We killed Them it was en masse and carried the emotional resonance of mowing a lawn. There was one excep-tion: that warlord was killed in a lovingly choreographed closing scene that recorded, up close and personal, his shock at being on the receiving end of one of those rocket propelled grenades. His death elicited tremendous applause and celebratory whoops from the audience.

I had a strong sense of déjà vu on exiting the theater. Although the movie I had just screened, a redaction of the U.S. Military's fatal 1993 mis-adventure in Mogadishu, had only just been released, I had an unshakeable sense that I had seen this *Black Hawk Down* before. And indeed I had, only a week earlier—*The Lord of the Rings: The Fellowship of the Ring*.

In that movie They were Orcs, but likewise a mass of undifferentiated dark bodies (albeit with jagged fangs, pointy ears and, perhaps most reveal-ing, black blood). This swarm also existed in only two states of activity. The first state was one of venal squabbling boredom, milling about vast blasted plains in search of captives to torment, torture, and rob. The second state was one of raving hostility. Herein, they took the form of a howling horde bent on wiping out anything within reach that was not part of Them, by means of siege engines, spears, swords, or even just bare hands. On the rare occasions when a figure stood out, it took the form of a relentless war-lord whose expressions ranged from the savage grin to the angry grimace and who barked orders for the destruction of his foes.

Sounding at all familiar yet?

The foe in this picture was a sorely outnumbered and exclusively white-bodied (and male) fellowship of nine more-or-less reluctant heroes from the West. These nine Men of the West were Our surrogates, replete with histories, biographies, hopes, feelings, and ambivalencies. We were impelled into combat for the good of the entire earth—Middle Earth, in this case—to eradicate the bloody panoptic chaos They strove to spread across the world. When They killed, it was on a one-by-one basis. It hurt. When Our fellowship killed, it was en masse, akin to swinging machetes through tangled underbrush. With the one exception of that warlord killed in a closing choreography that recorded, close-up, his slow and meaty demise by penetrating swordshafts and arrowheads. All to the tremendous applause and celebratory whoops of the audience.

Of course, these are just movies. Stories told in sound and vision for only a few hours each, shadowplays that are mere shadows of what they redact. Which is not to disparage the realities that came into being in Mogadishu that autumn of 1993—concretes far more complex and painful than those rescripted for reenactment in the set-decorated slums of Rabat, Morocco. But it is the fictionalizing translation of the one into the other, and that translation's consonance with other such stories, that is at issue. The Somalis I have know have been far more interested in feeding me sambusas and sharing my Islamo-industrial music CDs than in stripping my corpse of valuables. In fact, they have shown no interest in the latter whatsoever. True, I cannot say the same for Orcs, but that is merely because I have yet to meet one—or anybody who could be remotely mistaken for one. But what such people do in the flesh seems little related to what we have been convinced these people are terrifyingly prone do to our flesh should the opportunity present itself. So in the convergence of *Black Hawk Down* and *Fellowship of the Ring*, Orcs are realized in sight and sound as a corrupted and savage mass bent upon our bloody annihilation, Somalis are equated with Orcs through a narrative coincidence in the spatialities of the movie theater and the temporalities of release dates, and the whole then becomes a synecdoche for Them. And They will rend Us limb from limb should We step out there. And They will, no doubt, by Their very nature, seek to effect a similar rending should They enter in here.

Figure 4 Bless 'em.

Despite having recovered the storied descent of Somalis from Orcs, the onslaught of déjà vu had not abated. So I poked about back over the years (a full two of them, to be precise) and excavated an even deeper cinematic ancestry for Our atavistic aggressors. This one was not human to begin with, nor even independently sentient for the most part. Instead, They were a legion of identical, faintly corroded metal bodies, yet another swarm that existed with only two states of activity: off and on. When off, they did not do much of anything at all. Once switched on, They buzzed with instantaneous menace and formed into a phalanx single-mindedly committed to wiping out anything within reach that was not Them, by means of laser blasters and missile pods. These battle-droids all looked alike, and had no warlord. Instead, they were remotely controlled by a race of creatures with slitted almond eyes. These aliens dressed in elaborate Mikado-meets-Mandarin costumes and spoke with cartoon Asiatic accents. Neither grinning nor grimacing, these "Neimoidians" comported themselves with inscrutable diplomatic politeness while coldly plotting their galactic domination.

In this picture, *Star Wars Episode I: The Phantom Menace,* We took the form of a sorely outnumbered order of benign, quasi-mystical knights (but available, at least, in a range of skin colors including mint green and turquoise) charged with the task of compassionately policing the Galactic Order. Our knights came with histories, biographies, hopes, feelings, and ambivalencies—and mowed down the enemy in bulk, to no emotional effect. It is difficult, after all, to mourn the slaughter of battle-droids. But when They killed … Well, they did not really kill much at all, having clearly been manufactured with grossly defective targeting technology. Thus, the Neimoidian plot was foiled and the Neimoidians force-marched on a Walk of Shame into detention.

This story, of course, could be taken as particularly fantastical science fiction with no real-world correlate. But then I recall the belligerent rhetoric surrounding China's temporary confiscation of an off-course U.S. EP-3E Aries II spy plane two years later. All the rhetoric surrounding that event tacitly posited the threat of an emergent, and inscrutably duplicitous, Pax Sinica. So it seems willfully disingenuous to deny that the Neimoidian plot recapitulates every japanicked and sinophobic trope to have gained purchase in the prodigious ids of both the Pax Americana and the Pax Europaea. We know these tropes, and they have remained consistent throughout the decades. I recall, for example, the long-standing stereotype of the Red Chinese soldier or the Kamikaze pilot, look-alike fleshly fighting machines ordered out against their opponent in expendable waves. And shortly after screening *Phantom Menace,* I inadvertently reencountered Hergé's (1936) Tintin adventure *The Blue Lotus.* Set in China, depictions of the Japanese in this story take two forms: the conniving, dissembling diplomat, and the leering, decapitation-happy commandant.

None of this defends Japanese imperialism. The problem comes when attempts are made to declare Their empires bad but Ours good, assuming We are willing to declare Our empires imperial at all. Along these lines it is useful to page through Hergé's (1931) *Tintin in the Congo*. In this volume, We (in the form of Tintin and his friends, agents of the notoriously brutal Belgian Empire) arrive in the Congo to lend Our expertise and common sense to the natives. Throughout, these natives are aimlessly childlike or explicitly simian. They are readily prone to petty squabbling, except when incited by local witchdoctors and foreign adventurers into vicious armed assault en masse. One such assault is even directed against a cinematically projected image of Us, the savage mind here being seemingly incapable of distinguishing the representation from what it represents.

Sounding familiar?

True enough, Tintin's earlier adventures are relatively playful, and he emerges from them unscathed. In the Congo, he leaves the natives so grateful that they take to worshipping idols of both him and his dog, Milou (Snowy). But in its playfulness, Tintin is perhaps the most problematic of all. He is a candy-coating for empire, and I wonder how palatable that coating would have seemed to, say, deposed and assassinated Congolese Prime Minister Patrice Lumumba, or to the 160,000 Rwandans slaughtered during 1994 in what had been Belgium's Africa. (And then there is Tintin's own Euro-obsession with playing Cowboys-and-Indians; see Hergé, 1932.)

Tintin's early adventures and their constituent Thems, then, complement the concentrated banal nationalism celebrating Our superiority at sites such as Mount Rushmore. They comprise a *banal imperialism* that works deep in the background to justify and even render imperative the projection of Our superiority to and over Them. Simultaneously, it obscures the fact that such projection is indeed imperialism. Nor is this something relegated to the past. Narrative bloodlines link Tintin's Congolese and Japanese with our Neimoidians, Somalis, and Orcs. Furthermore, these latter characters do not remain confined to the realm of fiction. Their stories are told in conjunction with very concrete events from the south coast of China to Afghanistan and Iraq. Thus, banal imperialism begets what can be named a banal neoimperialism (assuming there is anything 'neo' about it) that suffuses our present, everyday lives. As an unnamed aid to the George W. Bush administration declared, "We're an empire now, and when we act, we create our own reality" (Suskind, 2004). It is on movie screens where valiant, vastly outnumbered armored celebrities simulate the defense of civilization against bloodthirsty (and invariably dark) hordes of extras that make-believe realities are acted out to create Our empire for real.

This act of creation is a slippery thing, conflating aliens with Africans with androids with East Asians as an imaginary whole, interbreeding the human with nonhuman, subhuman, and inhuman. The deeper one explores the more slippery it gets. Was not the director of *Black Hawk Down*, Ridley Scott, also the director of *Black Rain,* another film profiling Asians as inscrutable progenitors of ritualized violence? Did not Scott cast Congolese to play *Black Hawk Down*'s Somalis? Do not *Black Hawk Down, Fellowship of the Rings,* and *Phantom Menace* share common cast and crew members? Beneath the ever-increasing density of Scott, Tolkien, Hergé, and their fellows, I felt myself drawn inexorably beyond the event horizon of a collapsing century-old pop-cultural black hole. I was held captive in the singularity of an infinitely regressing procession of Thems, feeding off and reflecting and magnifying one another without ever touching ground with an actual Somali or flesh-and-blood Asian. (Much as Hergé himself, according to those Tintinologists I have queried, touched Africa only through the museum exhibitions of imperial booty on display in Brussels, Belgium.)

So mired in this deep primeval soup from which They germinate, one final observation struck me. Whether in the cinematic version or its literary (Tolkien, 1993) progenitor, the panoptic chaos reaching for the throat of Middle Earth's Men of the West is not spread by Orcs alone. In league with them are the militarized faceless Easterlings and the swarthy fanatical turban-clad Haradrim from the south. And there, consigned to the mythic geography of an imagined ancient world, sat caricatures of the steppe- and desert-dwellers who constitute the entirety of my own ancestry. With this observation, the collapse was complete. I, a native-born citizen of the Pax Americana's very homeland, an unequivocal Us, was also a ravening automaton-like black-blooded denizen of the savage horde that is Them. Which compels me to wonder, with each reflection I add: do I only make myself more so?

July 2002: Securities Trading

Since the visit to Mount Rushmore, worlds have been changed forever as if by divine providence. For some the change has been qualitative, a sense of unassailability lost, whether to the realized threat of death from above or to the threats whispered by each passing U.S.-flag-festooned SUV. For others half a world away, the change has been quantitative, with the bombarded rubble of already battered lives bounced and bounced again. All these changes have come as though delivered from out of thin air, figuratively and literally.

Nowhere has this aerial menace become more subtly omnipresent than at the hubs of air travel itself. Here, the federal state has assumed a godlike and indisputable omnipotence that seems to work in the most mysterious of ways. Airports have become sites of innumerable mundane disappearances, where the tweezers, lighters, knitting needles, or heirloom jewelry that was adjudged fit to fly the trip previous may become contraband the next, or vice versa. Indeed, in the earlier days of the U.S. Transportation Security Administration, some wags asserted that TSA stood for They Steal Anything. And these are but the meanest of disappearances, with travelers vanishing during stopovers and turning up fresh from ghost-flights in far-distant outsourced interrogation chambers (e.g., the case of Maher Arar; see CBC, 2005).

The resulting sense that one's existence may be impinged upon at any moment from any quarter is especially pronounced for those of Us who may also be Them. Will my lighter be apprehended en route, or will I? Will my flight arrive at its destination or terminate in midair? Which insecurity am I prepared to trade for which other? Can I even have the choice? We who are also They seem especially liable to have it both ways, without ever knowing why. And even if we do not end up having it at all, it is enough to be abidingly conscious that we might. *That* is insecurity.

These bedevilments danced through my head as I awaited check-in for a research expedition from the United States to the Pax Europaea's ever-expanding eastern frontier. And as the line crawled forward, they were afforded plenty of dancing space. But when I finally arrived at the counter, I discovered there was nothing to worry about. The flight was not departing at all. Rather, I would have to await another, on account of what was

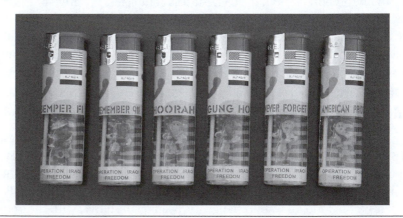

Figure 5 Lighters on parade.

described as some generic 'mechanical failure.' Some prodding, however, revealed the specifics of this failure—the antiterrorist lock on the cockpit door, something that not so long ago would have been considered a paranoid excess, would not lock. For our own protection, a replacement plane had to be delivered. In the process I would miss my connecting flight, but was to be put up in a luxury hotel at the airline's hub city and provided with an expense allowance for the inconvenience.

The terrorists, I realized, had won … me a complimentary, all-expenses paid evening in one of Europe's hippest urban hotspots. It was only a matter of moments, however, before it became apparent that one person's gain was another's loss. That loser was the fellow traveler in line right behind me.

She looked thoroughly beaten down, with the tic of an added expectation that some further blow was waiting to land upon her at the next inopportune moment. It was apparent she spoke very little English, and was having a good deal of difficulty negotiating just what the delay would mean for her connecting flight which, evidently, departed once every couple days. After checking her in, the desk clerk asked me if I, as the nearest traveler at hand, would accompany this fellow traveler through the security checkpoint and deliver her to her departure gate.

So we set off to walk the labyrinth of switchbacks and examinations that stood between us and the departure lounge. In pantomime and fragments of English, I helped my newfound associate perform the arcane rituals of submitting her carry-ons (from which nothing, despite an unusually thorough search, was confiscated), passing on cue through the metal detector's sanctuary arch and, once on the other side, negotiating the complexities of complimentary calling cards and gerrymandered area codes to apprise relatives of her indefinitely delayed arrival.

After a fraught phone conversation, the fellow traveler collapsed against the terminal wall and began to bawl with what seemed an endless reservoir of frustration. In broken English mixed with Farsi expletives, she wailed "I am not a terrorist, I blow nothing up. Why do they treat me like this!?" She let loose with the story of how she had lived in the United States and been, as she put it, a "good guest" in the country. She had respected the law, amassed a life's savings and deposited them in a local bank, and then returned to Tehran to discover that the entirety of her assets had been frozen. How she had made this trip back to the United States, been ushered through an infinity of government offices, and, with every meeting, had been told via translators that she could not have her savings back, but was never given an explanation as to why or what she might do about it. And now, her visa reaching its end, she was compelled to return to Tehran no better off than she had been when she had first arrived. Cathartically purged, she wiped her eyes, looked at me, and reiterated, "I am Irani, not terrorist, just because I am Irani does not make me terrorist. I do not hate you."

I struggled to explain how I felt about what she had told me, how disturbing it was, even how I had voted in the previous election. But it was evident that despite her impromptu eloquence in describing her own misadventures, she understood very little of what I was saying. Still, she was appreciative and, so calmed, we entered the departure lounge and found a Farsi-speaking family who shared my companion's itinerary and adopted her into their party. That was the last I saw of her.

Did she ever get home and get her savings back? Under just what rationale were they disappeared in the first place? I still sometimes wonder, and when I do these questions turn my mind to an oddly similar story of disappearances, one found in many parts of Latin America. It tells of a type of human-looking but vampirish creature that preys on the indigenous populations. In some earliest versions, from the time of 'first contact,' the vampires are foreigners whose pale skin testifies to their bloodlessness, and who require the local people to rectify this deficit. In later versions, the creatures steal not blood but body fat, *greases*. They sell these greases at a profit to local elites and to the affluent up north for the purposes of lubricating industrial machinery. In versions more recent still, the creatures take the form of rich North American tourists who come ostensibly to adopt orphans, but in truth are looking to disassemble them for transplantable organs. This later version has resulted in violent assaults upon numerous would-be adoptive mothers who have traveled from *El Norte* to the village orphanages of Central and South America (Radford, 2000; Honeyman, 1999).

Most recently, this tale has resurfaced half way around the world, with rumors flying across U.S.-occupied Iraq that teams of American and British physicians are extracting transplantable organs both from Iraqi casualties in the field and from prisoners held at Abu Ghraib Detention Facility (Harper's, 2005).

Although I am in no position to vouch for, or debunk, these stories, and am dubious of their literal truth, there is something about their mythic content that empowers them as a counternarrative to the stories told by Tolkien or Scott. The greases-thief and the baby-parts hijacker encapsulate the everyday sensibilities and anxieties of those—like my Tehrani fellow traveler—who have found themselves consistently on the Other side of empire, those whose metaphorical greases have indeed been appropriated to serve distant imperial interests. Can any of us, with a straight face, tell the people of the 'Near East' that their grease in a very literal sense isn't being taken from them? And just where have my fellow traveler's greases ended up?

December 2004: Secure the Blessings of Liberty

In an oblique way, all this brings me back to some semblance of how I started. I was somewhere around Barstow on the edge of the desert when the traffic started to take hold. Suddenly there was a terrible roar all around me and the road was packed with what looked like huge rolling billboards, an endless caravan of 40-foot-long intermodal cargo containers going at about a hundred miles an hour to Las Vegas. And a voice, my voice (or was it? n.b. Thompson, op. cit.), was screaming: "Holy Jesus! What is in these goddamn things?!"

Greases, of course. In the gas tanks. Lubricating the engines. Transformed into bottomless truckloads of souvenir refrigerator magnets, buffet fixings, cold-cast resin miniature replicas of triumphal arches and statuettes of Augustus and Julius Caesar. Within a few days, one of these miniature imperial busts would accompany me back along this same road, to join the collection of decapitated dictators resident atop my mantelpiece.

All roads once led to Rome. Radiating from the heart of the *Pax Romana*, mighty legions used these conduits to forcibly export imperial authority to the furthest provinces. In exchange, the animal, vegetal, and mineral wealth of the provinces was removed back to home. Now new roads lead to a new Rome, a high-rise palace for Caesar's fed by an endless convoy of tractor-trailers. This Caesar's Palace sprawls widely across the Nevada desert,

Figure 6 Coliseum.

a continuously metastasizing city unto itself. To visit it is to become lost in a maze of dreamlike architecture that shifts with each visit, a place that interleaves different Romes materialized through the sensibilities of different eras (Raento & Flusty, 2006; Douglass & Raento, 2004). In the brief time since my last visit, this eternal city had sprouted a coliseum and, more startling still, a monumental basilica on a previously empty sidewalk. And in keeping with the shared temperament of that long-ago imperial age and this one, this US$71.8 million, 175,000-square-foot (Southwest Contractor, 2004) basilica—the Forum Shops Expansion—was devoted entirely to the rituals of consumption.

The entrance to the Forum Shops was grandiose. An ornately corbelled triumphal arch studded with black marble(esque?) columns and Corinthian capitals, heads of lions rampant and laurel wreaths all in gilt—an irruption of classical architecture entirely at odds with the supposed democratizing modesty of its Jeffersonian forebears. The interior was more ostentatious still. An atrium of four over-high stories supported by bare-breasted caryatids, sprinkled with statues of emperors and senators in poses of tremendous gravitas, layered with bas reliefs and ornate *trompe l'oeil* murals. Akin to Rome at its height, the entirety deployed ancient idioms to bespeak great luxury and, perhaps, access to vast pools of affordable labor. Although going ancient Rome one better, say artisans of my acquaintance, labor costs were cut further by producing only some fraction of the murals by hand, replicating them digitally at full scale, and then affixing these printouts to the basilica's interior surfaces. Furthermore, the *SPQR* could never have imagined spiral escalators, let alone two pairs of them custom-engineered by Mitsubishi Electronics.

The Forum Shops, then, is a *Pax Romana* condensate. And, doing as the Romans did, guests here freely consume all that the world has to offer—the senatorial togs of *Versace,* the planet's herbaria blended into cosmetic potions (their distant provenance carefully called out, as with a skin crème "handcraft[ed] … in remote monasteries in Europe") as *fresh.* But most telling of all is *Villa Reale.* This boutique, devoted to lavish home furnishings and accessories, features amongst its Louis XIV, Napoleonic and Spanish Imperial churrigueresque housewares reproductions of the bejeweled eggs created for the Czars by Carl Fabergé. Czar, of course, was a slavicization of the term Caesar, the Czars bore a version of the latter Roman Empire's emblematic double-headed eagle, which is itself prominently displayed in the window of *Villa Reale.* So here, at a simulacrum of the Pax Romana, deep in the underbelly of the *Pax Americana*, sits replicated regalia of the Third Rome, the Russian Empire. Nor is this unique to Caesar's Palace. Rather, it is stamped across the dissimulated desert by such exhibitions as "Russia! The Majesty of the Tsars: Treasures from the Kremlin Museum"

Figure 7 Home free.

at the Venetian casino-resort, itself a simulacrum of the merchant empire of the 'Serene Republic' that was Venice.

Despite this densely layered concatenation of empires, one commonality is carefully avoided—the fact that all of these empires have long ago crumbled into ruins. At Caesar's Palace, with the exception of a peripherally located hourly sinking of Atlantis, we Caesars all are immersed in *Roma Eterna* as though it truly was eternal, an ancient imperial Rome that is *Our* imperial Rome. It is well repaired and maintained, free of decaying stone fascia and fallen columns. Nowhere is there any indication that empires collapse, inevitably and invariably.

It is, however, what empires do. Or more correctly, it is what they do to themselves. The same reach that projects legions to the far corners of the Pax, and so brings its spoils back to us, becomes overreach and, in so overreaching, empires rip themselves apart (Kennedy, 1987; Modelski, 1987; Wallerstein, 2003). Like the colossal statue of Constantine dissected into stony anatomical extremities strewn through the Palazzo dei Conservatori in Rome, Italy, the imperial body politic is one destined for dismemberment. Such dismemberment, however, is more akin to vivisection. Empires come apart kicking and screaming. These flailing death throes are expressed in the form of a belligerent combativeness that only further depletes the coffers and hastens the collapse. It is a long-established vicious cycle, but a no less contemporary one. Now, the legions of the *Pax Americana* stretch from the Korean Peninsula and Singapore the long way around due east to Kyrgyzstan (GlobalSecurity, 2006). (Alternately, we may also think of this reach as obtruding upon the eastern and western bounds, respectively, of the *Pax Sinica*.) In Iraq alone, the resultant hernia-tion of the *Pax Americana* hemorrhages an advertised US$7.4 million per hour (AP, 2004) and, according to the U.S. Department of Defense's own confirmation list, an average 64 soldiers per month. All this to suppos-edly secure a second century of American Pax (e.g., PNAC—Project for the New American Century).

This is not a pretty reality to face for those accustomed to the spoils of empire, and to seeing those spoils as anything other than spoils. Hence the 365-day-per-year, 50,000-person-per-day (Ziegler, 2004) bacchanale that carries on, punctuated only by surprise blips in the day's terrorist threat level, within the luxuriantly triumphal facades of fora like Caesar's Palace. This benumbing cocktail of orgiastic self-absorption plus a dash of learned helplessness transmutes *Pax Americana* into *Paxil* Americana, within which shopping becomes an apotrapaic practice—a comforting talisman against imperial collapse and the barbarian hordes just beyond the hori-zon off whom we have done quite well and who, in our deepest and most denied atavistic fears, will come upon us like Vandals in the night to get their own back. Indeed, our leaders have been explicit that in bellicosely pursuing our new century against the specter of impending collapse, it is each of our patriotic duty to "spend, spend, spend" (Carlson, 2001; Vardie and Watty, 2001).

In the intensifying sheer forces created by this occlusion of conquest, consumerism, denial and desperation, new rips open up across the scrim of normalcy that conceals empire from our view. I am thinking, for instance, of a recent newspaper front page emblazoned with the image of a pair of bemasked and camouflaged U.S. soldiers standing over two screaming Iraqi children. Their parents had just been mistakenly shot dead by those soldiers' comrades. And in the sidebar of this same page, immediately adja-cent this photograph, is the lead-in for an article on the best local places to go for the "cuisine delights" of the Middle and Near East (*Toronto Star*, 2005). Apparently, editors do not think to bat an eye at the neoaphoristic possibility of having our cake while killing the cook. And apparently, we have strayed quite far from the sermon on Mount Rushmore.

Of course, an early-twentieth-century Filipino or a middle-century Haitian (to give just a couple of many possible examples) would not see this detour as anything new or remarkable at all. The body of Mount Rushmore itself has been flawed from its inception, the presidential colossi riddled with continually opening fissures that demand constant applications of silicon caulk lest the entire edifice fall away in granitic shards. So in some ways, this is all an old, familiar tale.

What is novel, however, is the appearance of ruptures so mind-boggling that neither duct tape nor silicon caulk could repair them were we to apply it thickly across our own eyes. Most notorious of these are the photo-documentations of animal attacks, physical assaults and sexual humiliations to have emerged from the Abu Ghraib Detention Facility. I remain unable to shake the snapshot of Military Police Specialist Lynndie England grinning through her cigarette and giving 'thumbs up' while standing before a lineup of naked and restrained prisoners, their heads inserted into what look like nothing so much as shopping bags. And that is just me. Imagine how the same snapshot must read to the families and friends of those bagged prisoners—an American woman standing above a humiliated pile of stripped local men, communicating to the viewer an invitation in the regional gestural parlance to sit on her stiffened male member. Something Spc. England and her superiors knew full well, assuming they had familiarized themselves with their military-issue 'culture smart cards' (e.g., MCIA, 2004). In our own parlance, and in keeping with President George W. Bush's cavalier "bring them on" challenge to the Iraqi resistance in July of 2003, this is what is commonly termed "asking for it." Or, perhaps more concisely, "hubris."

Of course, we are indeed seeing these things, and so ourselves become party to a reappearance of the disappeared. Furthermore, this is a reappearance that actively (or *activistically*) refuses to redisappear. Consider, for example, the specter of he who has come to be known simply as "Abu Ghraib Man" or, as christened by his captors, 'Gilligan' (Salon, undated). He perches precariously atop a cardboard MRE (Meals Ready to Eat) shipping box, clad in a black poncho and a faceless hood adapted from a sandbag, wires hanging from his fingers and appearing to terminate at an electrical junction box immediately behind. This prisoner has become an icon of empire and against it, dramatically reenacted in street protests and inserted graphically into the interstices of everyday life by means of assorted posters reproducing his outline on everything from traffic light junction boxes to construction-site walls. At their cleverest, these reappearances depict head-on the confluence of conquest and consumption, as with the parodies of Apple iPod's postering campaign featuring dancing bodies silhouetted in black against solid florescent-hued backgrounds, with the signature white lines of iPod headphones trailing from their ears. Interspersed with these posters, it is now not uncommon to find on a similarly florescent background the black silhouette of Abu Ghraib Man, white lines trailing from his fingers above a logo reading "iRaq."

There has been a long-standing tendency to think of empire at its most vulgar as a thing of the past. But as Abu Ghraib Man insistently points out, the imperial present (cf. Gregory, 2004) now cannot but be widely acknowledged and, in ever more precincts, acknowledged for what it is. Of course, we do still tend to think of empire as dependant upon parading phalanxes of kevlar-armored legionnaires and mighty fleets of missile-studded galleons, the collection of retailable tribute and the dispatch of proconsuls to distant protectorates on freshly reinscribed maps (e.g., Flusty on "praetorian globality," 2004). And, indeed, empire *is* these things. But it is no less legible in, and no less reliant on, such everyday banalities as 18-wheeled intermodal amphorae laden with exotic oils or the box office blockbusters that inventively separate the *populus americanus quiritium* from the *barbarus* (while perhaps bringing over those of us caught in the frontiers between, see Ross, 2005; McKinley, 2005).

Empire is comprised of all these many pieces and more, pieces that must be forced back together again and again as the entire assemblage grows ever more unwieldy and strains to burst apart at the seams. Such force, in turn, makes plain that the term "imperial pax" is an oxymoron. *Pax*—peace—under these conditions will only be maintained for such a necessarily finite time as the violently inherent insecurities of empire are exported to others, elsewhere. And, in so doing, and so being, we trade the very possibilities of freedom and security for futility, an impossible perpetuation of empire and its perquisites that, in the last analysis, is the most insecure arrangement of all.

Figure 8 iRaq.

Acknowledgments

To Dean Martelli for the continuous source-feed; Pauliina Raento for editing and for on-site expertise from the Black Hills to Brussels via Vegas; and to John Sergeant for getting me out to the movies more.

References

AP (Associated Press). "Clock in NYC Shows Cost of Iraq War." August 26, 2004. Unpaginated, available online.

Billig, M. *Banal Nationalism.* Sage: London. 1995.

CBC (Canadian Broadcast Corporation). Maher Arar: Timeline. October 27, 2005. Unpaginated, available online.

Carlson, M. "Patriotic Splurging." *Time Magazine.* October 15, 2001. Unpaginated, available online.

Douglass, W.A., & Raento, P. "The Tradition of Invention: Conceiving Las Vegas." *Annals of Tourism Research* 31/1. 2004. pp. 7–23.

Flusty, S. *De-Coca-Colonization: Making the Globe from the Inside Out.* London, New York: Routledge. 2004.

GlobalSecurity. *U.S. Military Facilities* (see "Central Command" and "Pacific Command"). http://www.globalsecurity.org/military/facility/index.html.

Gregory, D. *The Colonial Present: Afghanistan, Palestine, Iraq.* Oxford: Blackwell. 2004.

Harper's. "Hearts and Brains, a Reading." *Harper's Magazine.* July 2005. Unpaginated, available online.

Hergé (Remi, G.). *Tintin au Congo.* Tournai: Casterman. 1970 (1931).

Hergé (Remi, G.). *Tintin en Amérique.* Tournai: Casterman. 1957 (1932).

Hergé (Remi, G.). *Le Lotus Bleu.* Tournai: Casterman. 1946 (1936).

Honeyman, D.D. *Lynch Mobs and Child Theft Rumors in the Guatemalan Highlands.* Unpublished thesis. 1999.

Kennedy, P. *The Rise and Fall of Great Powers: Economic Change and Military Conflict from 1500 to 2000.* New York: Vintage. 1987.

MCIA (Marine Corps Intelligence Activity). *Iraq Culture Smart Card: Guide for Communication and Cultural Awareness.* 2004.

McKinley, J. C. Jr. "Mexican Pride and Death in U.S. Service." *New York Times.* March 22, 2005. Unpaginated, available online.

Modelski, G. *Long Cycles in World Politics.* Seattle: University of Washington Press. 1987.

PNAC (Project for the New American Century). http://www.newamericancentury.org/.

Radford, B. "Kidney Devils." *Fortean Times.* #138, September 2000. Unpaginated, available online.

Raent, P. and Flusty, S. "Three Trips to Italy: Deconstructing the New Las Vegas." In Minca, C. and Oakes, T. (eds.) *Travels in Paradox: Remapping Tourism.* Lanham: Rowman and Littlefield. 2006.

Ross. J. Mexico: "The Pentagon's Proxy Army in Iraq." *Counterpunch.* February 21, 2005. Unpaginated, available online.

Salon, Undated. "The Abu Ghraib Files: Electrical Wires." http://www.salon.com/
news/abu_ghraib/2006/03/14/chapter_4/index.html.

Southwest Contractor. "Nevada Top Projects: Forum Shops at Caesars." July 2004.
p. 64.

Suskind, R. "Without a Doubt." *The New York Times Magazine*. October 17, 2004.
Unpaginated, available online.

Taliaferro, J. *Great White Fathers: The True Story of Gutzon Borglum and His
Obsessive Quest to Create the Mt. Rushmore National Monument*. New York:
PublicAffairs. 2002.

Thompson, H.S. *Fear and Loathing in Las Vegas: A Savage Journey to the Heart of
the American Dream*. New York: Random House. 1998 (1971).

Tolkien, J.R.R. *The Lord of the Rings*. London: Harper Collins. 1993 (1954–1955).

Toronto Star. "Faces of Anguish," and "Food Mecca." January 19, 2005. P.1.

Vardy, J. and Wattie, C. "Shopping is Patriotic, Leaders Say." *National Post*. September 28, 2001. Unpaginated, available online.

Wallerstein, I. *The Decline of American Power: The U.S. in a Chaotic World*. New
York: W.W. Norton and Company. 2003.

Ziegler, E. "The Forum Shops at Caesars Adds More Bang per Foot." *View Neighborhood Newspapers*. November 24, 2004. Unpaginated, available online.

Urban Operations and Network Centric Warfare

M. CHRISTINE BOYER

"If the natural utilization of productive forces is impeded by the property system, the increase in technical devices, in speed, and in the sources of energy will press for an unnatural utilization, and this is found in war. The destructiveness of war furnishes proof that society has not been mature enough to incorporate technology as its organ, that technology has not been sufficiently developed to cope with the elemental forces of society."

Walter Benjamin
"The work of art in the age of mechanical reproduction"
Illuminations [New York: Harcourt, Brace & World, Inc., 1968]: 242.

Urban Operations

Contemporary architect/urbanists like to praise the wild unruly nature of urban growth, believing that order will emerge spontaneously from a city's chaotic condition. An unbounded expanse of urban substance has erased from their minds any desire to impose a rational plan or regulatory control over the disorganized urban terrain. It is impossible for them to conceptualize the future of cities when all differences, identity and tradition have been discarded in the dust bin of outmoded practices. If the architect/urbanist can no longer sustain the idea of projective city plans, or theorizing about urban development and population characteristics in emerging nations, this is not so for the U.S. military which over the last decade has developed a strange juxtaposition of urban planning procedures, geographical imagination and military strategies termed 'military operations on urbanized terrain' or 'urban operations.' It has long been an assumption of military planners that fighting in urban areas has its pitfalls. In repetitive citations, almost all the military journal articles placed under review in order to discover what is meant by 'urban operations' make reference to the ancient master of war Sun Tzu who advised as early as 500 B.C. that

> the worst policy is to attack cities. Attack cities only when there is no alternative ... [T]hose skilled in war ... capture his [enemies'] cities without assaulting them and overthrow his state without protracted operations.[1]

Modern sensibilities chafe at the widespread collateral damage and killing of noncombatants that urban warfare necessarily entails.[2] Yet urban operations seem unavoidable and inevitable and so the 'transformation in military affairs' is concerned not only with how to operate on urban terrain but how to deploy the most highly advanced information technology to guarantee that strikes are swift, collateral damage minimized, and violence sanitized. In fact urban operations and net-centric warfare are so intimately intertwined in the minds of military strategists that one cannot be described without the other. It is hoped that information technology will bring about the virtualization of war carried on at a safe distance with minimal casualties inflicted except on the enemy where accurate records seem not to be kept. (In the Gulf War, 270 Americans lost their lives; in the Mogadishu raid, 18 Americans were killed; in the Kosovo campaign, no lives were lost; there are no accompanying lists for enemy losses.[3])

Perhaps the 1991 Gulf War was the last war to be fought on a traditional battlefield, planned and strategized on two-dimensional maps. Carried out in its purest form, as a war on a sand table in open terrain, it may have been the last war in which cities such as Kuwait City, Baghdad, Tel Aviv, while under attack, were incidental to the planning of military strategy. Operation Desert Storm proved that high-tech capabilities of air power are not only dominant but decisive, and Iraqi military leadership learned that fighting a conventional war in the wide-open spaces of the Arabian Peninsula was a hopeless strategy.[4] It is now assumed that warfare is information-based, giving technological superiority to the force that can collect, process, and disseminate an uninterrupted flow of information yet deny its adversary the ability to do the same.[5]

Operation Iraqi Freedom in 2003 was the first serious test of this assumption. Beginning in the spring of 2002, the U.S. army began to collect and archive all relevant national imagery and commercial digital terrain data for Iraq: data on vegetation, water resources, elevations and size of buildings, satellite imagery, maps of all varieties, and so on. Correlated databases provided a common operating picture of the battlefield and enabled the U.S. Army to achieve a stunning victory over the Iraqi army.

During the invasion of Iraq, U.S. military commanders constantly gathered and analyzed intelligence on the enemy in real time from many different sources. About 3,000 commanders shared "a tactical intranet" with a map overlay, which always let everyone know where everybody was. They could offer an operational assessment down to the level of the corps. Special forces with cellphones provided news that was used to stop demolitions of oil wells or dams; they monitored enemy signals, used imagery and GPS as the leading source of tactical intelligence. A "warfighting web" linked Air Force Space Command with ground forces equipped with 100,000 GPS receivers, one each to most squads of nine soldiers or five Marines.[6] Soldiers on the ground, however, were left without the ability to receive, much less process, such complicated data flows during the fluid and rapid tempo of combat operations. Just taking a few seconds to check or retrieve data could produce error and sudden tragedy.[7] Nevertheless, and in spite of these drawbacks, the belief remains unshaken that U.S. technological superiority will guarantee military dominance on any geographical terrain.

It is not the U.S. military that desires to fight in cities where its technological supremacy may become useless. To counter U.S. military superiority, especially that of aerial warfare and overhead surveillance, the Iraqi enemy developed innovative modes of attack or unconventional responses that avoided directly confronting the wall of U.S. military might. They selected a strategy of chaos hoping to achieve victory by avoiding defeat. Their key objective is to convince the U.S. that no clear solution or endstate is possible except the cessation of chaos.[8] The U.S. military may have decapitated Saddam's regime, but in the aftermath insurgents or urban guerillas understood that the asymmetrical power of U.S. technological superiority could be thwarted, even neutralized, by taking refuge in complex and uncertain urban terrains. They quickly moved the battlefield into Iraq's sixteen largest cities, which together hold 70 percent of the country's population. The conclusion is simple, as one military commander put it: "We have seen the future war, and it is urban."[9] The days of warfare defined by Carl von Clausewitz as fought on open fields between two symmetrical armies are over. Warfare once again has entered the city.

Three data sets underscore the impact worldwide urbanization has had on U.S. military operations. United Nations population statistics and urban growth rates project that population growth between 2000 and 2030 will be concentrated in urban areas. Sometime within the next two decades one out of two people will live in urban environments, and one out of two will live in water-stressed areas. By the year 2054, it is projected the world's population will reach the 9 billion mark. Sixty percent of these people will live in Asia, 20 percent in Africa, only 7 percent in Europe. In addition, documentation by the Heritage Foundation on the number of military units assigned to countries between 1950 and 2003, plus data collated by the Defense Department on U.S. military responses to oppositional situations around the world between 1990 and 2002 combine to yield an overall picture that U.S. military engagement in rapidly urbanizing areas of the world is dramatically increasing.[10]

Thus, the U.S. military understands that future warfare will not only be fought on urban battlefields, but because it considers itself to be a force-projection power, is likely to face adversaries on foreign soil, amid alien and possibly unfriendly noncombatants in unknown and complex urban terrains. It is easy to conclude that the complexity of urban systems, their vulnerable infrastructure and volatile populations have become a new focus for military strategists. Whether for military or peace-keeping engagements, whether to calm ethnic clashes or stabilize competition for resources and suppress criminal anarchy, urban operations require revolutionizing military operations to deal effectively with complexity, uncertainty, and chaos.[11] It is essential now to answer two vitally important questions: is it possible to seize and control a city without reducing it to rubble and what strategies are necessary to achieve military success on urban terrain?

The military bases its strategy for urban operations on two major assumptions. In order to take a city apart, one has to first know how to put it together, to understand the relative importance of its component parts and how these interact.[12] Urban geography and processes of urbanization must be studied and known. Without any architects/urbanists noticing, a shadow system of urban research has been established and funded by the military.[13] Military advisers now suggest that students of urban warfare study the highly related but little explored literature of urban design, city planning and municipal management. Analytical insights must then be brought to bear on military strategies because the process of planning a city and strategies of urban warfare are closely related. The vastness of built-up areas of cities makes uniform application of assets and forces ineffective unless military advisers understand at what points of the cityscape they should focus and how much pressure they can apply. The second assumption is that urban warfare has a long history, and this history must also be studied, the advantages and disadvantages of specific urban designs on strategies must be understood, and lessons drawn from forces facing similar problems and effecting similar or different solutions.[14]

Nevertheless, cities still present major barriers to warfare and have conventionally been viewed as an inferior kind of military terrain, usually a distraction from the main military effort. Wars are seldom won in cities, and it has long been assumed the moment an army crosses the line between landscape and cityscape, the terrain quickly turns against the invaders, transforming routine operations into operations that are anything but routine. Cities and armies are antagonistic to each other: for the army a city offers opportunity for unopposed violence and plunder; for the city the army is a monster, bent on its annihilation.

Modern military operations on urban terrain reach back to the nineteenth century to the time when cities expanding in population burst beyond their protective walls. For example, the last wall around Paris, the fifth system of fortification, was built in 1840–1841, built as much for protection against invaders as it was for defense against internal disorder. In fact, the deterrent effect of these fortifications seems to have been ineffective. Marshal Bugeaud-d'Isly was well aware after the year of revolutions in 1848 that the military had to be trained to combat civil discord in the streets of Paris, to overcome the troop's paralysis when confronted with a milling crowd of agitators, malcontents and delinquents revolting against the rule of law and usurping the sacred name of "the people."[15] Bugeaud knew that time was essential in 'the war of the streets': that every hour given to the agitators enabled them to raise their barricades, perfect their lines of command and communication, even augment their morale. Plans must be prepared to guard the major symbolic locations, always under attack in civil unrest, major points such as the Hotel de Ville, the National Assembly, or the Tuileries. And plans must be developed to occupy in advance principal houses that commanded a view along several streets, guarding major arteries and bridges that serviced a district day and night. Each house must be conceived as a permanent small fortress, provided with food, water, ammunition and manned around the clock so that at the slightest provocation soldiers could pierce the wall of resistance, break down barricades, repave streets, and care for the wounded. With prudent foresight insurgents would never gain the advantage of time, be allowed to rebuild their barricades at night, or retake terrain that had been abandoned.

Yet Paris remained the classic city of rebellion and revolution haunted its present and future throughout the nineteenth century. Three monarchies, three republics, and two empires would be overthrown in just over 80 years. No doubt, threat of insurrections yet to come was in the mind of Napoleon III when he commissioned Baron von Haussmann in the 1860s to modernize the city. Haussmann's improvements made sure that working-class neighborhoods where barricades had once been erected were demolished as he pierced major new boulevards through pockets of urban resistance, allowing military troops to circulate with ease, and water, air and light to cleanse unsavory conditions. Such aggressive 'haussmannization' making rubble in the streets an everyday reality only cemented the link between revolution and urbanization and raised the specter of dramatic disruptions and reconfigurations yet to come. The fall of the empire in 1870 and the bitter military defeat of France by the Prussians closed the century of revolutionary combat in the streets.

Instead, the Franco-Prussian War of 1870 and the storming of Paris [1870–1871] introduced the modern age of siege warfare. The French had been routed in a series of field battles, Napoleon III had been deposed by a popular uprising, and the city was surrounded by the German Third Army, so it was expected that Paris would soon capitulate because its seething populace bottled up within the city would bring about its own demise. But quite to the surprise of General Helmuth von Moltke, the chief of the Prussian Great General Staff, nothing like that took place. Instead, French irregulars were attacking Germans lines of communication outside the city from the rear while the meagerly armed forces and citizen soldiers inside Paris were planning for a long and self-sacrificing resistance. They hoped to lure the Germans into the city where they would be entrapped. The Germans, on the other hand, had no intention of storming Paris, but expected that rioting and mutiny within the irregular French army would bring the city to the negotiating table. To hasten such inevitability, the Germans decided to force Paris to surrender by hunger alone. Intended results were not immediate so the impatient Germans began to bombard the city. For one month, they sent 300 to 400 shells per day with little damage or results except to improve the morale of the French.

There was no military reason for this bombardment: French rations were low and starvation threatened. The Germans, however, believed that time was against them. As war dragged on and the French both inside and outside the city kept up their resistance, European opinion began to turn against Germany and in favor of France. Although the resistance had little hope of breaking the siege and reversing the German military success, still von Moltke understood that winning on the battlefield itself was a thing of the past unless an invading army was willing to reduce a city to rubble. A new dawn of urban warfare had been born: henceforth battles were fought to create conditions in which war would be won on the tables of diplomacy. Pounding the city with bombs would hasten this result. Thus armistice was soon declared, and on the 1st of March 1871 German troops entered the city of Paris.[16]

With the advent of the airplane as a new instrument of warfare during World War I, military strategists began to imagine how battles might be won by air power alone. While considering plans for the future development of Moscow in 1930, Le Corbusier was strikingly aware that a formidable new menace threatened all urban existence. Lieutenant Colonel Vauthier had just given him a copy of his book entitled *The Aerial Danger and the Future of the Country.* Le Corbusier understood that the air would be the new theater of military operations and that the threat of aerial warfare emanated not only from explosive projectiles that could destroy a city's built structures, but also from poison gas and chemical warfare that could asphyxiate its inhabitants, and from flammable liquids that could spread a firestorm beyond imagination. A city could be destroyed all at once. But it just so happened, quite without realizing it, that Le Corbusier had already provided a necessary defense against this new danger of aerial warfare in his studies for *Urbanisme* [1925] and in his book *Precisions* [1930].

He proposed the construction of housing in reinforced concrete, a material strong enough to withstand the impact of bombs and also fireproof. He also proposed these structures be isolated in great open spaces, that housing, commerce and industry be located in separate zones, and that the entire built surface of the city be reduced. These were essential conditions needed to lessen the exposure of built structures to aerial attack but also to contain the spread of any conflagration. To avoid the disaster of poisonous gas, his proposal for suppressing meager courtyards and narrow corridor streets, along with the provision of wide open spaces and housing raised on piloti, would allow sufficient wind and water from protected hydrants or large open air swimming pools to cleanse the air. Le Corbusier asked Colonel Vauthier to speak at the fifth CIAM congress gathering in Paris in 1937 to discuss the problems of housing and leisure. From the triple viewpoint of explosive projectiles, firebombs, and poisonous gases, he explained, it was necessary to reconsider architecture and urbanism.[17] Such defense measures, decreed for the safety of urban citizens, would ensure the realization of rational town-planning schemes. "Or, vice versa, in rationalizing a plan for the city. ... to save her from the shameful chaos into which she is now plunged, we shall automatically satisfy the need for aerial defense."[18]

Le Corbusier's rational town planning schemes, however, were never implemented and so were of no help to save London, the world's largest city in 1940, from the first aerial siege in history. Earlier that year, the Luftwaffe had raided the port of Rotterdam, killing a thousand citizens and destroying some 20,000 buildings, creating sufficient havoc to bring about a Dutch surrender. So it was expected that the Battle of Britain, an aerial bombardment of defenseless civilians, would be fought and won or lost as the result of air attacks alone. London brought a check to this optimistic belief. For five weeks, the Germans flew 12,000 sorties over the city but Londoners quickly adapted to even the most destructive raids. The underground tube stations quickly turned into bomb shelters where some 100,000 people sought safety every night. Nothing like the projected casualties—physical or psychological—was ever generated. Although gas was expected to play a major role in aerial attacks, the worst problems came from fire and unexploded bombs, which inhibited emergency services and public traffic from operating effectively. Aerial siege continued until early May 1941, when the German army finally understood that "London's fundamental cohesion, the city's capacity to function as a highly integrated metropolis, was not irreparably damaged by the German air campaign for one reason: physical destruction was not the same as systems destruction."[19]

The damage wrought on London was little compared to the havoc wreaked by Allied bombers sent against German and Japanese cities: 79 percent of Bremerhaven was destroyed, 75 percent of Hamburg, and 50 percent of numerous other cities. Tokyo suffered the most destructive aerial attack: 83,000 were killed and more than 15 square miles of its city center destroyed. Nevertheless no city in World War II was ever subdued by air attack to the point that it stopped functioning, including Hiroshima and Nagasaki. The cities attacked were too big to be eradicated completely, even if their heart had been annihilated. World War II taught the military that urban complexity worked to the advantage of a large city: complexity meant redundancy of basic operations. Knock out one aspect of its functioning, such as part of its transport system, it would quickly divert traffic to other parts of the system. A complex city remained robust, absorbing destruction and continuing to function as an urban entity.[20]

Yet nuclear warfare with its strategy of massive retaliation questioned the very 'survivability' of cities. U.S. deterrent strategists decided that cities over 100,000 in population would be the logical targets of a nuclear war, only their size and economic importance justified the use of expensive atomic weaponry.[21] They thought in terms of "city busting": cities would receive the direct hit and would absorb it in such a manner that damage would not spill over to survival areas, whereas the ensuing destruction would take care of other social problems as well. Defense planners after 1960 were adamant about the necessity to sacrifice the city. So it was argued "any effort to defend the American city by protecting its residents from attack is extremely dangerous to the national security. All analysts agree that such efforts ("hardening" the city) will be interpreted by the Soviet Union as an offensive move on our part, that is, as a sign that we are preparing for a *first strike*.[22] The official U.S. plan was to move people away from target cities, or suggest they move themselves, before a nuclear attack. Not surprisingly middle-class suburbs were built in the 1950s, followed by the upper middle class relocating to small towns beyond the urban fringe, and into exurbia by the 1980s. The postwar investment in highways, and disinvestment in rail transport, the breakup of a centralized phone system into smaller companies and cellular phone operators, the rise of personal computers and the World Wide Web, can all be interpreted as preparation for nuclear attack on the congested centers of cities. Left behind in the centers of cities, the urban population would be wiped out along with its substandard housing, impoverished neighborhoods, crime ridden streets, high mortality rates, and so on. The threat of the bomb and the policy of 'city busting' obviously generated paradoxical effects.

With the end of Cold War brinksmanship in 1991, the tumbling of walls and rending of iron curtains, nuclear deterrent strategies became anachronistic. Some other phantasm had to be conjured up because the nature of the aggressor had changed and with it the framework of military engagement. Kazakhstan, a recent breakaway state from the former Soviet Union, became the first 'Muslim' state to possess nuclear capability in December of 1991.[23] In addition to this new fear of terrorists with weapons of mass destruction, megacities had burst on the scene with their challenge of complexity and uncontrollability, and a new city built by information had arisen as well.

Air–land battles assume their primary objective is to throw the enemy off balance with a powerful blow from an unexpected direction and to follow this up with other strikes so that the enemy cannot recuperate. The doctrine was tailored for fighting the Soviets in NATO Europe, but was also deployed in the first Gulf War.[24] Currently, the military deploys an operational strategy that conceives of a military campaign as a "highly coordinated sequence of interrelated tactical actions that would move one's war toward the attainment of strategic objectives. ... The operational art presupposes also that all action is always under one's positive control even in the extremities of violence that the modern battlefield is sure to produce."[25] Not only must all military actions be synchronized over space and time but, in addition, the challenges of an urban campaign have to be met.

Contemporary cities are daunting environments that must be analyzed and understood by an invading army: they contain a maze of urban canyons and underground tunnels that restrict troop movement, change the rules of engagement, and diminish technological superiority. Buildings and manmade constructions superimposed on the terrain block lines-of-sight essential for deploying precision weapons; they interrupt radio frequencies and make GPS satellite positions difficult to obtain. Because the enemy controls the location of the conflict on what they consider to be friendly terrain, the invading force is required to maneuver in long columns along fixed routes, alleyways, and dead-ends with increased exposure from multiple points of attack without the ability to concentrate their firepower. These are the same streets and alleyways that offer the enemy routes of escape into which they can vanish. The invaders, moreover, have to operate within buildings, with no prior knowledge of their layouts, and are exposed to guerrilla tactics such as ambushes, kidnappings, booby traps, sniper fire, and improvised explosive devices. This calls for a new type of verticalized warfare visualizing the urban terrain in all three dimensions from underground tunnels to the high ground of rooftops, from surface street level to urban airspace. Solids must be seen through as if they no longer block lines of sight, buildings must be visualized from inside and soldiers must be able to assess what the invisible enemy is up to and decide if and when they need to strike.

This has caused the U.S. military to theorize about the complexity of cityscapes and the behavioral characteristics of urban populations. They have devised strategies of parallel not serial urban warfare, conceptualized the enemy as an organism with self-organizing and mutating behavior, and considered complex group movements to be modeled on flocking algorithms. The military has improved its urban mapping and simulation techniques for training soldiers for real-time operations. In short, the military is dealing with cities the way a planner once might have done: reaching backward to Ludwig von Bertalanffy's General Systems Theory of the 1950s, and forward to conceptualize cities as systems—actually systems within systems—whose parts can be manipulated and controlled by understanding the complex interrelationships between different levels within the system as a whole.[26]

Ground troops tend to think of cities as buildings, physical forms such as skyscrapers, houses, airports and harbors. Focused on terrain, they are likely to classify cities by their differences and assume that fighting in Munich would be more difficult than in Mogadishu. The latter so-called primitive city, however, was able to foil an international intervention while Munich was beat into submission after the fiercest war in history.[27] The key variable in cities is not just their physical structure but the complex behavior of human populations within the urban terrain. It is the complexity of people, like the citizens of Paris, which enables cities to withstand sieges lasting months or years unless their ability to survive is disorganized.

Hence, the military has started to classify different types of cities based on the behavioral characteristics of their population.[28] This typology of human architecture is only a starting point, a rough outline of the operational environment that awaits any occupying or stabilizing force. It is construed as an early warning system of some of the intractable problems that may lie ahead. The first type of city is called a hierarchical city, in which chains of command operate within broadly accepted rules of law—like American cities. These cities, with their united citizenry and accepted chain-of-command, can provide intensive resistance to an attacker yet once occupied can be the easiest to govern as soon as the population recognizes the benefits of collaboration. The cities of Germany and Japan after World War II were examples of this type—their populations fought fiercely but once defeated, were easy to govern and to reconstruct.

The second type of city is called a multicultural city and displays contending systems of custom and belief. These cities are cockpits of struggle aggravated by ethnic divisions and struggles for dominance. Power is diffused with partisans adhering to specific chains of command which are spread across ethnic networks, religious organizations, or terrorist groups. These cities squander their creative power, and tend to be intolerant of intercommunal exchange. Devoid of a shared community of values or experience in cooperative ventures, this type of city is unstable and ultimately self-destructive. The preeminent example is Jerusalem, where order is maintained only by force of the most powerful faction, inflaming the hatred of those excluded from power. Other examples can be drawn from South African cities under apartheid, the massacres of Hindus and Muslims on the Indian subcontinent, or cities in the collapsed Soviet empire. From a military standpoint a multicultural city may be easy to conquer, if not totally destroyed by the hegemonic group, but difficult to administer because compromise is literally unthinkable and a hardening of divisions between the contending groups an inevitable result.

The third type of city is labeled a tribal city and is growing in number. Cities of this type present the most difficult urban environment for military operations. Based on differences of blood or blood-based allegiances, these ethnic conflicts are the most intractable and merciless. It is difficult for outsiders to discern, yet alone fathom, the depth of hatred within clan fighting. Such conflicts as seen in Mogadishu, Kilgali, Karachi, or the former Yugoslavia represent a shift from slaughter between civilizations to slaughter of neighbors, from imperialist genocide to genocide against familiars. The military considers the tribe to be a basic killing organization with no will to compromise, or advantage to be achieved through cooperation. Tribal cities set up many 'inscrutable' obstacles for urban operations and are the most perplexing of city types. They may, however, become the predominant place of U.S. military engagement in the twenty-first century.

This simple typology is set up by the military to drive home a basic point: in urban operations the center of gravity for attack, "those characteristics, capabilities, or sources of power from which a military force derives its freedom of action, physical strength, or will to fight,"[29] is never a presidential palace, or a television station, or a bridge or barricade. Not physical objects, then, but something located inside the people and among the actions of the population. In urban operations, adversaries of the U.S. military are not only military actors but also can be crowds, political or economic leaders, criminal groups, terrorist organizations, and so on.

Cities offer the adversary the support of large and presumably friendly noncombatant populations which they can manipulate to their advantage. Thus, for example, the Egyptian defenders of Suez City in 1973 were able to rely on friendly noncombatants as couriers when other methods of communication were cut. The Israeli forces had no such option. Or Grozny in the winter of 1995: most Chechens were fighting in a city they had known since childhood. Working at night they laid mines, carried supplies and ammunition to the front, moved through back alleys, sewers, and basements. Circling around the Russians, they forced them to cling to their armored vehicles which they mistakenly thought offered some sort of security.[30]

Thus, it may not be surprising that strategists of urban operations focus on the psychological characteristics of populations and seek to evaluate the potential value of deception as an asymmetrical strategy of the underdog.[31] Clausewitz noted in 1873: "[t]he weaker the forces that are at the disposal of the supreme commander, the more appealing the use of cunning becomes."[32] Deception is a deliberate ploy meant to induce misperception in another. When utilized in conflict and war, its aim is to affect, confuse, even destroy, an enemy's decision-making process and as such becomes an integral component of intelligence operations. The classic arsenal of deception involves disinformation and camouflage.[33] Given the importance of navigation and orientation in urban terrain a major aim of disinformation is directed at mapping or navigational skills. For example the Soviets deliberately deployed cartographic disinformation affecting all maps of cities during the Cold War. Thus, detailed street maps of Moscow failed to identify major thoroughfares or locate important buildings making distances difficult to estimate and locations hard to pinpoint.[34]

Perhaps cities enhance and even facilitate the deployment of deception, trickery and guile because the U.S. military has utilized deception to throw the enemy off target. Thus in the first Gulf War the U.S. sought to convince Saddam Hussein that the Coalition's intention was to conduct its main offensive by attacking central Kuwait. It assumed the Iraqi's normal response to being attacked would be to counter-attack where it was struck. In order to lure Saddam into assuming that the U.S. had begun to strike, the military broadcasted tank noises over loudspeakers, set up dummy tanks and artillery pieces and simulated radio traffic so that its real intent to swing west of Kuwait and make a direct attack on Iraq was masked.[35] Again in Operation Iraqi Freedom, the enemy following media reports planted by the U.S. military was caught off guard by a sudden attack because they expected a long aerial war to be followed by a ground war. They did not expect a brief air attack nor the start of a ground war while the 4th Infantry Division was still in the Mediterranean. The U.S. military played mind games as well by intentionally wrecking Saddam Hussein's information feedback loop. If Saddam could not trust the information he was receiving, if he did not know what was happening on the battlefield, then he would not know if his soldiers were carrying out the war he had scripted. The initial air strikes on Saddam, and the highly publicized reports that information of his whereabouts was obtained from some of his trusted officers, were intended to unnerve other subordinates and disturb his lines of communication.[36]

Whether deployed by enemy or invader, deception in urban terrain must be carefully planned and monitored lest it be discovered and collateral damage the consequence. The U.S. military must be trained to perceive and counter enemy deceptive efforts through urban exercises and simulation models; its intelligence analysts must be able to discern signals from noise, and they must develop and know how to operate reliable and credible intelligence collection technology. The unrivaled advantage of the U.S. in information technologies allows it to deploy deceptive practices never thought possible before: "[i]n short, although a massive frontal assault may bloodily turn an enemy out of a prepared position in the city, if a well-orchestrated deception can accomplish the same thing without a shot being fired, does it not present a powerful resource to be tapped?"[37]

Network Centric Warfare

Network Centric Warfare conceptualizes the field of military operation as systems that are distributed, highly robust and dynamic, quick to evolve and adapt their behavior to ad hoc situations. Linked together via information technology, a network translates global governing principles into local rule sets, which in turn are governed by a deep understanding of battle force dynamics and urban environments. These systems encourage self-synchronization, connection, and recombination at the lowest possible echelons, so that learning via feedback takes place throughout the network and local challenges are met with innovative procedures across the operational spectrum.[38] Basically, netcentric warfare conceptualizes U.S. forces working as nets on the net, with data processing units at a distance operating as staff support through reachback and feedforward.[39]

Mathematicians call a *network* a collection of links and nodes, but they are not all equally robust or adaptable. A *chain*, for example, links nodes together one at a time, like a string of pearls, but is a brittle structure, not densely connected or clustered. Hence its links can be cut easily and its operational potential destroyed. A maximally connected network is high in redundancy with more than one way to connect all nodes together and thus is a robust system. Losing one or more links will seldom lead to catastrophe but the amount of communication required between nodes during an emergency can send this network into synthetic epilepsy. Recent research in the topology of networks has led to the discovery of a new class of networks: these have a few nodes with a large number of links (the commanders), a few moderately linked nodes (the airpower), and a large number of minimally linked nodes (the men on the ground). They are extremely robust networks; their hubs can easily be relocated, reconnected with only a few relinkages and therefore they are good candidates for logistical networks in complex environments such as cities.[40]

Thus, the assumption of network-centric operations is that with accurate and detailed real-time information, highly complex groups will organize naturally from the bottom up, generating self-synchronized operations that avoid top-down directive command. Such assumptions of behavior are modeled on flocking algorithms simulating the behavior of birds in flight. Autonomous units are programmed to avoid crowding their flock mates, always steering toward the average heading of the entire flock (i.e., one bird's movement makes use of information regarding the location, speed and direction of three or four closest members of the flock). Flocking behavior thus emerges from a few simple rules allowing for an effective coordination of actions without overt communication of intentions from top-down control. This is ideal for troops on the ground allowing them to adapt in real-time to the maneuvers of other unit members intent on achieving a common goal; it allows for a fluid flow of the virtual flock over terrain, and again leads to emergent properties and self-organizing efficiencies not attainable with top-down control.[41]

Robust networks are dependent on digitized, interactive forms of communication—such as instant video-feeds, satellite hook-ups, overhead surveillance systems, global mapping procedures, distributed computer profiling and more.[42] In Operation Desert Storm, it took two days for target planners to photograph a targeted object, confirm its coordinates, plan the mission and deliver it to the bomber crew. Operation Iraqi Freedom achieved real-time imaging of targets with photographs and coordinates transmitted electronically to aircraft already in flight. In Desert Storm, commanders located the movement of their troops on maps with grease pencils utilizing information from radio reports. In Iraq, commanders viewed real-time displays directly on their computer screens.[43]

It is currently assumed that persistent intelligence, surveillance, and reconnaissance [ISR] will achieve near perfect knowledge, will facilitate faster decision making at all levels of command and will remove uncertainty in war. When netcentric warfare is fully deployed, it is expected that a given enemy target will be unable to move, disperse, or break contact with the focused intelligence system which in theory will deny it any kind of sanctuary.[44] In this imaginary geography, there will be no point on the map of a city that is not under cover of intelligence, surveillance and reconnaissance with every force element, no matter how small, constantly collecting data and 'publishing' it over the military Internet.

Of course, this assumes that a wide range of geospatial information is extracted ahead of military engagement and then used to build as consistent a picture as possible of enemy networks, from imagery to electronic signals. The objective is to put a cursor over the target. Thus, it is essential that military planners map a city down to its street addresses, feeding as much information on strategic buildings and sites into a database so that during operations this preplanned playbook can be shared among air planners, aircrews, and ground forces as they work toward a common goal. But this assumes surveillance machinery that operates well ahead of military engagement.

It is just as critical to obtain real-time overview of the battle space during urban operations, allowing ground forces with direct feeds via satellite back to command centers to obtain a full-motion video perspective of the street battle. Data from airborne sensors lets troops virtually "see" around corners and over buildings, even to watch insurgents setting up mortars. There is both a grand view of the battlespace—its air defenses, threat radars, the disposition of enemy forces, ground moving targets and enemy communications—gathered from satellites and various platforms and more targeted micro views collected by ground fighters and unmanned aerial vehicles. For example, "haystack gatherers" collect vast amounts of data in a single gulp, while 'needles' gather more targeted information. The network remains sensitive to new sources of information as they arise, and has the new ability to pipe data without request to users who may need it. The system anticipates "what the warfighter needs before he needs it, just by virtue of knowing historical approaches and data."[45] It is expected that the future network will be both self-forming and self-healing showing when a satellite will become available and when a reconnaissance aircraft can be diverted to examine a pop-up point of interest.

Centers of gravity have always been a vital part of military strategy; now the flow of information into and out of a city, or the cybernetic signature of a city, becomes a new center of gravity in urban warfare with the strategy to cut the lines of communication as swiftly and definitively as possible so that the enemy's ability to act will be curtailed.[46] Hence, one of the tools of analysis is to think of the urbanized, operational world as a complex self-organizing system, one that evolves and mutates over time and thus is highly adaptable to a variety of complex environments. In other words, the same conceptualization of self-organizing systems used to reconceptualize U.S. military operations in netcentric warfare is also applied to the enemy and the city. These are both—to borrow the vocabulary from biological systems theory—believed to be autopoietic systems which achieve maintenance and stability over time.

This leads the military to a concept of 'parallel war' considering the enemy to be a system or organism with five organizational components: (1) field military operations at the periphery; (2) masses of civilians who are not direct combatants; (3) transportation infrastructure providing organic essentials; (4) organic essentials and productive capacity; and (5) at the center, the leadership controlling the entire system. These components are called five concentric rings and like a fractal, each of the rings contains all five components within it.[47] Air attack is thus focused simultaneously on the key nodes or centers of gravity within each of the rings in contrast to serial warfare where each ring is engaged in turn, moving from the periphery into the center, and it makes a sequential flow of command obsolete.

Although parallel aerial warfare was attempted in World War II, most often aerial targets were set serially—ball-bearing factories, then submarine pens, petroleum containers, airfields, rail and road networks. Parallel warfare attacks all decisive points in each ring simultaneously. The object is to destroy or render dysfunctional those targets causing a loss of the system's organic capabilities. The bolt that runs through all the rings and holds the system together is information—the most critical point to destroy, control, and influence. By cutting off the supply of information, or so it is assumed, the system's war fighting responses can be paralyzed causing the entire organic system to go into shock.[48]

Yet parallel warfare depends on airpower, which is a blunt instrument for urban warfare; its primary purpose is to act swiftly and critically turning buildings into rubble.[49] It considers the enemy to be a set of targets and when all the targets have been hit, it assumes that war will cease. Making rubble is an old idea in urban operations, precision targeting the new element and this relies increasingly on what can be called intelligence closework and street smarts. A precision target is an embedded component of network-centric warfare in which a computer network provides an integrated picture of the battlefield shared across all levels of the urban operation from the commander to the individual soldier on the street.[50] Network-centric operations constantly feed back to the common center via real-time surveillance and TV live-feeds information on the status and location of friendly forces, enemy forces, and other actors, which are subsequently rendered as icons on a map and displayed on a computer screen or eventually on a data wall where the tap of a cursor on a particular target in the territory of interest will immediately download all available information on that site. It tells the commander you have the Global Hawk here, U-2 there, and recommends he move assets over there or notify special operations 48 miles away, and so on. Network-centric warfare has a kind of futuristic hallucination to it and assumes that the U.S. not only will control the land, sea, air and space over which its forces and communications travel but will maintain a robust ability to keep thousands of interactive systems operating in parallel and functioning in unison.[51]

The military's concern, however, is that situational awareness and coordinated logistics even in short-range communications can be difficult at best in urban terrain. It is well understood that degradation of electromagnetic propagation in cluttered environments makes net-enabled operations complicated, that satellite links, wireless networks, and data-links all compete for frequency spectrum and that GPS coverage is generally limited to open areas. Still, it is expected that reliable airborne platforms or high ground relay stations and improved portable aerostat technology will soon provide deployable, reliable and secure communication services so essential to attain the superiority of net-centric warfare.[52] Even if there are limits in reality, the military assumes these will dissolve into air by conjuring future technical performances into existence. Its technophiliac performances are accumulative, both self-enhancing and self-reassuring.

War Games or Preparation for Urban Operations

Obviously, network-centric warfare demands elaborate training and simulation before military engagement.[53] In order to understand how the superiority of information can be utilized on the ground making urban operations more effective, the military conducts training sessions with digitized simulation models of urban terrain.[54] Such experimental war games test, or will test when they are fully developed, the military's ability to isolate and control the urban battlespace using precision strike weapons systems and situational understanding via network sensors. Played in real time, they allow players to coordinate joint maneuvers from supportive forces.

One such simulation model, labeled the "Urban Resolve Experiment," is based on cutting-edge modeling and simulation technologies. It considers three features of any given city: a complex man-made terrain superimposed on a natural terrain; a large and densely distributed population; and physical and service infrastructures. These three features interact, turning any given urban terrain into complex and dynamic systems of systems.[55] The synthetic environment of this war game is a representation of a three-dimensional real-world urban terrain of more than 1.8 million discrete buildings, 65,000 of which have the capacity for interaction with combatant players who can enter a building, maneuver inside and view the street outside. Weather conditions, traffic flows of civilian vehicles and pedestrian movements, even parking lots, are integrated into the model. More than 110,000 person-entities are simulated, about 35,000 displaying culturally appropriate behaviors. City streets and highways are affected by culturally specific traffic flows; for example, pedestrian presence increases around mosques at appropriate times for daily prayers.

A soldier is placed within any building contained in the program of the simulation model and provided with a virtual reality scene generator that presents a view of the interior of the presidential palace in Baghdad, for example, and locates the palace on a precisely drawn relief map of the city, and the room on a floor plan of the building.[56] He can visualize and understand all locational data inside and outside, down the street, and through the buildings. The players of such war games deploy sensors designed to enhance their line of sight, able to detect and track targets that move in and out of sight, to pick targets out of a dense background clutter, to discover concealed targets, and to discern military targets from civilian look-alikes.

The actions of players are coordinated through parallel processors working together on a supercomputer. Large computational tasks are broken down into clusters, parceled out to different processors, and reassembled quickly—thus simulating real-time network-centric warfare. This urban warfare simulation model greatly enhances the players' ability to gain situational awareness of where the enemy is located, what he is doing and what he might do in the future. It enhances commanders' view of how to shape the battlespace to their own advantage, how to understand key linkages and relationships in joint operations, and to understand the long-term implications of tactical decisions and maneuvers. It is hoped that such advanced knowledge and training procedures will lead to the minimization of collateral damage and the avoidance of culturally sensitive urban sites when battles do occur. So it is assumed: "[e]arly understanding of the cultural and geographical dimensions of an urban environment, along with precision engagement, eases the movement to stability operations."[57]

Homeland Security

Lest the reader think that the developers of netcentric systems theory are focused only on military engagement in foreign territory, the approach comes back to the U.S. via the politics of homeland security. After the terrorists' attack on September 11, 2001, the nature of warfare mutated into a full-blown Global War on Terrorism. Now it is feared the success of al-Qa'eda's relatively low-cost, highly organized, and synchronized operation to hijack four commercial jetliners and wreak havoc on a city and a nation will likely inspire other adversaries to attempt similar 'asymmetrical' assaults. Securing the homeland, particularly congested areas of population and the infrastructure of cities, against such terrorist enemies has become a major priority, one in which a new vulnerability becomes apparent.[58]

If netcentric warfare is sanitized virtual warfare because it is warfare at a distance giving America a false sense of technological superiority and a false promise to dominate in any military engagement—its twin is mirrored by the fear of failure to achieve security on the American homeland. This permanent fear provokes the United States to work through the dark side of impending catastrophe: suspending international laws governing the conduct of war, imposing security measures that violate civil rights, and engaging in a state of war against anyone that threatens its security.[59]

Terrorism generates the desire for security yet simultaneously fuels ever more insecurity and uncertainly. The fear is accumulative that the military might not be able to guarantee internal control over saboteurs—rogue states, insurgents, terrorists—a fear that the media's constant replay of disasters and real-time coverage of battle zones only fuels. As Agamben has noted, "[t]he thought of security bears within it an essential risk. A state which has security as its sole task and source of legitimacy is a fragile organism; it can always be provoked by terrorism to become itself terroristic."[60]

Like the military's urban operations, the war against terror focuses on the city and the technology of communication as the space of transgression. It applies the same conceptualizations to defensive operations as it does to force projective operations against terrorists. Thus, homeland defense is also a war against information technology, the same technology that is supposed to guarantee superiority and success in netcentric warfare. In other words, information, so essential in keeping the dream of netcentric warfare afloat and operable, turned upside down becomes a nightmare of the greatest vulnerability. Because of the terrorist's effective deployment of personal computers linked to the Internet, spiraling fears now center on the personal computer's awesome capacity and precarious power roughly equivalent to the entire computational power of the U.S. Defense Department in the mid-1960s.[61]

Evidence seems to suggest that plans for the 9/11 attack were organized via the Internet and that the al Qa'eda network of cells continues to communicate with each other across continents using Internet-based phone services. It has used the Internet to send encrypted intelligence reports on potential targets in the United States; it has gathered digitized imagery on these sites plus maps and diagrams on essential features so that it can virtually simulate catastrophic failure. Given al Qa'eda's cellular, dispersed organization, one able to decentralize battle orders over its mobile and mutating network, the U.S. military cannot fight these virtual strategists with conventional means. The war against the global network of terrorist organizations armed with laptop computers is not properly speaking a war but lies more in the realm of a protracted hunt based on intelligence work. Terrorists do not seize or hold territory, they do not engage the military in combat, and they often reveal impressive regenerative powers after being attacked.[62] Instead, as the White House defines it, "[t]he terrorist threat is a flexible, transnational network structure, enabled by modern technology and characterized by loose interconnectivity both within and between groups."[63]

It is just this specter of 'modern technology' that returns to haunt the vulnerability of homeland security. Al Qa'eda as a global insurgency has been able to turn the tables on netcentric warfare, moving the battlefield into cities, deploying information and disinformation as a weapon against American security, and instilling constant fear that the terrorists whoever they are may strike again, anywhere at anytime. The terrorists' global reach and staggering multiplicity, with different types of organizations and separate geographical locations, require a counterattack able to sever their communication links that constantly morph and change. Thus, the global war on terrorism is likened to walking through a maze whose walls are constantly rearranging as one walks.

Ironically, the Internet originally designed for American defense intelligence in the 1970s, but now transformed into a global communication system, in the hands of terrorists who seek to do harm to America becomes a digital menace.[64] The Internet offers all terrorists an effective command and control mechanism to coordinate and plan future attacks; it allows them to hide behind its anonymity, playing a shell game to cover up their identities and whereabouts. The U.S. government cannot censor or filter the Internet as they have done with newspaper coverage and television broadcasts, allowing the Internet to easily serve as the terrorists' media and tool of empowerment. Terrorists can broadcast their version of events, publish their sabotage handbooks, spread their fatwas [decisions on applying Muslim law], recruit new members to their cause, solicit donations and amplify all sorts of propaganda and disinformation through chat rooms, websites and various bulletin boards. Certainly, 9/11 was planned as a media event and its effect has been to generate within Americans not only fear but a sense of extreme vulnerability.

Terrorists understand the guerrilla tactics of cyberwarfare—to deform, distort, confuse, steal, even cut, the links of communication and feedback and send the enemy system into shock. Hence, the Patriot Act of 2001, an effect of terrorism, has added to its lists of intelligence matters computer crimes and has legitimized the use of enhanced electronic surveillance procedures, the interception of communication in computer hacking cases, and the acceptance of an array of evidence gathered electronically on those suspected of intent to cause damage. But a sense of security is thwarted by a growing awareness that wherever the terrorists are they can guide and plan their worldwide operations via the Internet without the need of physical meeting or even knowing who their recruits might be. Cyberoperations are just as distant and virtual as Urban Operations and they engender undemocratic means to stem their potential damage.[65]

Trapped within the labyrinth of cyberwarfare, there is no end to the U.S. hallucinations—an open society guaranteeing freedom of the press and information can never be secure enough when this same public information becomes a lethal weapon in the hands of the enemy. How easy it would be for terrorists to conduct word searches of newspaper articles trying to find vulnerable spots in the U.S. defense system: after newspaper articles, for example, reported that attempts to ship contraband through checkpoints at the Cincinnati airport were successful at least 50 percent of the time, a terrorist might consider that city to be a good embarkation point for its next operation. Noting other newspaper reports that Canadian garbage trucks to the U.S. receive little or no scrutiny, gaps along the 45th Parallel might be exploited to the terrorists' advantage. And imagine what terrorists might do when they learn from the media that New York City's allocation of money from the federal government to fight terrorism has been severely cut. Terrorists also can study how the United States collects, analyzes, and responds to information, they can interrupt this chain to introduce false information and then measure the U.S. intelligence response to find weak spots in its security net, or the type of technology used to uncover their encrypted false plans. The fears are recurrent that attacks by cyberterrorists against digital property and information systems might bring down airplanes, destroy the stock market, knock out the power grid, reveal Pentagon secrets, not to mention spread viruses via Internet-connected computers. The politics of security—or the war against terrorism—breeds an endless number of nightmare zones where the U.S. feels vulnerable and insecure and is forced to react.[66] The consequences are cumulative and hallucinatory: drawn into traditional assumptions about warfare, that one attacks after being attacked, a response creates more reason for terrorists to react.

And so the spiral grows, vulnerabilities increase, and reactions propel with no hope of winning the war on terrorism.

Conclusions

No matter how much fantasy is involved and how many debates even within the U.S. military over the feasibility of network-centric warfare, or technological omnipotence and worldwide military domination, it has been a very long time since simulation models, experimental design, and planning procedures, plus the latest communication technology and geographical imagination have been applied to peacetime urban operations in order to develop strategies for civilian populations—to enhance their quality of life or to understand the effects of different urban policies and plans. Priorities have clearly gone awry in the twenty-first century as the defense budget for 2007 climbs over a $550 billion mark.

Paul Virilio described the fall-out of events surrounding the explosion of the nuclear power plant in Chernobyl as a triptych of accidents. First came the substance accident (the event of the power station explosion); then the knowledge accident (nuclear physicists were outstripped by the accident); and finally the consciousness accident (no insight into this event, the event exceeded consciousness).[67]

The same, we might say, has taken place with respect to cities of Iraq and other rapidly urbanizing and highly contentious sites—there is the accident or the collateral damage of war that lays waste to a city's terrain; there is the knowledge accident where plans for demolition are present while those for reconstruction are absent; and there is also the consciousness accident, impossible for most of us to understand the military tactics of urban operations seen daily via real-time feedback over a variety of communication channels. Does overexposure dull sensibilities so that we are unable to fathom the reality of such accidents and events?

Military strategists are more pragmatic and realistic, eager to deploy all the knowledge they can glean about cities, the history of urban design and how this effects urban operations, plus all the information technology and systems theories available. All of this knowledge is grist for the mill of urban operations as they prepare to wreak havoc on cities that stand in their path. They appear to be the chief purveyors of the accident of urban events.

The third accident, that of consciousness, seems to have stunned architects/urbanists into silence—even though there are enormous consequences to bear for their decision do nothing about cities, to ignore and even to celebrate their unformed condition. The results of neglect can be catastrophic, as the Chernobyl accident revealed. All the while, the military studies an array of urban theory, develops and deploys information technologies so that war is sustained at a distance, severing the ties that bind consciousness to reality.

Perhaps this is the reason for this ramble through the recent history of urban operations and netcentric warfare. Neglect, confusion, mental disarray, failure of words, a sense of helplessness, even irony among the architects/urbanists are all accidents of consciousness. The casualties hardly need repeating: they are the world's cities, especially the poorest ones or those that sit astride valuable resources. The effects are inevitable: the reduction of buildings to rubble, the collateral damage of citizenry, the transgressions of international law, and the escalating war on terrorism and anxieties of vulnerability that feed ever accumulating desires for security. Without acts of consciousness to stop this madness, to become proactive and engaged in urban planning to improve the living conditions of cities around the world, then the military will continue to believe in its 'force-projection power' and its global domination. Yet there is no technological fix, never a guaranteed security of net-centric warfare, only growing awareness that the war on terrorism cannot be won on the battlefield and that cities and their citizens are the inevitable collateral damage.

Notes

1. "Military Operations on Urbanized Terrain [MOUT]" <http://www.globalsecurity.org/military/ops/mout.htm>
2. There is great need for improving preparations for urban combat. The U.S. Army's Field Manual 90–10, Military Operations in Urbanized Terrain [MOUT], issued in 1979, still trained troops for military engagement in small towns and villages, not major metropolitan areas. It was recently revised to FM90–10–1.
3. James Der Derian, "Virtuous/Virtual Theory" *International Affairs* 76, 4 [Oct., 2000]: 771–788.
4. Col. Richard Szafranski, USAF. Chap 5 "Parallel War and Hyperwar: Is Every Want a Weakness?" *Air & Space Power Chronicles* <http://www.airpower.maxwell.af.mil/airchronicles/battle/chp5.html>
5. Ralph Peters, "Human Terrain of Urban Operations" *Parameters* (Spring, 2000): 4–12; P. H. Liotta, "Chaos as Strategy" *Parameters* (Summer 2002): 47–56; John A. Gentry, "Doomed to Fail: America's Blind Faith in Military Technology" *Parameters* (Winter 2002–2003): unpaginated.
6. There were as well text-messaging systems and chat rooms on the classified military intranet system—used so often they threatened information overload and allowed rumor-spreading to be rife.
7. John Ferris, "A New American Way of War? C4ISR in Operation Iraqi Freedom, a Provisional Assessment," The Centre for Military and Strategic Studies, The University of Calgary (January 24, 2003): unpaginated. C4ISR = command, control, communications, computers, intelligence, surveillance and reconnaissance.

8. Liotta, "Chaos as Strategy."
9. Peter W. Wielhouwer, "Preparing for Future Joint Urban Operations: The Role of Simulation and the Urban Resolve Experiment." Command and Operations Group, USJFCOM/J9 (2004).
10. Wielhouwer, "Preparing for Future Joint Urban Operations."
11. Scott Gerwehr and Russell W. Glenn, *The Art of Darkness: Deception and Urban Operations* (Arroyo Center: The Rand Corporation, 2003).
12. Roger J. Spiller, "Sharp Corners: Urban Operations at Century's End." Combat Studies Institute [2001]: unpaginated.
13. Stephen Graham, "Urbanisation and Empire: The U.S. Military Confronts Global South Cities" (unpublished paper, 2005?); Russell W. Glenn, "Managing Complexity during Military Urban Operations: Visualizing the Elephant. (Arroyo Center: Rand Corporation, January 2004): 2–3.
14. Spiller, "Sharp Corners": unpaginated.
15. Maréchal Bugeaud, *La Guerre des rues et des maisons* (c1851) (Paris: Jean-Paul Rocher, 1997)
16. Spiller, "Sharp Corners": unpaginated.
17. Le Corbusier, 'Commentaires rélatifs à Moscow et à la 'Ville Verts' FLC A3–1-65 12–03–1930 "Communication observations of Colonel Vauthier, 5th Congress CIAM," FLC D2 [11].
18. Le Corbusier, *Sur les Quatre Routes* (Paris : NRF Gallimar, 1941) [English Translation : *The Four Routes* (London: Dobson, 1947): 51.]
19. Spiller, "Sharp Corners": unpaginated.
20. Spiller, "Sharp Corners": unpaginated.
21. Dean MacCannell, "Baltimore in the Morning ... After: On the Forms of Post-Nuclear Leadership" *Diacritics* 14, 2 (Summer, 1984): 32–46.
22. MacCannell, "Baltimore in the Morning": 40.
23. Roger Luckhurst, "Nuclear Criticism: Anachronism and Anachorism" *Diacritics* 23, 2 (Summer, 1993): 88–97.
24. Spiller, "Sharp Corners": unpaginated.
25. Spiller, "Sharp Corners": unpaginated.
26. Philip Misselwitz and Eyal Weizman, "Military Operations as Urban Planning," in *Territories Islands, Camps and Other States of Utopia* (Berlin: KW—Institute for Contemporary Art, 2003): 278; Lieutenant Colonel David W. Sutherland, "Systems Approach to Urban Operations" School of Advanced Military Studies. AY 02–03
27. Peters, "The Human Terain of Urban Operations"
28. Peters, "The Human Terrain of Urban Operations."
29. Quoted in Sutherland, "Systems Approach to Urban Operations": 30.
30. Gerwehr and Glenn, *The Art of Darkness:* 9.
31. Gerwehr and Glenn, *The Art of Darkness:* 2.
32. Clausewitz [1873]. Quoted by Gerwehr and. Glenn, *The Art of Darkness:* 10.
33. Gerwehr and Glenn, *The Art of Darkness:* 15, 18–19.
34. Gerwehr and Glenn, *The Art of Darkness:* 20.
35. Gerwehr and Glenn, *The Art of Darkness:* 34.
36. Glenn, "Managing Complexity During Military Urban Operations."
37. Gerwehr and Glenn, *The Art of Darkness:* 59.
38. Jeffrey R. Cares, "Distributed Adaptive Logistics," *Information Age Warfare Quarterly* 1, 1 [Winter, 2005]: unpaginated.

39. Ferris, "A New American Way of War?"

40. Cares, "Distributed Adaptive Logistics": unpaginated.

41. New tools are also needed to meet the challenges and necessary support for Urban Operations. DARPA's special projects is developing a low-altitude airborne sensor system [LAASS]—to find and target underground tunnels and facilities and ISIS [not specified]—the ability to track the movement of individuals for months enabling the military to reveal webs of connection between people and facilities, group meetings, unusual deployments. DARPA is also attempting to create a strategic mapping system that would offer troops detailed maps of the inside of buildings without entering buildings by utilizing wall-penetrating RF [not specified] radiation, plus the ability to sense and track activity within the structure by focusing on Doppler-shifted signals due to personnel movement and activity within a structure. The system would have to be portable, fast and integrated with other systems, sending back signals in real-time and returning with mapped information. DARPA is also interested in developing barrier materials that can be rapidly deployed by troops in the field, blocking routes with hardening foam that expands rapidly, blocking doors or roadways, yet can easily be opened by troops with chemical solvents. Or the use of slippery materials preventing enemy vehicles from gaining traction—oil or Teflon products work on asphalt, but not on dirt or gravel and they need to be neutralized. Troops on the ground need to detect then neutralize bombs at a distance, bombs made from a variety of energetic compounds—DARPA has remote RF-based triggering devices but it needs to develop triggering devices that are not RF-based such as a low power microwave emitter that can survey a crowd and detect a suicide bomber or electromagnetic pulse generator used to short circuit electronics (these need too much power and space, plus a truck to carry the equipment). Alternatively: rapidly deployable blast shields, directing the blast once detonated away from personnel, like a rigid foam that is strong enough to deflect blast, can be stored in a compact container and rapidly deployed. Paul Benda, "Assured Urban Operations" <http://www.DARPAtech2004/pdf/scripts.BendaScript.pdf>

42. Derian, "Virtual War/Virtual Theory"; Stephen Graham, "Urbanisation and Empire: The U.S. Military Confronts Global South Cities" [unpublished paper].

43. Lt. Gen Harry D. Raduege Jr. "Net-Centric Warfare is Changing the Battlefield Environment," www.stsc.hill.af.mil (January 2004).

44. Major David W. Pendall, "Persistent Surveillance and its Implications for the Common Operation Picture," Military Review [Nov.–Dec. 2005]: 41–50.

45. Lt. General William T. Hoabbins, the Air Force's deputy chief of staff for warfighting integration. Quoted by John A. Tirpak "The Network Way of War," Air Force Magazine 88, 3 (March, 2005): 26–31. Quote on page 28.

46. Spiller, "Sharp Corners": unpaginated.

47. Szafranski, Chp 5 "Parallel War and Hyperwar." Szafranski argues that Parallel War is not a new strategic conception or a new theory but has gained currency and is now being advanced by airpower advocates to enhance the power of aerial warfare.

48. Organisms are autopoietic; that is, they struggle to preserve themselves and evolve over time. Yet, parallel warfare is aimed at the initial organism, not

the evolved one. Contrary to the assumption, damage to the organism's information systems may deplete its ability to feedback how much damage was achieved; hence, other parts of the organism may not realize the system's paralysis nor behave as paralytic.

49. Acting in coordination with offensive operations on the ground, the technological superiority of airpower can back troops up by providing surveillance of the battlespace in real time, precision air strikes directed from the ground and command centers, plus airlift support. Rebecca Grant, "The Fallujah Model," *Air Force Magazine* 88, 2 (Feb. 2005): unpaginated; Tirpak "The Network Way of War." Yet airpower is limited against ethnic cleansing such as in former Yugoslavia, peacekeeping in Somalia, and stopping genocide in Rwanda. It is also not effective against 'third wave' information technology, such as distributed laptops which enable command and control centers to move about, even to offshore sites or nonbelligerent states. Miniaturization of satellite receivers and transmitters adds to the targeting challenge. And dual-use technologies confound the problem: that is, fermentation centers are needed for making beer, but also for biological weapons production. GPS has both military and civilian uses.

50. Nancy J. Wesensten, Gregory Belenky, Thomas J. Balkin, "Cognitive Readiness in Network-centric Operations" *Parameters* (Spring, 2005): unpaginated; Tirpak, "The Network Way of War."

51. Gentry, "Doomed to Fail."

52. "The Challenge of Command and Control in Urban Operations," *Search Defense Update* 1 (2006): 1–7.

53. Perhaps it is not surprising that Normal Bel Geddes, who is best remember for being the designer of the GM "Futurama" model at the 1939 World's Fair in New York, was also an inveterate war game player and prolific collector of information about military strategy and war maps. "Toward the close of the [first] World War M. Geddes was host every week to a group of military and naval men—Admirals, Generals and Strategists of the War College—who played this war game far into the night. It took six months to complete one 'game' or session. At the time, the U.S. War Department had ordered from Mr. Geddes, duplicates of his war game to be made and placed in every cantonment and training camp for the instruction and training of recruits." NBG. 45 Box 23 Folder 402.1 "Suggested material for war to be sent to prospective clients": p. 2. Memo Sept 27, 1939.

    In the mid-1930s, Bel Geddes designed a project for recording the world's great battles, utilizing slow motion color photography with narrative soundtracks, a method similar to animated motion pictures. The area of operations would be described on a layered relief map with various types of terrain made visible. River, plains, forests, meadows, marshes, railroads, paved and dirt roads, shoal and deep water marked its surface. The camera, for the most part stationary, focused on the map from an aerial perspective and was able to make close-up and distance shots. Exhaustive research of each battle would be carried out before the movie was to be shot. NBG.4 Box 1994 Folder 179.1 "A project for recording the world's great battles" [1935].

    Bel Geddes continued his interest in war games, designing in 1939 a model war map of northwestern Europe. This giant relief map, scaled one inch to eight miles, covered the entire terrain from south of Cairo to north of the Baltic Sea, all of the Black Sea and off the coast of Ireland. It was built in sections, with the Western Front, an area of about 250 square miles, built first. He planned to make photographs of the model available to newspapers so that readers could follow daily coverage of the maneuvers of war, tracking all fronts, translating obscure and vague communiqués into on the spot images of the battle action. A board of expert strategists would meet daily, culling over foreign news and explain the meaning of government communiqués and various military strategies. NBG. 45 Box 23 Folder 402.1 "War Map" Office Minutes Meeting, Sept 27 1939.

In 1944, Bel Geddes's War Maneuver Models was giving a showing at MoMA. As spectators looked down on the map from a runway above the gallery floor, model makers from Bel Geddes's office were seen building the woods on either side of a river, moving trees and other vegetation in place. Miniature tanks, jeeps, trucks, command cars, boats and other vehicles all modeled to scale and in exact detail, were constructed in sterling silver. Soldiers and officers of the opposing forces with rifles and other equipment appeared in white metal, soft enough to be twisted into realistic positions as they were placed on the field of action. There were four time-lapse phases to this display, each taking several days to complete: opposing forces drew up on either side of the river and engaged in artillery dual; next, pontoon bridges were put in place under gunfire and smoke; third, the first bridge was completed and close action fighting begun; and finally, after the second brigade was built, invaders crossed over in force. Each phase was photographed then reassembled for the next phase. On the opposite side of the runway, an enormous sea model of the South Pacific Theater was on display. [see Life Magazine close to Jan 26, 1944] NBG 47 Box 35 Folder 499.1.2.3.: "MoMA's War Maneuver Models Shown at the Museum of Modern Art" [Jan 26, 1944]. NBG 47 Box 35 Folder 499.1.2.3.

54. There are limits to war games. Sensors may track physical things that move and activities that have electromagnetic signatures, but they cannot identity enemy motives nor assess the importance of the data they gather. Electronic networks, moreover, are highly vulnerable to technical and operator-induced failures, they can be easily jammed or intercepted, and are open to attack. And network-centric warfare tends to focus on commander support, the protection of forces on the ground and the carrying out of specific missions. Gentry, "Doomed to Fail."

55. Peter W. Wielhouwer, "Preparing for Future Joint Urban Operations: The Role of Simulation and the *Urban Resolve* Experiment," U.S.JFCOM/J9 [2004].

56. Wielhouwer, "Preparing for Future Joint Urban Operations."

57. Wielhouwer, "Preparing for Future Joint Urban Operations": 16.

58. Robert J. Pratt, "Invasive Threats to the American Homeland," *Parameters* (Spring, 2004): unpaginated.

59. Bülent Diken, "The comedy of [t]erros" *http://comp.lancs.ac.uk/sociology/soc******

60. G. Agamben. Quoted by Diken, "The comedy of [t]erros."

61. Liotta, "Chaos as Strategy": 51.

62. Jeffrey Record, "Bounding the Global War on Terrorism," *Strategic Studies Institute monograph* (December, 2003): unpaginated.

63. Defined by "National Strategy for Combating Terrorism" The White House [September 2002]:1. Quoted by Record, "Bounding the Global War on Terrorism": 12.

64. Timothy L. Thomas, "Al Qaeda and the Internet: The Danger of 'Cyberplanning.'" *Parameters* [Spring, 2003].

65. Thomas, "Al Qaeda and the Internet."

66. Thomas, "Al Qaeda and the Internet."

67. Paul Virilio, *Unknown Quantity* (New York: Thames & Hudson, 2003): 201–202.

Planet America
Empire's New Land Grab

MARK L. GILLEM

> At some very basic level, imperialism means thinking about, settling
> on, controlling land that you do not possess, that is distant, that is
> lived on and owned by others.[1]
>
> **Edward Said**

Aboard the USS *Abraham Lincoln* shortly after the "collapse" of the formal
Iraq resistance in May 2003, U.S. President George W. Bush proclaimed,
"Other nations in history have fought in foreign lands and remained to
occupy and exploit. Americans, following a battle, want nothing more
than to return home."[2] The members of the advance team should get an
award for setting the stage for this audacious statement. Facing the President stood the proud men and women of the U.S. Navy. Above him was
a colorful banner declaring "Mission Accomplished." He wore a military
flight suit and was clearly invigorated by an extremely brief jet flight from
nearby San Diego. Although what he said is true for American soldiers
wanting to return home, this is certainly not the case for the neoconservative supporters of the new American Empire. Since 2001, these supporters
have been quite busy expanding empire's reach through retaliatory raids,
preemptive wars, and one-sided realignments. Although they justify their
actions in national security terms, they also place greater burdens on U.S.
soldiers and generate new demands for land.

In this chapter, I present the overseas footprint of the U.S. military, discuss recent realignment proposals, and focus on two cases that illustrate

how the new American Empire is using foreign land. I conclude by suggesting that the United States has implemented a new model to manage its dominion. Empires long ago abandoned policies of assimilation, a model of consciously eliminating local cultures. The more recent approach has been association, with empires reluctantly acknowledging the cultural norms of their "hosts." Now, a frightened U.S. military is realigning its forces and retreating into increasingly isolated but well-appointed compounds. Avoidance is the goal. September 11 and the fear it unleashed among military planners is in part responsible for this shift. But this is also the result of the United States seeking even more freedom in exercising, unilaterally if needed, its new policy of preemptive war—freedom that the Bush administration argues is hampered by the existing network of overseas bases.

Empire's Footprint

Since September 11, 2001, scholars have published numerous books on empire. On the political left, the wars testified to imperial hubris. America was acting largely alone without the consent of the global order.[3] On the political right, the wars were seen as a justifiable use of imperial power.[4] What is largely missing from these accounts is a discussion of the spatial impacts of projecting imperial might. The ability to wage the most recent wars in Afghanistan and Iraq was due largely to the positioning and existence of America's overseas outposts located in 143 countries. The United States operates over 860 permanent overseas sites on 676,491 acres that support a total population of 302,179 soldiers, civilian employees, and family members (Figure 1).[5]

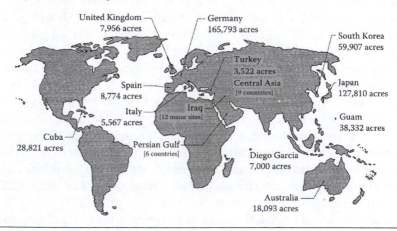

Figure 1 The imperial footprint.

The impact of these bases involves a complex web of spatial, social, cultural, and political factors. If one considers only South Korea, there are 95 sites, including 47 major outposts, in a nation half the size of the state of Washington. One of the largest installations is in the heart of Seoul. What would Americans think of a South Korean military base in Washington, DC?

In most of these countries, the United States has a "permanent" presence, which means they operate out of permanent buildings rather than tents. In the Persian Gulf area, the Afghan region, and Iraq, the numbers are for currently "temporary" outposts using a mix of tents and buildings (see Figure 1). The United States undoubtedly will leave some type of permanent presence in this region—it seems that "to the victor go the spoils," from oil contracts to base leasing rights.[6] This follows America's imperial history. After all, the United States left bases in Japan, Germany, and England following World War II, South Korea following the Korean War, and Saudi Arabia, Kuwait, and Qatar following the first Gulf War.

This imperial reach comes with a shocking price tag. The U.S. defense budget is now roughly equal to the combined defense spending of the rest of the world—all 191 countries.[7] In fiscal year 2004, defense related spending totaled $461.3 billion, consuming 20 percent of the federal budget. This bloated spending occurs in an era of record breaking federal budget deficits, $475 billion in 2004.[8] This is a *Mortgaged Empire*. At least one thing comes cheaply for the United States—the land America's outposts occupy. Following historical precedent, the United States does not pay directly for using another nation's land. Rather, the nations hosting the U.S. military must foot the bill.

Realigning Imperial Power

In another Hollywood-quality production, with American flags (actual and virtual) behind and to his sides and an enthusiastic audience at the 2004 Convention of the Veterans of Foreign Wars in front, President Bush announced a major shift in the basing strategies of the U.S. military.[9] The most significant changes will result from moving soldiers around in Asia and Europe. A cynic may notice two patterns in this realignment. First, the United States is reducing force levels in countries that are not supporting its imperial ambitions: Germany and Turkey are the most obvious cases. Second, the realignment policies leave unchanged force levels in many countries that are paying more than 50 percent of the costs of hosting the U.S. military and reducing forces in countries that pay less.[10] Japan pays more than the Defense Department's cost-sharing target of 50 percent and sees little change in U.S. troop levels; South Korea, on the other hand, pays less than the target and sees a reduction of 12,500 troops (34 percent of them).[11]

In Europe, the realignments officially began in December of 2005 with U.S. Secretary of State Condoleeza Rice signing a basing agreement with Romania. The United States will use Mihail Kogalnice Air Base in southeast Romania near the Black Sea, a strategic location given the growing importance of the region in the global oil distribution network.[12] Although the United States will get access to an airfield unencumbered by many of the environmental and political constraints found in Western European countries, the Romanian government is hoping the "facility" will bring diplomatic and economic gains to the former communist country. According to Romanian Defense Minister Teodor Atanasiu, "It is very important to us to have U.S. military bases on our territory. ... From the government's point of view, there is no reservation. From the parliament, it is OK. From the military's point of view, there is no reservation, and from the population, there are no major issues."[13] But, given the experiences of the U.S. military elsewhere, it is only a matter of time before many Romanians grow weary of their imperial guests. The United States also hopes to "share" military facilities in Bulgaria and signed an agreement in late 2005 that allows for U.S. use of Manas Air Base in Kyrgyzstan.[14] The new outposts in these countries will be unlike those in Asia. They will be for unaccompanied tours—Defense Department terminology for assignments where soldiers cannot bring their families. Without families, the United States will not need to build family housing, schools, day care centers, elaborate hospitals, or large shopping centers.[15] Although the Bush administration and its supporters advertised this approach as a way to save money and improve the military's strategic position,[16] the Congressional Budget Office concluded that the plan would cost $7 billion and offer little strategic advantage because the new installations are not significantly closer to potential areas of conflict.[17]

In Asia, the realignments build on negotiations that have been ongoing since the late 1990s. For instance, in both Japan and South Korea the shift is to locations in less developed areas—tucked away in remote places where the United States can avoid confrontations that inevitably result from the U.S. military's incessant spillover. From well-publicized sex crimes to long-term environmental contamination, the U.S. presence is hard to miss. Given the wide array of spillover that results from American actions, one could easily misread the concerns of those living with imperial "protectors." Moreover, given the focus on prostitution and all its ills, it would be justifiable to place this at the top of the list in terms of negative spillover.[18] However, that would be premature. A survey of 1,200 South Koreans living near U.S. military bases tells a very different story—one

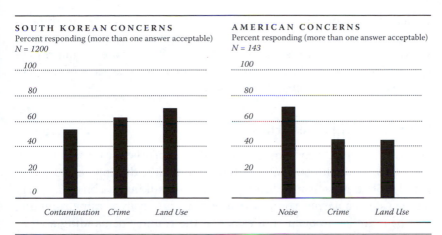

Figure 2 Comparing attitudes about spillover.

that goes largely unreported in the United States because it would require new ways of thinking about empire's impact. Americans are more interested in the accounts of crashing planes and women forced to work against their will as prostitutes. In the survey, though, these were not the most pressing concerns. The top concern was the U.S. military's excessive use of Korean land. In a similar survey of planners and architects working for the U.S. military, the result was quite different. They thought South Koreans would be most concerned about noise from military operations (Figure 2). The results of these two surveys are a mirror image of misunderstanding. Americans, used to living with ample land, appear blinded to the importance placed on land use by residents of other nations.

Despite the finding that the local residents stuck living with imperial spillover are most concerned about excessive land use, the United States continues to plan for new and expanded installations with little regard for the spatial cost of this approach. As part of the global realignment of the U.S. military, these plans supported Secretary of Defense Donald Rumsfeld's mandate for transformation as well as a new approach to war. The United States has shifted from containing its enemies to actively seeking them out. In 2002, the Bush administration published a revised *National Security Strategy of the United States of America* that calls for preemptive war. The United States, according to the strategy, "will not hesitate to act alone, if necessary, to exercise our right to self-defense by acting preemptively ..."[19] The presumed security of the United States overrides the sovereignty of another nation. The leadership in the Pentagon clearly dislikes the old basing structure since it relies on installations in countries that detest the preemptive approach or in locations that would be too vulnerable following preemptive strikes. In discussing the realignment,

Undersecretary of Defense for Policy Doug Feith brags, "Everything is going to move everywhere. There is not going to be a place in the world where it's going to be the same as it used to be."[20] These are the musings of an *Ambitious Empire*. Perhaps the most controversial aspects of the plan are the efforts now underway in South Korea.

South Korea: The Land Partnership Plan

On June 13, 2002, Army Sergeant Mark Walker crushed two South Korean schoolgirls under his 50-ton armored vehicle while driving near the 38th parallel. Shim Mi-son and Shin Hyo-sun were walking to a birthday party on the side of a narrow country road when a U.S. convoy came rumbling by. The event led to public rallies across the country demanding a withdrawal of U.S. forces.[21] In light of this turbulent sociopolitical context, South Korean and U.S. officials have agreed to a phased withdrawal of 12,500 soldiers from the peninsula, a return of over 32,000 acres of land, and a reduction in the number of main operating locations from 41 to 23.[22] The South Korean National Assembly ratified the land component of the plan four months after the accident that killed the two schoolgirls.

The two governments called the land use agreement the Land Partnership Plan (LPP). The crux of the plan calls for relocating U.S. soldiers away from the demilitarized zone (DMZ) and into the central and southern parts of the country. Many of the soldiers facing realignment are within artillery range of the DMZ and act as a "tripwire," ensuring a swift and substantial retaliation if Kim Jong-Il acts aggressively.[23] Of course, some soldiers are not enthralled with that prospect and look forward to relocation. "I know a lot of the infantry there feel that they're just there to die in place," said Staff Sergeant Ralph Yates speaking from Camp Henry in Taegu, a safer location in the southern part of the country. He added, " ... their mentality is, 'We're gonna be wiped out.' So spreading them out on the peninsula is good."[24] Some South Koreans, however, are less enthusiastic. "South Korean officials," according to one report, "see the move as part of an elaborate American scheme in which the United States could then feel free to stage a preemptive strike on North Korean nuclear facilities without fear of North Korean artillery."[25]

Although the majority of land the U.S. will return under the LPP is mountainous terrain with little potential for development, the United States wants 3,000 acres of prime urban land on which it plans to build even more sprawling compounds for its soldiers. On the new acreage, according to Army Colonel Russell A. Bucy, who was a senior commander in South Korea in 2002, the Army will use several billion dollars from South Korea to create new planned communities with housing areas, schools, and shopping centers.[26] In effect, the United States will use South Korean tax revenue to build a military version of suburbia. On-base hotels will replace "contract quarters" off-base. On-base housing will replace leased units off-base. And on-base shopping malls will reduce the demand for off-base excursions. Unfortunately, the model for these planned communities mimics low-density suburban developments in the United States; so even the ample land the United States does control will not suffice. This is yet another justification for empire's new land grab.

This pressure to build on-base responds to three issues. First, in this age of international terrorism, commanders believe that retreating onto increasingly self-contained enclaves is one way to reduce exposure to potential attacks. Although perhaps relevant to installations in the Middle East, in South Korea and Japan the record does not support this belief. In these two countries, individuals living and shopping off-base have not been terrorist targets. Rather, protestors have aimed their wrath at sprawling bases rather than individual soldiers. Ironically, when coupled with new planning regulations that require substantial setbacks between buildings and roads to mitigate potential damage from vehicle bombs, the move onto these bases will require that military bases have an even bigger footprint. The net effect will be even more animosity between the locals and the United States.

Second, in today's "married military," families are seen as a mellowing influence. Their presence corresponds to a noticeable reduction in crimes committed by U.S. soldiers. Quite telling from a sociospatial perspective is the variation in crime rates within the military community. The annualized rate for the period between 1999 and 2002 is quite instructive. In South Korea, there were 11.2 crimes per 1,000 U.S. soldiers. In Okinawa, Japan, there were just 2.4 crimes per 1,000 U.S. soldiers.[27] Why the striking disparity? Differences in the individual soldiers are minimal—in both countries they are generally men in their 20s and 30s, two-thirds with families. They rotate in and out of the United States, Japan, South Korea, and Europe. In Japan, 72 percent of the tours are accompanied, which means families can live with the sponsor or military member assigned to Japan. In South Korea, however, the ratio is nearly reversed; 90 percent of the "tours" are unaccompanied.[28] Without the land on which to build homes, day care centers, schools, hospitals, and shopping malls, families stay in the United States. The drastic difference in crime rates indicates in part that the needs of family life occupy off-duty hours in Japan.

Third, the price of staffing South Korea has become especially high in a married military. Two-thirds of the soldiers assigned to South Korea are married but less than 10 percent of them can bring their families since bases have few facilities to support family life.[29] This is one of the main reasons why South Korea is, according to one commander, the country soldiers most hate to live in.[30] In one three-year period, half of the 60,000 soldiers given orders to South Korea refused, opting to leave the military instead of their families.[31] Home, schools, and parks are motivational tools because their availability supports more accompanied assignments. In addition, these assignments can be longer, thereby reducing the cost of frequent moves. In South Korea, the military recognizes that it cannot afford to lose so many highly trained soldiers in a time when it is calling the Guards and Reserves for extended periods of active duty to serve across the globe. Hence, military leaders hope to build their way out of the problem. By 2010, they plan to have enough homes and support facilities to allow 25 percent of the soldiers to bring their families. By 2020, the goal is 50 percent.[32] Colonel Bob Durbin, assistant deputy chief of staff for U.S. Forces Korea explains, "To improve the quality of life of our servicemembers here means you've got to build things."[33] The plans call for building many "things," including 3,799 apartments in 10 years.[34]

The urban area most impacted by the realignment will be Pyongtaek around Osan Air Base where the South Korean government has already acquired 408 acres for U.S. use.[35] The expansion of the air base and neighboring Camp Humphreys has stirred emotions on all sides. For landowners who will sell their holdings, the new development could prove to be lucrative because just the announcement of the move sparked a 10 percent rise in real estate values in the area between January and April of 2003.[36] But for opponents, economic gains do not justify imperial expansion. The Korea Confederation of Trade Unions, for example, has coordinated the efforts of 600 citizens under a "buy one *pyong* movement" to acquire land just outside Osan Air Base as a symbolic foothold against its growth.[37] One pyong is 35.585 square feet. Like the Japanese tsubo (which is 35.583 square feet), this measure is a telling example of the value of land. American planners typically measure land in terms of acres. One acre is 43,560 square feet. Although land has been plentiful in America, the units of measure in South Korea and Japan reveal that land is a precious resource. After all, banks do not measure gold by the ton but by the ounce.

Japan: Special Action Committee Okinawa

On September 4, 1995, three U.S. Marines stationed in Okinawa, Japan raped a 12-year-old Japanese girl. The event brought U.S. and Japan relations to a postwar low—85,000 Okinawans rallied and demanded that the United States remove its forces from the island. The rally adopted by acclamation a resolution condemning the United States for an "occupation mentality."[38] Given that the U.S. occupies 20 percent of the land on the

0   1000'

Figure 3 Building figure-ground plan of Kadena Air Base (upper left) and Okinawa-chi (lower right).

island of Okinawa, this claim is understandable. But the U.S. military is unlikely to leave any time soon. The United States has a substantial investment in Japan, where 81,149 Department of Defense personnel operate out of 158 locations on 127,378 acres.[39] However, the rallies and subsequent political fallout did lead to some changes. Two months after the rape and accompanying protests, the governments of Japan and the United States established the Special Action Committee Okinawa (SACO) to "reduce the burden on the people of Okinawa."[40] The burden is a heavy one. In addition to the social costs, the spatial costs are magnified by the incompatible presence of expansive U.S. outposts surrounded by Okinawan urban development (Figure 3).[41]

What the above image from a section of Kadena Air Base and neighboring Okinawa-chi illustrates is that the United States has imported American sprawl, replete with isolated land-uses, widely spaced buildings, and auto dependency. As is typical of America's outposts worldwide, Kadena is a low-density enclave surrounded by dense urban development. As measured by the Floor Area Ratio, Okinawa-chi supports eight times the density of Kadena (2.4 vs. 0.3). This means that for every 100 square meters of land, there are 240 square meters of building off-base and just 30 square meters of building on-base. The difference is not a result of high-rise

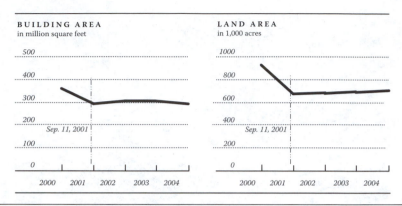

Figure 4 The U.S. military's footprint on Japan.

construction; rather, it is a result of layouts that are more compact. Average building height on the base is two levels; adjacent to the base it is three levels. New military construction following this low-density model drives up the demand for land.

The United States and Japan had hoped that the SACO process would address the disparities in land use between Okinawa, the rest of Japan, and the U.S. military. Negotiations lasted over a year and concluded in the SACO Final Report published in 1996. As part of the process, the United States agreed to return 21 percent of the land that it used (12,361 acres).[42] Even with this reduction, Okinawa's share of the total area used by the U.S. military in Japan will only drop from 75 percent to 70.2 percent.[43] Reduction, however, remains an illusive goal (Figure 4). Moreover, the building area controlled by the United States has increased dramatically since 2002.[44]

Two of the primary SACO proposals were to build up Kadena and close Futenma Marine Corps Air Station. While Futenma remains open, consolidation has begun at Kadena, where the spending difference between the United States and Japan is substantial. Since 2000, the Japanese taxpayers have funded roughly $300 million in nonhousing construction projects, whereas the U.S. taxpayer has funded less than $10 million. But this program is minor compared to what the government of Japan has agreed to fund for housing. "SACO housing is a $2 billion program," said Ryan Martini, a planner at Kadena Air Base.[45] In 1996, as part of the SACO process, the two governments agreed to replace 1,473 homes at Kadena Air base and 1,777 units at nearby Camp Foster. So, what started out as a response to a rape ended up being a major housing construction program, providing new homes at no cost to the new American empire and its representatives.

In addition to these projects at Kadena, the two governments began the process of planning for the relocation of Futenma Marine Corps Air Station. The 1,188-acre outpost takes up one-quarter of Ginowan, a city of over 82,000 in an area of 4,821 acres,[46] which results in a population density for Ginowan of 5,633 people per square kilometer. This is over five times higher than the air base. The SACO report called for the replacement to be an airfield located off the east coast of the main island of Okinawa.[47] Under the plan, over 2,500 personnel would transfer to the floating airfield or other sites up to an hour away, where housing, shopping, and medical facilities would be located.[48] About 70 aircraft from Futenma would move to the airfield and its 4,200-foot runway (Figures 5 and 6).

The plan, however, faced many obstacles. In addition to substantial environmental, technical, and security challenges of building a floating airfield, a Government Accountability Office (GAO) report found that annual operations and maintenance costs could be over 70 times more expensive at the proposed site than at Futenma ($200 million versus $2.8 million).[49] Throughout the controversy that has developed around this proposal, the United States maintained its position that it was up to the Japanese to find a site and build a replacement for Futenma. Given the problems with the proposal, the United States agreed to a scaled-back plan in October 2005 that calls for the Futenma mission to relocate to Camp Schwab, an existing U.S. base located in a rural section of Okinawa.[50] But this plan requires reclamation of areas of Oura Bay, which presents its own set of environmental problems. Regardless of Futenma's fate, the status of the SACO

Figure 5 A proposal for a sea-based facility. (*Source*: Government Accountability Office.)

Figure 6 A proposal for a sea-based facility. (*Source*: Government Accountability Office.)

recommendations is not encouraging. Although the government of Japan has funded substantial reconstruction at Kadena Air Base and several other U.S. installations targeted for expansion under SACO, the United States has yet to give back any significant amount of land.

In the End: Avoidance

The first plane slammed into the north tower at 8:45 a.m. The second plane struck the south tower 18 minutes later. Soon after, half a world away, military police began knocking on doors. "Get your family together, pack one bag for each person and get on the bus," one police officer told Sergeant Michael Nutter. He was living with his wife In Suk and their four sons in a housing area about twenty minutes by foot from Osan Air Base in South Korea. "We're moving you on the base."[51] Military police gave the same order to several hundred families living off-base. The heavily loaded buses brought the shocked and terrified families to the base where commanders thought they could better protect their troops. These relocations ushered in a new era of imperial land use.

In the past, imperial powers, from the Japanese to the French, have implemented policies of assimilation. Colonizers consumed the cultures of the colonized. They would transform languages, legal structures, and building practices, by force if needed.[52] The model changed, however, when imperial powers encountered stiff resistance; association became the norm.[53] They reluctantly acknowledged the cultural practices of the colonized and integrated them into the imperial model when it suited the imperial power. The new model is neither assimilation nor association, rather the new American Empire practices avoidance. Increasingly secluded in their own gated enclaves, American military forces overseas are avoiding contact altogether. This withdrawal into an isolated yet, paradoxically, heavily engaged empire, presents its own set of contradictions.

Although September 11, 2001 was a significant marker, new thinking about base planning actually began after the 1996 bombing of Khobar Towers in Dhahran, Saudi Arabia. After this incident, the U.S. military relocated its 6,000 soldiers from Dhahran to a vacant airfield in the desert. In congressional testimony shortly after the Khobar Towers bombing, Secretary of Defense William Perry previewed the new policy of avoidance and said the following:

> We now know that we face an unprecedented threat. We must fundamentally rethink our approach to force protection. First, we are relocating. The location at Khobar Towers made defense against such an attack almost impossible. Therefore, we are moving our combatant forces to the Prince Sultan Air Base, whose remote location permits much more extensive security protection against terrorist attack.[54]

Although the United States would not withdraw from Saudi Arabia at that time, it certainly could retreat to the desert. The image of the world's only superpower hastily relocating to the desert symbolized to some a new imperial weakness. As Nan Ellin argues, "form follows fear."[55] Will relocating to the hinterlands or floating airfields make the U.S. military safer? In Graham Greene's Vietnam, the threat came from hundreds of bicycle pumps converted into small plastic bombs.[56] Will bikes be the next vector to eliminate? Is it possible to avoid all probable threats and remain an effective military force? This exercise in avoidance could be a never ending one.

One could use numerous adjectives for today's empire: *arrogant, supersized, extravagant,* and *isolated* to name a few. There is another adjective that Pentagon strategists disdain: *entangled.* This is yet another justification for avoidance. American policy-makers do not want their war-fighting options limited. The United States wants to avoid global alliances, dismiss concerns of long-standing allies, and isolate its soldiers from the very people they are presumably defending. Since the 1990s, both Bush administrations concluded that they had little freedom to act unilaterally, even though George W. Bush has done just that.[57] The military analyst Adam Siegel notes that "host" nations have placed myriad constraints on U.S. power, including denying war planes the right to fly over their airspace, restricting use of U.S. bases on their soil to specific purposes, or establishing limits on the types of personnel and weapons at American outposts.[58] Admittedly, there are some restrictions, such as Turkey's refusal to support offensive operations against Iraq, but the United States has demonstrated the capacity to work around these "constraints."

Strategists in the Department of Defense are busy inventing ways out of the need for alliances so that unilateralism and preemptive military force will continue to work. The Bush administration's realignment policy for Eastern Europe is one element. It rewards more compliant nations with military bases and their economic benefits. Relocating the remaining soldiers in South Korea away from the heavily armed demilitarized zone is another element that can free the hand of military planners, who would not have as much concern about instant retaliatory strikes on soldiers within artillery distance of the North Korean army. Safely out of the way, U.S. soldiers could be less limited in their options for dealing with North Korea. Seoul, however, remains in the deadly middle, which may be one reason why South Korean President Roh Moo-Hyun is planning to relocate all functions of the national government 100 miles south of Seoul in a new capital city.[59]

In one important respect, the United States has an incoherent approach to this realignment. In Asia, military planners are trying to increase the number of family members that can accompany U.S. soldiers. Given the advantages in terms of crime reduction and retention of highly trained personnel this is a valid goal. But to achieve this goal, the United States wants more land to build its sprawling compounds, filled with massive retail centers, multilane bowling alleys, tract homes, and impeccably manicured golf courses. The United States apparently cannot figure out how to accommodate more families without getting more land. But annexing this land is controversial and will lead to more calls for U.S. withdrawal from disaffected residents of the "host" nations. By contrast, in Eastern Europe, the proposed new bases will be "remote" assignments with few amenities and no families. The results seem predictable: more crime and dysfunction will inevitably lead to another round of costly reconstruction.

Edward Said reminds empires that, "… domination breeds resistance, and that the violence inherent in the imperial contest—for all its occasional profit or pleasure—is an impoverishment for both sides."[60] Is the insurgency in Iraq a harbinger of events to come elsewhere? The United States has made its new land grab when its troops are increasingly unwelcome in the very nations hosting them, which requires new investments and new strategies regarding military bases. The United States has mothballed many of its outposts in "unsupportive" nations such as Saudi Arabia and Turkey and closed bases in Western Europe where the environmental and political constraints are too demanding for a Defense Department in search of its own version of freedom—freedom to plan and execute its war plans without interference from the "host" nations. Hence, the United States has shifted to building new bases in Eastern Europe while expanding and relocating bases in parts of Asia. While today's empire desires implicit control over global affairs, it need not have explicit control over entire countries. Rather, to project its power, it wants self-contained and isolated outposts strategically located across the planet. This is the new face of imperial land use.

Notes

1. Edward W. Said, *Culture and Imperialism* (New York: Random House, 1993) p. 90.
2. The White House, *President Bush Announces Major Combat Operations in Iraq Have Ended* (May 1, 2003 {cited October 5, 2004}); available from http://www.whitehouse.gov/news/releases/2003/05 /iraq/20030501-15.html.
3. See Noam Chomsky, *Hegemony or Survival: America's Quest for Global Dominance* (New York: Henry Holt and Company, 2003); Chalmers Johnson, *The Sorrows of Empire: Militarism, Secrecy, and the End of the Republic* (New York: Metropolitan Books, 2004); Rashid Khalidi, *Resurrecting Empire: Western Footprints and America's Perilous Path in the Middle East* (Boston: Beacon Press, 2004); Michael Mann, *Incoherent Empire* (London: Verso, 2003); and Arundhati Roy, *An Ordinary Person's Guide to Empire* (Cambridge, MA: South End Press, 2004).
4. See Thomas Barnett, *The Pentagon's New Map: War and Peace in the Twenty-First Century* (New York: Putnam Publishing Group, 2004); Dinesh D'Souza, *What's So Great About America* (New York: Penguin Books, 2003); and Niall Ferguson, *Colossus: The Price of America's Empire* (New York: Penguin Press, 2004).
5. See United States Department of Defense, *Base Structure Report* (Washington, DC: 2004). For numbers of deployed personnel by country, see United States Department of Defense, *Worldwide Manpower Distribution by Geographical Area* (2004).
6. For a discussion of future outposts in Iraq and Central Asia see Lutz Kleveman, *The New Great Game: Blood and Oil in Central Asia*, 1st ed. (New York: Atlantic Monthly Press, 2003).
7. Fareed Zakaria, "The Arrogant Empire: Age of Generosity," *Newsweek*, March 24, 2003.
8. Office of Management and Budget, *Budget Summary* (Washington, DC: 2004).
9. For a transcript of the speech, see The White House, *President Bush Announces Major Combat Operations in Iraq Have Ended* (2003).
10. United States Department of Defense, *Report on Allied Contributions to the Common Defense* (2003).
11. Joseph Giordono, "S. Korea to Set Aside Land for Base Growth," *Stars and Stripes*, August 21, 2004.
12. See Kleveman, *The New Great Game: Blood and Oil in Central Asia*.
13. Cited in Russ Rizzo, "Romania Moving Closer to Base Access Deal with U.S.," *Stars and Stripes*, July 25, 2005.

14. Jonathan Beale, *U.S. Gets Deal on Kyrgyz Air Base* (BBC News, October 11, 2005 {cited January 15, 2006}); available from http://news.bbc.co.uk/2/hi/asia-pacific/4332234.stm.
15. Charlie Coon, "Treaty with Romania Will Allow U.S. Forces to Use Bases," *Stars and Stripes*, December 6, 2005.
16. For Bush's remarks on cost savings see The White House, *President Speaks at V.F.W. Convention* (2004 {cited August 18 2004}); available from http://www.whitehouse.gov/news/releases/2004/ 08/20040816-12.html. Also see Jack Spencer, *Statement of Jack Spencer Senior Policy Analyst for Defense and National Security the Heritage Foundation before the Overseas Basing Commission* (1 September 2004 {cited January 20, 2006}); available from http://www.heritage.org/Research/NationalSecurity/ tst090104a.cfm.
17. Congressional Budget Office, *Options for Changing the Army's Overseas Basing* (2004 {cited July 7, 2004}); available from http://www.cbo.gov/ftpdocs/54xx/doc5415/05-03-ArmyOBasing.pdf.
18. See Saundra Pollock Sturdevant and Brenda Stoltzfus, *Let the Good Times Roll: Prostitution and the U.S. Military in Asia* (New York: The New Press, 1992). Also see Cynthia Enloe, *Bananas, Beaches & Bases: Making Feminist Sense of International Politics* (Berkeley: University of California Press, 1990). For a discussion of how the U.S. military in Asia is contributing to forced prostitution and sex trafficking, see William H. McMichael, "Sex Slaves and the U.S. Military," *Air Force Times*, August 19, 2002.
19. The White House, *The National Security Strategy of the United States of America* (17 September 2002 {cited October 5, 2004}); available from http://www.whitehouse.gov/nsc/nss.pdf. p. 6.
20. Cited in Esther Schrader, "Pentagon Plans Major Shift of Troops Throughout Asia," *Pittsburgh Post Gazette*, June 1, 2003.
21. See Don Kirk, "2nd U.S. Sergeant Is Cleared in the Death of 2 Korean Girls," *The New York Times*, November 22, 2003; James Brooke, "First of 2 G.I.S on Trial in Deaths of 2 Korean Girls Is Acquitted," *The New York Times* 2002. Also see Joshua C. Ray, "Higher-Ups Put Safety Second: Letter to the Editor," *Stars and Stripes*, 22 November 2003.
22. United States Forces Korea, *U.S.F.K. Press Release No. 021004* (2004 {cited 7 July 2004}); available from http://www.korea.army.mil/pao/news/021004.htm.
23. For the concept of tripwire see Doug Bandow, *Tripwire: Korea and U.S. Foreign Policy in a Changed World* (Washington, DC: Cato Institute, 1996).
24. Jeremy Kirk and Franklin Fisher, "Army: No Timetable for South Korea Move," *Stars and Stripes*, 10 June 2003. p. 1.
25. Don Kirk, "U.S. Pushing Realignment of Troops in South Korea," *New York Times*, 1 June 2003.
26. Cited in Franklin Fisher, "Commander Proud of Improving Life in Korea's Area I.V.," *Stars and Stripes*, 9 July 2002.
27. David Allen and Chiyomi Sumida, "Okinawa: Crimes by Americans on Rise," *Stars and Stripes*, 15 September 2002.
28. Yoo Yong-won, "U.S. Soldiers Avoid Service in Korea: Research," *Chosun Ilbo*, 22 January 2002.
29. Franklin Fisher, "Giving Back Land," *Stars and Stripes*, 17 July 2001.

30. Cited in Staff Report, "U.S.F.K. To Regroup Troops into 7 Areas of the Country," *Seoul Yonhap*, 11 January 2002.
31. Yong-won, "U.S. Soldiers Avoid Service in Korea: Research."
32. Jan Wesner Childs, "G.Is, Spouses See Need for Plan to Improve, Expand Housing in S. Korea," *Stars and Stripes*, 23 July 2001.
33. Cited in ibid.
34. Yoo Yong-won, "U.S.-Korea Meet on Base Housing Plan," *Chosun Ilbo*, 12 December 2001.
35. Seo Soo-min, "Expansion Plan for Osan Sparks Controversy," *Korea Times*, 28 April 2003.
36. Ibid.
37. Ibid.
38. Paul Eckert, "Okinawans Want Reduction of U.S. Base," *Reuters*, 21 October 1995.
39. United States Department of Defense, *Base Structure Report* (2004).
40. Government of Japan Ministry of Foreign Affairs, *The Japan-U.S. Special Action Committee Interim Report* (1996 {cited 17 June 2003}); available from http://www.mofa.go.jp/region/n-america/us/security/seco.html.
41. David Allen and Chiyomi Sumida, "Japan Defense Minister Visits Okinawa to Address 'Military Related Problems,'" *Stars and Stripes*, 26 August 2001.
42. United States General Accountability Office, *Overseas Presence: Issues Involved in Reducing the Impact of the U.S. Military Presence on Okinawa* (1998 {cited 16 June 2004}); available from http://www.gao.gov/archive/1998/ns98066.pdf.
43. Staff Report, "Final S.A.C.O. Report Announced," *Okinawa Times*, 9 December 1996.
44. United States Department of Defense, *Base Structure Report* (2004).
45. Ryan Martini, Personal Interview, 5 June 2003.
46. Size of Futenma from United States Department of Defense, *Base Structure Report*. Size and population of Ginowan from Government of Japan, *Okinawa Prefecture Population Data* (2000 {cited 1 October 2004}); available from http://web-japan.org/stat/category_01.html.
47. Special Action Committee Okinawa, *The S.A.C.O. Final Report on Futenma Air Station* (2 December 1996 {cited 15 May 2004}); available from http://www.niraikanai.wwma.net/pages/archive/ 21296.html.
48. United States General Accountability Office, *Overseas Presence: Issues Involved in Reducing the Impact of the U.S. Military Presence on Okinawa*. Also see David Allen and Chiyomi Sumida, "Frustration Reigns over Futenma's Future," *Stars and Stripes*, 19 April 2004.
49. United States General Accountability Office, *Overseas Presence: Issues Involved in Reducing the Impact of the U.S. Military Presence on Okinawa*.
50. David Allen and Chiyomi Sumida, "Mayoral Election Could Be Key to Japan Realignment Plan," *Stars and Stripes*, 18 January 2006.
51. Cited in Jim Lea, "Military Families in S. Korea Deal with Displacement from Off-Base Homes," *Stars and Stripes*, 15 September 2001.
52. For a discussion of how the Romans assimilated their new subjects see Mann, *Incoherent Empire*. The French polices of assimilation in North Africa are described by Shirine Hamadeh, "Creating the Traditional City: A French

Project," in *Forms of Dominance*, ed. Nezar AlSayyad (Brookfield, VT: Avebury, 1992). The Japanese aggressively practiced policies of assimilation as well. See Steve Rabson, "Assimilation Policy in Okinawa: Promotion, Resistance and 'Reconstruction,'" in *Okinawa: Cold War Island*, ed. Chalmers Johnson (Cardiff, CA: Japan Policy Research Institute, 1999).

53. Paul Rabinow argues that the French in Algeria practiced a policy of association that was based on less direct use of force. See Paul Rabinow, *French Modern: Norms and Forms of the Social Environment* (Cambridge, MA: MIT Press, 1989). Also see Michele Lamprakos, "Le Corbusier and Algiers: The Plan Obus as Colonial Urbanism," in *Forms of Dominance*, ed. Nezar AlSayyad (Brookfield, VT: Avebury, 1992). The Italians implemented similar practices in Libya. See Mia Fuller, "Building Power: Italy's Colonial Architecture and Urbanism, 1923–1940," *Cultural Anthropology* 3 (1988).

54. Senate Armed Services Committee, *Opening Statement by Secretary of Defense William Perry*, 18 September 1996.

55. Nan Ellin, *Postmodern Urbanism* (Cambridge, MA: Blackwell, 1996). p. 145. Ellin argues that in the postmodern world, form follows function, finance, and fear. She links the growing trend toward privatization of public space to the increasing fear of uncontrolled urban life.

56. Graham Greene, *The Quiet American* (New York: Viking Press, 1956).

57. Cited in Zakaria, "The Arrogant Empire: Age of Generosity," p. 21.

58. Adam Siegel, "Base Access Constraints and Crisis Response," *Air and Space Power Chronicles* (1996).

59. Jong-Heon Lee, "S. Korea Roils over Capital Relocation," *Washington Times*, 11 August 2004. South Korean President Roh Moo-Hyun argues that the purpose of the $40 billion project is to relieve overcrowding in Seoul and reduce Seoul's dominance over South Korea. Security analysts support the plan, noting that Seoul is just 25 miles from the heavily armed DMZ.

60. Edward W. Said, *Culture and Imperialism* (New York: Random House, 1993). p. 288.

Waiting in African Cities

ABDOUMALIQ SIMONE

Waiting for What

Urban analysis has privileged notions of urban mobility—people and things on the move, circulating, crossing frontiers and sectors of all kinds as frontiers become more proliferate. Clearly cities have been penetrated in perhaps unprecedented ways by diasporas and restless cognitions. Particularly across Africa, the predominant stories that get told in cities concern those on the move, or at least trying to move, as the impediments and surveillance are more proficient, and thus the tactics applied to getting somewhere become more desperate. Of course, the vast majority of people trying to make ends meet in the now highly urbanized Global South do not move, would never be able to mobilize the resources necessary in order to move even if the tightening of borders and transportation hadn't taken place. This stasis doesn't necessarily mean that their aspirations to move are any less than those who do; it simply means that they have to put together a way to wait. We tend to know little about such processes of waiting. Given the scrutiny to which any place or any person can be increasingly subjected to, and the associated apparatuses of confinement that grow up around such scrutiny, waiting increasingly becomes a modality of living in cities that needs to be enacted in new ways as a site of possibility.

Of course, waiting has substantial histories, as people have waited for many things—for freedom, prosperity, covenants, and opportunities. As many wait today in order to resume the pursuit of movement or wait for conditions to no longer make movement such a necessity, what is one to make of all the waiting that has already occurred—as a kind of commemoration of waiting? Waiting has entailed prolonged periods of endurance, tolerated only because there was faith in a specific future—a future capable of redeeming the hardships endured. Although it is important to always recognize what was endured, it is also important that such attention not crowd out certain implications of the endurance—that is, that the resourcefulness and implications of another past were not actualized. It is not that these possibilities were precisely defined, as in a revolutionary program or set of policies. Rather, they act as a spatial language that permits extension into the larger world. It is a language that doesn't represent a people's dimensions in clear compartments but a language that includes the gestures, the positionalities, the intonations, and the rhythms that can constantly remix socialities, crossing and intertwining the particularities of the city in shifting webs of "upstream" and "downstream" circuits, assembling, disassembling, using all parts to piece together new machines that are constantly taken apart so those parts can be used and assembled elsewhere.

If there was an opportunity lost, and if there is a certain social possibility that continues to haunt the city, it is this capacity to become many things. In this way, cities do not operate simply as a modernity yet to be made or the evidence of its failure. There are worlds to assume outside of structural adjustment, incessant low-intensity warfare, good democratic governance, or rampant piracy. Commemoration is memory of this capacity. This is a capacity to wait for the right moment, a moment that has no map, no specific signal announcing its arrival. This is a capacity to wait for the supposed benefits and freedom that liberation purportedly means now that the moment has come. "How long, not long" is the incessant query and response constituting the rhythm of duration, for even if the waiting has been long, there is much that has happened along the way that reiterates the yet to come as almost here, even if somehow everything that had been thought about in terms of what that arrival would look like may have long slipped into the past.

Unlike the hushed tones and reverence conventionally associated with it, commemoration is rather a capacity that is heretical. It refuses to be polite. For it asks those who remember to act as if what did happen never did.[1] Liberation only means something in terms of how far a community has moved away from the period of confinement. Yet to move far away also means that the originary power of the moment of liberation—that moment when all of the efforts, the struggles, and the blood are concentrated at a rupture where they, too, are subject to finitude and die—will have been mediated and reworked over and over again. For after all, it is the waiting itself which is commemorated, that patient marking of time that focuses attention and prompts some form of tactical resilience. It is

the waiting which is the real testament to the singularity that is to desig-
nate the liberation of a particular people, and not any integral character or
set of aspirations embodied by them. "We are because we have waited to
be what we are."

This moment waited for will be invoked for a multiplicity of agendas.
It will be used to discipline citizens seen to be getting out of hand; it will
be used to justify claims and privileges of all kinds; it will be reinterpreted
and reframed in light of new information and events; it will be qualified
and even demeaned as repetitions of old authoritarian or corrupt ways
become visible in the present. So if commemoration is to be the memory of
duration and as such, a capacity to become many things, then an attitude
of generosity—to what may or may not have occurred and to what may
or may not occur—must prevail despite the accumulated trauma. All of
the complicity among groups and identities that were necessary to pull off
decades of colonialism and neocolonialism—that necessary supplement to
the proficiencies of social engineering and state terror—could have pointed
to many futures, not just the one they were marshaled to secure. For at every
dinner table that was the site of a decision to go out and do something—to
feed a family, to make a mark, to get a head start, or to be free—there was
a social gathering, perhaps not always civil, but with all the incipient and
indeterminate possibilities that such sociality entails. Because waiting was
its own discipline; it needed no additional proofs and supplements, and
thus to wait meant a certain freedom to bide one's time, to consider all
kinds of diversions because what demanded compliance and rigor was that
which was to come, not that which could be played with now.

To keep people in a place, under control, requires a very physical engagement, an excess of the tactile. Yet, even when this physicality becomes very
violent, something else is fostered, some other compassion, some other
opportunity to both the purveyors of violence and their victims to become
something unrecognizable. For every extrajudicial killing and arbitrary
detention and for every unnecessary eulogy there was always some other
mode of excess, of going beyond what existed, ready to show its face, but
not able to be grasped in freedom songs, liberation charters, five-year
plans, or new development agendas. It is to these excesses that generosity
is required.

In many colonial cities, the overgrown ruins of administrative buildings and logics, and the free-standing pavilions set in lush urban gardens
all exude a certain generosity of persistence and uselessness. They do not
go away, but they do not endure to make any specific point and forward
any specific agenda. People come and go across the overgrown lawns; a
final wooden column is removed from the sunken porch; some laundry
is hung out to dry. Down the road, there may be construction sites for a

Holiday Inn or a new merchant bank. Scaffolding from a hurriedly completed stadium is being dismantled, and perhaps soon these remnants will be gone. But, in most ways, African cities remain ruined and generous in their capacity to remake the times to come.

On the Waiting to Be Remembered

Djibouti

Some places have seemingly been content to wait, even when it appears that they have had little choice. Africans from the Sahel have made their homes in the *Ish Ish Felatas*[2] of Djibouti city for generations, their progenitors having traveled long distances on their way to *hadj,* almost reaching Makka, but not quite. Although they may have run out of money, although they may have intended to take just a temporary respite from the journey, and though the geopolitics of the cross from the Horn to Arabia may have been often fraught with peril, stories told even to this day point to other more ephemeral impediments. Despite the fact that Makka operates as an overwhelming gravitational force for both the devout and the perfunctory, the closer these Sahelians got to Makka the more wary they became, the more they feared being drawn into some vortex of dessication they couldn't quite put their fingers on.

Hadj does come with its own concomitant discourses of preparedness, of being ready to participate in this affirmation of the *umma,*[3] of this acknowledgment of sacrifice of everything that has enabled one to know oneself as something discrete and particular. And the sheer logistics of the long journey eastward compelled those who undertook it to be ready to become something different, to face the prospects of never returning home. Yet even after this journey and all that it entailed, the Sahelians sensed that it was crucial to keep a distance from this power, to remain at the periphery, in the shadows, with the Middle East always just barely in view.

The stories of the Sahelians convey without fail the desire to reach the destination, and of course, many of the offspring have come and gone many times; but there are still others who protect their reticence and who counsel the wisdom of charting the outer circumference, that imaginary line where one can still bask in the prospect of some superseding belonging which *Hadj* and *Makka* offer but which can also, at a moment's notice, be opted out of; where the devout can make an easy exit into being forgotten and invisible. And for generations the *felata* of Djibouti city have been invisible, burrowing their way into the Arhiba, Yousef Kounoun, and Baahanabi quaters of the town. As Djibouti had long been a backwater port, there was little to disturb this invisibility; often the only arguments among them were whether to build their shacks continuing to face Makkah or away from it, back toward some by now mythological point of origin.

Just two weeks before independence in 1977, the French mayor of the town approached Hassan Gulaid Abitidoon, the future president, and asked him to employ a Mr. Romani as his finance advisor, someone linked strongly to the Corsican Mafia. By the time that Ismail Omar Ghelle, the former head of the secret police became president in 1999, Djibouti had become a state for the mafia, its banks laundering international drug money, its barren landscape a repository for toxic waste dumping. From the Borre Group which traffics in counterfeit cigarettes, Somalian banknotes to Comad, which ships arms, to Liban Omer, which owns nightclubs from small cities in South Africa to the Seychelles to Salim Al-Mudhi, who runs prostitution rackets to Marine Transportation of the infamous Monfried family trafficking drugs—Djibouti had itself become the crossroads of the illicit.

The *felata,* as the country's senior group of strangers, then could broker a wide variety of relationships amongst the various wayfarers, pirates, prostitutes, smugglers, and surplus labor that poured into the city as a by-product of these ventures, and after generations they managed to come into their own, advising immigrants and sojourners alike where to go, who to see, how to move on or stay put, again always at the fringes of the major trades and scams; they arranged marriages and households, work crews and discussion groups. As there were few institutions, no nationalist ideologies, and the only discernible trend being the jogging habits of the French legionnaires, there were few constraints to rework the refuse of flailing Horn economies and refugees from conflicts into some ragtag carnival of preachers, circus performances, snake charmers, sages, poets, astrologers, and hip hop crews that toured the local streets in qat[4] fueled performances lasting from late afternoon to the early hours of the morning in a world that rarely worked and had little to defend.

Yet, by 2001, the new center of the Arab world, Dubai, brought loads of cash to further "disseminate" itself and take over what was Djibouti's best asset—its port, developing a free trade zone and sinking some $400 million into extending the port's capacity for container ships and oil tankers. Dubai became powerful by virtue of making a space available through which the rest of the world could configure largely unimpeded articulations with each other. This process of centering largely derives from the engineering of a certain vacancy. Standing back from imbuing a space with particular ideological constructs or icons of identity, sovereignty is enunciated as what it is—the decision to act arbitrarily constituting a space of exception and exemption. The Jebel Ali Freetrade Zone, Dubai Media City, Dubai Internet City, Dubai Maritime City permit 100 percent foreign ownership,

100 percent guaranteed repatriation of capital and profits, state-of-the-art urban infrastructure, education, medical services, and housing, one stop for everything regulation as well as state-of-the-art telecom, support, bandwidth infrastructure—a space where economies of all kinds and proficiencies, as well as every element of the value chain, seem to intermingle with unparalleled fluidity.

In post–9/11 Djibouti, the Americans have been quick to follow Dubai, establishing a base from which to watch the links between Arabia and the Horn, and in this surveillance try to fracture the historic articulation among them. This project has punished the very people who were content to wait in the shadows, content to remain at the periphery, where the articulation was more ephemeral or even spiritual, where there was vigilance to elaborate a different kind of connection some time in the future. Even though the connection was based on the gravitational pull of Makka, it was not necessarily centered there; it was something more diffuse. But this waiting has been dispersed, and in September 2004 the Djibouti government, once the exemplary Mafia state, expelled over 100,000 strangers, many of whom had made it their home for generations.

Marseilles

Moving to another periphery at some distance but, in a stretch of the imagination, within the same zone, I want to say a few things about Marseilles,[5] another port town, now reputed on its way to becoming the new "hip" city of Europe. Even though the scores of makeshift mosques across the city make the liberation of Palestine the first in the list of to-dos that mark every Friday *jummah khutba*,[6] the real priority perhaps rests elsewhere.

Marseilles is the base of the renowned hip hop crew IAM, which stands for *Independenista Automes Marseilles, Imperial Asiatic Men,* or *Invasion Africaine de Mars,* depending on the mood of the crew. Five Muslim men are at its core plus associates; Muslims from Sicily, Tunisia, Gambia, Algeria, with pre-Islamic names such as Akhenaton, Shurik'n, and Menelik who claim Marseilles as an extraterrestrial place—taking the politics of verticality that so punctuate and puncture Palestine to a new spatial arena. Marseilles becomes Mars—more than the abbreviated nickname for the city, but a city that belongs nowhere; a place where one suspects life to exist but it is not clear what life has existed or could exist. At the same time, the concrete realities in IAM's songs of the concrete zones of HLM projects[7] built on the almost lunar landscape to the north of the city are conveyed as intergalactic video games that render the wounds of the street, the emptiness of unemployed futures and the territorial constrictions exerted by competing gangs and political mafia like a cartoon, disembodied from history, denied politics, but at the same time extricating the icons of non-Western civilization from the obligation to conventional historical narratives.

Akhenaton thus can play the part of an *imam*[8] in the "hood," whose sister's head is properly covered even if her ass isn't. It is this willingness to face one's situation with the determination of ethics even if one knows one lives in nothing more than the "joint," the prison where no discourse, no violence can really cover one's back. Like the *Beurs* movement that initially promoted a pro-integrationist strategy for Arabs in France, IAM would claim, "*J'aurais pu croire en l'Occident*" (I could have believed in the West) but refused because it would have rendered the notion of belief impossible. In other words, the precariousness in the relationship of French Arabs and Africans with Europe is not because of the impediments to belief. They were prepared to believe; they wanted to believe but they were "sliced" out of the picture, instructed as to what could be made visible, what could be talked about and how. As a result, Freeman of IAM raps, "take all that which is visible and visualized—lives, targets, mirages … defend with fervor all this which is mistargeted and bizarre, spent casings and face emaciated, visible features, heritages, missiles, and trails, missive and visa, illegible epitaph."

Although there are many songs of Palestine in the IAM oeuvre, Shurik'n says, we are what Palestine has been waiting for: "… all of those which survive, mothers Muslim or Jewish who do not dream of power; all of those without affection, people without aversion who keep the history as if a furious and deforming version of it … a limpid strategy, not the apology of emptiness."

Unlike those who apologize for the emptiness of the Marseilles suburb, Solidarité, that huge expanse of concrete barriers, squatted flats, vacancy, and regimentation—either those who are sorry about the conditions in which Africans and Arabs, French or non-French are condemned to live or those who are apologists for the styles of emptiness, the drugs, the rape, the bitterness—IAM say something else. They speak as Muslims to the abandoned industrial parks and wasted infrastructure as spaces waiting to happen, as gifts to the process of bringing into play various influences, logics, moral sensibilities, and ways of making money and lives.

IAM are the offspring of a generation that had to delink themselves from tradition in order to immigrate and to reinvent a truncated, disembodied tradition in order to compensate for the inability to really participate in a modernity responsible for the very inadequacy of that tradition. Muslim youth are caught in a space where family cannot be denied. But neither can they embody a partial sense of connection to a past that is unable to really connect. At all costs, one cannot be an instrument or occasion for French "moderns" to criticize Islam. So most Muslim youth of Marseilles have little but their individual initiatives to consider as a way of making life better.

All else has fallen away; there is nothing to defend but their capacity to act. Islam then enters the scene of Marseilles, as it does in many cities across the South of Europe, as the precise criterion through which social engagements worked out at the local level try to have something to do with each other, converse with each other, to forge some instruments of solidarity and political mobilization capable of operating outside the local context. To take Jacques Ranciére out of context, this is not a matter of self-reflection by an entity that already exists for itself. In this way, Islam is a work in progress, and the remembrance of Palestine becomes a marker of the fundamental precariousness of this task, and that whatever the similarities of the encampments of Marseilles to the encampments of Gaza, what ensues here will be inevitably different, must be different in order to work.

Palestine and the City

The politics of verticality that have characterized the respatialization of the West Bank—with its infrastructural disarticulation of surface, ground, and air—is a logic at work in the fragmentation of the infrastructural grids and their effects on the coherence of the physical city almost everywhere, both from the point of view of residents and from that of planners. But this raises the question of how the physical environments of infrastructural systems are actually used in differentially capacitated neighborhoods. "Heretical" uses of infrastructure and the "counterurbanisms" they generate stand in stark contrast and opposition to "infra-cities"—those hi-tech and privileged enclaves of unbundled and disconnected infrastructures whose speculative construction is seen to be driving new economies and new social conditions in the era of globalization.[9]

The push and the pull of these two kinds of urbanisms (or forms of city-building)—the one associated with repair, breakdowns, dereliction, obsolescence, and environmental catastrophe and the other with the wired and wireless universe, with the cutting-edge, high-speed, high-connectivity information transfer and with the inauguration of an era in which the movement of things can become the object of a continuous logistics[10]—are joined together by new kinds of security concerns. Cities everywhere become articulated and interwoven with cities elsewhere. At the same time, the internal coherence of discrete cities is substantially fractured, in part, by these very articulations, and, as such, many unanticipated threats, difficult to detect and track, can ramify far beyond the administrative border and ecological domains of a given city.

Faith and the Sahel

Let us return to the Sahelians, not those historically implanted in Djibouti but, rather, the Senegalese, Malians, Burkinabe, and Nigerians on the move today, extending circuits of transactions from Dakar to Johannesburg to Bangkok to Sao Paolo to New York to Naples to Marseilles to Libreville, Gabon. Increasingly, the Sahelians are the wild cards for the Islamic world. For in both their willingness and proficiency in moving across Muslim and non-Muslim worlds they provide concrete entrepreneurial shapes to heuristic notions concerning new forms of Islamic mobility and instantiation. In this way, the locus of what is to be nurtured and defended is not so much the "seat" of some superseding religious or cultural authenticity, but its capacity to seep into the crevices on uncharted and weakly surveyed urban spaces and economies.

A significant part of the economy of the Sahel has of course long revolved around the multifaceted dimensions of travel. Today, these dimensions include the securing of documents and tickets, the deployment of remittances, the negotiation of obligations and remuneration, as well as the lengthy process of saving the money required for leaving. Even before children reach secondary school, there is a common assumption that energies must be spent preparing to leave. This preparation is an often complex process which frequently requires protracted periods of almost "indentured" labor to relatives or family associates who are prepared to help, or simply to cultivate potential offers of assistance.

One of the primary motivations for emigration is to attain the space necessary to accrue some savings outside of the tightly knit family networks that can quickly eat up any earnings made at home. Accordingly, individuals must insist on some flexibility in how they manage their livelihoods, social lives, and movements. The prevailing "common sense" is that groups can only provide and support each other as long as they have some flexibility to pursue various alliances, contacts, and activities. They can pursue these new alliances just as long as they don't endanger their associates. Such flexibility adds an additional comparative advantage. Seemingly nonconvergent activities can be articulated in new and unconventional ways. In other words, finding ways of putting together disparate activities within an overall framework of the trust and solidarity that prevails among immigrant groups expands opportunities.

Soninke[11] traders, originally based in Dakar, Senegal, and Conakry, Guinea, also have cultivated a wide range of activities in Southeast Asia, particularly in the importation of textiles, clothing, and electronics. They have built up substantial contacts at ports in Dubai, Jidda, Durban, and Mombassa, which allow the circumvention of custom controls under simulated repackaging deals where containers are supposedly destined elsewhere. By bringing together these formerly distinct networks, Soninke entrepreneurs can manipulate loading and off-loading of varying goods depending on relative prices and market opportunities. Continuous adaptations have to be made in this process, given the fluid situations that predominate especially in Africa. Flexibility is maintained through keeping options open. One must be willing to take risks in forging new groupings and deals, many of which don't pan out. Sometimes, especially middle-level informal traders incur heavy losses. To compensate for the prospect of such losses, entrepreneurs must stay close to a wide range of contacts and activities. Small-scale entrepreneurs also have to be cautious about larger syndicates muscling-in and absorbing the trade routes and practices that they have opened up. These syndicates are often formidable in scope and size. They use their links to governments and to powerful religious organizations to secure dominance over particular sectors and domains of trade. Competition among syndicates does exist. Still, existing religious, political, or fraternal organizations are effectively appropriated as the vehicle for trading and other commercial activities by previously unaffiliated actors, or the continuing (or nascent) elaboration of activities of such groupings into transnational trade. This is particularly the case among the predominantly loose-knit, more provisional associations made up of actors and groups essentially pursuing different agendas but amenable to different forms of coordination on various occasions, producing shifting alliances and "memberships."

Particularly in Africa, the appropriation of borders, weakly guarded military bases, cross-border flows and fluidly configured social conflicts become critical elements in the elaboration of new economies that operate outside, yet in tandem, with national regulatory frameworks. These parallel economies intersect with national regulatory frameworks by reinventing economic and cultural practices that once predominated in regions such as the Chad Basin,[12] the Futa Jalon,[13] and the Swahili Coast—that is, raiding and smuggling. A sense of continuity or relinking is constructed, but one which entails a rupture with prevailing formal power relations.[14] Here, as Janet Roitman indicates, the *real* fiscal subject exceeds the fiscal subject of the state since it has moved into more diverse and unpredictable relations with emergent figures of regulatory authority. These newly reinvented (and largely familiar) modalities of accumulation—through smuggling, raiding, and parallel taxation—undermine the regulatory logic of development, national progress, social welfare, and their concomitant institutions. Accordingly, local populations invest in new forms of security and welfare. In return, national regimes endure, in part, because they are not encumbered with having to sustain or operate exclusively within distinctions between near and far, inside and outside, of the licit and illicit. Rather, such binaries often act as "internal markers" of rather solid arrangements that take place over a broad set of diverse actors, territories and identities. Something then is always emerging, always in struggle to actualize specific connotations and outcomes. It is little wonder, then, that the Sahel has been the object of such concern by the U.S. military, which has quickly sought to conclude arrangements with Mali, Algeria, Mauritania, and Niger to permit the operations of various high-tech surveillance systems and clandestine rapid intervention forces.

Largely informed by their own urban upbringings, Sahelians prove particularly adept operating in contexts where state administrations and civil institutions have lacked the political and economic power to assign the diversity of activities taking place within cities—that is, buying, selling, exchanging, collecting, dissembling, stealing, importing, fabricating, residing, and so on—to specific bounded spaces of deployment, codes of articulation, or the purview of designated actors. The incomplete, truncated, or deteriorated forms and temporalities of various, seemingly incompatible institutional rationalities and modes of production—from the bureaucracies of civil administration, the workshop, the industrial unit, subsistence agriculture, private enterprise, to customary usufruct arrangements governing land use—are intersected as a means of stabilizing a social field of interaction. As a result, they continuously readapt their actions to engage the open-ended destinations that their collaborations have produced.

Yet, Islam still always waits for them and these collaborations. Islam seems to know that for Muslim Africans, Islam will be the vehicle—no matter how many accidents, no matter how many cannibalized parts are used to put it together—through which multiple social engagements worked out at local levels will seek to consolidate broader levels of solidarity and political mobilization that cut across ethnic and national levels.[15]

Across Europe, it is possible to witness the implantation of a wide range of religious, social, and entrepreneurial projects broadly connected to this engagement with constituting a European Islam in the peripheral suburbs, the increasingly vacated industrial districts, decaying inner-city neighborhoods, and small towns now part of larger urban systems. Whatever Sahelians have experienced that prepares them to potentially deal creatively with changing urban worlds is largely deployed through highly localized maneuvers to maximize opportunity and livelihood within the domains of usually informal work and underresourced urban territories in northern cities. For, it is hard to predict just what skills and performances will be necessary in order to eke some kind of advantage from territories that are both under more proficient surveillance yet, at the same time, often off the maps of policymakers and developers. Yet, if long-term changes of lives and creative engagement are to be viable, these singular local operations must be articulated across platforms of mobilization and belonging that value these singularities at the same time they network them in coordinated actions and investments.[16]

In this way, Islam—that which is unyielding in all waiting—operates as a gestational form of urban correspondence. For it relates the initiatives, styles, interpretations, and experiences of different kinds of Muslims, opening up circumscribed resource bases onto a wider range of opportunities, even under conditions of intense scrutiny and fear. Far from the claims of some that it is something in danger of being destroyed and compromised, Islam is something never entirely born, for it waits patiently for the next journey, the next aspiration to pass on, always deferring its own realization to be available to the exercising of an incipient wholeness of potential applications, which is *Tawhid*.[17] Again, this is an act of generosity, as it points elsewhere, as it gives other dimensions, experiences, and actors their chance. Islam exemplifies the ability to wait, to be ready to affiliate, join it, and play whatever part may be necessary to make something different happen. As such, Islam's most significant principle, that of *Tawhid*, is precisely the recognition that all that is waited for is always already here.

Notes

1. G. Agamben 1999, *Potentialities: Collected Essays*. Stanford University Press.
2. A somewhat derogatory term commonly used to refer to the places where people of the Sahel settled in the towns of Sudan, and other countries of the Horn; people who were lumped together as Fulanis (Felatas).
3. The global community of the Muslim faithful.
4. An herb widely chewed across the Horn of Africa for its mildly narcotic effects.
5. A major French urban center on the Mediterranean.
6. The weekly Friday afternoon prayer obligatory for all Muslims.
7. Large-scale public housing for low-income households.
8. The leader of prayers.
9. V. Rao (forthcoming) *Infra-City: Siting the New Economy in Post-Industrial Mumbai.*
10. M. Wark 2004, *A Hacker Manifesto*. Cambridge, MA: Harvard University Press.
11. A peoples originating in the confluence of Senegal, Mali, and Mauritania.
12. The border region of Chad, Cameroon, and Nigeria.
13. A historically important area for Fulani economy and culture located in the foothills of the Futa Jallon.
14. J. Roitman 1998, "The Garrison-Entrepôt," *Cahiers d'Ètudes Africaines* 150–152, xxxvii-2–4: 297–329.

15. J. Cesari 1999, "The re-Islamisation of Muslim migration in Europe," in G. Martin Muñoz (ed.), *Islam, Modernism and the West: Cultural and Political Relations at the End of the Millennium,* London: Zed Books, 211–223; J. Cesari 2003, "Muslim Minorities in Europe: The Silent Revolution," in J. Esposito and F. Burgat (ed.), *Modernizing Islam: Religion in the Public Sphere in the Middle East and in Europe,* New Brunswick, NJ: Rutgers University Press, 251–269; P. Mandaville 2000, "Information technology and the changing boundaries of European Islam," in F. Dassetto (ed.), *Paroles d'islam; Individus, sociétés et discours dans l'islam européen contemporain,* Paris: Maisonneuve-Larose, 281–297; J. Nielsen 1999, *Towards a European Islam,* Houndmills, Basingstoke, Hampshire: Macmillan in association with the Centre for Research in Ethnic Relations University of Warwick.
16. C. Saint-Blancat 2002, "Islam in diaspora: between reterritorialization and extraterritoriality," *International Journal of Urban and Regional Research* 26: 138–151.
17. A key concept in Islam referring to the fundamental interrelatedness among all things.

Border Tours
Strategies of Surveillance, Tactics of Encroachment

TEDDY CRUZ

The New Global Border

Tracing an imaginary line along the U.S.–Mexico border and extending it directly across a map of the world, what emerges is a *political equator* that roughly corresponds with the revised geography of the post–9/11 world. This revised geography is, in accordance with Thomas P. M. Barnett's scheme for *The Pentagon's New Map,* in which he effectively divides the globe into "Functioning Core," or parts of the world where "globalization is thick with network connectivity, financial transactions, liberal media flows, and collective security," and "Non-Integrating Gap," "regions plagued by politically repressive regimes, widespread poverty and disease, routine mass murder, and chronic conflicts that incubate the next generation of global terrorists."

Along this imaginary border encircling the globe lie some of the world's most contested thresholds: the U.S.–Mexico border at Tijuana/San Diego, the most intensified portal for immigration from Latin America to the United States; the Strait of Gibraltar, where waves of migration flow from North Africa into Europe; the Israeli–Palestinian border that divides the Middle East, along with the embattled frontiers of Afghanistan, Iran, Iraq, Syria, and Jordan; the Line of Control between the Indian state of Kashmir and *Azad* or free Kashmir on the Pakistani side; and the Taiwan Strait, where relations between China and Taiwan are increasingly strained as the Pearl River Delta rapidly ascends to the role of China's economic gateway,

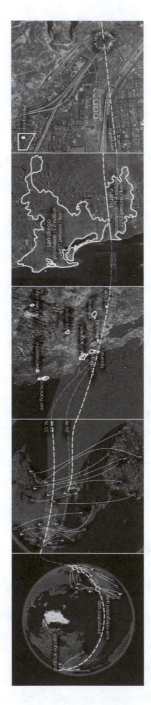

Figure 1 New global border. (Courtesy of Estudio Teddy Cruz.)

supported by the traditional centers of Hong Kong and Shanghai. These are only a few of the critical thresholds of a world in which the politics of density and labor are transforming not only the sites of conflict, but also the centers of production and consumption, whereas unprecedented sociocultural demographics rearrange flows of information and capital.

It is also along this imaginary border that the most dramatic socioeconomic global dynamics are witnessed as a series of two-way hemispheric crossings. On the one hand, the increasing migration of people across this border represents an illegal flow from the nonintegrating gap in search of the "strong" economies of the functioning core setting in motion a sort of "reverse colonization." On the other hand, the redistribution of centers of manufacturing and production moves in the opposite direction, as the functioning core targets the nonintegrating gap as the site to enact its politics of outsourcing and its search for the world's cheapest labor markets. Furthermore, as migrant communities from Latin America, Africa, and Asia move northward, they unleash a southbound flow of capital—informal subsidies—to support the fragile economies of their countries of origin. In Mexico alone, these informal subsidies amount to US$16 billion annually, and now account for its largest source of domestic revenue.

These are only a few of the critical thresholds of a world in which the politics of density and labor are transforming both the sites of conflict and the centers of production and consumption, whereas unprecedented sociocultural demographics rearrange flows of information and capital. The dramatic images emerging from the political equator are intensified by the current political climate in which terrorism and its opposite, fear, set the stage for the current confrontations over immigration policy and the regulation of borders worldwide. The result is an urbanism born of surveillance and exclusion, casting these geographies of conflict as anticipatory scenarios of the twenty-first century global metropolis, where the city will increasingly become the battleground between control and transgression; formal and informal economies; and legal and illegal occupations.

Critical Thresholds: Strategies of Surveillance

Latin America is currently reconfiguring itself within this world, ideologically and economically polarized across national, continental, and global scales. The political transformations emerging in many South American capitals, including La Paz, Brasilia, Caracas, Lima, and La Asuncion, are eroding the established institutions of control and influence that had traditionally aligned many of these countries with Washington, DC. Actions by presidents, including Bolivian Evo Morales announcing the insertion of illegal coca production into the official national economy, Brazilian

Figure 2 Critical thresholds. (Courtesy of Estudio Teddy Cruz.)

Ignacio Lula awarding property titles to thousands of slum dwellers in Rio de Janeiro and Sao Paulo, and Venezuelan Hugo Chavez catapulting a demagogic war against the Bush administration and promising to give huge oil revenues to the poor of his country, all point at a very different sociopolitical and economic landscape in Latin America—and one that was hard to imagine barely 10 years ago.

In a certain way, the blockade against current U.S. unilateral politics being formed in many of these countries is beginning to shape an expanding cartographic figure of resistance whose 'spill' ends at the border between Latin America and the United States. In this context, the deflection of the Washington, DC–Latin America axis is further bent through the prism of the current politics of fear manifested at the border between the United States and Mexico. As the U.S. Congress passes regulations to build 700 more miles of border wall and pours billions of dollars into increasing surveillance infrastructure at the different border checkpoints across the continent, it is clear that the current policies emerging from Washington, DC, are consolidating antiterrorist and antiimmigration agendas in the United States and fostering a xenophobic urbanism of division.

In the context of these transformations, the centralization of unchecked and unchallenged police power in Washington, DC, has made Homeland Security the new national planning department and the Patriot Act its social and environmental blueprint, making many disenfranchised inner-city neighborhoods across the United States a renewed focus of police repression and disinvestment, and transforming the 11 million illegal laborers who live in them into criminals.

These forces of division and control are amplified in particular critical thresholds along the political equator's trajectory, such as the San Diego–Tijuana border region. It is at critical junctures such as these that global shifting sociocultural and economic dynamics can be found at the scale of the neighborhood and reflected on the politics of urban development, anticipating the transformation of our normative notions of housing, city, and the territory.

The international border between the United States and Mexico at the San Diego/Tijuana checkpoint is the most trafficked in the world. Approximately 60 million people cross annually, moving untold amounts of goods and services back and forth. But as it has occurred at different stages of its history, the intensity of this sociocultural and economic funnel is once more being suppressed as the federal government is quietly planning to close the gaps and fortify or "harden" the San Diego/Tijuana border checkpoint. This is one of the most recent and symbolic post–9/11 urban interventions, and it is with this project that Homeland Security is continuing to further divide the U.S. from its Mexican neighbor.

The initial plans for the new checkpoint, ironically part of the General Services Administration (GSA) Excellence in Design program, have revealed, once more, the subordination of the social and the cultural to the politics of fear and the atrophy of institutional thinking. Promising to increase the capacity of car lanes and the construction of massive parking structures to service the increasing army of immigration officers and national guards at the border, as well as the expansion of the detention and revision areas for suspects, these plans fail to include the perpendicular urban dynamics of the binational communities that have historically framed this passage. Instead, it installs a parallel 'highway of surveillance' along the border wall's path. Construction of this highway has been accelerated with the mandate of the federal government, and with the excuse of the current national security its construction is overriding every single environmental policy that has protected the land reserves along the border Tijuana River Estuary for decades.

As the initial studies of the new check point suggest, this major intervention—at the threshold between the Tijuana River (the natural) and the geopolitical borderline (the artificial)—will remain indifferent to the transborder ecologies that perforate this barrier. The intensity of the binational social and economic flows and the borderless ecological networks (Kevin Lynch's 1970s vision study for San Diego identified the natural ecologies shared by the two cities as the armature for the border's future growth) indicate the co-dependence between Tijuana and San Diego as well as the missed opportunities for strengthening these transborder urban dynamics. As one San Ysidro neighborhood representative recently put it at a community workshop concerning the new checkpoint planning: "I hope that the architects designing the new border crossing will deliver a nice looking building, one that does not look like a jail"—referring to the character of the existing checkpoint. "But even if that is the case, have the architects and engineers working in the project considered the performance of crossing? Can they think of a more efficient system of revision so that no one should be required to wait in line more than 15 minutes?"

The current barricading of the continental border thus mirrors the inefficacy of urban planning and architectural institutions in the context of these sociopolitical realities. The checkpoint is being planned without the collaboration of these two border cities. Additionally, not one single municipal agency is acknowledging the temporal and socioeconomic systems that flow beneath the wall, not one single transborder land use map nor planning strategy and not one single shared infrastructure. In a recent San Diego mayoral forum, the five top candidates were asked to name the current mayor of the border city that lies barely 20 minutes away from

San Diego's City Hall. None of them could answer. The current border-crossing transformation and its highway of surveillance promise to further exacerbate the division of these border cities and the perpetuation of their governments' indifference.

This massive transformation of the border ecology inspires a chronological retracing of the border's 30-year evolution, as well as of the urbanisms that have emerged from this zero set back condition. The physical transformations of this edge range from the time when the landscape between Tijuana and San Ysidro was uninterrupted, to the construction of the first chain link fence, to the building of a 10-foot high steel wall in the early 1990s. Because this steel wall has proven to be very inefficient (its corrugation runs horizontally, allowing people to easily climb it, and its solidity made it a perfect place to hide), it is currently being replaced by a more functional version. The newest wall, currently under construction, can be called the longest Panopticon in history: A very hygienic and efficient wall made of concrete columns strategically spaced to allow maximum surveillance and minimum human slippage and crowned by an electrified fence. The border's transformation, from light to solid, evinces the powerlessness of contemporary architecture and urbanism's search for lightness and nomadism. It also will define a radically conservative cultural agenda in years to come, incrementally reinforcing a rigid grid of containment instead of a fluid bed of opportunity. In other words, the hardening of the wall has occurred in tandem with the hardening of a social legislature toward the public, producing a discriminating urban policy of exclusion and division. The divisive 'cut' that the wall as an artifact inflicts on this binational territory is reproduced a thousand times in the rest of San Diego, dividing the city into urban and administrative islands and perpetuating an urbanism of distance separation or "setbacks" between large (freeway) and small (neighborhood), public and private resources and across local, state, and federal agencies.

The perennial alliance between militarization and urbanization is reenacted and epitomized by the solidifying of this border wall, further transforming San Diego into the world's largest gated community. But, although in the context of the history of urbanism this historic alliance between systems of control and urban development is nothing new, what dramatizes its effect in the post–9/11 city is the complicity between the military—industrial establishment and the increasing neoliberalist economic policies of privatization and homogenization. This 'ownership society' and the promise of the 'free' market forces that support it are also engendering particular divisive tensions in terms of social and economic inequalities across communities, nation-states, and hemispheres.

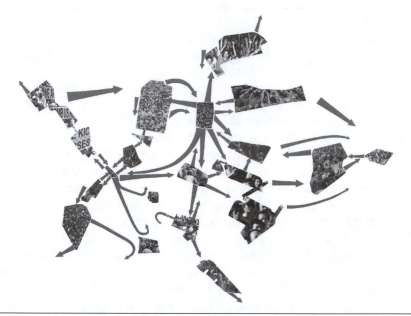

Figure 3 Guy Debord(er). (Courtesy of Estudio Teddy Cruz.)

Practices of Encroachment

Relational Architectures: Micro Urbanisms

Five Mini Tours

It is primarily in territories of conflict, such as this one, where critical urban and artistic practices are emerging. This is an art and urbanism of transgression that infiltrates itself beyond the property line—a migrant, small scale activism that alters the rigidity of discriminatory urban planning via illegal uses, informal politics and economies, and that searches for new organizational strategies across the untapped resources found within diverse jurisdictions, communities and institutions. What comes to mind are certain anticipatory actions scenes from a world to come that have already been staged in the transborder urban context of Tijuana and San Diego, two-way journeys out of which new 'micro-heterotopias' will unfold over time, negotiating the border that continues separating social responsibility and artistic experimentation.

By zooming into the particularities of this volatile territory, traveling back and forth between these two border cities, we can expose landscapes of contradiction where conditions of difference and sameness collide and overlap. For, despite the apocalyptic implications of a more fortified border with intensified surveillance infrastructure, the growing tension between the various communities of San Diego and those of Tijuana have elicited a multitude of insurgent responses—new opportunities for constructing alternative modes of encounter for dialogue and debate, sharing resources and infrastructure, recycling at the most outlandish levels the fragments and situations of these two cities and constructing critical practices of encroachment into the increasing privatization of the public realm.

Brief back-and-forth tours into Tijuana and San Diego can reveal the double paradox of a transborder urban cluster that simultaneously wants to be divided and fluid. As we move through these landscapes of contradiction, we witness two kinds of urbanisms which collide and overlap daily: one of difference, one of juxtaposition. If San Diego is emblematic of an urbanism of segregation and control, epitomized by the master-planned and gated communities that define its sprawl, Tijuana's periphery has evolved as a collection of informal, nomadic settlements or favelas. This contrast is not reductive if one considers that the steel border wall is the ultimate symbol of a puritan planning tradition made of social exclusion and separation.

The contrast between these two cities is further dramatized by the unfolding of their different histories, narratives and identities. Their centers, for example, which are only 22 miles apart, represent entirely different socioeconomic and political universes. Whereas San Diego calls itself "America's Finest City," Mexico views Tijuana as a decadent hybrid and transient world unto itself, distinct from (and somehow inferior to) the rest of the country. Whereas San Diego has always been perceived in the United States as a picturesque resort town, a point of arrival for migrating populations looking for a nice *cul-de-sac* in which to retire, Tijuana has traditionally been perceived in Mexico as a threshold leading to the 'other side,' a contemporary Sodom and Gomorrah.

By contrast, we can simultaneously witness how the differences between these border cities dwindle and urbanisms of juxtaposition emerge as San Diego's signature mini-malls spring up on Tijuana's street corners and San Diego style gated residential communities fill in the city's periphery. At the same time, Tijuana's random patterns of density, mixed-use and informal economies begin to appear in neighborhoods of San Diego. The following mini tours will reveal how as these cities further divide, they also begin to contain each other. Unavoidably, in every 'first world' city a 'third world' exists, and every 'third world' city replicates the first.

Tour 1—South under North

The Fictional Cartographies of an Urbanism 70-feet Deep   When Kevin Lynch was commissioned by a local environmental group to come up with a "regional vision plan" for the U.S.–Mexico border zone in 1974, he dreamed of a *temporary paradise*. Addressed to the City Planning Commission of San Diego, his binational planning strategy focused on the network of canyons and watersheds that traverse the landscape on both sides of the San Diego–Tijuana border. Lynch could never have predicted that neither the natural landscape *nor* city planners would define the real action plan for transborder urbanism, and that instead it would be an emergent network of underground tunnels masterminded by drug lords and "coyotes" and quietly and invisibly effacing the formidable barrier that separates the two cities. Now, 34 years later, at least 30 tunnels have been discovered, a vast "ant farm"–like maze of subterranean routes criss-crossing the border from California to Arizona—all dug within the last eight years. At the very least, this creates a *permanent hell* for the U.S. Department of Homeland Security.

An archaeological section map of the territory today would reveal an underground urbanism worming its way into houses, churches, parking lots, warehouses, and streets. The most outlandish and sophisticated of these tunnels, discovered by U.S. border officials in January of this year, is clearly the work of professionals: up to 70 feet below ground and 2,400 feet in length, its passageways are five to six feet high and four feet wide to permit two-way circulation. Striking not only for its scale but also for its "amenities," the tunnel is equipped with ventilation and drainage systems, water pumps, electricity, retaining reinforcements, and stairs connecting various levels. In addition to being used by drug traffickers, it also was "leased out" during "off" hours to coyotes transporting illegal aliens into the United States, making it perhaps the first mixed-use smuggling tunnel at the border. Some might see this as a marvel of informal transnational infrastructure, but most locals understand it as just another example of the vigorous Mexican–American economy at work.

Beyond the sensationalism that might accompany these images, it is the undeniable presence of an informal economy and the politics of density that are exposed here. As we insert the actual location of these illegal tunnels into an official border map, a different image of the borderline appears. The linear rigidity of the artificial geopolitical boundary, "flat-lining" the pulsations of the living complexity of the natural, is transformed into a complex set of porous lines perpendicular to the border. As these lines puncture the borderline in our fictional cartography, they almost restore the primacy of the network of existing canyons, juxtaposing the natural with the socioeconomic flows that continue to be 'under the radar' in our official modes of urban planning representation.

In other words, our institutions of representation across government, academia and development have not been able to critically observe and translate the logic of the informal socioeconomic dynamics at play not only at the border itself but also within the city at large. The official documentation of land use at any city agency, whether in San Diego or Tijuana, for example, has systematically ignored the nonconforming and self-organizing dynamics of these environments by continuing to advocate a false, bidimensional land-use convention based on abstract information rendered at the planners' table. In these plans, retail is represented with red and housing yellow, safely located adjacent to one another in the best of scenarios, since they are typically very far apart.

If, by contrast, one were to map the *real* land use in some of the San Diego neighborhoods that have been impacted in the last decades by waves of immigration from Latin America, Africa, and Asia, examining them parcel by parcel, block by block, what would emerge is a land-use map with at least ten or more 'zone colors,' reflecting the gradation of use and scale of the diverse social composition and nonconforming small businesses and social exchanges that characterizes these culturally intensive areas of the city. We also would find a three-dimensional zoning based not on adjacencies but on juxtapositions, as dormant infrastructures are transformed into usable semipublic spaces and larger than 'needed' parcels are illegally subdivided to accommodate extra dwelling units. In other words, the appropriation and negotiation of public and private boundaries remains anathema for conventional code regulation, ignoring the potentialities of this stealth urbanism. How to alter our conventions of representation in order to absorb the ambiguity of these forces remains the essential question in the negotiation between the formal and the informal city.

Similar to the cartography of cross-border illegal tunnels, then, an accurate binational land-use map does not currently exist. If we were to 'cut and paste' the existing land-use documents from Tijuana and San Diego without marking the border wall itself, a borderline would again 'appear' between the two cities as the larger land-use 'chunks' of San Diego come side to side with the smaller pixilation of Tijuana's Land Use map. A fictional cartography of this 'collision' would invite one to speculate a way of representing the transformation of some of the San Diego neighborhoods impacted by informal patterns of development. This new map would show the higher pixilation of Tijuana's three dimensional and multicolor zoning crossing the borderline and forming an archipelago of difference within the sea of the current homogeneous sprawl that defines this city's periphery.

What this phenomenon points out, then, is the fact that our institutions of representation are unable to mediate the multiple forces that shape the politics of the territory or resolve the tensions between the top-down urban strategies of official development and the bottom-up tactics of community activism. The micro heterotopias that are emerging within small communities in the form of informal spatial and entrepreneurial practices are defining a different idea of density and land use. Making visible the invisibility of these nonconforming forces and their operational potential to bridge between the formal and the informal, the wealthy subdivisions and the enclaves of poverty (service communities) in the city, would be the only point of departure needed to construct a different idea of density and sustainability. We need to engage new conceptual and representational tools that can allow us to transcend the reductive understanding of density as an abstract amount of units/inhabitants per acre, and instead reaffirm it as an amount of 'social interactions and exchanges' per acre.

Tour 2—North to South: Migrant Housing

How San Diego's Waste Builds Tijuana   In many ways, Tijuana builds itself with the waste of San Diego. One city recycles the "leftover" of the other into a sort of "secondhand" urbanism. Tijuana's informal settlements are shaped by these cross-border recycling dynamics and by organizational tactics of invasion, allowing settlers to claim underutilized territory. Whereas San Diego's vast sprawl is incrementally made of gigantic infrastructure to support loosely scattered units of housing, in Tijuana's edges dense habitation happens first so that incremental small infrastructure can follow.

This temporal, nomadic urbanism is supported by a very sophisticated social choreography of neighborhood participation. Hundreds of dwellers called "*paracaidistas*" (parachuters) invade, en masse, large public (sometimes private) vacant properties. As these urban guerillas parachute into the hills of Tijuana's edges, they are organized and choreographed by what are commonly called "urban pirates." These characters, armed with cellular phones, are the community activists (or land speculators) who are in charge of organizing the first deployment of people at the sites as well as the community in an effort to begin the process of requesting services from the city. Through improvisational tactics of construction and distribution of goods and ad hoc services, a process of assembly begins by recycling the systems and materials from San Diego's urban debris. Garage doors are used to make walls; rubber tires are cut and dismantled into folded loops, clipped and interlocked, creating a system that threads a stable retaining wall; wooden crates make the armature for other imported surfaces, such as recycled refrigerator doors, and so on. After months of construction and community organization, the inhabitants of the neighborhood begin to request municipal services. The city sends trucks to deliver water at certain locations and electricity follows as the city sends *one* official line, expecting the community to "steal" the rest via a series of illegal clippings called "*diablitos*" (Little Devils). These sites are threaded by the temporal stitching of these multiple situations, internal and external, simultaneously, making the interiors of these dwellings become their

Figure 4 Migrant housing. (Courtesy of Estudio Teddy Cruz.)

exteriors, expressive of the history of their pragmatic evolution. As one anonymous resident put it, "Not everything that we have is to our liking, but everything is useful."

But it isn't only small, scattered debris that is imported into Tijuana. Entire pieces of one city travel southward as residential ready-mades are directly plugged into the other's fabric. This process begins when a Tijuana speculator travels to San Diego to buy up little postwar bungalows that have been slated for demolition in order to make space for new luxury condominium projects. The little houses are loaded onto trailers and prepared to travel to Tijuana, where they will have to clear customs before making their journey south. For days, one can see houses, just like cars and pedestrians, waiting in line to cross the border. Finally the houses enter into Tijuana and are mounted on top of one-story metal frames, leaving an empty space at the street level to accommodate future uses. These floating houses define a space of opportunity beneath them, a space that will be filled, through time, with more homes, a taco stand, a car repair shop, or a garden. One city profits from the dwellings that the other one discards, recombining them into fresh scenarios and creating countless new possibilities. This is how the border cities enact a strange mirroring effect. Although the seemingly permanent housing stock in San Diego is turned disposable from one day to another, the ephemeral dwellings in Tijuana want to become permanent.

Ultimately, this intensive recycling urbanism of juxtaposition is emblematic of how Tijuana's informal communities are growing faster than the urban cores they surround, creating a different set of rules for development and blurring the distinctions between the urban, the suburban, and the rural. As notions of the informal are brought back, recycled by the fields of architecture and urbanism in debating the growth of the contemporary city, let's hope that it is not only the figural 'image' of the ephemeral and nomadic that is once more seducing our imagination, but the complex temporal, evolutionary processes beneath them, whose essence is grounded on sociopolitical and economic dynamics.

In other words, what is missing from our institutions of urban governance and development is precisely what gives shape to this informal urbanism: the notion that any physical intervention in the city should be preceded by a social imprint made of collaborations across agencies and institutions as well as the negotiation of territorial boundaries and private and public resources. These transborder urban dynamics are evidence of how guerrilla urban tactics, whether in the hands of common citizens or artistic practices, are incrementally reshaping the city out of an infrastructure of acupuncture, a temporal urbanism of small parts, of social and economic contingency.

Figure 5 Illegal zoning. (Courtesy of Estudio Teddy Cruz.)

Tour 3—South to North: Illegal Zoning

The Search for Infrastructures of Ambiguity   After years of being absent from our main institutions of representation and display, we are all again drawn to the city, yearning to recuperate it as a site of experimentation, a laboratory of cultural production. The current desire of our cultural institutions to move from the notion of city as a static repository of objects—whether seen as autonomous architectural artifacts or as sculpture in the middle of the plaza—to a more 'complicated' idea, one that is inclusive of the temporal dynamics of social and ecological networks as well as of the politics and economics of density and urban development has been unavoidably provoked by a new world in flux that is beginning to redefine, once more, the role of architecture in relationship to the larger territory. The changing geopolitical boundaries across continents, the unprecedented shifting of sociocultural demographics, the migration of labor and the redeployment of centers of manufacturing across hemispheres are conditions that are currently provoking many architects and artists to construct alternative practices, particularly within geographies of conflict such as the Tijuana–San Diego region. So this return to the city, then, and to critical thresholds such as Tijuana might ultimately be a reflection of our need to critically redefine established notions of public culture.

But, as we return to the city, it is clear that across the fields of government, academia, and private development, the focus of attention continues to be two-fold: the return to the downtown core, on one end, and engaging the challenge of sprawl, on the other—whereas the territory that continues to be ignored is the space in between, the inner city, the *mid*-city. Even though the return to the center is a welcome agenda after the urban flight to the periphery of past decades, the economic strategies that are generally driving these re-development energies are engendering a project of gentrification on a massive scale. The downtown revitalization projects in many American cities, a widespread phenomenon occurring from New York to San Diego, are ironically importing into city centers the very suburban project of privatization, homogenization and "theming," accompanied by "loftlike" luxury housing, stadiums, and the official corporate franchises that are always brought with this kind of development. At the other end of the spectrum, the interest in suburbia of recent years is equally a welcome attitude, mainly when the institutions of architecture and urbanism have been overtly discriminating against such environments, calling them uncivilized and benefiting the center as the privileged site of urban culture. Many efforts to engage sprawl end up merely supporting a repeating project of gentrification. The proliferation of McMansions everywhere continues to be made possible by the construction of huge freeway infrastructure subsidized by our own tax dollars and indulged by architecture's own indifference to the economic forces that shape these recipes for development.

The emphasis on these two extreme areas of development in many cities around the world mirrors in some way the urgency for many metropolitan centers to engage the relevancy of new economic models of revitalization through privatization. But, as Saskia Sassen has pointed out, when the "new economies" of globalization hit the actual ground, it divides into two projects: on the one hand, the "mega project of glamour" (every city wants its Times Square, its grand stadium) and, on the other, the "project of marginalization" (the service sector needed to support such projects). At the time when these mega projects of redevelopment are becoming the basis for the skyrocketing of the real estate market in many city centers across the United States, creating a formidable economic bubble of land speculation, practically no one is asking *where* the cook, janitor, service maid, busboy, nanny, gardener, and many of the thousands of immigrants crossing the border(s) to fulfill the demand for such jobs will live—or what kinds of rents and housing markets will be available to them. There are not too many options when we are reminded that, according to the last housing census, San Diego is the second least affordable housing area in the country, with only 11 percent of households capable of affording a median-price home at $500,000.

So, although left over rubber tires, garage doors, pallet racks and disposable houses flow southbound to construct an urbanism of emergency, immigrants flow toward the north, searching for one of the strongest economies in the world, the state of California, with the assurance that such economic power still depends on the cheap labor only provided by them—a supply and demand logic. The increasing waves of immigrants from Latin America have had a major impact on the urbanism of many American cities, not to mention the economic and social life of this country. Already, Los Angeles, for example, is home to the second largest concentration of Latin Americans outside the capitals of Mexico, Guatemala, and El Salvador. Current demographic studies have predicted that Latin Americans will comprise the majority of California's population in the next decade. As the Latin American Diaspora travels north, it inevitably alters and transforms the fabric of certain neighborhoods in cities such as Los Angeles and San Diego. Immigrants bring with them diverse sociocultural attitudes and sensibilities regarding the use of domestic and public space as well as the natural landscape. In these neighborhoods, multigenerational households of extended families shape their own programs of use, taking charge of their own micro-economies in order to maintain a standard for the household, generating nonconforming uses and high densities that reshape the fabric of the residential neighborhoods where they settle. Alleys, setbacks, driveways, and other underutilized infrastructures and leftover spaces are appropriated and activated as the community sees fit. This results in the emergence of a temporal public domain encroaching into private property: Social spaces begin to spring up in large parking lots, informal economies such as flea markets and street vendors appear in vacant properties, and housing additions in the shape of illegal companion units are plugged into existing dwellings to provide affordable living. Together, these 'plug-in' programs and architectures pixilate with a finer socioeconomic grain than the discriminating land use that has maintained the social and the formal at a distance.

It is not a coincidence, then, that the territory that continues to be ignored is the inner city. This is the area where most of the immigrants coming from Latin America, Asia, and Africa have settled in the last decades, making these neighborhoods the service communities for the newly gentrified center and the expensive periphery. Not able to afford the high-priced real estate of downtown or the McMansion of the new sprawl, waves of immigrant communities have concentrated themselves in the inner- or mid-city neighborhoods of many American cities in recent years. The temporal, informal economies and patterns of density promoted by immigrants and their sociocultural and economic dynamics have fundamentally altered what was the first ring of Levittown-type suburbanization of the 1950s, transforming its homogeneity into a more complex network of illegal socioeconomic relationships. By critically observing how these temporal and contingent urbanisms have contaminated the rigidity of zoning within these older fabrics, can we anticipate how the one-dimensionality of the McMansions now sprawling in the third, fourth, and fifth rings of suburbanization will be retrofitted to accommodate difference in the next five decades?

If our planning and architecture institutions were to seriously acknowledge these mutations, then, the question of how to anticipate density would have to redefine our processes of intervention in the city. By bridging between the planned and the unplanned, the legal and the illegal, the object and the political ground, Tijuana's informal urbanism could become an instrument to research and further understand the patterns of density and programmatic intensity that are redefining the American metropolis. The cataloging, for example, of the small prototypical nonconforming appendages, spatially and programmatically, that have erupted illegally from the official planning of the mid-city, would point out that the future of the edge, sprawling city will be determined by the tactics of an urbanism made of retrofitting. Small programs, spaces and infrastructures will be injected into the homogeneity of these environments as a result of micro-political and socioeconomic transformations in urban policy. In other words, the future of these environments might be determined by a more strategic relationship between the socioeconomic, the political and the spatial tactics that can frame and support such transformations, and by urban policies and infrastructures that can support levels of ambiguity and open-endedness.

The current need to engage the politics of land use, then, has been provoked by the realization that no advances in housing design can be accomplished without advances in the transformation of urban policy. In other words, the ultimate site of intervention is *planning regulation* itself, and the contamination of zoning in the form of alternative densities and transitional uses, informal politics and economies, and in a search for new organizational strategies across the untapped resources found within diverse jurisdictions, communities, and institutions. It is in fact the political and cultural dimension of housing and density as tools for social integration in the city that can inform an urbanism of transgression that infiltrates itself beyond the property line, a migrant, micro-urbanism that can alter the rigidity of the discriminatory public policies of the American city. The effort has been to create a participatory practice that can enter the politics of information and public debate about the city: What do we mean by density? What is the meaning of housing?

But the future of housing and its needed transparency and triangulation across social and ecological networks in the United States is currently not in the hands of the federal (the Bush administration) or state (Schwarzenegger administration) governments, which have overtly indicated their indifference to the social and environmental project as well as to the public institution. Nor is it in the hands of private developers, most of whom continue perpetuating the equation of minimum investment–maximum profit and perceive investing in the public realm to be antidemocratic because it reduces their economic "freedoms." Instead, the most experimental work in housing in the United States is in the hands of progressive, community-based, nonprofit organizations, as well as small communities across the continent. These agencies engage the social dynamics of many mid-city neighborhoods daily, mediating between their histories and identities and the planning policies that shape their destiny. It seems appropriate that these nongovernmental organizations (NGOs) become the future developers of affordable housing and a new public realm within these environments because their sociocultural agendas can translate into unique organizational and spatial strategies, inclusive of the specificity of individual communities and places. It is this sense of emergency in shaping alternative practices that can erode the increasing privatization of the public domain and mobilize new triangulations among institutions across the border, negotiating private and public resources and straddling both sides of the San Diego–Tijuana border between the politics of zoning and the strategies of the informal.

Figure 6 North into south: the counterinvasion. (Courtesy of Estudio Teddy Cruz.)

Tour 4—North into South: The Counterinvasion

Tijuana's Mini Gated Communities and the Purchase of Baja

1. The World's Aquarium for Sale (segment in collaboration with Enrique Martin-Moreno)   As millions of Latin American immigrants flow North to work illegally for 'unwanted' jobs, U.S. citizens, armed with millions of dollars, run southward in an unprecedented land rush to purchase the peninsula of Baja California, as this unspoiled corner of Mexico, whose internal 'sea of Cortez' was once called "the aquarium of the world" by the renowned oceanographer Jacques Cousteau, is for sale. North American developers are rushing to cross the border to buy large sections of land in such a volume that a string of mega luxury waterfront residential subdivisions and resorts have begun to emerge in the last five years, all along the Baja peninsula, from Tijuana to Cabo San Lucas. As xenophobia once again prompts the American Public to denounce illegal immigration, calling it an invasion, one could claim that the Baja California colonization, currently in the hands of land speculators, represents the beginning of a counterinvasion.

This buying frenzy has been primarily sponsored in recent years by FONATUR, the Mexican Federal Tourism Bureau, which installed the "Nautical Ladder," an integrated network of 29 ports along the peninsula. But the acceleration of the sale of Baja began when the neoliberalist economic policies of Mexican President Carlos Salinas de Gortari amended the Mexican Constitution in 1992 to allow the selling of *Ejidos* or communal land that had been given to peasants as part of the post-1910 revolution's agrarian reform. The owners of these waterfront properties have been living in poverty for decades as the land they own has proven unproductive—the desert and saline lands make agriculture impossible and cattle raising difficult. But now under the new economic logic of the global tourism industry, these waterfront lands have become attractive for beach resort development. These developments are characterized by 'economies of extraction' such as the ones found in similar tourist strips strung along the Caribbean coast where, for example, according to the urban research group SUPERSUDACA, for each dollar spent in a Caribbean resort, only 3¢ trickles into the local economy.

Although it is still prohibited for foreigners to own land near the coast, real estate agents have developed strategies for giving Americans the equivalent of ownership, even if they cannot hold formal title to their houses. In the most common arrangement, banks buy houses and then hold them in a trust for the foreign "buyers." A trust, under recent amendments to the law, can now last 50 years and can be renewed at the end of that term. The bottom line is that a "buyer" can expect to retain a property in perpetuity. If the bank fails, the trust can be transferred to another bank.

These changes in the financial and political structures that until recently maintained a check and balances framework, indirectly protecting these ecologically sensitive zones, have unleashed a real estate speculation frenzy that no longer asks whether the communal lands will be sold but 'when.' Around the Bay of Loreto, for instance, most *ejidatarios* (communal land owners) have already sold their land, especially if they have access to the water. In an article for the Mexican Newspaper *La Jornada*, José de Jesús Varela, director of the NGO Kuyima, describes a recurring dynamic as people see the amazing possibility of a short term profit: "the American developers give them about $800,000 pesos (about US$80,000) and the first thing the Ejidatarios do is buy a new truck—a Ford Lobo—then they throw a big party and then they change their wife. Very soon, they are left without money, without a wife and without land. They are left with nothing." Soon Baja Californians will become the gardeners or the bellhops of the resorts built on the land they once owned.

It is here, in the Bay of Loreto, where developers are building a 5,000-unit resort designed by Andres Duany, who is selling it to the world as 'the first ecologically friendly subdivision.' In a typical New Urbanist appeal, this mega development is customized as an authentic Mexican Village, completing the invasion of Loreto Bay by not only a mono culture of upper-middle-class North American land owners who can afford this island of pleasure, but by 'Seaside' and 'Celebration' type of planning, making this the official arrival of New Urbanism in grand scale to the Mexican West Coast. Beyond issues of architectural style, however, it is tragic that these mega developments, as ecologically responsible and manicured as they can be, are indifferent to the social and economic inequalities they will engender, as these 'all inclusive' and gated environments might be eventually surrounded by the shanty towns built by their own service providers. This phenomenon will add to the strange asymmetry at the border and along the political equator's trajectory, as this will become another instance of the kind of neoliberalist urbanities worldwide that continue to be supported by cheap labor (service sector), on one end, and the emergence of expensive real state (enclaves of wealth), on the other.

2. Little San Diego in Tijuana   But the most dramatic physical manifestation of the importation into Tijuana of these neoliberalist economic policies of privatization and the urban planning values of security and sameness that accompany them can be found in the newly built mini-master-planned gated communities sprawling to the southeast of the city. As Tijuana grows eastward and is seduced by the style and glamour of the master-planned, gated communities of the United States, Tijuana is building its own version—miniaturized replicas of typical suburban Southern California tract

Figure 7 Little San Diego in Tijuana. (Courtesy of Estudio Teddy Cruz.)

homes, paradoxically imported into Tijuana to provide "social housing." Thousands of tiny tract homes are now scattered around the periphery of Tijuana, creating a vast landscape of homogeneity and division that is at odds with this city's prevailing heterogeneous and organic metropolitan condition. These diminutive 250-square-foot dwellings come equipped with all the clichés and conventions: manicured landscaping, gate houses, model units, banners and flags, mini-setbacks, front and back yards.

This process is the result of the privatization of new social housing in Mexico. The Mexican Federal Housing Commission, INFONAVIT, is now awarding contracts to private developers and speculators to develop public housing in Tijuana and in other cities across Mexico. These developers have adopted and are selling the image of individual houses on individual lots, even if they are miniscule. The urban code of Southern California is imported here, as in the rest of the world, to build the periphery of the twenty-first-century city. But, although the gated communities of Southern California remain closed systems as a result of stringent zoning that prohibits any kind of formal alteration or programmatic juxtaposition, housing tracts in Tijuana quickly submit to transformation by occupants who are little hindered by comparatively permissive zoning regulations. The ways in which occupants customize their tract houses and parcels—filling in setbacks, occupying front and back yards as well as garages with more construction to support mixed use and more usable space—mirror the urban tactics common to older informal communities of the city rather than the idealized suburban dream house. Even if designed with a fixed stylistic recipe by developers—beige units irresponsibly thrown in the landscape, lacking an infrastructure of public space and transportation—these tracts are transformed through time by their occupants into open systems, allowing them the freedom to activate higher-density, mixed uses and the negotiation of a new public realm. A small business fills in the front yard; an overhang appears, extending beyond the right of way, creating a public shade by a main sidewalk; two, three, four stories unfold through time, morphing the tiny prototype original model from an autonomous object into a series of interlinked spaces and patterns. Sometimes, beneath the many layers, one can view the original house, hidden away as a silent witness of its transformation.

The tactics of encroachment Tijuana residents have taken here may prefigure the fate of urban densification in many cities around the world, where redevelopment has been driven by privatization, homogenization, and theming. The cataloguing of these improvisational additions and ad hoc public domain tactics could begin to give us clues as to how to imagine the redefinition of future cross-border development to accept programmatic contingency and spatial transformation. The radical physical

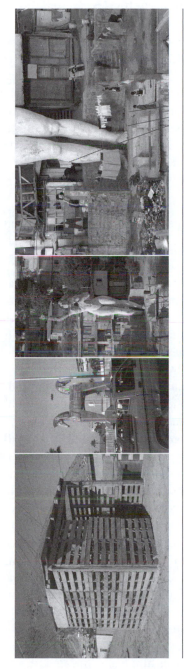

Figure 8 Architectures of desire. (Courtesy of Estudio Teddy Cruz.)

transformation of these developments in the last five years suggests an 'urbanism beyond the property line,' becoming the kind of laboratory to search for tactics of intervention in the contemporary city that can anticipate densification and diversification of social and economic composition. In other words, by critically observing and measuring the mutation of these environments, we can begin to redefine the degree of criticality in the field of architecture today, which, within this context, might be better measured, not by what forms we can produce, but by the social formations we can engender, as these tactics also encroach into the one-dimensional modes of thinking of the official institutions shaping the city.

Tour 5—South Only: Architectures of Desire
House, Horse and Doll

> "Here, unlike any other place, dreams have broken steps as if they were old ladders."

House (Case Study by Marcos Ramirez, ERRE)   Jose Hernandez builds a house. He has wrapped it with pieces of cardboard that he picked up from the trash at the 'curios' market where he works. It was there where he was also able to find other left over 'stuff' to build the rest of his walls—approximately 40 pallet racks that his neighbor's boss sold him after retrieving a shipment of clay figurines from Guadalajara, mysteriously abandoned by a truck driver before he was paid. Jose has gotten a couple of blue canvases from the flea market that comes to his neighborhood every Tuesday and used them to fabricate a temporary roof. The type of blue he has chosen is a bit stronger than the blue of the sky, but useful for stopping the water leak that has been dripping on the corner that he is currently using as kitchen.

At the house's entrance, there is a nice patterned cotton curtain that, from the inside, hides a crooked door that cannot close all the way, but can, in any case, by connecting to a wooden post with a chain, allow him and his wife to sleep peacefully at night. Jose also was able to pay monthly installments to his neighborhood's hardware store for a couple of French windows, the ones that have multiple mullions, so that he doesn't have to replace the whole thing if the window breaks. In terms of furniture, Jose has a strange mixture of styles and colors, which he wants to edit immediately after taking care of the most pressing necessities. It is useless, he says, in order to console himself, to have strong, uniform furniture when you don't have an appropriate floor surface. Jose's floor is made of compacted dirt that he has to water constantly to avoid the dust cloud that makes everything dirty and makes him feel suffocated.

But there is a refrigerator. Jose does not tolerate warm beer. His wife and two daughters need this appliance a lot more than he does, which is as indispensable to them as the $30 television set that Jose bought for his wife Teresa on their last wedding anniversary. The Hernandezes also have a battery operated radio and a camping stove that works with a small gas cylinder that allows them to cook for two weeks at a time. The rest of their house wares, including clothing, appliances, utensils, dishes, blankets, and linens, they have acquired either by buying them or by receiving them as gifts. They just arrived a few months ago to this location and with time they will save more money to finish painting their house. This will only happen after they finish building a fence and a place for washing. But this will not happen until they finally receive official electrical service—which up to now they have been stealing like everyone else. Among their other priorities is to replace the parabolic dish that the wind took away the other night when it wouldn't stop raining, but this will not happen until their uncle, who is the leader of the neighborhood's liberal political party, fulfills his promise to finally give them the property title to their small lot.

Horse   On the 26th of September 1997, as part of a binational art project called InSite, Marcos Ramírez Erre, one of the most far-sighted artists to emerge in Tijuana, rolled an enormous Janus-headed Trojan Horse into the midst of the traffic waiting to cross the border on both sides. The horse appeared out of nowhere, and, in the same way, it vanished. It was positioned to straddle the border, with two legs resting on the U.S. side, one head looking north, while the other legs remained rooted in Mexico, the other head gazing southward. Erre inserted his horse into the decentered, deterritorialized, and multidirectional flows that constitute the border, where it dwelled for a brief moment (impossibly), occupying both sides at once in defiance of the dialectic forces that govern the space. Representing both arrival and departure, stasis as well as movement at a crossroads, the Trojan Horse, in the words of Erre, was:

> The fragile 'anti-monument,' ephemeral and translucent because in our time there is nothing to hide, we already know all their intentions towards us, and they know our intentions towards them. It is a universal symbol, which was modified to indicate the uncertainty of a time in which the only way to conceal the truth is to overwhelm us with information. When there are no more sufficient caretakers of censorship to control the avalanche of doubts, and when one does not know anymore where the truth has been buried, everyone has a version of it, and that is where creativity begins. This should be the best response

for those who still believe that it is possible to establish rigid custom houses, and protect cities and their images with judicial decrees.

Doll   In 1989, Armando Muñoz, a Tijuana citizen who Michel De Certeau would have called 'a common hero,' paid homage to the 100th anniversary of his city by erecting a home-made 'statue of liberty.' La Mona (the Doll) appeared from one day to the next from within Colonia Libertad, one of Tijuana's oldest informal, favela-like communities. Her arms reaching for the sky, La Mona invokes the irony of liberty in this context, but she also stands for the political role of women in the city. La Mona was not only a monument to Armando Muñoz's city—it is also a permanent addition to his own house. As the Situationists imagined it, the ultimate avant-garde action occurs the moment that an average citizen is able to appropriate the spaces and the materials of the city.

Muñoz's "monument" and Erre's "antimonument," the Trojan Horse, remind us that the contemporary city is still able to elude the absolute ordering devices that attempt to render it homogeneous and one-dimensional. Spontaneous gestures such as the Horse and the Doll allow us to glimpse the subjective and collective struggles of a community locked into conflicts that are being played out in the border zone: the most derelict and unexpected places have the potential to become sites for light occupations that challenge the massive colonization of traditional urbanism. For San Diego as well as for Tijuana, the Horse and the Doll have ironically become political symbols that remind us of the opportunities opened up by an insurgent, flexible urbanism that insinuates itself into the most rigid contexts using simple strategies of transgression and appropriation. How to appropriate the empty spaces of the city—defunct infrastructure, abandoned industrial buildings, and brown fields—and how to activate the potential of the void are still, as Catalunian urban theorist Ignasi de Sola-Morales noted in his seminal text *Terrain Vague*, the crucial questions for contemporary artists—and also for architects and urban planners.

In a certain way, the status of the Mexican border today is just one more casualty of 9/11, in the sense that the events of that day permanently altered the U.S. government's position on its international borders, throwing long-standing and politically charged immigration issues relating to illegal labor into high relief against the backdrop of terrorism. Contradictions inherent in revamped protectionist agendas were further dramatized in 2004 when George W. Bush rolled out his new policy on immigration. Proposing to issue temporary work visas that would allow immigrants to work legally in the United States for a period of three years, with a renewable second three-year term, after which workers would have to return to their home country, this 'open-door' policy professes to "legalize" the status of hard-working people who currently fill a seemingly insatiable demand for cheap labor (in California alone, if every nanny, housekeeper, waiter, bus boy, cook, gardener, janitor, construction and agricultural worker stopped working for 24 hours, the whole state would come to a standstill). However, labor organizers contend that by denying the possibility of citizenship, the proposed policy merely (re)produces a labor underclass. Is this just a rerun of the Bracero program that invited over 12,000 documented Mexican workers into the country in 1942? Although it is true that in little more than two decades, these workers transformed the growing fields of America into the most productive in the world, one shouldn't forget that the Bracero program was abolished in 1964, when then Department of Labor official Lee G. Williams indicted it as a system of "legalized slavery."

Public reaction to the dysfunctional nature of the border is reflected in the actual death of one pedestrian attempting to cross the border from Tijuana into San Diego early one morning in May 2007. A man hanged himself from one of the pedestrian bridges currently under construction by the city of Tijuana as part of an effort to address the chaotic flow of foot traffic on the Mexican side of the checkpoint. The body dangled as it hung directly over hundreds of cars waiting in endless lanes of bumper-to-bumper rush-hour traffic to cross into San Diego, while countless vendors swarmed through the traffic jam selling curios. No one knows for sure why he decided to take his own life in this way. Some speculated that he had grown increasingly desperate after many failed attempts to cross the border to reach family from which he had been separated for months. Whatever the reasons, this surreal scene became emblematic of the lack of interest on the part of the U.S. government in the functionality of the border on which many citizens and businesses depend and the absence of binational agencies to protect the human rights of the millions of people who cross this border annually, legally and illegally.

The new millennium's utopian dream of a borderless world of cities whose urbanism is founded on cultural contact and exchange, whose social landscape is enriched by advanced informational technologies, whose infrastructure is shared, and whose interinstitutional and jurisdictional alliances and collaborations are ensured has been compromised. So, reentrenched anti-immigration sentiment in the United States converges with the ongoing post-9/11 anti-terrorist agenda at the Mexican border in the most recent sequel, "Homeland Security and the Minutemen against the Eminent Invasion." The general perception of this "imminent invasion from south of the border," as County Commissioner Robert Vasquez of Idaho called it in a *New York Times* article in May 2005, is what has galvanized anti-immigration and antiterrorism as the new emblem of patriotic nationalism in the United States and the manifesto for a new urban code that promises to exacerbate the already rampant NIMBYism ("not in my backyard") in many American cities.

It is at this critical juncture, where we witness the foreclosing of shared horizons, that alternative urban and artistic practices must cross the property line and enter into the public and political debate in order to denounce the incremental privatization and erosion of public culture.

Restating the Obvious

RUTH WILSON GILMORE AND CRAIG GILMORE

Et puis, comme on trouve toujours plus de moines que de raison—

Pascal

Introduction

The announcement that 14 alleged terrorists would be relocated from secret CIA prisons to the military prison at Guantánamo seemed to some a welcome move away from black ops and extraordinary renditions and, however haltingly, toward the rule of law. At the same time, the Bush administration proposed significant changes in court rules in order to allow secret testimony, the use of hearsay, and evidence obtained using so-called alternative interrogation techniques. "There's agreement on the goal," Senator John Cornyn (R, Texas) said, "that we continue to comply with our international treaty obligations and all of our domestic laws, but at the same time not tie the hands of our intelligence officials" (Zernike 2006). Many legislators, including some Republicans, balked at the proposed revisions to rules of evidence and the unilateral redefinition of the Geneva Conventions' definition of torture. What ensued has been an extended public flap about whether the current government should be able to change what the state does legitimately—which means, practically and normatively, whether the government should change what the state *is*.

Although this particular public fight may have been extraordinary, significant changes in the state justified by wars—on terror or crime or drugs—have been commonplace throughout U.S. history, and have sped up during the last quarter century. Domestically, the war on crime has been changing the state in broad daylight. Let's start with some numbers to give a sense of the raw dimensions of this complex development. Since 1980, the number of people held in custody in the United States has grown tenfold, topping 2.3 million presently. In 1980, about 1 of every 800 people in the United States was in prison or jail; currently that number is about 1 of 130—not including the thousands held by the U.S. Marshal and immigration and customs enforcement (ICE). During the period of intense growth, which continues as we write, the racial composition of U.S. prisons has changed: although absolute numbers are up across the board, a shrinking *percentage* of prisoners is white and upward of 70 percent are people of color. About 10 percent of prisoners are women of all races. The United States, comprising about 5 percent of the world's population, holds 25 percent of the world's prisoners and more than half the world's wealth.

The case of the Guantánamo 14 offers us a chance to pause and consider how legal protections under the law are not protections *from* the law, a point well illustrated by the unprecedented increase in numbers of people legally held in cages in the United States.

We propose that a key way to understand what the state has become, and a fundamental structure of the expansive neoliberal, or as we call it "antistate state," is to consider the expanded use of cages as catch-all solutions to social and political problems. What are the ideological and material components of this extraordinary proliferation of cages and the policing, courts, belief-systems, and pundits who make them seem so naturally a part of the contemporary landscape? Prisons are symptomatic and emblematic of antistate state-building, and they are therefore concrete manifestations of a dour future for all insofar as they congeal within both novel and reworked state apparatuses a deadly present for many.

For some, prisons are an aberration, something to be talked away using a set of policy papers, rational alternatives and lobbying days. For others, the state is a massive but simple cudgel of the corporations who rule the world, fading in importance as corporate power grows. Prisons in this view are simply a means by which public wealth is transferred to private hands. As milieu or tool the state in these views is characterized as rather statically insensate—a type of thinking that has roots in what Stuart Hall (1988) dubbed a "low-flying economism," which perpetuates the ideological misdirection neoliberal antistate statism requires to grow and grow. Following the lead of Stuart Hall et al.'s indispensable *Policing the Crisis* (1978), we wish to raise the vantage point on prisons so that our view takes in the state's tricky, complicated, obvious yet often caricatured central role in all aspects of the prison political economy. If we follow the details (and not just the money, but that too) we'll see in greater specificity how the antistate state has arisen and normalized extreme and exceptional relationships. The presumptions guiding popular acclaim for instituting the rule of law in Guantánamo belie a regrettably underdeveloped awareness of what's been happening in the domestic criminal system. There's a good excuse for this: what circulates about the growth in prisons, as we'll discuss below, is quite often more distraction than head-on analysis. As our brief caveat agitor in the Guantánamo case suggests, and this chapter aims to demonstrate, prisons and jails are central indefensible spaces: politically, socially, economically, morally, and ideologically they are what the growing neoliberal state is made of. They're big. They're horrible. They're tentacular. And they're not inevitable.

Stateless World, Hahaha

"States matter not simply because of the goal-oriented activities of state officials. They matter because their organizational configurations, along with their overall patterns of activity, affect political culture, encourage some kinds of group formation and collective political action (but not others), and make possible the raising of certain political issues (but not others)."

—Theda Skocpol 1985

"The state is not univocal: the relations between state power, which is in a constant process of formation, and actors, social groups and local communities are highly diverse and complex."

—Béatrice Hibou 2004

A state is a territorially bounded set of relatively specialized institutions that develop and change over time in the gaps and fissures of social conflict, compromise, and cooperation. Analytically, states differ from governments: If states are ideological and institutional capacities that derive their legitimacy and material wherewithal from residents, governments are the animating forces—policies plus personnel—that put state capacities into motion and orchestrate or coerce people in their jurisdictions to conduct their lives according to centrally made and enforced rules. Through the exercise of centralized rulemaking and redistribution, a state's purpose (at whatever scale—municipal, county, national, etc.) is to secure a society's ability to do different kinds of things: such as tax, educate, support, connect, exclude, criminalize, segregate, equalize, make war, and make profits. As such, states interact with individuals and with other types of institutions (e.g., religious, familial, corporate, union), while at the same time seeking to maintain, through consent or coercion, supremacy over all other organizational forms in the social order. A key feature of that supremacy lies in the state's singular control over who may commit violence, how, and to what end.

Modern states came into being during the long bloody process of staking out control of the planet's surface. Today's geopolitical structure is the residue of conflict—the material and ideological effects of domination and rebellion characterizing the massive dislocations of slavery, genocide, land theft, colonialism, imperialism, industrialization, urbanization, the cold war, and capitalism. These conflicts, widely explained and resolved through perpetually redefining insiders and outsiders—and normalizing ways of seeing who is in or out—shaped the central contradictions of modernity, from racism to class struggle.

Indeed, the modern nation-state—organized through fictive and real blood-soil relationships of particular territorial residents ("nations")—consolidated into the fundamental political and economic unit of the Earth's surface in the late eighteenth century. At about the same time, the modern prison arose in the landscape as an easily reproducible, large-scale, impersonal yet individualized institution of total control (Gilmore 2006; cf. Goffman 1984). The connection between the rise of the nation-state and the rise of the prison is located in the contradiction between mobility and immobility: when the conditions attending on a global system that requires constant motion (i.e., capitalism) clash with challenges to maintain order, spatial fixes such as racialization and criminalization temporarily settle things through complicating insider-outsider distinctions with additional, rights-differentiated hierarchical schemes (Gilmore 2002; cf. Moore 2005, Hesse 2004).

The racial state is a category of analysis taken up by a number of theorists following the lead of sociologists Michael Omi and Howard Winant (1984). The racial state signifies not simply the rac*ist* state—the Jim Crow or Apartheid state—but, rather, more generally the way the institutions comprising the state develop and act, legislatively, juridically, and administratively, through the establishment, regulation, and differentiation of racial formations that through assertion as well as ascription (as Koshy 2001 argues) themselves change over time. These days in the United States, at all scales, the racial state operates ironically (but without a hint of mirth) through the mode of "colorblindness" (HoSang, 2001, 2004). The state's management of racial categories is analogous to the management of highways or ports or telecommunication: racist ideological and material practices are infrastructure that needs to be updated, upgraded, and modernized periodically: this is what is meant by racialization. And the state itself, not just interests or forces external to the state, is built and enhanced through these practices. Sometimes the practices result in "protecting" certain racial groups, and other times they result in sacrificing them. In any event, racialization is a key part of U.S. governance, and the state's role as the sole determiner of legitimate violence has played a key part in management through racialization.[1]

Given the reach as well as the hesitations of the racial state, it is in the folds of the state's institutions—where inequality gathers its strength, speed, and stamina—that activists have sought and secured the energy to redirect social capacity and thereby social wealth. Many have remarked on how "colorblindness" works, on how politics and policies recode "color" (a standard though slippery proxy for race) to, for example, "urban" and "immigrant" in order to avoid the nasty stench of past outrage while perpetuating cruel practices and their predictably negative consequences into the future. But, oddly, in the case when such changes fall into the category of non-reformist reform, then redirection does not settle the matter but rather enlarges the scope of activity through which our everyday existences might be reconfigured. Nonreformist reforms—or what Avery Gordon calls "abolitionist reforms"—are systemic changes that do not extend the life or breadth of deadly forces such as prisons (see also Gorz [1968] and Mathiesen [1974]).

How is such engagement possible? A useful way to think about the state's complexity in power-terms is to consider it as a contradictory set of institutions able to act with some autonomy and some impunity. Thus, the state is not only "not univocal," as Hibou says, but also fraught by intrastate antagonisms—put into play by the very kinds of forceful disputes and alliances constantly bringing the state into being as a centralizing structure in the first place. In other words, if states are the residue of struggle, then the institutions comprising states are the same substance: partly realized and partly failed attempts to make general certain modes of social being whose underlying contradictions never fully disappear (more of this below). But in addition to the state's inner complexity, there is also the fact that at any historical moment, the people and ideas, parties and prejudices, interests and purposes that coalesce into "who" controls the state (the government) is a varied grouping. This formation, or "bloc" as some call it (following Gramsci 1974; see also Hall 1978), achieves for a time general control of the state (if not thorough control of all state agencies) by appearing to be the "legitimate" steward of the public good.

Legitimacy, then, is an important feature of the state—whatever it does can only be sustained if enough of the people whose opinions count (whether voters or rioters, investors or mothers) agree that the direction in which the society is going makes sense to them. Such sense need not be coherent or, even if coherent, demonstrable, but it needs to exist. Crime is the problem for which prisons are the solution is a version of such legitimating sense today, and it is virtually impossible to get through a meeting on prison reform (much less abolition!) without having somebody predict "but we'll always have prisons."

States make territories governable and predictably so, and they do it at a series of "removes" from the most local or immediate milieu. At different levels states do different things, not only because of the rationalization of state-activity fought out over time (and continually revised—consider today's resurgent federalism that seemed, 65 years ago, to be decisively withering), but also because of the ways in which ordinary people's lives are enmeshed in a variety of overlapping and interlocking jurisdictions and political economic scales. Thus, a local planning commission might help a community stop a prison but will have no sway over the municipal judge who sentences children of that community to long terms in cages; yet the judge might stand for election on the same ballot as the commission members, and the ballot might also contain language for approving certain kinds of taxes, debt, or other social income-producing schemes to build prisons or parks.

The variety of political geographies, themselves differentiated and hierarchical, is cross-cut, materially and ideologically, by both elite and everyday understanding of what the state should be. Presently, the dominant if not consensual view of the state in the United States is what we have called the "antistate state." The antistate state is both producer and product of the prison and jail expansion; it gathers and deploys the wherewithal to normalize particular bureaucratic and fiscal capacities that put such spaces into motion as places.

A widely repeated tale runs in the opposite direction from what is actually happening. The fable tells us the state's in demise because tyrannical multinational corporations or free democratic societies don't find it useful anymore. The new end of history has been repeated from Thatcher and Reagan to Blair, Clinton, and Bush and by critics of globalization no less than by its boosters. One way to measure whether the state is shrinking or growing is to compare government spending as a percentage of the gross domestic product (GDP) in constant dollars. In the United States, state spending at all levels (federal, state and local) has increased as a percentage of GDP by around 10 percent (from about 30 percent of GDP to about 33 percent) since the start of the prison-building boom (Smelzer 2005).

Although the state-as-economic-actor is not an invention of capitalism, there has never been a minute in the history of capitalism lacking the organized, centralized, and reproducible capacities of the state. Those capacities did not merely preexist the struggles between capitalists and workers but, rather, in many instances came into being, or expanded, or shifted, as a result of the antagonisms inherent in a mode of production that requires inequality to thrive. The history of the United States is, in large part, the history of capitalists figuring out how to develop and use large-scale complex governmental institutions to secure their ability to get rich. A cursory study of any period in U.S. history—the Civil War, the Progressive Era, the New Deal, the postwar New Frontier/Great Society—reveals examples of the ways that capitalists helped develop "the state" in order to disable monopolist adversaries, secure access to raw materials and new markets, murder indigenous people, outlaw or circumscribe worker-organizing, or socialize the cost of protections against calamity and opportunities for advancement in order to minimize vulnerability to wage demands. Workers of all races and conditions weren't gifted with concessions but, rather, won them through fighting hard, sometimes together and sometimes not.

The antistate state's fable promising its own demise is a central part of the *rhetoric* of neoliberalism. As Peter Evans and others have argued, telling and retelling the story is part of the discourse of globalization, a crucial part of the current attempt to normalize market ideology in order to reshape and renew global domination. Ideology matters: the ways people think about the world, and understand themselves in it, define in large part what they do to endure or change the world. As Evans elaborates: "Today, the untrammeled hegemony of Anglo-American ideological premises is one of the most salient forces shaping the specific character of the current global economy, including the extent to which globalization is viewed as entailing the eclipse of the state" (Evans 1997: 64).

Central to our concerns here, and we would argue to the project of state rebuilding more generally, is the way that the state's ability to erect barriers, enforce boundaries, patrol borders, and create enemies is rejigging the dynamic categories of poverty, race, and citizenship and imposing new threats on the life chances of the world's working people.

More specifically, the post-Cold War state is deriving considerable legitimacy and concrete impenetrability through its punishment-enabled growth and consolidation in the gaps opened by the dismantling of the Cold War welfare state. The general imperatives that are the motivating force for any state have not faded from the territory: defense, internal pacification, infrastructural coordination, and communication (see Mann 1988).

How exactly is the state changing? The literature on states and globalization is enormous and some tendencies in the U.S. model are clear. Although we see some programs such as welfare being eviscerated, it is a mistake to imagine that the state is simply withdrawing resources from the management of the poor. As Jamie Peck says of welfare reform, "In terms of the regulation of poverty and poor subjects, this is not less government but *different* government" (Peck 2003: 224).

How and why the state has turned to prisons and away from welfare as a means of managing the poor is beyond our scope here. It should be clear, however, that states have transformed the functions of certain agencies— such as welfare and housing. The agencies haven't disappeared: they do different things. Resources have been shifted from agency to agency, and agencies—from public student aid to income supports—have expanded their policing practices whatever their original social mandate. Twenty-five years ago, California spent 2 percent of the state budget on prisons. Today, it spends 8 percent. That increase signals a profound change in the state's priorities—away from public education, away from health care, away from affordable housing and environmental protection—and toward prisons, jails, policing, and courts.

Very few people are against schools or health care. But to shift resources away from those departments, to lower their priority, residents whose opinions count need to be convinced. One commonly hears of politicians being afraid of voters—afraid to look soft on crime, for example. The fact is that it is often politicians or other employees of the state who create public opinion in the first place.

Mark Purcell and Joseph Nevins show that one of the key players in the creation of the hysteria over illegal immigration was the Western Regional Commissioner of the INS, Howard Ezell. In addition to his many public statements fanning the flames of racist nativism, Ezell founded the not-for-profit Americans for Border Control—the solution to the problem that Ezell helped to create in the public's mind—more funding for the INS, more Border Patrol agents. "So in everyday practice, certain factions of state actors engage key factions of the citizenry to produce expectations and pursue particular agendas" (Purcell and Nevins 2005: 217–218).

An important part of the legitimation of an expanded INS was to create fear in the minds of U.S. residents. Part of that process was to change the ways certain people are seen. The creation and enforcement of new laws and the reimagining of peoples are mutually reinforcing. Thus, people are arrested because they are bad, and one knows they are bad because they've been arrested. "The goal of state violence is not to inflict pain; it is the social project of creating punishable categories of people" (Nabengast 1994: 122; see also Feldman 1991). Part of the infrastructure buildup along the U.S.-Mexico border has been renewed racist and nativist images of immigrants, or as Nevins calls the process, the "illegalization" of unauthorized entrants. In other words, the wall along the border was built to create fear and legitimize the state that built it.

Capitalists have always understood the usefulness of the state for their practices, and their constant groaning against "the state" is against particular ways that the social wage is collected rather than against the kinds of institutions necessary to negotiate and guarantee currency and trade, ensure open markets, raise tariffs, seize oil fields, build infrastructure, regulate competition, educate workers, support retirees, open or close borders, and so forth. The development of any state capacity is the outcome of struggle, and that struggle includes governmental actors who enliven and enforce the policies of their institutions and agencies. We can say that the state is a "relatively autonomous" (Poulantzas 1973: 1978) institution, whose economic role is complicated and to some degree doubles back on itself since its ability to perpetuate itself (via access to adequate resources) depends on how well it achieves legitimacy through guaranteeing economic capacities for certain workers or capitalists.

At the same time, state legitimacy is not the outcome of simply calculated economic benefit, and the appearance of benefits of other types can offset seemingly broadly held beliefs about what the state "should" do. Thus, for example, under today's neoliberal regimes, the "problem" of immigrants and nonimmigrant poor people is rhetorically posed as economic in nature—competition over scare jobs or costly social welfare benefits—whereas the antistate resolution of the problem—criminalization and incarceration—widely embraced as correct, provides no economic security (or any other safety, for that matter) for most of those who are allegedly the proper objects of the state's care.

Thus, the coincidence of the breathtaking incarceration of people of color, erection of border walls, uncontested stolen presidential elections, and international military excursions cannot be understood as simply the actions of a racist state or of a state acting in response to racist corporations or voters. In the struggle to produce its own legitimacy, the U.S. state, through multiple governments, employs or delegates violence to name and resolve distinctions—and imprisonment is a machine and a purpose for these outcomes, while racism is the consequence of this interplay of relationships rather than the reason for which they developed. In the next section we will discuss the political economy of prisons, paying special attention to the multiplicity of elements and categories that add up to what has popularly come to be known as the Prison Industrial Complex.

The Political Economy of Prisons

"A good theory in theory might be a bad theory in practice."

—**Toni Negri**

Ten years ago, nobody used the term "prison industrial complex" (PIC) to talk about the elaborate set of relationships, institutions, buildings, laws, urban and rural places, personnel, equipment, finances, dependencies, technocrats, opportunists, and intellectuals in the public, private and not-for-profit sectors that synergistically make up the PIC. The term gained wide popularity after the historic 1998 "Critical Resistance—Beyond the Prison Industrial Complex" conference and strategy session in California; but almost as rapidly it lost its meaningful breadth. By becoming too narrow, PIC became less accurate. The phrase, intended to resonate with rather than simply mimic "the military industrial complex," has not fulfilled its potential to help people theorize adequately how the PIC shapes political and social life for everyone. As a result, it has yet to become a broadly useful tool in mobilizing opposition to the complex's continued expansion.

We must note that the hollowing out of the term, and the skewed political vision thus implied, has often come from those who use the term with the most enthusiasm. Along the way, the meaning of 'industrial' shrank to 'profit' and the state disappeared behind the specter of immoral gain. In this view, the outcome of capitalist activity stands in for the complicated relationships that enable or change that outcome. This low-flying economism misses some key facts about where we are now.

Of those 1 of 130 U.S. residents in prison, 95 percent are in institutions that are wholly public, and 100 percent of all prisons are publicly paid for. Of the prisoners who work (and fewer and fewer do), 97 percent work for the public agencies holding them in bondage. Prisoners' families indeed pay extra for everything: phone charges, soft drinks on visiting day, gifts, and cash. These poverty taxes have often been designed by public prison operatives in order to produce income for the agency; vendors come along to put the tax into practice, rather than as instigators. We're always happy to bash telephone companies, corporations who exploit anybody's labor, and private prison corporations. But those are not the principal players who have created the PIC and sustained its growth. Although campaigns against such adversaries might accomplish great things, shrinking or destroying the PIC is not one of them. In this context, it should be obvious that private prison firms and other corporations are opportunists slurping at the public trough rather than the prime movers behind this extraordinary period in U.S. history.

Given that the United States has always been capitalist and always been racist, the question arises: why prisons now? Each element in the PIC is either an aspect of the state (a rule or a government agent or agency) or derives its power (or powerlessness) in relation to the state and its capacities. Because prisons and prisoners are part of the structure of the state, they enable governments to establish state legitimacy through a claim to provide social "protection" combined with their monopoly on the delegation of violence. The state establishes legitimacy precisely *because* it violently dominates certain people and thereby defines them (and makes them visible to others) as the sort of people who should be pushed around. In modeling behavior for the polity, the antistate state naturalizes violent domination—as Archer and Gartner (1984) have demonstrated.[2] What's important is the transformation of relationships between and among the elements that make up the PIC, producing and projecting into the unforeseeable future a set of dependencies—in the form of domestic militarism—that rely on harming individuals and communities in the name of safety.

If, as many researchers have shown, the state's specific role as an economic player is changing rather than diminishing, then as Toni Negri predicted at the beginning of the current period of globalization and the PIC, "the counter-revolution of the capitalist entrepreneur today can only operate strictly within the context of an increase in the coercive powers of the state. The 'new Right' ideology of laissez-faire implies as its corollary the extension of new techniques of coercive and state intervention in society at large" (Negri 1988: 183).

Imprisonment—the involuntary loss of self-determination and mobility, and the consignment of human lives to cages—depends on coercion. As a result, although the political economy of prison crosses back-and-forth between the "public" and "private" (a line generally as depthless and invisible as an international boundary), it is always fully connected to the state while not wholly defining or motivating the state. The legitimacy for this unbroken connection derives, in part, from achieved consent concerning whose lives and bodies should be vulnerable to the destructive force of prisons. If the fiscal and bureaucratic capacities making mass imprisonment possible are strictly and unequivocally state capacities, and the ideological capacities are articulated through and by the state, then for analytical purposes, it is useful to think of the state in broad categories: in terms of actors, agencies, rules, bodies, and the contradictory crises through which change is generated.[3] The state, then, is not only site and weapon, it is both adversary and, in a few corners at least, ally—as the examples here demonstrate.

The Budget as Battleground

"Changes in taxation necessarily lead to modifications in the logics of extraction and redistribution, and thus transform modes of unequal accumulation or redistribution that legitimize the political."

—Béatrice Hibou 2004: 24

The era of the PIC and globalization has been in the United States a period in which the popularity of taxes dipped ever further. There is always considerable antipathy to handing one's money over to the state, but we can mark the election of Ronald Reagan as president as a time in which that tendency became even stronger. As with the panic around immigration, public emotions about taxes were fanned by state actors, none more important than Reagan himself. As a result, for much of the last 25 years, discussion of public spending has taken place as though it were a zero-sum equation: If we must spend more money here, we must spend less elsewhere (because we can't raise taxes).

It is in this period that the ideological mask of the new state makes its debut for a national audience. Too much state interference in our personal lives. Too much state interference in the economy. The state is a burden, a threat. We must shrink the state and restore liberty and markets. Although no doubt there were and are some true believers in this libertarian-lite rant, most of those who spout it, and all of those in power, have no intention of shrinking the state. Rather their intent has been and continues to be to remake the state to do other things. I have called this ideological construct "the anti-state state": a state that grows on the promise of shrinking.[4]

"The relative burden of taxes and the division of state expenditures between different social classes," argues James O'Connor "are the fundamental class issues of state finance." He continues "Every important change in the balance of class and political forces is registered in the tax structure. Put another way, tax systems are simply particular forms of class systems" (O'Connor [1973] 2001: 162 and 203).

The difficulty in raising taxes is the threat of increasing delegitimation of the state, or at least of substantial state functions. That delegitimation has been a key part of the Right's attempt to remake the state. Discredit those programs we want to change or destroy. Portray the rest as necessary and open only to the most technical discussion of means and methods, not of priority. The closure of discussions of alternatives to Right policies in the 1980s was so successful it produced an acronym, generally credited to Tory Prime Minister Margaret Thatcher: TINA, or There Is No Alternative (see Hall 1988).

Even if the state seems incapable of raising taxes to generate more income, there continue to be fights over how the money coming in will be spent. As the recent indictments of Congressman Randy "Duke" Cunningham and lobbyist Jack Abramoff show, some of that fighting is still happening the old-fashioned way, by bribing politicians. Other tactics also take place behind closed doors but might involve campaign contributions of money or labor in exchange for votes or access. There is also a fight for public opinion.

Antiprison activists seeing the budget crisis that hit U.S. states after the dot-com crash of 2000 tried to take advantage of the opportunity by educating those with a stake in public spending to demand cuts in prison spending. Here in California, the budget crisis continues into its sixth year. The results of our work are unclear. Apart from the Delano II prison, on the boards since the early 1990s and greenlighted by Gov. Gray Davis at a time when there was no budget crisis (Davis inherited a surplus of hundreds of millions of dollars when he took office in 1999), California has neither built nor planned any new prisons since the budget crisis began—a substantial contrast to the 22 built in the previous two decades.

In the first year of the budget crisis, we helped teachers, students, and parents from the Bay Area organize a lobby day in the state capitol. Tens of thousands of teachers were sent pink slips that spring, giving them notice they would not be employed the following fall. We descended on the capitol with students asking legislators why the state was willing to spend hundreds of millions of dollars for a new prison but was laying off teachers.

Students from the University of California Students Association and groups from other state colleges and junior colleges demanded that funds be taken from the prison budget in order to avoid increases in student fees. They lost that fight, student fees at state universities were increased 40 percent and fees for junior colleges by 67 percent. Over 100,000 students were forced out of state community colleges because of that one year's fee increases.

Who was most hurt by the cuts in public school funding? By increases in college fees? By cuts to state health programs? The poor, people of color, and the state's substantial immigrant population.[5]

Back in 2003, Julie Falk argued that activists who hoped to shrink the prison system through the budget crisis were probably misled. Instead, she warned, prisons would simply become leaner and meaner, with more cuts to education and counselling programs. During California Governor Arnold Schwarzenegger's first year in office, it appeared that Falk was right. His solution to overspending in California prisons was to propose cutting the number of meals prisoners were served in a week (Falk 2003).

As we have argued elsewhere, the targeting of the overlapping categories of people of color, noncitizens, and the poor cannot be explained simply by the convenience of their lack of power (Gilmore 2006; Gilmore and Gilmore 2003; Braz and Gilmore 2006). Peter Evans argues that contemporary state managers, trying to secure state legitimacy, sacrifice "the capacity to deliver services that the affluent can supply privately for themselves (for example, health and education)." What the state promises to deliver is protection. "In turn, delivering security means devoting more resources to the repression of the more desperate and reckless among the excluded, both domestic and international" (Evans 1997: 84–85; see also Gilmore 2006).

We can take Evans a couple of steps further. First would be to point out that by diverting resources away from education, health care, mental health services, and so on, the state is increasing the numbers of "the more desperate and reckless among the excluded." Or, as Tony Fitzpatrick puts it, "The contemporary state consists of a series of punitive responses to the chaos it has facilitated" (Fitzpatrick 2001: 220). That chaos includes freeing racism from both state definition (as in Jim Crow laws) and state disapproval (Civil Rights laws, which have become so narrowly adjudicated as to be nearly unenforceable), as a result of which the proliferation of certain kinds of laws that do not specify "race" has resulted in the most enormous roundup of people of color in the history of the United States, and many poor white people have been caught at the margins. The people in prison, and their kin outside, lacking "services the rich provide themselves" are increasingly vulnerable to premature death sanctioned by the state through the policies of aggressive, iron-fisted abandonment.

Second, we would add that as in any protection racket (Tilly 1985), the protector requires the threat from which we need protection: gang members, meth labs, immigrants. If they didn't exist, they would have to be invented. From Willie Horton to Mara Salvatrucha, politicians, bureaucrats, agencies, and unions heavily or exclusively representing police and prison guards have made certain that the public understand the need for protection from "people like that." These days, it is hard to distinguish the union representing California's prison guards—the CCPOA—from Crime Victims United. Both campaign very effectively for more criminal laws and longer sentences and against any reform of the prison system that would reduce time served, all in the name of protecting public safety.

"He stole something. We don't know what it is yet."
Watermelon Man

Here's another example of the ideology of the antistate state playing out in the realm of current policing policy.

So-called Broken Windows policing grew out of a magazine article from 1982 written by a couple of arch-conservatives, James Q. Wilson and George Kelling. William Bratton made the theory famous during his high-profile term as head of the NYPD, and now in his double role as head of the LAPD and as an international consultant, he is exporting Broken Windows policing around the world.

One of the central tenets of Broken Windows policing is that long-term crime reduction depends on neighborhoods in which people are in the streets, know each other and take some responsibility for their neighbors and neighborhoods. This belief is not unique to the conservatives who espouse Broken Windows policing.[6] Indeed, looking at the model in a wider context, we can see how the ideology of Broken Windows plays into the fable of the disappearing state and the related celebration of the public sphere as a sort of third space neither market nor state.

Broken Windows policing aims to remove not only broken windows and graffiti but also the people who are, as Fred Moten puts it, themselves broken windows: those who make others uncomfortable, those who spend too much time in the streets. As Bernard Harcourt and Joe Domanick remind us, much of the practice of Broken Windows—rounding up the usual suspects, checking for their outstanding warrants, keeping them off the streets and on the defensive—is not new to the policy. In fact, most of what is new is the name and the justification—both for increasing the number of involuntary encounters with police and the level of police aggression in those encounters (Domanick 1994; Harcourt 2001).

Broken Windows advocates argue that the only way to achieve neighborhoods in which neighbors reduce crime by hanging out and knowing each other is, like any other antistate state project, by hiring more police, and arresting, convicting, and incarcerating more people. In this scheme, we get to depend on each other more only if we first depend on the state, and on an even more punitive version of the state, first.

What the research of Dina Rose and Todd Clear and their colleagues shows is that saturation policing—arresting, convicting, and imprisoning too many people from a neighborhood—actually has negative impacts on the crime rate. Why? Because taking so many people out of a neighborhood—and returning many of them years later after the horrors of prison—disrupts the very neighborhood ties that Broken Windows purports to strengthen.

Although Chief Bratton campaigns to hire more police in Los Angeles, his consulting firm and its competitors and colleagues are selling U.S. style policing across the globe. He and his former boss, ex-NYC mayor Rudolph Guliani, have helped seed such projects as Mano Dura ("Strong Hand") in El Salvador and Honduras. Mano Dura, a near cousin of Broken Windows, is also Zero Tolerance policing. Police stop "the suspicious" in Central America—often those with tattoos—and arrest and detain at every opportunity. The crackdowns on youth in those countries have led to massive overcrowding in prisons, the reemergence of death squads and what appears to be the state-organized mass murder of alleged gang members in prisons (Hayden 2004; Zilberg 2004).[7] El Salvador will host the new International Law Enforcement Academy, which depending on who you listen to, will either help to modernize and depoliticize Latin American police forces, making it an important tool in the move toward democracy, or it will be the School of the Americas II, where police (and military) will share lessons of social cleansing, mass arrests, and deportations that stay carefully within contemporary human rights boundaries. Globalization? Yes. The eclipse of the state?

What about the State-as-Ally?

The massive economic dislocations of globalization, combined with anticipatory tax revolts waged by banks and corporations in the late 1960s, and by a segment of workers (especially aging homeowners) in the late 1970s, threw California's social wage—its general fund—into deep imbalances that are still to be worked out. The result, as we have noted earlier, has been the proliferation of "zero-sum" rhetoric around state spending, as though a political entity and a household were identical in their ability to produce income. The result in the shift of spending to prisons and policing and courts and jails, and away from postsecondary education and social welfare programs, has hit public service workers hard and put many who are not direct participants in the prison industrial complex—teachers, nurses, clerical staff, and others—on the defensive.

But even direct participants have seen the writing on the wall. Several years ago, a career teacher in the California prison system reached out to several antiprison activists and organizations to try to sound the alarm over what, in his view, was happening inside the system that would in the end not only jeopardize his job but also accelerate prison growth. Everybody knows that education, along with employment and strong emotional support (family, friends, community groups) enable people who have been to prison to overcome the devastation of that experience, and the causes that may have made them vulnerable to it (such as drug dependency), and stay in the free world. The expansion of the California Department of Corrections, initiated by political elites but maintained by the CCPOA—which became the state's largest political contributor—minimized to the point of near-extinction meaningful education, health, and other rehabilitative programming inside.

The teacher, a member of the Service Employees International Union (SEIU), decided that enough was enough. As a member of the California State Employees' Local 1000, he worked hard to persuade his State Council, the local leadership, and the rank and file to consider what might seem unthinkable: to work with anti-prison activists to shrink the system. After many false starts, a coalition developed including the SEIU state council, SEIU local 1000 that significantly shifted the terrain of battle at the state level. Why? Because the state employees declared their willingness to do battle with the guards, not only for a share of California's social wage but also because their complexity as an organization, representing more than half a million workers in many different public sectors (cities, counties, as well as the State of California) told the union that what was ultimately at stake is the future of public service and the kinds of social well-being public workers such as themselves might be able to offer both to prisoners and to people in the free world. They also concluded that opportunities for workers with their skills—instructors, health care providers, locksmiths, secretaries—could readily translate into other kinds of public jobs, and it was only the guards, with their single specialty, whose motive to expand the state prison system, whose vision for the future could not be tempered by alternative visions of future workplace opportunities. Given that total California SEIU membership outnumbers that of the guards union by an order of magnitude (500,000 vs. about 50,000) it seems possible that the ongoing alliance between antiprison activists and the union holds great promise.

In the early 1970s, James O'Connor theorized that public sector workers and their clients might find the contradiction between them not antagonistic at all, and a shift in solidarity would change the ground of political activism especially with respect to the state. Odd that such a shift seems to be proceeding on the most antagonistic-imaginable grounds—prison—and it is exactly that oddity to which activists should pay attention. Indeed, about a decade ago Paul Johnstone (1994) argued that it is in the public sector (along with low-wage private sector—such as Justice for Janitors) that true social movement unionism has grown and flourished, while in the ranks of the old labor aristocracy membership decline and many unions' capitulation to double-tiering has weakened the unionism that flourished briefly during the Golden Age of American Capitalism. What's the dynamic here? How do the members of public sector and low-wage unions overlap with the communities most impacted by criminalization, and what is the possible basis for invigorating organizations already attuned to understanding labor struggles as not merely workplace, "bread-and-butter" issues to oppose the proliferation of cages? How might organizers develop outreach to organized public-sector health, welfare, and education workers whose frontline experience working with people vulnerable to criminalization may well hold as rich potential for nonreformist reform strategies as was found among SEIU prison workers?

Fanon (1963) tried to convince his readers to think hard about the many ways that people in conditions of crisis can be understood categorically—that is, as classes or groups—and in so thinking to look beneath the surface and ask what the possibility might be for cooptation, on the one hand, and differential alignment, on the other. Fanon, like DuBois (1935) before him, examined how various groupings cohere internally and connect externally—what calls them to identify in some ways but not in others, how those relationships might change, and to what end. This is the great challenge for antiprison activists who can engage the state in surprising ways, and in particular expand the repertoire of such engagements beyond the narrow, technocratic rehearsals of "experts" at hearings. Marx wrote that ideology becomes a material force when it grips the masses; and broadly based public-sector unions might be a way to proliferate active understanding of prison as a machine that produces premature death for prisoners and their kin rather than safety for the types of vulnerable communities who have gained a measure of *real* security through social movement unionism and other innovative organizing.

Conclusion

"Gramsci was interested in what he called the autonomous state life, one in which the transformation of politics transformed the state. Yet it was also one in which a transformed state transformed politics."

—Harney 2002

If, as we have argued, the state is remaking itself using the newly vast prison system's coercive powers on some parts of the population to produce consent, among others, there are implications for political activists.

Those already struggling against police and prisons need a clearer and deeper picture of why the state does what it does to their family members and neighbors. Thinking about state violence, and especially racist state violence, as an aberration to be reformed away misses the way that states work and the work that states do. Many activists in Critical Resistance warn us not to think of the prison system as broken. Rather, they insist, we should imagine it is working and think about what that means. The political implications demand an understanding of why the system does work this way, and of how, as Gramsci argues, we can change the state enough to make real changes in it—or what we have been calling nonreformist reform.

For those involved in other social justice work, we would suggest that there is great risk in not incorporating some analysis of how the state is becoming or has become a "penal state" (Peck 2003). It is not clear that the growth of the prison system will reach some natural plateau. If the state seems to require more enemies, who will be next? And where will the funds be found to pay for the next rounds of increased staff of Border Patrol, Marshalls, prison guards, police, ICE, not to mention the prisons, jails and border fences yet to be built? The prison buildup is a key, perhaps *the* key, political attack on the political ground created in the New Deal and Civil Rights eras.

Our opposition has mastered the Gramscian puzzle of changing the state to change politics and changing politics to change the state. We have to go deeply into the state in all its aspects—its legitimacy, the ideological apparatuses it wields to normalize the everyday horror of mass incarceration, its budget process, its inner contradictions, its intrastate antagonisms and frictions. All of these places are sites where activists can set their feet to fight the fight. And the sites are, as well, locations where we meet others struggling to piece together lives torn apart by poverty, illness, undereducation, war, long-distance migration, flight. Here, where we fight, is where the state is.

Acknowledgments

For continuing guidance, thanks to Dana Kaplan and Avery Gordon; and for translation and much more, thanks to Tiago Pires e família.

References

Archer, Dane and Rosemary Gartner. 1984. *Violence and Crime in Cross-National Perspective*. New Haven: Yale University Press.

Braz, Rose and Craig Gilmore. 2006. "Joining Forces: Prisons and Environmental Justice Organizing in California." *Radical History Review* (96): 95–111.

Dikeç, Mustafa. 2006. "Two Decades of French Urban Policy: From the Social Development of Neighborhoods to the Republican Penal State." *Antipode* 38 (1): 59–81.

Domanick, Joe. 1994 *To Protect and to Serve: The LAPD's Century of War in the City of Dreams*. New York: Simon and Schuster.

Du Bois, W. E. B. [1935] 1992. *Black Reconstruction in America, 1860–1880*. New York: The Free Press.

Evans, Peter. 1997. "The Eclipse of the State? Reflections on Stateness in an Era of Globalization." *World Politics* 50 (1): 62–87.

Evans, Peter B., Dietrich Rueschemeyer, and Theda Skocpol, eds. 1985. *Bringing the State Back In*. Cambridge: Cambridge University Press.

Falk, Julie. 2003. "Fiscal Lockdown, Part I." *Dollars and Sense* 248: 19–23, 45.

Falk, Julie. 2003. "Fiscal Lockdown, Part II." *Dollars and Sense* 250: 32–35.

Fanon, Frantz. 1963. *Wretched of the Earth*. New York: Grove Press.

Feldman, Allen. 1991. *Formations of Violence: The Narrative of the Body and Terror in Northern Ireland*. Chicago: University of Chicago Press.

Fitzpatrick, Tony. 2001. "New Agendas for Social Policy and Criminology: Globalization, Urbanism and the Emerging Post-Social Security State." *Social Policy & Administration* 35(2): 212–229.

Gilmore, Ruth Wilson. 1998. Globalisation and U.S. Prison Growth: From Military-Keynesianism to Post-Keynesian Militarism. *Race and Class* 40 (2–3): 171–187.

Gilmore, Ruth Wilson. 2002. "Race and Globalization" in R. J. Johnstone et al., eds. *Geographies of Global Change, 2nd Edition*. Oxford: Blackwell: 261–274.

Gilmore, Ruth Wilson. 2007. *Golden Gulag: Prisons, Surplus, Crisis, and Opposition in Globalizing California*. Berkeley: University of California Press.

Gilmore, Ruth Wilson and Craig Gilmore. 2003. "The Other California." In *Globalizing Liberation: How to Uproot the System and Build a Better World*. Ed. David Solnit. San Francisco: City Lights Publishers: 381–396.

Gramsci, Antonio. 1971. *Selections from the Prison Notebooks*. New York: International Publishers.

Goffman, Erving. 1984. "Characteristics of Total Institutions" in Delos Kelly, *Deviant Behavior*, New York: St. Martin's Press: 464–77.

Gordon, Avery. 2004. *Keeping Good Time*. Boulder: Paradigm Publishers.

Gorz, Andre. 1968. *Strategy for Labor: A Radical Proposal*. Boston: Beacon Press.

Hall, Stuart, et al. 1978. *Policing the Crisis: Mugging, the State and Law and Order*. London: Holmes and Meier.

Hall, Stuart. 1984. "The State in Question." In *The Idea of the Modern State*. Ed. Gregor McClellan, David Held and Stuart Hall. Milton Keynes: The Open University Press: 1–28.

Hall, Stuart. 1988. *The Hard Road to Renewal: Thatcherism and the Crisis of the Left*. London: Verso.

Harcourt, Bernard. 2001. *Illusion of Order: The False Promise of Broken Windows Policing*. Cambridge, MA: Harvard University Press.

Harcourt, Bernard and Jens Ludwig. 2005. "Broken Windows: New Evidence from New York City and a Five-City Social Experiment." *The University of Chicago Law Review* 73: 271–320.

Harney, Stefano. 2002. *State Work: Public Administration and Mass Intellectuality*. Durham, NC: Duke University Press.

Hayden, Tom. 2004. "'Homies Were Burning Alive,'" accessed May 1, 2006, at http:libertadcondignidad.org/inthenews/inthenews.html.

Hesse, Barnor. 2004. "Im/Plausible Deniability: Racism's Conceptual Double Bind." *Social Identities* 10 (1): 9–29.

Hibou, Béatrice. 2004. "From Privatizing the Economy to Privatizing the State: An Analysis of the Continual Formation of the State." In Béatrice Hibou, ed., *Privatizing the State*. New York: Columbia University Press: 1–46.

HoSang, Daniel. 2001. "Hiding Race." *Colorlines*. Volume 4 (4): 6–9, accessed May 1, 2006, at http://www.arc.org/C_Lines/CLArchive/story4_4_03.html.

HoSang, Daniel. 2004. "The End of Race in California? Ward Connerly, Multiculturalism, and the Politics of 'Racelessness.'" Paper presented at the Western Political Science Association Annual Conference, Portland, OR, March 17.

HoSang, Daniel. n.d. "'De-racing' Civil Rights: The 2003 California Racial Data Initiative and the Future of Political Discourse on Race." Unpublished ms.

INCITE! Women of Color Against Violence, eds. Forthcoming. *The Revolution Will Not Be Funded: Beyond the Non-Profit Industrial Complex*. Cambridge: South End Press.

Johnstone, Paul. 1994. *Success While Others Fail: Social Movement Unionism and the Public Workplace*. Ithaca, NY: ILR Press.

Katzenberger, Elaine, ed. 1995. *First World, Ha Ha Ha!: The Zapatista Challenge*. San Francisco: City Lights.

Koshy, Susan. 2001. "Morphing Race into Ethnicity: Asian Americans and Critical Transformations of Whiteness." *Boundary* 2 28:1: 153–194.

Mann, Michael. 1988. *States, War, and Capitalism*. Oxford: Blackwell.

Mathiesen, Thomas. 1974. *The Politics of Abolition: Essays in Political Action Theory*. London: Martin Robertson.

Moore, Donald S. 2005. *Suffering for Territory: Race, Space, and Power in Zimbabwe.* Durham, NC: Duke University Press.

Nagengast, Carole. 1994. "Violence, Terror, and the Crisis of the State." *Annual Review of Anthropology* 23: 109–36.

Negri, Tony. 1988. *Revolution Retrieved: Writings on Marx, Keynes, Capitalist Crisis, and New Social Subjects (1967–83).* London: Red Notes.

Nevins, Joseph. 2002. *Operation Gatekeeper: The Rise of the "Illegal Alien" and the Making of the U.S.-Mexico Boundary.* New York: Routledge.

O'Connor, James. [1973] 2001. *Fiscal Crisis of the State.* New Brunswick, NJ: Transaction Books.

Peck, Jamie. 2003. "Geography and Public Policy: Mapping the Penal State." *Progress in Human Geography* 27 (2): 222–232.

Poulantzas, Nicos. 1975. *Political Power and Social Classes.* London: NLB.

Poulantzas, Nicos. 1978. *State, Power, Socialism.* London: NLB.

Purcell, Mark and Joseph Nevins. 2005. "Pushing the Boundary: State Restructuring, State Theory, and the Case of U.S.-Mexico Border Enforcement in the 1990s." *Political Geography* 24: 211–235.

Rediker, Marcus. 2007. *The Slave Ship: A Human History.* New York: Viking Penguin.

Retort. 2005. *Afflicted Powers: Capital and Spectacle in a New Age of War.* London & New York: Verso.

Seigel, Micol. n.d. "Prison Connections Across the Americas." Unpublished ms.

Skocpol, Theda. 1985. "Bringing the State Back In: Strategies of Analysis in Current Research." In *Bringing the State Back In,* ed. Peter B. Evans, Dietrich Rueschemeyer, and Theda Skocpol. Cambridge: Cambridge University Press: 3–43.

Smelzer, Daniel. 2005. U.S. Government Spending as a Percentage of GDP—Updated, accessed June 15, 2005, at http://carriedaway.blogs.com/carried_away/2005/04/us_government_s.html.

Solnit, David, ed. 2003. *Globalizing Liberation: How to Uproot the System and Build a Better World.* San Francisco: City Lights Publishers.

Tilly, Charles. 1985. "War Making and State Making as Organized Crime." In *Bringing the State Back In.* ed. Peter B. Evans, Dietrich Rueschemeyer, and Theda Skocpol. Cambridge: Cambridge University Press: 169–191.

Trouillot, Michel-Rolph. 2001. "The Anthropology of the State in the Age of Globalization: Close Encounters of the Deceptive Kind." *Current Anthropology* 42(1): 125–138.

Wolch, Jennifer R. 1990. *The Shadow State: Government and the Voluntary Sector in Transition.* New York: The Foundation Center.

Zernike, Kate. 2006. "White House Drops a Condition on Interrogation Bill." *New York Times,* accessed September 20, 2006, at http://www.nytimes.com/2006/09/20/washington/20detain.html.

Zilberg, Elana. 2004. "Fools Banished from the Kingdom: Remapping the Geographies of Gang Violence between the Americas (Los Angeles and San Salvador)." *American Quarterly* 56(3): 759–779.

Notes

1. For a discussion of an attempt to construct an anti-racist state, see Harney 2002, especially chapter 1.
2. The circulation of money through prisons might appear to function according to capitalist imperatives. Mostly it does not. The social expense, as James O'Connor (1973) named social wages squandered on prisons and policing, does not produce the means for producing more of anything. By contrast, because states are, by definition, in the work of redistribution, the fact that lots of people make their living from state income is not the reason we should raise our eyebrows and fists.
3. This discussion of the political economy of the PIC leaves out an important sector—the nongovernmental organizations (NGOs) or the not-for-profit sector: foundations, think-tanks, activist organizations, service providers, intellectuals on all sides of the issues. The role of NGOs in the PIC deserves considerable study. According to Michel-Rolph Trouillot, "Haitians say in reference to NGOs: 'yo fè leta' (literally, 'they make the state') … The same word can mean 'state' or 'bully' in Haitian" (Trouillot 2001: 132). For more about NGOs and their relation to the state, see Wolch 1990 and INCITE! forthcoming.
4. For more about the antistate state, see Gilmore 2006, Introduction.
5. For more about Education not Incarceration, see http://ednotinc.org/. For other coalitions working on California's prison budget politics, see the Coalition for Effective Public Safety at http://www.effectivepublic-safety.org/ and Californians United for a Responsible Budget at http://curbprisonspending.org.
6. See Harcourt 2001 and the many essays of Dina Rose and Todd Clear and their colleagues.
7. For more about Mano Dura and crackdowns in both the United States and in Central America, see both http://homiesunidos.org and http://www.libertadcondignidad.org.

The Threat from Within
Protecting the Indefensible from the Indeterminate

KATHI HOLT-DAMANT

Before 9/11, Australia had been off the radar of large-scale terror activities. Separated from the rest of the Western world by four oceans and between 13 and 27 hours of flying time, Australia had previously enjoyed a fair amount of security in its isolation. Its location within the Pacific Rim followed by its empathy and compliance with the United States and Great Britain has increased its vulnerability in the region.

Since 9/11, a series of attacks have consolidated Australia's involvement in the 'war against terror.'

A year later came the unexpected and shocking Bali Bombings of October 2002, where the location and choice of target shattered all myths about Australia's security within Southeast Asia. Bali had long been favored as an inexpensive, exotic but safe, holiday destination for school leavers, honeymooners, or football teams—a piece of Australia abroad. This attack focused on an expatriate night club and beer garden as well as the public space of the street outside, and in doing so rippled through the Australian psyche threatening our 'way of life.' Jemaah Islamiyah (JI) took responsibility for the Bali bombings, which killed 90 Australians and just over 100 people from around the world.[1] Two subsequent attacks on commuter transportation, in Madrid (March 2004) and in London (July 2005), reinforced a new global trend of terrorist attacks. That terrorism could disrupt the order and livelihood of three world cities at the same time as it produced mass casualties has been a major concern for the rest of the Western world.

The New Threat to Australia—JI

Along with other countries comprising "the coalition of the willing," the Australian government has responded to the global war on terrorism (GWOT) by waging a marketing and research campaign targeting the threat from within.

> Australia's security environment has changed. We are now directly threatened by a new kind of terrorism. It is transnational and it is perpetrated in the name of a Muslim extremist cause ... It is epitomized by al-Qaeda and, in our region, Jemaah Islamiyah ... Australia is a target.[2]

This campaign calls on the community to play its part in identifying suspicious behavior. On the one hand, the message is propaganda (public warnings, posters, television commercials and repeated updates in the media) and, on the other, an enforced engagement with the general public as a community. One quotation appearing in a white paper on a government Web site frames the threat to Australia as distinguishable for being an unknowable but inventive enemy of indeterminate size and identity:

> Australia must also now face the threats of ambiguity and the unknown. This is part of the "asymmetric" nature of terror. This transnational terrorism works through the loose networks rather than through hierarchy or within borders. It is neither dependent on nation-state sponsors, nor responsive to conventional deterrents. To defeat one is not to defeat all. It is constantly evolving, with a capacity to regenerate and adapt where its forces are degraded. There will be new individuals, groups and networks that we simply do not know about.[3]

There has been a growing concern with the tactical agility of Jemaah Islamiyah, the widely dispersed but well-networked group of Islamic extremists who have developed a strong operational base within Southeast Asia. Although JI emerged out of the early separatist movements in Indonesia in the 1950s, it is now strongly aligned to Osama bin Laden's ideology and philosophy both of which have spread rapidly throughout Southeast Asia.[4]

The Australian government has reiterated that: "We must not let these terrorists set the agenda. We must fight the battle of ideas. They should not be allowed to have the final word ..."[5]

To advocate that the war on terror is really a battle about ideas, strategic and tactical, acknowledges that there are certainly issues to be interrogated. One of these ideas worth examining further is whether these attacks—branded as the war on terror—can be considered more generally as warfare against Australia or not?

Two Types of Warfare

Although the Australian government argues that there is nothing in history that can be drawn on to inform its current situation, new recruits to Jemaah Islamiyah are known to have trained in camps in Afghanistan and Pakistan from the mid-1980s. The random and resourceful nature of attacks perpetrated by al-Qa'eda and JI, indicate that such tactical training employed in these camps might have more historical roots that any recent warfare strategies suggest.[6] Apart from the rugged terrain, hostile environments and opium trade, Afghanistan is renowned for its sustained frustration of invading Soviet forces in the 1980s.[7] This location as a training hot-house, resonates with the early nomadic wars of Manuel De Landa's *War in the Age of Intelligent Machines*, in which he writes:

> Throughout human history there have been two distinct ways of waging war, and two primary methods for organizing armed forces. On the one hand is the war machine assembled by the nomads of the Steppes, such as the armies of Genghis Kahn, which invaded Europe in the thirteenth century; on the other hand is the war-making machine invented by sedentary peoples, like the Assyrian, Greek and Roman armies from which modern armies have evolved.[8]

The recent U.S.-led invasion of Afghanistan not only produced a temporary destructuring of the Taliban through sheer fire-power, but also saw the unfathomable escape of Osama bin Laden. Unable to deal tactically with breaking information, Western forces were powerless to consolidate what should have been an easy victory—arguably evidence of both modern and traditional nomadic strategies of warfare.

Tactics of Nomadic Warfare Translated to the Urban Condition

In remembering De Landa's account of such warfare, we can establish some parallels between more recent terrorist attacks and these early nomadic tactical traditions—a key element being an ability to act and react within multiple coordinated actions.[9] When applied to the urban environment, attacks employing surprise, stealth, and flexibility become significantly treacherous. Ordinary, everyday urban elements replace open plains, or mountainous rugged slopes—the choice and number of potential targets expand as do the elements for concealment: street furniture, vehicles of transportation, tall buildings, railway corridors, streets, lanes, or public urban space.

If we take the organization of the nomadic armies into account, we can find further correspondence in terrorist networks that are built up from small groups or cells, each with their own leader who reports up the chain of command. Each group has a degree of autonomy in making decisions, and will incorporate new recruits as well as experienced activists, which may not be selected from a single ethnic group. Like the armies of Genghis Kahn these networks rely on waystations that are set up to supply communications, intelligence and supplies to mobile groups. In this way, the networks are fluid but maintained.[10]

The shape of random and opportunistic terrorist attacks on Western centers in part reflects the confusion caused by the nomadic armies on the phalanx of war machines:

> In contrast to the extreme mobility of the nomad army and its ability to enter into multiple coordinated actions, the phalanx had a very limited ability to maneuver on the battlefield and, for the same reason, could no longer be controlled by a commander once the order to engage with the enemy had been given.[11]

Where modern armies appear to have engaged selective tactics from nomadic warfare, these methods have been contained purely within military organizations. Because terrorist attacks are more often located within urban centers, an understanding of the strategic structure behind such threats should be a priority.

Target Selection: Object versus Space

The tragic events of terrorism have heightened the impact associated with the selection of target. The idea that a target could be either object or public space and effect maximum destruction presents a dangerous trend of unpredictability in urban centers. The iconic objects selected for the 9/11 attacks—the World Trade Center, the Pentagon, and the White House—hit at the nerve center of an entire nation. With the Bali bombings, the target selection shifted from object to public space—a tactic successfully employed by waiting until the first bomb had scattered people from inside the establishment out into the street before the second bomb was then detonated leveraging maximum destruction. Bali showed that rather than attacking political objects, the assault on public space rendered our cities ever more defenseless against militant groups desiring disruption, destruction, death, and disablement.

Although mass surface transportation (MST) has been the target of various random attacks for many years, the most recent assaults in Madrid and London have underscored the vulnerability of critical infrastructure in any country. MST is susceptible to attacks of this nature because of its accessibility and the fact that it has to move millions of people on a daily basis: "The culture of transportation is never to shut down, to always keep people moving, to keep the system going at all costs."[12] According to Dr. Peter Chalk an open system such as any rail network, or bus system, offers opportunities for disruption and large numbers of soft target casualties.

With nearly 200 people being killed in the Madrid bombings, and 243 in the suicide bombings in London, the number of fatalities and significant injuries, not to mention the disruption to the city, have concentrated Australia's efforts on safeguarding its mass surface transport as one of the more vulnerable soft targets within Australia. But what does this really mean for mass surface transport?

Railway stations (and to a lesser extent bus stations) present a critical point of interchange for hundreds of thousands of daily commuters. To do this, the stations need to operate on two levels simultaneously: to provide a recognizable symbol for mass transit (object) and at the same time an effective set of urban spaces able to accommodate large numbers of people for short periods of time. For the most part in Australia, railway stations have failed at both levels—losing their significance to the community they serve. Yet to undergo the radical design transformations seen in Europe and Japan, current rail stations offer little in the way of supporting a community. Services can be irregular, amenities are minimal and public space is generally leftover residual space between poorly fitting administrative functions—an environment not conducive to transient commuters. Moreover, stations as key centers are often invisible as buildings within the community.

One opportunity for public space in mass transit over other types of urban space is that it is used by a defined group of people—a transient community. It acts as a conduit between the suburbs and larger urban centers, often excluding car-related activities. This collective network of spaces is also a semiclosed system bringing together people who would normally not aggregate—similar to an airport or shopping mall rather than a civic square. In this regard, the public space of mass transit has a social function tangential to the working life of a city. This amplifies the difficulty of protecting an indefensible space from an indeterminate enemy.

Urban Governance versus D Tactics (Disruption, Destruction, Death, and Disablement)

When the threat of an attack, such as a planned bombing (even a hoax), is made against critical infrastructure the response system relies on city or urban governance to make consequential decisions (state government, city councils, railway companies). The speed by which a city can react to an attack has in the past proved to be severely encumbered by their governance structures. For example, in the London bombings, it was reported that "it took 27 minutes before an amber alert to curtail all underground operations was issued."[13] In another more vivid example, Tokyo suffered an even higher number of casualties during the 1995 sarin nerve gas attacks which were carried out on the subway trains killing 12 people but injuring 1,200.[14] It was reported that "in one case one of the trains ran all the way to the end of the line, reversed, came back—carrying bags of sarin—got to the end of the line, reversed and came back a third time, an hour and a half later before it shut down."[15] Examples like this highlight the difficulty that large organizations have in assessing and responding to threats—real or not. For each threat, the hierarchical flow of information across the various networks and governance structures impedes any rapid decision making. This in itself is problematic because it is a symptom of democracy.

Because tactics most frequently displayed in recent terrorist attacks have not been deciphered for urban governance, cities as the preferred sites of attack are generally left defenseless. Even if the number of deaths is few, the impact of an actual attack can be measured in many other ways that affect the city's economy: loss in productivity, confidence, and revenue in mass transit; fear; suspicion within the community; and breakdown of community networks. But what about hoaxes or benign threats made against critical infrastructure—how are these treated within the system and what do they mean for public space?

The Hoax

On November 14, 2005, Brisbane experienced several bomb threats to its public transport system. This recent hoax highlighted the confusion and disruption that followed. Here, the threats and responses verified the unnecessary complication, contradiction, and duplication of directives taken.

According to a recent research report undertaken for the Emerging Futures Project[16] by counterterrorism expert Dr. Peter Chalk: "Four calls made to QP [Queensland Police] Headquarters at 10.30 that morning warned IEDs had been placed on four buses and four trains and would detonate at noon." Brisbane City Council and Queensland Rail "both took the unilateral decision to suspend all surface transit services at 11:55 am.[17] A fifth call then came in claiming that the timing of the supposed attack had been pushed back and would now occur at 5 pm—the height of the afternoon rush-hour—when it was more likely to cause disruption and fatalities. No further details were given, either with respect to specific targets or attack locations. This time it was the Department of the Premier and Cabinet that reacted, suspending all bus and train operations between 4:45 and 5:15 pm. As with the earlier threat, the afternoon passed without incident."[18]

The public and employees of the various transport companies (rail, bus, and ferry) were not informed of the developing situation. When the shutdown occurred, confusion reigned: buses stopped precisely where they were—some parked at the side of busy arterial roads, others under bridges or next to petrol stations, and so on. Public spaces in and around stations filled with commuters simply waiting for the system to revert to normal. Had the bomb not been a hoax, many experts speculated that the casualty rates and disruption to the city system could have been enormous.

This hoax demonstrated not only the flaws in the security system but also that in emergency situations current urban governance hierarchies are ineffective at responding to such threats. Internal divisions within single organizations further add to the confusion in response time.[19] On the one hand, such hierarchies are desirable for city life and suit the myriad of administrative functions required of them, but, on the other, can explain much of the confusion experienced in recent incidents. As with the Brisbane hoax, these organizations tended to resemble the hierarchical structures of the Napoleonic phalanx armies that were easily thrown into disarray under the pressures of the battleground, rendering them ill-equipped to retort.

HOAX: A Humorous or Malicious Deception[20]

How far the 'threats of ambiguity and the unknown' were framed by government security agencies to include provision for hoaxes is unclear. Although the government is calling on the community to flush out real threats of terror from within, they appear to have no strategy for dealing with hoaxes.

I am interested in the idea of a hoax for its obfuscation of what is first assumed to be an act of terror. It is difficult to ascertain how many foiled terror attacks would have remained as hoaxes rather than been converted to actual attacks since they were not played out to completion.

At one level, the outcome of a hoax is similar to a terrorist attack—without sacrificing lives or causing mass destruction associated with an actual attack the *hoax* can have an equally disruptive and terrorizing effect on the community, the economy of a city, and its governance.

In the case of actual terror attacks, the perpetrators tend to articulate a clear, and usually politically aligned, motive. They are usually part of a larger network or organized group and are often distanced from the event itself by suicide bombers or front-runners, whereas the perpetrators of a hoax come from a wider range of backgrounds, are often independent of any political alignment, and are committed to a *bluff* being called and played out to some degree. They are nearly always caught, prosecuted, and punished severely for their actions—often unable to show any clear motives for the hoax. Rarely are hoaxes ever taken to be humorous by the public, police, or government agencies.

Because Australia's level of threat is set at medium, no threat can afford to be overlooked. This in itself raises further questions about the idea of a hoax—is there a symbiotic relationship between a hoax and urban governance? Who are the beneficiaries of a hoax? Does a hoax move closer to an act of terror or is it considered more like a drill exercise? Is it more useful, or less useful to Urban Governance, or does it play into the hands of terror groups to create further confusion, disruption, and fear? If the hoax works on heightening the perception of fear, it nevertheless guarantees public safety—is this a good thing or a bad thing? We certainly know it is costly.[21]

Be Alert, but Not Alarmed—the New Public Space of Mass Transit

During the last five years, urban design has had to embrace this inscrutable force influencing the way cities and infrastructure need to be secured for the future. Although designs of all new major buildings around the world are being carefully assessed for terrorist attacks, there are far fewer ideas for securing public space other than deploying state of the art surveillance systems.

Even though the network of public space within mass transit is considered susceptible to the growing 'threat from within,' these spaces are more at risk from hoax threats.

In this arena, the impact of any hoax is temporary but cumulative. The more frequent the hoaxes are, the less these events terrorize, instead producing complacency and endorsing a "she'll be right" attitude.[22] If there were more hoaxes and fewer acts of terror, could we ensure that the public space of mass transit be made more defensible by detecting gaps in security? It is unlikely because the nature of any attack is so unstable and constructed from multiple actions that Chalk proposes:

> ... the objective should rather be the development of a set of "tools" and practices that are able to manage the risks within acceptable boundaries.[23]

When the threat of an attack (hoax or otherwise) is leveraged at mass transit, the sequence of these actions is suspended and replaced with directive actions. Where the threats are unanticipated, as in hoaxes, the question of who is our community is thus challenged and contested. For public space, the act of waiting, interchange/connection, embarking/ disembarking, or meeting people requires a set of actions explicitly associated with mass transit rather than air travel. Unlike facilities catering for air travelers, the cost of searching and screening each and every passenger and their baggage is prohibitively high and cannot be offset by ticket increases. With few exceptions, Israel being one, it is unlikely that this would change in the foreseeable future.

Queensland Rail has recently adopted a British system for the assessment of potential threats by their employees: "Hot or Not?" Designed to increase the powers of surveillance by employees of the transport companies, this system enables a policy of rapid detection to be carried out. After completing a 20-minute online introduction course personnel are able to respond to three key questions: Is the person and/or object hidden? Is the person/object obviously suspicious? Is the person/object typical for the area? Based on these questions, any suspicions are relayed back to the command center for further investigation, either by patrol or CCTV. However, a young fashionably dressed university student with a backpack/bag and mobile phone in hand is neither hidden, suspicious, nor atypical for any area within the commuter belt in any city in Australia—which suggests that these questions might be lacking in depth. Such an obvious gap in the broad sweep detection strategy suggests that many more marginal profiles could fall through the cracks.

The threat to urban space is not confined to what terrorism has delivered to date, with the demise of public space becoming one of the most serious threats to the social structure of the community. In line with new attitudes to ensure greater public safety, surveillance cameras in stations, trains and buses are in operation 24/7 to deter antisocial behavior and potential threats. Apart from the quality of public space being downgraded by increased levels of lighting required for surveillance cameras, the choice of fixtures and vandal-proof fittings offers little in the way of comfort to public spaces.

Australia's mixture of analogue and digital CCTV recordings have had no real bearing on crime prevention—petty crime and drug related offenses are on the increase, and a lack of real-time transparency in CCTV footage means that perpetrators of petty crimes are often unable to be identified and prosecuted. Although the success of incident-based surveillance has been analyzed extensively, there is no clear evidence that surveillance has ever produced real-time security for these urban environments. As a result of the prohibitively high costs of installing, outsourcing and maintaining real-time digital surveillance systems, it is probable that they will be co-opted for market research—your preferred brand of coffee, choice of newspaper, demographic makeup of friends, selection of brand clothing, mobile phone, music, and so on.

With these new trends, the corollary for public space in Australia is concerning because all activities will be recorded, stored, transferred, and controlled by independent groups. Where air travel has systematically developed passenger profiling through identity documents, finger-printing, and facial photographic data-basing, train travel cannot. Instead, the invisible surveillance already mushrooming under the new smart card technology may offer some alternatives for security, if not public space, in mass transit systems. But, without effective public space in these mass transit zones, the community cannot participate in its own surveillance.

Smart-card technology has been operational in Southeast Asia and Europe for some years now. With the newest advances enabling every legitimate user (purchaser of ticket) of the rail network to contribute up to 37 pieces of personal information that are stored on the card in 96 bytes of memory and relayed to a central database that will be kept, for purposes not yet specified, for up to 10 years.

Hong Kong and Singapore have had two versions of these smart-cards in place. What began with economic convenience in the "octopus card" used in Hong Kong, and enabling small purchases, membership fees, and paying bills, has expanded to a more comprehensive contact-less ticketing system. Highly appealing with recent spread of disease such as SARS and bird flu in Southeast Asia, what was once a closed but vulnerable system in mass transit can now theoretically become an open system that is both healthier and better secured.

In Australia, the contact-less smart-card technology has yet to be embraced but could offer some real benefits to opening up and securing indefensible space where the current measures of surveillance have had very little impact.[24] Along with the public spaces of mass transit, the railway station as a significant building type needs to be reinvented as a new and vibrant space-form that will challenge its present demise. If the public spaces are recast as community-oriented and combine contact-less (smart card) ticketing and face recognition technology with free Internet access, e-mail, and Web-based activities, such as chat rooms and shopping, perhaps these new interactive environments could produce both *security* and *spectacle* that are cooperative and supportive of transient commuter communities.

Furthermore, apart from mounting the aggressive marketing campaigns seeking community involvement, government departments really need to review their own phalanxlike hierarchies for what is really at stake here.

Notes

1. Eighty-eight citizens, three residents, and then 111 people from 18 other countries. [http://www.dfat.gov.au/publications/terrorism/overview.html p. 3]
2. 'Transnational Terrorism: the threat to Australia,' Overview, p. 1, Dept of Foreign Affairs and Trade, Australian Government, http://www.dfat.gov. au/publications/terrorism/overview.html [last accessed, 19 June 2006]. See also http://www.safeguardingaustralia.org.au/index.html and http:// www.nationalsecurity.gov.au/agd/www/nationalsecurity.nsf.
3. 'Transnational Terrorism: the threat to Australia,' Overview, p. 1, Dept of Foreign Affairs and Trade, Australian Government, http://www.dfat.gov. au/publications/terrorism/overview.html [last accessed, 19 June 2006]. Two additional information sheets showcase the differences and similarities between al Qaeda and Jemaah Islamiyah (JI), the two groups responsible for the 9/11 and the Bali bombings, respectively.
4. http://www.dfat.gov.au/publications/terrorism/is4.html [last accessed, 19 June 2006].
5. http://www.dfat.gov.au/publications/terrorism/overview.html p. 6 [last accessed, 19 June 2006].
6. "Genghis Khan and his generals made advances in military disciplines, such as mobility, psychological warfare, intelligence, military autonomy, and tactics. Genghis Khan and others are widely cited as producing a highly efficient army with remarkable discipline, organization, toughness, dedication, loyalty and military intelligence, in comparison to their enemies and by defeating one of the most powerful and largest armies, empires, tribes and dynasties besides being militarily outnumbered in almost all of them. The Mongol armies were one of the most feared and militarily ruthless forces ever to take the field of battle. Operating in massive sweeps, extending over dozens of miles, the Mongol army combined shock, mobility and firepower unmatched in land warfare until the modern age. Other peoples such as the Romans had stronger infantry, and others like the Byzantines deployed more heavily armored cavalry. Still others were experts in fortification. But none combined combat power on land with such devastating range, speed, scope and effectiveness as the Mongol military practicing advanced tactics, strategies and toughness." Quotation taken from: http://en.wikipedia.org/ wiki/Genghis_Khan (military) [last accessed July 2006].
7. "The Soviet war in Afghanistan was a nine-year war between the Soviet forces and the anti-government Mujahideen insurgents that were fighting to depose Afghanistan's Marxist People's Democratic Party of Afghanistan (PDPA) government. The Soviet Union supported the government while the insurgents found support from a variety of sources including the United States and Pakistan"; also "The initial Soviet deployment of the 40th Army into Afghanistan took place on December 25, 1979, and the final troop withdrawal took place between May 15, 1988, and February 2, 1989. On February 15, 1989, the Soviet Union announced that all of its troops had departed the country." Quotations taken from: http://en.wikipedia.org/wiki/Soviet_ invasion_of_Afghanistan [last accessed July 2006].
8. Manuel De Landa, *War in the Age of Intelligent Machines,* Zone Books, New York, 1994, p. 11.

9. 'The tactics of the nomads were based on a combination of psychological shock and physical speed. They were the first to integrate the swift sudden movements of loose cavalry formations with the deadly effects of intense missile power. The nomads combined the skills of highly mobile archers and horsemen with flexible tactical doctrine that utilized every feature of the battleground for ambush and surprise.' De Landa, p. 11.

10. See also http://en.wikipedia.org/wiki/Genghis_Khan 'organisation, terror and communications' [last accessed July 2006].

11. De Landa, pp. 11–12. See also http://en.wikipedia.org/wiki/Genghis_Khan 'organisation' [last accessed July 2006].

12. Brian Jenkins quoted by Dr. Peter Chalk, Unpublished report on SEQ Railway Infrastructure, for the ARC funded Emerging Futures Project (2005–2007), UQ and Columbia University (NY), 2006, p. 11.

13. Alan Cowell, "Subway and Bus Blasts in London kill at least 37; 700 are wounded." *The New York Times,* July 8, 2005; reported by Chalk, Unpublished report on SEQ Railway Infrastructure, p. 11.

14. Dr. Peter Chalk, Unpublished report on SEQ Railway Infrastructure; see also David Kaplan and Andre Marshall, *The Cult at the End of the World,* Crown Publishers, New York, 1996, pp. 244–251.

15. Brian Jenkins, in Chalk, Unpublished report on SEQ Railway Infrastructure, p. 11.

16. Dr. Peter Chalk, Unpublished report on SEQ Railway Infrastructure; Emerging Future Project: The project is an interdisciplinary study of railway corridors, transit-oriented development and strategies to combat urban sprawl and congestion in SEQ. The project is funded by the Australian Research Council (ARC) and two Linkage partners: Queensland Rail and Queensland Transport. The team comprises researchers based at the University of Queensland, Columbia University, New York, and Rand Corporation, Los Angeles: Dr. Kathi Holt-Damant UQ; Professor Phil Charles, Centre for Transport Strategy, UQ; Dean Mark Wigley Columbia University, New York; Associate Professor Mojdeh Baratloo, Columbia University, New York; Dr. Peter Chalk, RAND Corporation, Los Angeles.

17. Brisbane City Council and the two railway companies (Queensland Rail and Queensland Transport) responsible for the public transport system (rail, bus and ferry) are the largest government bodies in their respective positions in Australia. The BCC operates under the single directorship of the Mayor of Brisbane, and the rail companies under multiheaded groups responsible for passenger travel, freight, and rail land ownership.

18. Dr. Peter Chalk, author interviews, January 2006: "The perpetrator of the hoax was Rodney Bruce Watson, courier driver who was arrested within 24 hours. ... The motive for his actions remain unclear." See also http://en.wikipedia.org/wiki/November_14_2005_Brisbane_Bomb_Hoax.

19. The railway network in SEQ is owned and operated by a group of government agencies: Queensland Rail (rolling stock, passenger, and freight services); Queensland Transport (Land), Translink (revenue from integrated ticketing on rail bus and ferry services).

20. *Concise Oxford Dictionary,* Oxford University Press, London and New York, 2001.

21. Australia has subsequently introduced tough new laws in 2006 to prosecute perpetrators of terrorlike hoaxes.
22. Australian slang for a combined meaning of "don't worry" with a view that "everything will take care of itself in its own time."
23. Chalk, Unpublished report on SEQ Railway Infrastructure, p. 35.
24. To examine more thoroughly this intersection between public space, passive surveillance and security, an interactive installation has been designed for testing in an inner city railway station in Brisbane. As part of the Emerging Futures project, this installation aims to scrutinize the public space of mass transit by focusing on public reactions to visual surveillance and data mining through strategically positioned cameras.

    The installation is designed to capture both the natural trajectories of pedestrian movement and the typical waiting patterns associated with the public space of mass transit. Using the subject as object and inverting the two, the overt and covert surveillance cameras will record and reveal both the conscious and subconscious responses to events such as random searches, security personnel, smart-card technology tech trials, hoaxes, and petty theft. Transient commuter communities will be recorded intermittently over a 10-day period (covering on- and off-peak travel and in-between periods). A selection of recorded times will attempt to cover as many communities using the station as possible. Community responses will be grouped, sorted, discussed and debated by a panel assembled from different disciplines areas: philosophy, social and cultural studies, ethics, international law, security, counterterrorism, architecture and urban studies, local and state government.

Blank Slates and Disaster Zones
The State, September 11, and the Displacement of Chinatown

LAURA Y. LIU

The garment shops on Bowery that are being renovated probably won't be garment shops [after the renovation]. I overheard someone at the senior center say, "Chinatown in the future won't be called Chinatown."

—**Mrs. P**
Chinese Staff & Workers' Association organizer, August 9, 2001

The revival will move further south … making the great leap over Delancey Street that has always seemed impossible. … I like Allen Street. South of Delancey, it's really got soul. These great old, *underutilized* buildings, open spaces. Allen's like a European street, with that great, green divider down the middle. You watch: people are going to start opening up new places down there. *It's Chinatown, but it's not really. … It's a blank slate.*

—**Dewey Dufresne, restaurant developer and owner**
quoted in "Hipification: How a Neighborhood Goes from Down and Out to Extremely Cool, Block by Block" by Jim Nelson, New York Times Magazine, October 6, 2002, emphasis added

Without question, the events of September 11, 2001, reconfigured the landscape of urban development in Lower Manhattan. But community-based groups in New York City's Chinatown had been actively engaged in organizing against community displacement long before 9/11. Real estate forces, interested in Chinatown's residential, commercial, and industrial spaces, had characterized the area as a "blank slate" for development, ignoring the community and economic activities that had been and are under threat of displacement. The World Trade Center disaster exacerbated many of these displacement issues for community organizers. Chinatown, often politically constructed as self-isolated, was structurally isolated after September 11 and it proved to be a heavy burden on a community otherwise interconnected with the rest of the city and with other cities and regions at various scales. Several factors, including this isolation of Chinatown, exacerbated the problem of community displacement for Chinatown.

This chapter examines the state's response to September 11 and the role of community elites and community organizations in shaping or contesting that response.[1] At issue is the use of spatial strategies of control by the state, business interests, and community leadership. The militarization and spatial demarcation of the "disaster zone" restricted mobility for immigrant workers, for goods into and out of production sites, and created a general sense of fear and intimidation. In addition, the state's poorly implemented assistance programs resulted in uneven and inadequate distribution of disaster aid to workers, residents, and small businesses and contributed to the further isolation of certain parts of Chinatown. Beyond that, community elites and the state took advantage of the 9/11 disaster to accelerate redevelopment and changes in commercial and industrial use of space. Post-September 11 relief policies produced a contradictory moment of "shadow state" incorporation (Wolch 1990) for immigrant community-based organizations, even as it reinforced undocumented immigrants' precarious position. Examination of the state's contradictory and differential treatment of immigrants reveals the state to be nonunified, shifting, and incoherent (Burchell et al. 1991; Mitchell 1991) in ways that suggest possibilities for organizing. Ultimately, community contestation of state policy and of the spatial boundaries of "disaster" repositioned Chinatown in a wider debate around redevelopment and community displacement.

The context for this chapter is the interaction between a local campaign to stop the displacement of the Chinatown community out of Lower Manhattan and the state's responses to the events of September 11 in terms of security and disaster assistance. This straightforwardly named Anti-Displacement Campaign, organized by Chinese Staff and Workers' Association (CSWA), a Chinatown-based community organization, together with other local community-based groups,[2] focuses on fighting the displacement of jobs, housing, and services out of downtown's Chinatown. Examination of this campaign and other organizing activity both before and after the events of September 11 highlights the state's shifting and contradictory relationship to immigrant labor and communities.[3]

Exclusionary States

By questioning and challenging the U.S. government, we aren't being unpatriotic. I think we are being patriotic. We're saying we love this country, because we love what it could be and what it should be.

—Mrs. W,[4] CSWA organizer, September 16, 2001

On the morning of September 11, 2001, the scheduled date of the New York State primary, many CSWA organizers and members had come to Lower Manhattan to help take other members to the Chinatown polling places. That morning, the towers of the World Trade Center were attacked with passenger airplanes and both towers collapsed. When the first tower fell, many organizers and members were outside in the streets and felt the thundering explosion as the huge structure gave way, then eerily dropped from view. In the pandemonium, they converged at the CSWA office in Chinatown. Some members went to the Chinatown polling sites to gather other members and bring them back to the CSWA space, where they remained for most of the day, huddled around the radio. News reports from government officials told New Yorkers to stay calm and stay put. Roads were closed and subways were shut down. Chinatown is less then one mile from the World Trade Center site and, like all of New York City, was shaken. Early in the afternoon, members heard an announcement on the radio that the American Red Cross needed volunteers to give blood. A group of CSWA organizers and members (I was among them) went to Foley Square, a public plaza surrounded by courthouse and civic buildings in downtown Manhattan, where they waited with masses of other volunteers. After almost three hours, a Red Cross representative announced that the blood donation supplies had still not arrived and volunteers might not be able to give blood. Wanting to rally the crowd, he thanked them for their patience and added, "We won't let them get away with this!" As the Chinese immigrants, workers, and students looked around, they wondered, "Who were 'we' and who was 'them,' and where did CSWA fit in?"

At the same time that some members had gone to Foley Square to give blood, a separate group of CSWA workers from CCWA (Chinese Construction Workers Association), a subgroup within CSWA, had volunteered to help move debris. That first day, they, and hundreds of others, were turned away because the recovery effort was not yet organized. For the next three days, CCWA workers returned to offer assistance. Although a couple helped, most were continually turned away by the volunteer coordinators.

In the days and weeks following, CSWA was alive with debate about exactly where the organization and Chinatown fit into the "us"/"them" scheme. On September 16, 2001, five days after the disaster, organizers called members to a general meeting to analyze the disaster and discuss its effect on CSWA's organizing work. Some of the CCWA construction workers voiced their frustration at being shut out of the rescue and recovery efforts. Mr. K, for instance, said, "The television coverage shows the rescue volunteers as all white people from Yonkers, from New Jersey. But they don't want Chinese people to help! This is our community, too. Why can't we be part of this? We must demand the right to help!" The construction workers' demand to take part in the recovery work opened the question of whether Chinatown should or even could be part of the national or New York City "we." Mr. K's demand disproves the assumption that immigrant organizing is about extracting benefits from the withering U.S. welfare state, during a time characterized by Ruth Wilson Gilmore as a shift from "military Keynesianism" to "post-Keynesian militarism" (Gilmore 2007; Gilmore 1998).

To the extent that the Red Cross as a nonprofit organization acted on behalf of the state in coordinating relief efforts, this example reflects another instance of the exclusion of Chinese immigrants from the civic body. CSWA organizers wanted the right to be part of a collective volunteer effort but were repeatedly denied, and thus prevented from joining the "thousand points of light" invoked by George H. W. Bush in his January 1989 inaugural address expounding on the American virtues of civic voluntarism. Hardly coincidentally, this voluntarism was being championed in conjunction with neoliberal policies that promoted privatization in place of the state taking responsibility for a range of social and economic inequalities. As this chapter will demonstrate, the Red Cross, Salvation Army, and other nonprofit organizations would exemplify the manifold problems of the state's outsourcing of relief work as one part of this constellation of responsibilities. Sadly, these problems would replay in New Orleans and along the Gulf Coast in the tragic aftermath of Hurricane Katrina in 2005. As Jennifer Wolch has effectively argued in *The Shadow State* (1990), by moving away from welfare state functions in the post-Fordist period, the U.S. state concomitantly altered the volunteer sector in troubling ways. As nonprofit organizations have taken on welfare state functions, such as disaster and relief assistance, they have become a shadow arm of the state. Yet through mechanisms such as distribution of state funding, awarding of government contracts, monitoring of tax-exempt status, and so on, the state very much maintains control over the nonprofit shadow state.

Returning to the scene of CSWA's internal debate, when the conversation came around to the near future of the organization's various campaigns, some of which clearly target the state, the discussion grew more heated. Many members felt the campaigns should be set aside to prioritize the 9/11 victims and their families' needs. Others noted that the imposition of martial law and the restriction on civil liberties in and around Chinatown signaled a change in the tenor of the state's attitude to civil disobedience and acts of opposition. They feared violence from the state or from others if CSWA appeared "unpatriotic." In response, however, several organizers, like Mrs. W quoted earlier, insisted this was exactly the time when the campaigns mattered most. This faction, some of them injured workers, did not see a distinction between the victims of September 11 and other workers who had been injured or killed on the job before 9/11.

This proved to be a crucial time for CSWA as an organization and especially for its Anti-Displacement Campaign, which was both invigorated and disrupted by the organization's efforts to offer immediate disaster relief to the Chinatown community. In the climate of George W. Bush's domestic and international "War on Terror," the organization grappled with questions about the role of protest and opposition for immigrant workers, especially in terms of targeting the state. Whereas other moments had raised similar issues about the state's relationship to Chinese immigrant workers, the post-9/11 period heightened internal discord over issues of U.S. nationalism and immigrant labor policy. The organization has never shied away from dissent among its own and mostly welcomed the friction as an opportunity to refine its political goals. Although silent dissent foments organizational disunity, one organizer told me, open dissent is the precursor to "consolidation within the organization."

In awareness of the transnational backdrop to local and urban conflict, some organizers noted how strategic differences over how and whether to oppose the state reflected the organizers' differing political outlooks resulting partially from their places and regions of origin. Some immigrant organizers from China, for instance, exhibited harsh views on state repression, and advocated for more open opposition to the U.S. state in the context of its perceived political freedoms. Some organizers from pre-1997 Hong Kong and Taiwan, by contrast, suggested more conciliatory approaches, perhaps reflecting their sense that they had come from relatively open societies not too dissimilar from the United States. Organizer's speculations on these differences remind us that immigrant organizing reflects political formation where people come from as much as in the United States. These differences and the internal conflict that accompanied them were heightened by organizers' awareness that September 11 was likely to intensify the regulation of immigrant communities, as indeed it has.

Disaster Zones, Gentrification, and the Insecurity State

Chinatown has been a disaster zone this whole time, [even] before September 11.

—**Mr. W, CSWA organizer, October 7, 2001**

Before the events of September 11, 2001, as the forces of industrial change, redevelopment, and gentrification threatened to displace New York City's Chinatown, the fear that the area would change so drastically that it "won't be called Chinatown," anymore, as Mrs. P overheard, had Chinese workers throughout the city fighting displacement. The World Trade Center disaster, however, exacerbated many of the displacement issues CSWA organizers had been confronting. The state's immediate response to 9/11 was a physical lockdown of Lower Manhattan below 14th Street, which includes all of Chinatown and several other neighborhoods. By the following day, multiple scales of the state's police and military power collected on the street corners of major intersections in Chinatown and throughout Lower Manhattan to enforce restrictions on movement and stand guard. The physical convergence of the state's various scales of soldiers included U.S. federal marshals, Federal Bureau of Investigation (FBI) agents, Bureau of Alcohol, Tobacco, and Firearms (ATF) agents, the National Guard, New York State Troopers, Port Authority Police, and New York City Police (NYPD), who clustered together in packs displaying a diverse array of beige, tan, green, blue, and black uniforms, all accessorized with clearly visible weapons of many shapes and sizes. The gathering of might was reminiscent of what Mike Davis calls the "militarized New Urban Order" that followed the Los Angeles rebellion of April 1992 and was characterized by the influx of an unprecedented range and number of federal agents and military personnel on top of local police and sheriffs (Davis 1993: 150–154).

Because of Chinatown's proximity to federal, state, and city buildings, including several courthouses, City Hall, the Municipal Building, and the New York City Police Department Headquarters, tight security remained highly concentrated on the main streets into and around Chinatown for months. For the first few weeks, residents and workers had to show identification at checkpoints and explain their reasons for coming or going. The continued police presence was an intimidating sight and resulted in an extended period of anxiety and fear for residents and workers, including CSWA members and organizers, especially those who were undocumented immigrants. Chinatown, often seen as self-isolated (see Chen 2003 for an analysis of this political construction), was now being isolated by the state's imposed restrictions on movement. But unlike in wealthy neighborhoods of Lower Manhattan, such as Tribeca, this isolation threatened to exacerbate the displacement of the community already underway. Given Chinatown's role as the core of the wider urban immigrant community, the implications of such displacement would be far reaching, affecting the whole city and surrounding region. With its concentration of Chinese businesses and services and its mix of industrial and service jobs, Chinatown functions as a work, consumption, and service hub for Chinese immigrants and workers in Manhattan's Chinatown, in the satellite Chinatowns (Chinatowns located in the outer boroughs of Brooklyn and Queens), in non-Chinatown neighborhoods throughout the boroughs, and in suburban and exurban areas outside the city. Should Manhattan's Chinatown be displaced, immigrants throughout the metropolitan area would lose a central place of community. An examination of CSWA's fight against community displacement before 9/11 demonstrates fears of such a loss and shows that state forces, industrial capital, and real estate capital had already shaped the spatial threat to Chinatown's continued presence in Lower Manhattan.

The threats to Chinatown that existed before September 11 (and became heightened post-9/11) are the same ones that threaten working-class neighborhoods throughout the city: gentrification and speculative development based on the "rent gap" between current commercial and residential rent and potential future rents (Smith 1987a; Smith 1987b; Smith 1984, 1990 ed.); the decline of manufacturing jobs in the city (Mollenkopf & Castells 1991); and city and state subsidies for redevelopment (Fitch 1993). Numerous scholars have looked at the Lower East Side of Manhattan or sub-neighborhoods within it as case studies of gentrification and neighborhood change (Mele 2000; Abu-Lughod 1994; Smith, Duncan & Reid 1994). Most do not focus on changes in Chinatown specifically,[5] although Janet Abu-Lughod sets up a curious opposition, by saying:

> On the east-west cross streets between Third Avenue and Avenue A, particularly south of East Twelfth Street, are buildings in various stages of rehabilitation and restoration, and it is from these cross streets that *minority* populations are increasingly being displaced by whites and, most recently, by *Asians* who may be moving there as vanguards from Chinatown. (Abu-Lughod 1994: 346, emphasis mine)

It is curious that Abu-Lughod excludes Asians from "minority"[6] in this picture. In doing so, she invokes model minority discourse (often used to elevate some people of color out of the larger category "minority") while simultaneously ejecting Asians from the U.S. nation-state with a refusal of the term "Asian-American," a phenomenon Mia Tuan refers to as being cast as either "forever foreigners" or "honorary whites" (Tuan 1998). This is a typical effect of the contradictory positioning of Asian-American racial triangulation between blackness and whiteness (Kim 1999; Kim 2000) and the tendency to employ different racial discourses around immigration or immigrant settlement and segregation (Liu 2000). In this case, the triangulation suggests that Asians (and Asian-Americans) from Chinatown are themselves *part of* the forces of displacement, rather than possibly vulnerable to them. Of course, none of this makes sense without a consideration of class and capital.

By contrast, for instance, Jan Lin explicitly considers displacement in and of Chinatown in his analysis of the Lower East Side's changing economy. Although Lin says, "the continuing flow of poor rural immigrants into Chinatown perpetuates a human din and third world grittiness that mitigates against ... gentrification," he notes that:

> Garment industry representatives and planners have warned that rising rents on industrial space and conversion of manufacturing lofts into upmarket residential condominia greatly threaten the continued viability of garment contractors in the Chinatown production center. Speculative land market activity by overseas investors, some in secretive dealings, has also inflated commercial rents, endangering the livelihood of many petty street-level enterprises. Exorbitant "key money"[7] payments are required supplements to most leases. Low-income tenants are plagued by poor building services and some are harassed by landlords eager to displace them in favor of new tenants who must pay higher decontrolled rents. There are signs that redevelopment and economic restructuring in Chinatown, even if temporarily slowed, are moving inexorably forward. Dozens of medium-scale condominium projects have been built. (Lin 1994: 57–58)

Lin's grim description from the mid-1990s of the forces that threaten displacement has become exacerbated, "human din" and "third world grittiness" notwithstanding. As gathered from the restaurant developer Dufresne's quote that opened this chapter, to outsiders, Chinatown offers a sense of *blankness* that can be translated into possibility for development. In other accounts, contrary to Lin's prediction, the exoticism of Chinatown is a draw or, at least, not a drawback. A neighborhood profile of Chinatown that appeared in the *Village Voice* a month after the "Hipification" article in the *New York Times Magazine* (both articles came out after 9/11) comments that:

> Non-Asian hipsters have begun to filter in, nesting in buildings tucked among Chinese greengrocers, fishmongers, and dim sum houses. Time was, the only way you could score a walk-up in this clamorous, exotic enclave was to inherit it from your Chinese grandmother. For a rent-stabilized pad, that's still the way. But a few newly converted lofts or recently renovated walk-ups offer decent-to-luxurious digs at market rates. ... *While community activists complain that immigrants are being squeezed out, the landlords are mostly Chinese, so there aren't the*

usual gentrification wars along ethnic lines. And the ma-and-pa character of the old Chinatown is subtly changing anyway, says Insignia-Douglas Elliman broker Nancy Loo, who notes, "Five of the Chinese restaurants on Mott Street are now owned by corporations located outside the neighborhood." (Russo 2002: 139, emphasis mine)

Echoing Lin's analysis that speculative capital from outside Chinatown is a major force in its transformation, this article (complete with average rents, best bars, and crime statistics) uses the coethnicity of Chinese landlords pushing out Chinese tenants to put prospective new residents at ease. The subtext is, "Don't feel bad about gentrification in Chinatown. The Chinese are displacing their own." Reflecting the often mutually beneficial relationship between the New York City real estate press and the real estate industry, this article aims its rosy portrait at potential "non-Asian" renters and fails to note any relationship between neighborhood displacement and the effects of September 11. Campaigns against displacement in Chinatown belie this sanguine view.

As it turns out, Mrs. P, whose quote also opened this chapter, *is* a Chinese grandmother who used to live in a one-bedroom rent-stabilized apartment on Bowery. Her story complicates Russo's story of benign neighborhood transition. Instead of passing the apartment on to her grandsons, in 2001, in the months before September 11, Mrs. P was evicted by her Chinese landlord after her elderly mother, the original tenant, passed away. In June 2001, I accompanied Mrs. P to housing court to attend an eviction hearing on her case. Mrs. P tried to get onto the apartment's lease based on family member succession rights which allow close relatives to take over rent-stabilized apartments if they live in the unit with the leaseholder for a period of two years. However, the landlord contested Mrs. P's claim. The landlord's attorney argued that Mrs. P's electricity bills were too low for her to have been living there. Mrs. P explained that she had spent the last several months at the hospital every day with her mother before she passed away, and consequently had not used as much electricity as before her mother fell ill. The landlord's attorney claimed there was no documentary evidence to connect Mrs. P to her mother's address: no leases and no bank statements. The utility bills were in Mrs. P's daughter's name, reflecting common practices when language issues prevent older generations from opening accounts. In the end, the judge ruled for the landlord, who used Mrs. P's frugal habits and lack of documents against her. Two months later, after she left, Mrs. P reported that she heard that the landlord raised the rent from $410 a month to $600, and then to $1,000. She said that once the landlord pushed out the remaining tenants, he would raise the rent for all the units in the building.[8] One-bedroom apartments renting to Chinese tenants for $300–$400 would soon rent for $800, prohibitive for many new Chinese immigrants.

Besides being a "Chinese grandmother," Mrs. P is also the mother of Mrs. L, an organizer and board member of CSWA. When Mrs. P noted overhearing that "Chinatown in the future won't be called Chinatown," she was participating in an internal CSWA organizing discussion in August 2001 about the direction of the Anti-Displacement Campaign. Though she herself was residentially evicted, Mrs. P echoes Jan Lin's emphasis on both housing *and* jobs as key components in the displacement of a *community*. This is the crucial distinction CSWA organizers make to distinguish their approach to fighting displacement from other tenants' groups, mutual housing associations, and nonprofit low- and moderate-income housing developers. CSWA argues that these groups focus too narrowly on housing as the crux of displacement. The following exchange among CSWA and NMASS organizers at the meeting with Mrs. P reflects the process of arriving at what they call a "holistic" approach to fighting community displacement:

Franklin: What meaning does displacement have? In the past, it was about pushing tenants out. So it was just organizing tenants, very individually focused.

Ms. L: The issue [of displacement] is very new, but also very old. [Organization A], [Organization B],[9] they have worked on it a lot and for a long time. But a lot of people don't trust them. They'll offer a lawyer; it's very reactive. The usual tenant organizing groups are bad.

Zach: But isn't [displacement] just a consumer issue? How is housing different from other things people can't afford?

Mr. R: People don't know how to fight [displacement]. They are too focused on housing. As workers, we should fight displacement as both a consumption *and* production issue. It has to be a bigger issue about the loss of the whole community. When you see it as the entire community, if housing is expensive, then commercial rent is also expensive. Small businesses will also be impacted. Goods will be more expensive. You'll only be able to buy expensive things. There will be no daycare, no low-income housing. Services will be more expensive. Nearby services for the poor will be pushed out. This is a low-income area so the government services are here. Don't we need to protect the whole community? Lots of people don't see the big picture.

Roger: It's difficult—some people just look at housing. CCWA just looks at [displacement of] jobs. The CCWA construction workers came together to fight for jobs, but then nothing more.

When Ms. L notes that confronting displacement is "very new, but also very old," she references its historical centrality as a concern for urban immigrant communities. Unlike the many authors who depict Chinatown as the embodiment of static continuity and bounded insularity tied to its exoticism and culture (for a particularly Orientalist account, see Kincaid 1992), Ms. L recognizes a history of neighborhood change in Chinatown, and of contestation. It is the approach to this contestation that these organizers debate. Mr. R, a seasoned organizer, highlights that Chinatown's commercial, job, and service functions are as vulnerable to displacement as housing. Roger is self-critical of CCWA, the Chinese Construction Workers Association he belongs to that mobilized workers to help with clearing debris post-9/11, but were denied. CCWA formed in the early 1990s to fight the exclusion of local construction workers, specifically immigrants, women, and people of color, from building projects in and around Chinatown and the Lower East Side. One of their significant victories was winning jobs on the construction of two multimillion dollar federal buildings on Foley Square, the triangular plaza surrounded by the federal and state courthouses where volunteers gathered to donate blood on September 11. This was a significant victory to establish jobs for local residents in the Chinatown area. But here Roger concludes that the exclusive emphasis on jobs is as short-sighted as the exclusive emphasis on housing. By looking at three forms of displacement—jobs, housing, and services—and by bringing "worker" and "resident" identities together, CSWA organizers offer a broad understanding of what constitutes the Chinatown community. CSWA organizers include their own workers' center as one site of service that must fight displacement. It is this broad view of community and of its displacement that suggests the continuities between the new insecurity state's policies and older state formations need to be drawn out.

Organizing Amid Shifting Relief Policy

The state's response to September 11 was one of uncoordinated assistance programs with narrow eligibility requirements, leading to uneven and inadequate distribution of disaster aid. Several state agencies and charities offered assistance to victims, but the guidelines remained a work in progress for months as the agencies and organizations scrambled to establish relief policies. Ad hoc, disorganized, and inconsistent, these efforts amounted to a shifting terrain of disaster assistance destined to fail many immigrant workers and residents in Chinatown. It was in response to these rapidly changing programs that CSWA organizers acted in the weeks and months following September 11. CSWA's organizing after 9/11 also developed in response to Chinatown workers' and residents' immediate needs.

In addition to those who had died or lost loved ones at the site, CSWA real-ized there were thousands of indirect "economic victims," affected by the loss of work. Faced with a dizzying array of applications and poor transla-tion services for assistance from the various groups, CSWA predicted that Chinatown residents and workers would be shut out from the aid. They launched an effort to help community members apply for assistance and, within days, the organization was inundated by potential new members.

The agencies and nonprofits established Disaster Assistance Centers (DAC) in a few locations throughout Manhattan. One at the corner of Worth and Centre Streets off Foley Square was just a few blocks from the CSWA center. Another DAC was set up at Pier 94 at 54th Street on the East Side of Manhattan. The agencies included the Federal Emergency Manage-ment Agency (FEMA); Human Resources Administration (HRA), which oversees Medicaid, Disaster Medicaid, and Food Stamps; the Small Busi-ness Administration (SBA); the New York State Department of Labor (NYS DOL), which oversees Unemployment Insurance and Disaster Unemploy-ment Assistance[10]; and the New York State Workers' Compensation Board (NYS WCB). The charities and nonprofit organizations included Safe Horizon, which serves victims of crime and abuse, the Red Cross, and the Salvation Army.

Although disaster relief included both state aid and charitable assis-tance, the way relief was administered very much reflected the incorpora-tion of the charitable organizations into the shadow state. They occupied the same space in the DACs, which were generally run by FEMA, and, to some extent, shared information and application procedures. Although significant differences in rules about eligibility distinguished state and charitable organizations—most notably, the Red Cross and Salvation Army gave assistance to the undocumented—the voluntary organizations working in the DACs still acted as the shadow state in administering aid.

Members who had sought assistance at the centers were critical of the disorganization and inconsistency they encountered. One organizer who had been helping members at the center said in frustration, "It's changing day by day, week by week. Last week there was no [Chinese] translation, but they gave out all these forms. This week, there was translation, but no forms!" While helping members and organizers apply for relief, CSWA began to demand Chinese language translation and question the shifting grounds of eligibility criteria. By the end of the third week, to CSWA's sur-prise, operators at FEMA and Safe Horizon were telling Chinese speaking callers to call CSWA *directly*, in a clear example of the organization's instant and unwilling incorporation into the shadow state. When she learned that the relief centers were giving out CSWA's phone number, one young organizer said simply, "They can't do that. No way. They're deflecting responsibility."

By refusing to take on additional shadow state functions, CSWA organizers were intent on retaining an oppositional position to the state's implementation of relief policy. They continued to assist members in applications for aid, and worked closely with Catholic Charities, which had money to give and wanted to distribute assistance to the Chinatown community, but did not know how to outreach to or screen applicants. In the process, CSWA organizers highlighted the distinction between service for its own sake (e.g., service-focused community-based groups) and service as a tool for organizing (e.g., organizing-focused community-based groups). As one organizer said:

> What is the ultimate goal of this? Doing all this [9/11] service is only useful insofar as it relates to raising consciousness and organizing the community. If someone comes to us and we work with them, and then they leave for good, it's not their fault. It's our fault. We failed to challenge them and bring them in. Our goal must be larger than service.

Through the relief work, CSWA came in contact with thousands of Chinatown workers who had never come to the organization. Ever-focused on organizing, CSWA organizers asked prospective members not only what they needed, but also what they could do as potential new organizers, thereby echoing Mr. K's demand that the Chinatown community be included as a part of the relief work. This demand refutes the construction of Chinatown's identity as solely the location of need. Instead, organizing centers on what the community can do for itself. The direct contact with workers provided an opportunity to gain valuable information about what was happening in industries and worksites throughout Chinatown, the very reason organizers prioritize grounding in local conditions and a local base.

Based on the interactions with existing members and potential members, organizers concentrated on three groups that were hit especially hard by the disaster: garment workers and restaurant workers—two groups CSWA had always focused on organizing—and car service drivers.[11] Each group faced unique difficulties in their industries. The garment industry was hit especially hard by restrictions on vehicular traffic below 14th Street. Without supplies coming in or manufactured goods going out by truck, production slowed drastically and bosses[12] cut workweeks from six or seven days down to three or less. Many workers could not document their losses, however, for one of several reasons. Some bosses paid workers in cash. Others delayed checks so that they progressively built up more time between the work done and the wages paid. This is what organizers call a "sweatshop tactic" because it is used in cases where bosses engage in micro-scale geographic mobility, an ultralocal version of capital flight. After closing up shop, claiming bankruptcy, and moving to another location, workers are left unpaid. The longer the time period between the check and the pay period, the more the boss evades paying. Another reason garment workers could not document losses is a practice known as "check buying." It is a system where workers actually pay bosses in order to then be paid their wages by check (as opposed to cash), in order to submit paystubs to the Union of Needletrades, Industrial and Textile Employees (UNITE), the garment union.[13] UNITE uses the checks to document eligibility for health insurance. Because purchased paychecks may not reflect actual earnings, the practice of "check buying" is a substantial obstacle for garment workers in proving loss of work in order to get disaster assistance. Workers reduced to three days of work a week were working more than allowable to receive Disaster Unemployment Assistance, but less than they could survive on, reflecting the disconnect between the state's approach to relief and conditions within the community.

For the restaurant industry, although the news media focused on the lack of tourism which was surely a factor, restaurant workers told CSWA it was the absence of garment and other workers eating lunch and dinner in the area on a daily basis that was most damaging to business. That the loss of production work in the garment industry affected the restaurant industry so greatly highlights the integration of Chinatown's service and production economies and shows that, should garment jobs become significantly displaced out of Lower Manhattan, other Chinatown industries will suffer.

The relocation of financial services workers out of Lower Manhattan severely cut business for car service drivers, most of whom had relied heavily on regular clients in the Wall Street financial district. Based on discussions with car service drivers and agencies, organizers estimate that 5,000 to 6,000 drivers, and of those, one thousand Chinese drivers, serviced the World Trade Center area before 9/11. As a target group for organizing, car service drivers proved to be a unique group to organize in terms of where and how they work. Although their issues did not overlap significantly with the Anti-Displacement Campaign, organizing this group did raise interesting issues about the placement of these workers in the category of "subcontractor." Drivers work for car service agencies, but must file IRS Form 1099 (instead of Form W-2), as self-employed independent contractors. CSWA organizers say agencies, like garment manufacturers, use the subcontracting system as a way to deflect providing benefits and paying taxes for drivers, who they do not consider to be self-employed but, rather, to be *workers*. How then did the state respond to car service workers' demands for assistance after September 11? Initially, state agencies used the unrooted nature of car service work against the drivers. Even though Manhattan-based drivers' work was heavily concentrated in Lower Manhattan, FEMA and other agencies claimed that car service drivers were not eligible for assistance because they could find work in other parts of the city. They also said that, as subcontractors, they could not receive Disaster Unemployment Assistance. After being told he was ineligible for assistance, Joseph, a CSWA board members' son and a car service driver, came into the Chinatown CSWA center. He said:

> Well, supposedly we drivers are self-employed. So I haven't been laid off. I just have no business, and no income! On top of that, they're telling me if I work more than three days a week, I wouldn't be entitled to Unemployment anyway. Well, it's not an issue of the number of days a week I work. I can work seven days a week, but I'm still not going to make any money! All our business was there [at the World Trade Center].

Although they came to CSWA in relatively small numbers, Chinatown street vendors and other self-employed workers faced the same restrictive guidelines. At most, they could receive small business loans from the SBA if they showed that their work was affected by 9/11. For car service drivers, that meant providing evidence that their dispatcher was located below Canal Street and that the majority of their customers were from the Wall Street area, which excluded many of them nevertheless impacted by the disaster.

Enforcement of policy was highly inconsistent. Within the first few weeks, drivers reported what they described as a "run-around." In the early weeks, the DACs required that workers come in just to make an appointment for another day. Many waited for whole days at the DACs, only to be told they were ineligible based on their status as "self-employed." Others went to the downtown Worth Street DAC, but were told that only the Pier 94 DAC would see car service drivers. On one particular day in mid-September, FEMA representatives at Pier 94 categorically stated that car service drivers were ineligible for Disaster Unemployment Assistance, but the Worth Street DAC had backed off from sending drivers to Pier 94 and had begun scheduling new appointments for them. Each driver came into CSWA with a different story. By the end of September, CSWA began organizing car service drivers to approach the DACs *collectively,* rather than individually, the basic strategy of all mass-based organizing. They noted that, given the individual inconsistencies of drivers' experiences, the only way they could push state agencies would be to act as a group. At a meeting of drivers, Joseph called for an organized, collective approach:

We must bring people together collectively within [CSWA], but also with other groups. If you go individually to the relief center, then you take your chances. But if we assemble people together, say one thousand Chinese car service drivers, then you show how big [a loss] this is. We've each lost $2000 of income in one month. With one thousand drivers, that's $2 million for only one month! FEMA still hasn't established a way to deal with the massive number of claims. And a lot of people don't know they're eligible. It's better to bring people together, share our experiences and information, and pursue an outcome as a group.

CSWA also began working with the Urban Justice Center (UJC), a nonprofit legal advocacy group focused on providing legal assistance to community-based organizations. UJC began collecting names and denial letters from all the drivers who had applied for Disaster Unemployment Assistance and been denied to make one case for a *pattern* of inequality.

By October 5, 2001, CSWA learned that the New York State Department of Labor (NYS DOL) had changed the rules so that self-employed workers, like car service drivers, could collect Disaster Unemployment Assistance and Workers' Compensation. The change was relatively unnoticed by the media, but CSWA organizers recognized its massive implications. Mr. C noted:

The state is being very quiet about these changes. There is no publicity. What are we doing? We're raising the issue. We're talking to papers. We're talking to elected officials. We're changing the rules. We don't want to accept the rules as they are. Now all of a sudden, the self-employed can get Unemployment. So the government *can* make changes if they want to. How come if you're a boss, you can get a small business loan, regardless of whether you yourself are undocumented? Because they are looking at the business entity. They don't call that Unemployment. They call it a small business loan. Now the undocumented are eligible for Workers' Comp, but not Unemployment. If the self-employed can now get Unemployment, then why not give it to the undocumented? Whatever the boss calls you, whether he gives you cash or not, you should still be entitled to Unemployment. The self-employed never pay Unemployment Insurance, but now they're eligible. So why not the undocumented?

Mr. C and other CSWA organizers identified the openings made possible by the state's various contradictory positions on eligibility for various forms of assistance. Post-9/11 conflicting policies of Disaster Unemployment Assistance, Unemployment Insurance, and small business loans, regarding the self-employed and the undocumented, allowed Mr. C to reiterate a broad understanding and identity for workers, whatever bosses or the state might name them. This was part of a more general strategy of using the irreconcilability of state policy regarding immigrant workers to challenge the state's production of worker and immigrant identities.

On November 13, 2001, the U.S. Department of Labor (U.S. DOL) formally clarified the Disaster Unemployment Assistance guidelines for "unemployment as a direct result of the major disaster" to include a broader range of workers. In the new guidelines, the U.S. DOL explicitly included "self-employed individuals" and offered two contrasting examples based on taxicab drivers:

> ...a taxicab driver would be potentially eligible for DUA [Disaster Unemployment Assistance] where a majority of his or her business depended on providing transportation services between points which include areas cordoned off because of the physical damage of the major disaster or because facilities were closed or commandeered by the federal government. On the other hand, DUA eligibility must be denied a taxicab driver who cannot establish that a majority of his or her livelihood depended on providing transportation services between points which include areas cordoned off because of either the physical damage of the major disaster or the closing or commandeering of the facilities by the federal government. (U.S. Department of Labor 2001)

The contrasting taxicab examples provided by the clarification to the Disaster Unemployment Assistance provision of the Stafford Act placed the distinction between eligible and ineligible workers around another crucial axis: the spatial boundaries of the disaster. By using boundaries to delimit eligibility, the state opened up a larger question of how to spatially limit the effects of September 11.

Just as the state's eligibility requirements for car service drivers changed dramatically over the weeks after September 11, spatial boundaries used to define the disaster zone for residents and workers also shifted. In the months following 9/11, the Lower Manhattan Development Corporation (LMDC), the city and state-appointed corporation charged with responsibility for the redevelopment of Lower Manhattan, together with various agencies such as FEMA, de facto established a zone organizers referred to as the "Chinatown bubble." They used this term to denote that only part of Chinatown was considered by the state to be within the official disaster zone. By arbitrarily setting limits and boundaries on the disaster zone, the agencies, together with politically powerful voluntary organizations in Chinatown, established terms against which organizers could fight.

CSWA organizers, concerned that differential relief policies would marginalize Chinatown as a whole, began to contest the demarcation of the disaster zone. To many Chinatown workers, the idea that the impact of the disaster could be so neatly contained was untenable. Even more glaring was the arbitrary use of Canal Street, a major east-west commercial street within Chinatown, as the northern boundary of the bubble. As one organizer said angrily in October 2001, "Why is the boundary at Canal? The majority of garment factories [in Lower Manhattan] are *north* of Canal!" This prompted other organizers to dispute the idea that a worker in a factory south of Canal Street was a legitimate economic victim of the disaster, but one on the other side of the street was not. Organizers interviewed workers who came to the 9/11 intake clinics, and also conducted door-to-door economic surveys of factories outside the official disaster zone. The surveys showed that a third of the factories had closed down (and this did not count factories not included in the survey), whereas factories that avoided closure had laid off half of their workers. It was many of these workers left ineligible for assistance if the factories were north of Canal Street. CSWA's criticisms were especially directed at the Red Cross, who had already rejected Chinatown volunteers in the cleanup effort, and also failed to mobilize relief in residential sections of Chinatown, claiming language barriers and the inability to evaluate need. In challenging the state and shadow state determination of the disaster zone, CSWA also criticized the relief efforts for not reaching or trying to reach the neediest immigrant families. As one organizer put it in a membership meeting in April 2002:

> It's a failure of the agencies, like FEMA, and the charities. They're ignoring Chinese people. They gave a half a billion dollars to companies, but only if they are bigger than two hundred people and located south of Canal Street. This effectively excludes Chinatown because the companies in Chinatown are small. The government said they wouldn't help garment factories north of Canal because they were [already] closing in the months before 9/11. But it was the "low season." The government is using this as an excuse.

By December 2001, organizers had responded by mobilizing affected workers in factories north of Canal Street, to demonstrate that Canal Street should not be used as the boundary. Yet, state agencies and the big charities still refused to give assistance to many of these workers.

In reaction, by January 2002, CSWA was working with three charity groups to provide assistance to those workers not served by the Red Cross: Catholic Charities, the Brooklyn Bureau of Community Service (BBCS), and World Vision. Unlike the Red Cross, at least in its initial efforts, these groups wanted specifically to reach low-income immigrants, especially non-English speakers. Working with these charities, CSWA helped to interview and evaluate applications from thousands of garment workers, eventually facilitating the distribution of over $2.3 million to at least 2200 workers. Even so, the three charities were only a small part of the relief apparatus and, overall, the state and shadow state had largely failed Chinatown.

Unfortunately, the government was not alone in using September 11 in ways that would accelerate redevelopment. Certain landlords and garment factory bosses also took advantage of 9/11 to encourage turnover of leases and further exploit workers, contributing to the decline of local Chinatown industries. One small boss reported to his workers that, because the bank had been closed in the weeks following the disaster, he could not pay them. By this point, workers knew the bank had reopened. In one case that exemplified the trend, a landlord for a garment factory launched a campaign of harassment to push the tenant out of the space, offering money and other incentives to relocate the tenant to Sunset Park. Restaurant workers reported increased harassment from bosses who also claimed the lack of business meant they could not pay their commercial rent and therefore could not pay workers. Post-September 11, the combination of abuses by landlords and by their commercial tenants, the garment bosses, created conditions of heightened exploitation for some workers and increased the departure of garment factories from Chinatown. By viewing these practices as a continuation and acceleration of pre-9/11 community displacement, organizers were able to mobilize at a time when many felt the pressure to stifle criticism and support the state and even small bosses.

Yet, the results for different groups of workers varied. Perhaps because they were not fixed to particular worksites like restaurants and factories, car service workers, a mobile workforce, had offered a challenging case for organizers post-9/11. Organizing the car service workers proved to be instructive to the organization in terms of conceptualizing political goals in terms of the state. The car service organizers were ultimately quite successful in receiving assistance and relief from the state agencies and charities. Garment and restaurant workers, as collective groups challenging the state's requirements, were much less successful. One organizer explained to me that the response to the car service workers from the state, from other workers, and from others in the community was very positive because by organizing the car service workers, CSWA organizers were "not asking anyone to take on the bosses." By not threatening the larger structure of the system, car service workers represented a "safe" organized group. At the same time, the car service case showed CSWA's ability to resist shadow state incorporation while still expanding the scope of some of the state's benefits. And the disparity in assistance between car service workers, some of whom received repeat payments, and garment workers, many of whom worked north of Canal Street and received no payments, revealed yet another contradiction in the way the system treated different workers. Mobile workers, considered to be subcontractors or "small business," fared better than workers fixed to worksites in Chinatown, suggesting that organizing the car service drivers did not necessarily advance the Anti-Displacement Campaign as much as hoped.

Eventually, CSWA's organizing the disaster relief would converge more closely with the Anti-Displacement Campaign in targeting the shortcomings of the Lower Manhattan Development Corporation (LMDC). Established after September 11 to coordinate the rebuilding of Lower Manhattan, the LMDC is perhaps best known for its ineffectual handling of the 9/11 memorial and rebuilding of the World Trade Center site. The LMDC also oversaw the Residential Grant Program, which it began in August 2002. The program, approved by the Department of Housing and Urban Development (HUD) and granted $281 million in federal monies, was established to retain and attract residents to Lower Manhattan. Yet organizers claimed the grant application process excluded low-income Chinese and other East Side residents in favor of areas such as Battery Park City. Like the initial relief programs discussed above, the Residential Grant Program required official documentation in the form of leases, which many Chinatown residents (and others) could not provide. In April 2003, in response, CSWA helped to form the Lower East Side Chinatown Consortium (LESCC) to contest these requirements and establish a community-driven rebuilding agenda that encompassed environmental and health, housing and land use, and jobs and economic recovery concerns.

Ultimately, exposing the contradictions of the state's relief policies through post-September 11 organizing dovetailed with the political goal of demonstrating the state's overall contradictory treatment of Chinese immigrant (and other) workers. Contradictory immigration, labor, and other policies are continually negotiated and accommodated by the state, but at key moments, offer potential openings for political challenge. Examining the state's shifting approach to the regulation of immigrant communities suggests some of the implications for 9/11's lasting impact.

On September 20, 2001, George W. Bush established the Office of Homeland Security (OHS) to coordinate the administration of domestic security efforts. On November 25, 2002, Bush signed the Homeland Security Act of 2002 (Public Law 107–296) into law, establishing the Department of Homeland Security (DHS). Part of the law provided for dissolution of the Immigration and Naturalization Service (INS) (housed in the Department of Justice) and transference of its various roles to the DHS. This shift went into effect on March 1, 2003, and involved dividing the functions of the former INS between several bureaus within DHS. These include the U.S. Citizenship and Immigration Services (USCIS) (briefly known as the Bureau of Citizenship and Immigration Services [BCIS]), which handles immigration services such as permanent residency and citizenship applications. The policing aspects of immigration regulation, as indicated by the language of "enforcement," fell under two new bureaus under the Directorate of Border and Transportation Security (BTS). These are the bureau of Immigration and Customs Enforcement (ICE), which handles policing functions such as immigration violations and deportation; and the bureau of Customs and Border Protection (CBP), which merges regulation of customs with policing of national borders. These institutional shifts followed escalating criticism of the INS for bureaucratic inefficiency (the bureau had received increasing negative publicity for its severe backlog in processing applications) but also serve as a significant declaration that immigration policy encompasses three areas: taxation for revenue, promotion of "security" and policing of borders, and control of the flow of immigrant labor.

On October 26, 2001, two years before the establishment of the three separate bureaus, Congress passed the "Uniting and Strengthening America by Providing Appropriate Tools Required to Intercept and Obstruct Terrorism Act of 2001" also called the "USA Patriot Act," limiting civil liberties for immigrants suspected of engaging in terrorist activity. Congress renewed the Act on March 2, 2006. Together with placement of the three new bureaus within the newly formed Department of Homeland Security, continued congressional support for the Patriot Act reflects the state's current overt emphasis on security in immigration policy. The implications of this emphasis for immigrant communities are profound, especially for communities that include undocumented and otherwise vulnerable populations. Muslim and Arab Americans, immigrants or not, as well as others mistaken for members of these groups, are now especially targets of post-9/11 racial profiling, suggesting that the policing and invention of the national other flexibly accommodates the insecurity state's expanding reach (Nguyen 2005; Hagopian 2004; Tirman 2004; Cole 2003; Leonard 2003). In this context, it is perhaps all the more powerful to see that some undocumented immigrants will not be deterred from political activity.

Out of the Shadows: Organizing Undocumented Immigrant Workers

One of the most fruitful frustrations of executing ethnographic fieldwork is the discovery of the error of your original assumptions. Often the mismatch between the assumption and the empirical encounter is itself highly instructive. In my case, I assumed that stark distinctions would exist between documented and undocumented immigrants, both as analytical categories and as CSWA members.[14] I was skeptical that undocumented immigrants would be highly active as organizers, given their constrained position in U.S. society. This assumption was based on preliminary ethnographic research conducted with another community-based organization in Chinatown where I had witnessed very few undocumented immigrants coming through the organization's doors. That organization's focus, like most in Chinatown, was on permanent residents and citizens and its main goals centered on providing services (as opposed to organizing), placing them clearly within the shadow state sector.[15] Many Chinatown groups offer English classes, naturalization classes, job training, and so on, in keeping with the shadow state functions of voluntary organizations. CSWA occupies a very different position by opposing the state's formal structures of laws, policies, and so on. They also oppose the informal shadow state structures of other voluntary organizations, when they are seen as supporting repressive and oppressive policies of the state. At the same time, they themselves occasionally work with state agencies and politicians if doing so advances their political goals.

Differences between the service-oriented versus organizing-oriented community groups often center on comprehensive criticism of the state and analyses of state policy. This crucial difference became clear to me during one of my first encounters with Julie, a young organizer who immigrated from Hong Kong by herself as a teenager in the late 1980s and was now working as a paralegal for an immigration lawyer. Julie, like many of the organizers, was drawn into the organization by walking past a picket line in front of the Jing Fong restaurant in the early 1990s. The Jing Fong picket was a longstanding and successful protest against the massive Chinatown restaurant's poor labor practices. Julie became a leader in the Jing Fong student hunger strike of 1995 and continued to be an active leader in restaurant organizing and in what came to be known as the "Justice Will Be Served" Campaign targeted at abuses in the service industry. After a campaign meeting in early 2001 to prepare for a press conference about the conditions in a different restaurant (this one a suburban New Jersey restaurant), Diane, a white woman organizer with the National Mobilization Against SweatShops (NMASS), who was herself a restaurant worker and former security guard and was to speak at the press conference in support of the workers, asked if the New Jersey workers were undocumented. Julie replied:

> Yes, but whether workers are undocumented is less of an issue for [CSWA] because the INS does not care when it comes to Chinese workers. [The government] wants Chinese immigrants here to do

work. There will be a fine, or there will be a ticket, but they will not deport Chinese [immigrant] workers because it's too expensive to send them back to China! Unlike for Mexican workers—Mexico is close by. It's easy for the U.S. to send them back. I do immigration work, mostly visas for skilled immigrants. Did you know the INS has a category for some immigrants called "aliens with extraordinary ability"? [She laughs.] You know, they want us here to *work*.

As Julie suggests, and as the preceding history of immigration regulations confirms, the position of Chinese immigrants in the United States has always been determined by the U.S. need for workers and relations between immigrant and native-born workers. Wage competition, labor conditions, and hostility toward native-born African American workers ensure that immigrant labor may coexist with surplus native-born labor, simultaneous with competition among immigrant groups. By contrasting the cases of Chinese and Mexican undocumented immigrants, Julie comments on the hypocritical nature of U.S. immigration and labor policy.[16] "Ability," of course, refers to skills. By linking "aliens with extraordinary ability" to undocumented immigrants in one breath, Julie shows that the same imperatives drive immigration and labor policy for both skilled and so-called unskilled immigrant workers, albeit with contradictory results. The USCIS and formerly the INS use the term "aliens with extraordinary ability" to describe one class of immigrants eligible for the highest priority employment-based visa (known as the EB-1 visa).[17] To demonstrate what they mean, the USCIS offers the example that an "alien with extraordinary ability" could be a Nobel Prize recipient, for instance. EB-1 visas also cover "outstanding professors and researchers," and, curiously, "certain multinational executives and managers." From there, skills-based preference decreases for categories EB-2 through EB-4.[18] Even so, for Julie and other CSWA organizers, the difference between the "abilities" of undocumented workers and these "extraordinary aliens" only highlights the U.S. need for foreign labor of all types. This need changes with labor surplus and shortage, as well as interacting with political discourse around belonging and nationhood.

I highlight Julie's comments to show that, both before and after September 11, CSWA organizers have been engaged in contesting the distinctions the state makes between undocumented and documented immigrant workers by highlighting the ways the distinctions differentially operate. They are critical of the ways immigration and labor policies reify the differences between undocumented and documented immigrants even as they undermine those differences. For example, the state divides these groups but documented and undocumented workers often face the same working conditions in the same worksites. At the same time, the state only deports certain undocumented immigrants and not others. A focus of CSWA's criticism, for example, is the Immigration Reform and Control Act of 1986 (IRCA), which exemplifies the state's schizophrenia toward immigrant workers through two sets of contradictory policies: one for what is known as "amnesty," where undocumented workers (considered "out of status") can apply to "adjust status" (to obtain permanent residency), the other for what are called "employer sanctions," which force employers to verify immigrants' authorization to work and in effect allows bosses to police immigrants.

CSWA organizers are critical of amnesty policies in the IRCA and of the way amnesty is implemented in general. IRCA includes provisions for two groups of undocumented immigrants to seek amnesty and apply for green cards: undocumented immigrants who had been in the United States continuously since at least January 1, 1982, and undocumented agricultural workers who had been in the United States for at least 90 days between May 1, 1985 and May 1, 1986. With amnesty, both groups could apply for permanent residency without being criminalized. The IRCA amnesty programs ended in 1988, but in 1994, as part of an appropriations bill, Congress passed Section 245(i), or what became known as a "mini-amnesty," that amended the Immigration and Naturalization Act to allow undocumented immigrants to remain in the United States while they seek permanent residency. Section 245(i) is considered a "mini-amnesty" and not actual amnesty because it merely allows undocumented immigrants to stay in the United States while seeking to "adjust status," and does not decriminalize them. Undocumented immigrants are usually required to return to their home countries to apply for an immigrant visa and, because of the violation, must remain out of the United States for 3 to 10 years. Under Section 245(i), undocumented immigrants are still considered in violation of immigration law, remain so until application for adjustment of status is filed (which can take months or years), and can be deported at any time. Section 245(i) was extended several times but expired on April 30, 2001. In the months following its expiration, several immigration advocacy groups fought for its extension. Some contacted CSWA seeking their support of another extension, prompting organizers to debate the idea of amnesty. Most CSWA organizers are critical of the ways that both amnesty and "mini-amnesty" laws work, in part because they actually reinforce the idea of legitimate and illegitimate immigrants, and because of their relationship to other laws that regulate immigrant workers, such as the employer sanctions. During a meeting with a community-based religious group that serves immigrants and endorses CSWA's campaigns, CSWA organizers discussed both issues:

Ms. J: [Undocumented status] doesn't matter that much one way or another because Chinese people without green cards can still work and working conditions do not necessarily change much for those with green cards. So documented and undocumented workers face the same working conditions much of the time. Often undocumented workers actually get paid more than documented union workers. Employers are violating wage and other laws anyway, so they figure, why not hire undocumented workers and violate one more law?

Mr. W: See, we don't divide the undocumented from the documented. That's part of why we are not in favor of amnesty. With amnesty, [the government] chooses a date and arbitrarily decides that everyone who was here before that is OK. But they're talking out of both sides of their mouth. Amnesty divides the community. One date divides who's OK and who's not. Immigration is a labor policy, a tool to control labor. For example, money and skills allow you in. We think amnesty just criminalizes the next generation. We would rather have a six-year cycle, for instance, where if someone commits no crime, then they automatically get "status," instead of a ten-year cycle, where politicians decide each time around. Another reason we are not in favor of amnesty is that the focus on amnesty has pushed back the focus on repealing employer sanctions.

Ms. B: Employers want to hire undocumented workers because then they have a tool against them. The sanctions allow them to hire slaves.

Mr. W: Another group we work with, [Coalition A],[19] their main focus is Latinos. They focus on workplace issues, especially INS raids. They are separate from [Coalition B], which is pushing for amnesty. [Coalition A] has a similar position to ours against employer sanctions. We are against criminalizing any section of the population.

Mr. W echoes Julie's comments. Part of why he and Ms. B do not divide the undocumented from the documented is that they identify the commonality of poor working conditions for both groups.

The employer sanctions provisions of IRCA were intended to legislatively reinforce the separation between documented and undocumented workers by penalizing employers who hire the undocumented. But the employer sanctions have had unintended effects. The IRCA's mechanism for self-enforcement of employer sanctions requires that employers verify authorization to work and document it on the now familiar USCIS/INS

Form I-9. CSWA organizers note that, because of the difficulty and lax execution of enforcement, the sanctions essentially allow employers to play off the state's contradictory policy by hiring undocumented workers, but firing or threatening to fire them at any time. The state's construction of the illegitimacy of undocumented identity becomes a tool for workplace exploitation. As Mr. W explains:

> I was undocumented for twelve years, but it wasn't as bad then; there were no employer sanctions. In 1985 and 1986, we campaigned actively against the sanctions before they passed. At that time, the AFL-CIO was totally for them. A few years later, they reversed their position, although they haven't done anything about it. Small businesses at that time didn't like the sanctions. But then, soon after, they loved them because they could use them to intimidate and control workers. You see, employer sanctions extend *powers of the state* to the *employer.* The employer becomes the police. The amnesty was only given in 1986 to "sweeten the poison" of the employer sanctions. How else did this happen during the Reagan years? And those who get amnesty still work like slaves. In Chinatown and in the U.S., documented workers become slaves.

Mr. W is not alone in his analysis of the manipulation of the employer sanctions by bosses to discriminate against workers. In March 1990, the U.S. General Accounting Office (GAO)[20] released a report that showed that the employer sanctions provision of the IRCA *produced* a "widespread pattern" of employer discrimination against documented, undocumented, and even citizen workers based on national origin and citizenship (U.S. General Accounting Office 1990). The GAO report said that an estimated 19 percent of employers reported *beginning* discriminatory practices because of the employer sanctions. Ten percent discriminated based on national origin and 9 percent based on citizenship status (for example, not hiring permanent residents). Rates were even higher in some heavily Asian and Latino/a cities such as Los Angeles (29 percent) and New York (21 percent) (U.S. General Accounting Office 1990: 38).[21]

The effect even reaches beyond workplace discrimination. Human rights groups confirm increasing discrimination because of the employer sanctions in areas beyond employment and suggest that the concept of "eligibility" within the employer sanctions provisions causes a ripple effect. They claim that landlords, banks, insurance agencies, and other service providers were more likely to discriminate after the employer sanctions guidelines were established (U.S. House of Representatives 2002). The discrimination ripple effect of the employer sanctions demonstrates the interplay between the material and discursive forces of the state, whether intentional or not. The language of the law produces a discourse about eligibility and legitimacy that, in turn, produces structural effects, such as increased discrimination in areas outside of employment. Although many of these employers and service providers may not be discriminating purposefully against workers, others surely are. It is an especially useful tool for retaliating against worker-organizers, which is why the AFL-CIO reversed its position on the sanctions, as Mr. W mentions above (U.S. House of Representatives 2002). CSWA organizers had come to this conclusion before the sanctions had even passed, partially based on their longstanding view that undocumented immigrants are a crucial category for organizing.

Organizing undocumented immigrant workers highlights the contradictions of labor-immigration policy that, on the one hand, reinforce the separation between the documented and the undocumented (for example, by dividing along arbitrary lines of pre-amnesty and post-amnesty, and then newer arrivals without amnesty) and, on the other, produce discrimination that bosses direct at *both* groups (undocumented and documented) without distinction, thus grouping them into *one* identity. By refusing to separate the undocumented from the documented in their analyses of labor-immigration policies, CSWA organizers put forth new understandings of undocumented identity. The illegitimacy of undocumented identity is disrupted by the authorization of worker identity. The political passivity of undocumented identity is remade by the political challenge of organizer identity. Undocumented immigrant worker-organizers recreate undocumented identity, but also claim legitimacy and rights for all workers. CSWA organizers see undocumented worker-organizers in a pivotal position to expose the U.S. contradictory immigration and labor policy. Another parallel can be drawn with the way organizing reworks the identity of Chinatown itself as a place. Its identity as "site of organizing" contrasts strongly with its purported identity as a "site of worker passivity." It is partly the assumption of this latter identity that enables some to see Chinatown as a "blank slate" for their use. Many organizers say, when undocumented workers do come forward to take on a boss, they are the strongest organizers because they have overcome a greater sense of intimidation and greater actual risks.

Because of this, CSWA has developed specific strategies for organizing undocumented immigrants and is often successful at doing so. One strategy involves identification with other lead organizers who are or have been undocumented. Organizers are deliberate about addressing undocumented workers' fears and devise strategies that protect them even as they showcase their strength. In the following exchange, workers discuss the difference between fear and weakness:

Mr. D: If feels like we aren't that strong. Dealing with [the state] is risky.

Mr. A: What risks are you afraid of? What is a workers' movement without risks? How else do we gain strength?

Ms. X: But afraid doesn't mean weak. If you are afraid and it stops you from acting, then that's weakness. If you are afraid and you still act, then that's strength.

Because organizers know that undocumented immigrant workers can face additional threats and have fewer rights than permanent residents, they encourage undocumented workers to organize but emphasize strategies for protecting them when they speak out in public spaces of organizing, such as demonstrations or press conferences. In the case of the New Jersey restaurant workers, the restaurant bosses had openly threatened the workers who organized against them by publicly offering money in exchange for photographs of the workers, implying that they would then use the photographs to hire organized criminals to do them harm. In preparation for a demonstration in August of 2001, CSWA organizers Ms. B and Mr. E talked with Ellen, Stuart, and Robert, three of the workers, about wearing masks to protect their identities during a public demonstration at the restaurant:

Ms. B: What if you are photographed by the press [at the demonstration]? Would that bother you?

Ellen: I don't know. The bosses will use the pictures to blackmail us.

Mr. E: Do you want to wear masks to cover your faces? At pickets where workers have been afraid of the police or of bosses, they have worn masks and picketed anyway. If you wear a mask, it does not mean that you are weak. The masks show how threatening the bosses have been. In fact, we use the masks to show that workers *are* afraid of the bosses, but *are not* afraid to stand up against them. It is very powerful to show the risks involved and that you still demonstrate publicly anyway.

Ms. B: The masks can help protect you against being blacklisted.

The masks provided a legitimate alternative for the workers who feared violence or being blacklisting among the tightly knit network of bosses. They also underscored the de-individualized power of public demonstrations and protests. It was not the workers' individual identities that mattered, but the *collectivity* of workers and their willingness to stand together. In the end, although they considered it, none of the workers decided to wear masks at the demonstration. But by discussing the option, the workers were able to see the larger point of the demonstration could have been accomplished while protecting their identities, which settled some of their fears. It is not just undocumented workers that are ambivalent about speaking out. But, because they are perceived by many to have the most to lose, organizers say undocumented worker-organizers set a powerful example for all workers.

In line with Mr. W's comment that CSWA's analysis does not "divide the undocumented from the documented," they have developed strategies that contest the undocumented status of documented immigrants. These strategies can be described as creating documents for the undocumented based on relations of work. As Mr. C describes it:

> The undocumented *can* be documented, in fact, *are* documented through business records, time cards, etc. There is no such thing as "undocumented." We help the undocumented *build* their documents. For example, we tell them they can file and pay taxes. Then their tax return becomes a document.[22]

The strategy of establishing documents grew out of years of fighting bad bosses during which CSWA helped immigrant workers, both documented and undocumented, provide evidence of labor violations based on their own records of wages, hours, and so on. Bosses themselves have long used documentation to their advantage, often keeping two sets of documents, one an accurate record of wages and hours used for payment, and another a false record should they be investigated. Bosses also use documents as one way to play favorites and divide workers. In one Brooklyn restaurant, for instance, workers reported that bosses arbitrarily filed IRS W-2 forms for some waiters, waitresses, and busers, but not others, even though some in the group that did not receive W-2s were documented.

Because bosses who violate labor laws often pay workers in cash, workers' own records provide valuable evidence of unpaid wages or overtime violations that counter bosses' claims. State agencies investigating labor violations have not always accepted workers' own records as valid documents. But after CSWA had worked together with agencies like the New York State Attorney General and the state and federal Departments of Labor to bring claims against exploitative bosses, they began to more regularly accept workers' wage logs, time journals, and notes as legitimate records. In the case of Chinese immigrant workers, CSWA helps translate and organize subpoenaed or discovery documents from bosses in Chinese, as well as workers' own records in Chinese. Through this process, organizers have long been rejecting the identity of undocumented immigrants as illegitimate and without recorded documentation. After September 11, organizers used similar strategies of document building to help undocumented immigrants (as well as some documented immigrants and naturalized citizens)[23] apply for assistance from government agencies and charities. Where successful, this strategy of building documents contested the state's narrow definition of "documentation," and reflected the way the organization adapted its experience to a new and difficult situation.

Even with such strategies, community displacement remains a very real threat to Chinatown in an era of continued state insecurity. Immigrants have, however, mobilized on a national and urban scale in massive numbers during the second George W. Bush administration, reflecting a potential movement against a domestically oriented attack on immigrant rights. Current political debates around guestworker programs, amnesty policies, and civil liberties for immigrants, both documented and undocumented, as well as for citizens, suggest the centrality of immigration politics at the national and local levels. Immigrant organizers are all too aware of the relationships between the gentrification and displacement of urban neighborhoods such as Chinatown and the so-called global "War on Terror."[24]

> The government is using 9/11 to further displace poor neighborhoods, to rob the poor and help the rich. The war [in Afghanistan] isn't just over there. There is a war is going on *here*. It's not just about overseas resources. International policy is just an *extension* of domestic policy. [The government] is fragmenting issues to divert issues outward instead of bringing attention inside. ... The relief agencies are pumping money into neighborhoods *selectively*.

> **—Mr. T, CSWA organizer, June 15, 2002**

By drawing together these international and national policies of the state, immigrant organizers conceptualize the insecurity state's apparatus of spatial control. By organizing and developing counterstrategies, they hold out the possibility of contesting community displacement for Chinatown and for communities under threat elsewhere.

Acknowledgments

I offer my deepest gratitude to Michael Sorkin for all his labor and vision in assembling this edited collection, and for including this piece, which has benefited tremendously from his editorial insight and intellectual advice. Thank you to Amy Freeman, who read an earlier version of the chapter and whose sharp comments helped enormously. I extend my appreciation to Linta Varghese for fruitful discussions on immigrant organizing which contributed to this piece. Thanks to Junaid Rana, who recommended key citations. Sustained guidance and support from Ruthie Gilmore and Robert Lake enabled me to think through the arguments here in an earlier form. To all the pseudonymous organizers and workers who generously shared their analyses, intellectual theories, political strategies, and more, usually with humor, I am eternally grateful.

Notes

1. It is drawn from a larger research project on organizing campaigns and the production of identity in New York City's Chinatown (Liu n.d.; Liu 2003).
2. One primary coalition partner is the National Mobilization Against Sweat-Shops (NMASS), which was founded in 1997 by youth members of CSWA as a project within CSWA. Their aims were and are to organize and mobilize youth, to encompass multiracial and multiethnic membership beyond Chinatown, and to address working peoples' issues at the national level. NMASS eventually spun out of CSWA to form its own independent organization, currently based in downtown Brooklyn and the Lower East Side. Although the two groups are now organizationally distinct, they work together on multiple campaigns and projects, including the ones discussed here. Overall, this research focuses on CSWA as the organization working primarily in New York City's Chinatown, but much of their joint work includes NMASS's role in developing organizing strategy and the complementary relationship between the two organizations in campaign and other organizing work.
3. The primary research for this chapter is drawn from 18 months of intensive ethnographic fieldwork in 2001 and 2002 on community-based organizing campaigns in New York City's Chinatown, as well as background research that preceded the intensive period and follow-up research since. The majority of this research was participant observation. Although I became and remain deeply politically identified with both the political goals and analysis of CSWA and see this research project as an extension of that identification, I refrain from using first person plural pronouns such as "we," "us," or "our." This should not be taken as either a disavowal of that identification or an attempt to create a pure objective distance between myself and the organization. Instead I wish to acknowledge the over-25-year historical development of the organization's purpose, form, methodology, and analysis and the length of commitment of many of the organizers to the work.
4. All of the organizers' names in this chapter have been changed to keep their identities confidential. In the work of organizing, many Chinese organizers are referred to by title and surname. As with the English titles of Mr., Mrs., Miss, and Ms., forms of address in Chinese refer to men, married women, young or unmarried women, and women whose marital status is unknown. Because there are relatively few surnames in Chinese, rather than assign false surnames to workers, I use abbreviated letters. For organizers who go by first names, whether English or Chinese, I have assigned first name pseudonyms. For non-Chinese organizers (Latino/a, African American,

Caribbean, Polish, and white), I have used this system of following how they are referred to in the work of organizing (i.e., by title and surname, or by first name). All of their names have been changed as well.

5. Peter Kwong's work is a notable and important exception (Kwong 1997; Kwong 1987, 1996 ed.).

6. Numerous scholars have criticized the use of the term "minority" for people of color as it reinforces "whiteness" as normative and reifies implications of subordination. Ruth Wilson Gilmore offers "international majority" as an alternative (Gilmore forthcoming n.d.).

7. "Key money" refers to illegal fees added to rents by landlords.

8. Following rent deregulation in the mid- and late-1990s, many rent-stabilized units in New York City become eligible for rent decontrol when rent-stabilized tenants leave, provided the landlord elects to forego the tax abatements associated with stabilization. In rapidly gentrifying neighborhoods, increasing rents outpace these tax benefits.

9. These are organizational pseudonyms. Organization A is a well-established Chinatown business group active in local politics. Organization B is a large nonprofit in Chinatown that develops moderate-income housing, among other projects.

10. Disaster Unemployment Assistance was established in 1988 as part of the Robert T. Stafford Disaster Relief and Emergency Relief Act (the Stafford Act). Disaster Unemployment Assistance is intended for workers who become unemployed because of a declared disaster but are ineligible for Unemployment Insurance. Unlike Unemployment Insurance, which is funded by both state and federal monies, Disaster Unemployment Assistance is entirely federally financed.

11. Also called livery cabs, car services differ from taxicabs in that drivers do not pick up riders who hail them on the street. Riders call the dispatcher, who then sends the car to a particular site for pick up. Informally, car service drivers do sometimes pick up fares on the street, but they are not supposed to.

12. Following organizers, I use "boss" instead of "employer" for several reasons. "Boss" is the translation used by bilingual organizers because "boss-worker" relationships suggest a wider range of conditions than "employer-employee" and imply the full hierarchy of relations. For organizers, bosses can include multiple actors in positions of power at the top of the subcontracting pyramid, rather than just the immediate person who employs a worker. For example, in some ways, a powerful landlord who leases space to a manufacturer could be considered a type of boss to the workers in that factory.

13. In 2004, UNITE merged with HERE, the Hotel Employees and Restaurant Employees International Union, to form UNITE-HERE.

14. Like CSWA organizers, I use "documented" and "undocumented" to avoid the implication of criminality associated with "legal" and "illegal." Some immigrant advocates use "unauthorized" instead of "undocumented" for the same reason. By using "undocumented," I do not intend to reify the notion of "documentation" or to deny that state policies tacitly authorize the presence of these immigrants.

15. Even in service and community development oriented organizations, uneven access to services produces what Lake & Newman refer to as differential citizenship (Lake & Newman 2002).
16. In some high profile cases of smuggling, the INS has deported Chinese immigrants (Kwong 1997). Organizers say these are the exception, not the rule, and that there are other high profile cases where the USCIS/ICE/INS does not deport Chinese immigrants.
17. Immigrant visas are required to apply for what is known as "adjustment of status" or getting a green card. "Nonimmigrant" visas are intended for temporary visits.
18. In addition to highly skilled "EB-1 Priority Workers" including "aliens with extraordinary abilities," the USCIS designates three other categories of employment-based visas in decreasing order of skill level and stated preference. There is a fourth category, "EB-5," called "Employment Creation" which applies to investors who establish a new business, invest a minimum of $1 million in that business ($500,000 in certain areas of high unemployment), and employ a minimum of ten U.S. workers full-time.
19. These are organizational pseudonyms. Coalition A focuses on human rights issues for immigrants. Coalition B focuses on a broad range of immigration issues throughout New York City.
20. Renamed in 2004 the Government Accountability Office.
21. Lawmakers recognized the potential for increased discrimination due to employer sanctions, evidenced by the antidiscrimination provisions added by amendment to the IRCA to address discrimination caused by the sanctions. The antidiscrimination provisions created an Office of Special Counsel (OSC) to investigate and prosecute illegal immigration-related discrimination based on national origin and/or citizenship status. The OSC is an inadequate countermeasure, however, as it operates under budget constraints, has limited jurisdiction, and focuses on outreach and education over litigation (U.S. House of Representatives 2002).
22. In another example of the power of local Chinatown bosses, Ms. J reports, "Chinatown accountants won't file tax forms or help workers who have been paid in cash. The accountants don't want to offend the bosses. They don't care about small clients like workers."
23. After all, documented immigrants and citizens may also lack official documentation of income loss, residency, and so on. For many of them, this meant that they also were shut out from disaster relief.
24. The controversies surrounding the awarding of federal contracts to Halliburton, through its subsidiary Kellogg, Brown, and Root (now KBR), to "rebuild" military bases and infrastructure in Afghanistan, Iraq, and the U.S. Gulf Coast, post–Hurricane Katrina, demonstrate public uneasiness with these connections between local and international "redevelopment."

References

Abu-Lughod, Janet L., Ed. (1994). *From Urban Village to East Village: The Battle for New York's Lower East Side.* Oxford: Blackwell.

Burchell, Graham, Colin Gordon, & Peter Miller, Eds. (1991). *The Foucault Effect: Studies in Governmentality with Two Lectures by and an Interview with Michel Foucault.* Chicago: University of Chicago Press.

Chen, PeiYao. (2003). The "Isolation" of New York City Chinatown: A Geo-Historical Approach to a Chinese Community in the United States. Ph.D. dissertation, City University of New York.

Cole, David. (2003). *Enemy Aliens: Double Standards and Constitutional Freedoms in the War on Terrorism.* New York: New Press.

Davis, Mike. (1993). "Uprising and Repression in L.A.: An Interview with Mike Davis by the Covert Action Information Bulletin." In *Reading Rodney King: Reading Urban Uprising.* Robert Gooding-Williams, Ed. New York: Routledge, 142–154.

Fitch, Robert. (1993). *The Assassination of New York.* New York: Verso.

Gilmore, Ruth Wilson. (forthcoming n.d.). "In the Shadow of the Shadow State." In *The Revolution Will Not be Funded.* Andrea Lea Smith, Ed. Boston: South End Press.

Gilmore, Ruth Wilson. (2007). *Golden Gulag: Labor, Land, State, and Opposition in Globalizing California.* Berkeley: University of California Press.

Gilmore, Ruth Wilson. (1998). "Globalisation and U.S. Prison Growth: From Military Keynesianism to Post-Keynesian Militarism." *Race and Class* 40(2–3): 171–188.

Hagopian, Elaine C. (Ed.) (2004). *Civil Rights in Peril: The Targeting of Arabs and Muslims.* Chicago: Haymarket Books.

Kinkead, Gwen. (1992). *Chinatown: A Portrait of a Closed Society.* New York: Harper Collins.

Kim, Claire Jean. (2000). *Bitter Fruit: The Politics of Black-Korean Conflict in New York City.* New Haven: Yale University Press.

Kim, Claire Jean. (1999). "The Racial Triangulation of Asian Americans." *Politics and Society* 27(1): 105–138.

Kwong, Peter. (1997). *Forbidden Workers: Illegal Chinese Immigrants and American Labor.* New York: The New Press.

Kwong, Peter. (1987, 1996 ed.). *The New Chinatown.* New York: Hill and Wang.

Lake, Robert W. & Kathe Newman. (2002). "Differential Citizenship in the Shadow State." *GeoJournal,* 58 (2–3): 109–120.

Leonard, Karen Isaksen. (2003). *Muslims in the United States: The State of Research.* New York: Russell Sage Foundation.

Lin, Jan. (1998). *Reconstructing Chinatown: Ethnic Enclave, Global Change.* Minneapolis: University of Minnesota Press.

Liu, Laura Y. (n.d.). Sweatshop City. Book manuscript in preparation.

Liu, Laura Y. (2003). Placing Identity: Chinese Immigrant Workers and the Politics of Community Organizing in New York City. Ph.D. dissertation, Rutgers University.

Liu, Laura Y. (2000). "The Place of Immigration in Studies of Geography and Race." *Social and Cultural Geography* 1(2): 169–182.

Mele, Christopher. (2000). *Selling the Lower East Side: Culture, Real Estate and Resistance in New York City.* Minneapolis: University of Minnesota Press.

Mitchell, Timothy. (1991). "The Limits of the State: Beyond Statist Approaches and Their Critics." *American Political Science Review* 85(1): 77–96.

Mollenkopf, John Hull, & Manuel Castells, Eds. (1991). *Dual City: Restructuring New York.* New York: Russell Sage Foundation.

Nelson, Jim. (2003). "Hipification: How a Neighborhood Goes from Down and Out to Extremely Cool, Block by Block." *New York Times,* Oct. 6, 2002, Sec. 6, p. 114–118.

Nguyen, Tram. (2005). *We are All Suspects Now: Untold Stories from Immigrant Communities after 9/11.* Boston, MA: Beacon Press.

Russo, Francine. (2002). "Close-up on Chinatown." (New York) *Village Voice,* Nov. 6–12, p. 139.

Smith, Neil. (1984, 1990 ed.). *Uneven Development: Nature, Capital and the Production of Space.* Oxford: Basil Blackwell.

Smith, Neil. (1987a). "Gentrification and the Rent Gap." *Annals of the Association of American Geographers* 77: 462–465.

Smith, Neil. (1987b). "Of Yuppies and Housing: Gentrification, Social Restructuring, and the Urban Dream." *Environment and Planning D: Society and Space* 5(2): 151–172.

Smith, Neil, Betsy Duncan, & Laura Reid. (1994). "From Disinvestment to Reinvestment: Mapping the Urban 'Frontier' in the Lower East Side." In *From Urban Village to East Village: The Battle for New York's Lower East Side.* Janet L. Abu-Lughod, Ed. Oxford: Blackwell.

Tirman, John. (2004). *The Maze of Fear: Security and Migration after 9/11.* New York: New Press.

Tuan, Mia. (1998). *Forever Foreigners or Honorary Whites? The Asian Ethnic Experience Today.* New Brunswick, NJ: Rutgers University Press.

U.S. Department of Labor. (2001). "Disaster Unemployment Assistance Program; Request for Comments; Interim Final Rule." *Federal Register* 66 (November 13): 56960–56962.

U.S. House of Representatives. (2002). Subcommittee on Immigration and Claims, House Committee on the Judiciary. "Statement of Wade Henderson, Executive Director, Leadership Conference on Civil Rights." Oversight Hearing on the Office of Special Counsel, March 21.

U.S. General Accounting Office. (1990). "Immigration Reform: Employer Sanctions and the Question of Discrimination (Gao/Ggd-90-62)."

Wolch, Jennifer R. (1990). *The Shadow State: Government and Voluntary Sector in Transition.* New York: The Foundation Center.

Back to Zero

Mourning in America

MICHAEL SORKIN

Looking down on the still-unbuilt cavity of Ground Zero, you can see, on the massive excavation's concrete floor, several hundred fluorescent orange rubber traffic cones, arranged to outline the two footprints of the vanished World Trade Towers. The frailty of this commemoration is a monument both to the excruciating incompetence of those charged with recreating the site and to the tenacity and uncertainty of memory. More than five years after the attack, little has been built and final plans remain unclear.

Much of the delay can be accounted for via familiar routines of power struggle, greed, self-interest, bureaucracy, double-dealing, and corruption—the inevitable stew of big projects, especially those with so very many chefs gathered around the cauldron to flavor the broth. Whereas the major players at Ground Zero are a who's who of the usual suspects, the line-up has been so long, with many of the perps standing so far away that, viewed obliquely and at a distance, they're barely visible through the one-way glass of public disenfranchisement. The never-endingness of this reconstruction "process" parallels the progress of the "war on terror" itself: no fantasy of build-out requires less than a decade to realize and the clash of unpredictability and interest has conveyed the idea of recovery toward dramas of enactment in which the realization of physical architectures becomes symbolically secondary.

The Panglossian early scenarios for the invasion of Iraq were untroubled by contingency. A Manichean parsing of values into ours and the "evil-doers'" imagined that conflict would simply evaporate, leaving behind the straightforward tasks of reconstruction à la Marshall Plan. Heady lists of projects for renewed infrastructure—especially for the extraction of petroleum—were published and contracts signed, many of them no-bid crony deals with monster firms like Halliburton and Bechtel for whom disasters—from Iraq to Katrina—are the fortunate (wind)falls of engorgement. All of this was administered with cowboy swagger and freewheeling incompetence by the suzerains of the Coalition Provisional Authority. Nobody seemed aware that there might be resistance.

The parallels with Ground Zero are instructive and deep. From the start, the discourse of rebuilding has been remarkably constrained conceptually. Just as the Bush administration has viewed Iraq as a fallow field for neoliberal economic cultivation, ready to burst into free-market bloom, so the planners in New York have insistently identified "recovery" with the restoration of the site's economic capacity. Discussion of the architectural alignments of the vessels for this renewal and the debate over the fraught niceties of one scheme or another have become surrogates for participation—for democracy—magnets for the expression of public fear, anxiety, and desire designed to have no bearing on fundamental agendas.

As in Iraq, management is formulated for slippery accountability, to evade the risks of more direct democracy. The Lower Manhattan Development Corporation—like the owner of the site, the Port Authority of New York and New Jersey—is an appointive body empowered to circumvent normal planning processes, constraints, and reviews in the name of efficiency and can-do, undergirded by the idea that some things are simply too important to be exposed to disagreement. This is a style of paternalism whose own Great Father was Robert Moses, the father who always knew best. The superagency format was further invigorated by Nelson Rockefeller who, along with brother David, was the key operative behind the construction of the World Trade Center itself. Although Moses made epic, unmatched, contributions—for both good and ill—to New York's infrastructure, the Oedipal backlash to his domineering, Olympian, style and unequivocal paradigms was as powerful as it was unavoidable and thus polarity between the unanswerable and the unsatisfiable forms the dialectical armature of virtually all planning in New York to this day.

The proliferation of agencies operating in this gray area marks the institutional architecture of both the national insecurity state and of the planning bodies charged with the spatial implementation of its priorities. Power is enjoying its perfect Foucauldian moment, using our freshened fears to universally extend its panoptic gaze. The dramatic expansion of urban infrastructures of command and control, now so visible everywhere, depend on the successful promotion and almost universal acquiescence in their core formulation: security, the "value" that trumps all others. The ideological power and capacity of this idea are demonstrated by its expansiveness, its ready appearance in many registers, and its domination of both our national project and the projects of urban planning and architecture. This new condition concatenates ideas of home/land/security into a single, universal, comprising ambition, agency, and anxiety. The rebuilding of Ground Zero has been framed by constant recourse to three securities: security from terror, economic security, and—to a lesser but useful degree—environmental security. These have now become planning's triad of authority, fixing the terms of its project both in their internal relations and in their exclusion of competing values.

Ground Zero's sublime embodiment of this security agenda operates both as a driver of form and organization and as its main metonymy. Ground Zero has become the great national research lab in the search to give meaning not simply to the event of 9/11 but to the larger project of social reconstruction for a future in which new forms of insecurity—terror, hurricanes, alien labor, loss of traditional values, unsatisfying employment—predominate in the everyday life world. It represents both the symbol and practice of resolve but also describes the new limits on autonomy and optimism of America after terror. And, as a great theater for the formalization of grief, it has served to define our mourning, the way we're to work through the meaning of the event.

This stage is set by the literal apparatus of safety and protection, the tactics with which the reconstruction seeks to steel itself against any repetition of the 9/11 attack. The police department has intervened to relocate the "Freedom Tower" away from the street and to fortify its lower stories and there is an on-going debate about the effect of a suicide bomber in the confined chambers of the memorial. In early 2006, James Kallstrom, former FBI deputy director and Senior Advisor for Counterterrorism to Governor George Pataki, wrote a confidential letter warning that "the memorial complex possesses an elevated level of risk and target attractiveness, as a result of its international stature and large public assembly capacity." This expansive statement is remarkably chilling in its vagueness, in its reflexive identification of public assembly with risk of attack and its anxious precaution against it. It's also somewhat ironic in the context of recent Department of Homeland Security cutbacks in antiterror funds for New York on the basis of the claim that the city lacks significant "icons."

At one level, the implications for building of such concerns are simply elaborations of the regulatory effects of fire or seismic codes, part of an on-going history of safe construction that has always been architecture's ethical duty. To the degree that the tectonics of security are to be legible— in the massive blast-proof base of the Freedom Tower, in the elimination of tightly enclosed spaces in the memorial, in the frenetic deployment of beefed-up bollards, hi-tech ha-has and ubiquitous check-points—they will function as mnemonics, recalling the event that inspired them, agents of fear itself. Their visibility and clear association with a form of terror that we have already known will act to confirm the necessity of fear and will characterize its privileged source in the implacable acts of another to be treated with vigilant wariness. These outward fortifications will also serve to enlist us in the far larger system of unfreedoms, a surrender of convenience and rights that depends on the constant relegitimation of fear.

When finally rebuilt, Ground Zero will hold one of the planet's most intense concentrations of surveillance and policing technologies: hypervisibility—submission to continuous screening and profiling by the "authorities"—will be the condition of entry to the site. No cranny will be out of view of security cameras, no threshold without its magnetometers, biometric scanners, pass-card readers, radiation detectors, bomb sniffers, and baleful security agents on the lookout for revelatory tics and demeanors. All of these detection devices will be networked and linked to enormous databases that will constantly measure and update our identities, ranking our level of risk—code yellow, orange, red. Ground Zero will be an intensified, idealized, highly legitimated version of a more generally pervasive environment, the utopia—the Disneyland—of fear. It will provide the icon to fulfill and justify Kallstrom's prophecy.

Ground Zero's symbolic—iconic—authority rises from its power to evoke memories of dread and vulnerability and from its embodiment of a collective expression of grief. The task of its memorial is not simply to commemorate but to sort out the meaning of our loss, to define the values that inform the practices of our mourning. The dead at Ground Zero are no longer simply victims, they are the agents through whom victimization is translated into endeavor, via both local acts of commemoration and the national projects of warfare and policing. They ask what suffering demands—how to apportion revenge and restraint. The fierce fight over what meanings are to be inscribed at Ground Zero—in its forms and institutions—is intensely political precisely because it is a struggle to define not simply the event but what the event makes possible.

From the first, Ground Zero was understood to be "hallowed" ground and the form of its reconstruction invested with the weight of the sacramental. Because sacred meanings were to be made explicit, all interventions and readings of the site were also always iconographic, freighted with representation. The surplus of meanings produced by the millions of private responses to the event had to be communalized, expressed in a language that could be shared and public. This meant drawing from a lexicon capable of wide understanding and assent, invested with civic gravity and capable of supporting a transformative mourning that would not be arrested in eternal melancholia.

Sacrality immediately attached to objects that remained: a twisted remnant of façade, the battered Fritz Koenig sculpture that had stood in the Trade Center plaza, an accidental crucifix of girders, the exposed retaining wall. The horrifying vaporization of bodies gave these surviving remnants representative force, endowing them with deep historic consequence. This, in turn, authorized their reading through the lens of "preservation," the official discourse of commemorative sanction for elements of the constructed environment and the means by which historic importance is fixed to places and objects. But because so little actually remained and because recovery was so insistently identified with economic reconstruction, a structured discussion of the issue of how Ground Zero might be recognized by the National Register of Historic Places was not convened by the LMDC until early 2004, well after the site had been cleared. The LMDC took the position that the site's historic significance "clearly" did "not depend on the presence of the original, or even the damaged, buildings and structures that portrayed the horror of that day."

By setting up this opposition of the physical and the virtual, the LMDC only reinforced the terms of a conflict put into motion by the differing implications of the removal of the remains of that day, by the decision to reproduce the preexisting program, and by the survival—and conservation—of many physical elements (including fragmentary, untraceable, human remains) that had been removed from the site. To date, over 260 major formal depositories of material have been identified—including the famous Hangar 17 at JFK where many large fragments, including the carefully conserved façade fragment and the steel cross (recently removed from the site) are stored—as well as an estimated 100,000 "collections" in various hands. And there is the enormous landfill on Staten Island to which rubble was removed and thousands of tons of recycled steel, including that used to construct a soon-to-be-launched American warship, plowshares into sword.

This definition of an historic place in which any defining physical elements of its original form were almost completely lacking—and in which the presence of such remains was seen as an impediment to the restoration of the site to its highest and best use—put an enormous weight on what little was left after clearance, including the massive slurry walls as well as the stubs of the towers' supporting columns, largely sheared away to facilitate clearance of the site but now conserved with archaeological rigor, and the last above-ground remnant of the Trade Center—the so-called survivors stairway—which the LMDC has now decided to demolish. It also set up the roiling debate about what is to be returned to the site as part of its still largely undefined museum and about the relationship between location and meaning. There is, for example, a proposal to move a fragment of the slurry wall to a more advantageous location for viewing by museum visitors. This would strip the wall of the circumstances of its structural meaning: holding back the forces of the Hudson River, an active equipoise that was widely seen as conferring special powers of symbolism on it.

Although our civic culture no longer offers an uncontested expressive default for it ceremonial architectures, Ground Zero held an iconographic ready-made that immediately acquired sacred status: the "footprints" of the twin towers. The horrific yet miraculous collapse of the towers on themselves mapped the resting place of most of the three thousand dead onto two killing quadrants. The unrecoverability of the remains of so many victims, despite the narrow confines of their demise, gave the footprints both the blood soaked authority of a battleground and the weight of an incredibly legible abstraction, square stigmata. Any memorial was predestined to operate within the iconographic terms of the double squares but was forced to deal with the simultaneity of the indelible memory of the towers and the near invisibility of their traces.

As Ground Zero was cleared, the present-ness of the footprints largely evaporated and they entered the symbolic lists as at once uneffaceable and almost completely virtual. What remained was the so-called bathtub, the huge concrete-lined excavation ringed by slurry walls identified as part of the sacral iconography of the site. Their symbolic resonance was not just the product of the metaphor of resistance but also an obvious association with a long history of walls of remembrance, including the Wailing Wall in Jerusalem and, especially, the Vietnam Memorial in Washington, widely admired for its iconographic concision and its succinct expressive relation to an event still shrouded in interpretive ambiguity.

The Vietnam Memorial—whose designer, Maya Lin, played a prominent role in selecting the design of the 9/11 Memorial—uses two particular strategies that have become expressive defaults for contemporary iconography and informed much of the discussion of the inscription of memory at Ground Zero. The first is an idea about "pointing" or directionality, a way of establishing the specific, local authority of abstract figuration. The Vietnam wall takes the form of a flat "V" (Vietnam? Victory?), with its arms pointing to other monuments on the Mall—the Washington Monument and the Lincoln Memorial—tying it in to the larger system of national commemoration, not via the previous homology of neoclassical architecture but through a highly pared geometric and cartographic relationship. By pointing to commemorations of great leaders, the monument vitiates the problem of marking a controversial war—ending in American defeat—by associating the soldiers it remembers both with purer forms of heroism and by relationally civilizing its society—pointing to presidents, not generals.

The masterplan for Ground Zero by Daniel Libeskind was originally slathered with such pointers, radiating lines oriented to the fire and police stations from which rescuers had approached the site and to celestial angles meant to prompt—like Stonehenge or the Great Pyramid—ritual solar illumination on an annual cycle, although on a spot away from the footprints. This was the same strategy that had informed Libeskind's best-known architectural work—the Jewish Museum in Berlin—in which such lines—joining sites of important locations in the history of Jewish Berlin—purported to define the shape of the building itself. In both cases, these "memory traces" marked invisible forces and substituted for the presence of actual physical traces of the events commemorated, metaphor trumping materiality as a source of material meaning. Similarly, the shardlike geometries of his plan and its architectural constituents were unmistakable, if generic, evocations of fracture and fragmentation, at once the height of architectural fashion and signifiers of something vaguely violent, incitements never to forget (as viewed from Starbucks across the plaza).

A second major element of the Vietnam Memorial—a memorial tradition dating to the nineteenth century—was the carving of the names of each of the 57,000 American dead in its surface. For the Ground Zero Memorial, it went without saying that all who perished would be named and that this would be done within the geometric frame of the recollected footprints of the Twin Towers. But how to list the names? At the Vietnam Memorial, the names appear in the chronology of their deaths and the experience of descent and ascent in viewing them evokes the bloody course of the war itself. Military ranks are given but—unlike memorials for many previous wars—officers and enlisted personnel are listed together.

Clearly, a chronological listing is neither possible nor relevant at Ground Zero. In the initial proposal for the memorial, the names were to have been incised in carefully random order on low walls surrounding the sunken reflecting pools that are to occupy the sacred space of the footprints. The placement below ground at the level of the water would have both imparted a funereal dignity associated with subterranean spaces and removed the experience of viewing from the hurly-burly of passing traffic on the big adjacent roadway above. Random order surely resonates with the character of the event itself and avoids the irrelevant priorities of the alphabet.

But this proposal has aroused considerable controversy, amplified by both the intrinsic emotional meanings of the memorial and by the fact that this is the only part of Ground Zero over which the public has some immediate influence. Survivor organizations—who, via their moving and inexhaustible activism, have become the conscience of the site—have banded together in a "Take Back the Memorial" coalition and a variety of objections—including a strong animus on the part of many to the idea of subterranean spaces of commemoration—have been expressed as the final design is buffeted by value engineering, aesthetic differences, security dicta, shifts in context, and other jostling values.

Not the least of these concerns is the random disposition of the names which, many protest, will not simply strip victims of their identity as individuals but will needlessly complicate finding the name of a loved one. Many survivors continue to urge that names be identified by the towers in which, the floors on which, and companies for which they worked—as well as by their ages. Members of the uniformed city services have called for both separate commemoration and for the inclusion of individual rank and service. It currently appears that the names will be grouped by tower and that uniformed rescuers will be set apart and grouped by unit and that there will be latitude for grouping coworkers together. And, as the result a recent cost cutting move that also reflects security anxieties, name-bearing walls are now being raised to grade. Dissatisfaction remains rife among many survivors.

Whatever the final outcome, the idea of a differential grievability is highly problematic. This is not to insist that it is inappropriate to recognize the special heroism of the 9/11 rescuers—or the huge loss of a Trade Center tenant such as Cantor Fitzgerald, a company from which 658 died—rather to evoke the slippery slope of the idea of commemorability that is made specific by the listing of names. The Vietnam Memorial, of course, does not include the names of the hundreds of thousands of Vietnamese dead, nor those of American civilians—journalists, aid workers, contractors—who died. It is a *military* memorial, a tribute to those who gave their lives for the country in the battles of a particular war, formalized by a beginning and an end. We will surely construct a similar memorial to those killed in Afghanistan and Iraq. And, it is not likely that we will ever commemorate with memorials, obituaries, even published lists, the names of the tens of thousands of civilian dead in Afghanistan or Iraq, victims of our own retributive violence.

Alone among the war memorials on the mall, the Vietnam Memorial offers a comprehensive list of the dead, a component that is not a part of the subsequent memorials to World War II (done in pompous, recherché, neoclassical grandiosity) and the Korean War (which, with its mass of realist sculptures depicting troops slogging though the rain, offers a definitely post-Vietnam perspective). The collective listing of names in their terrible length at the Vietnam memorial is a mnemonic that forces us to remember a war we'd like to forget. It is a cautionary accounting that transforms the political and ethical ambiguity of this mass sacrifice into something more abstract. The architecture is funereal rather than heroic: its walls are somberly black and the whole is sunken into the earth. This descent into a symbolically delineated void to attend to a message whose gravity comes via an iterative accumulation of names is the same strategy of meaning that was to have organized the 9/11 memorial, a commemoration of disaster rather than of victory.

The arguments about how to organize this list of victims and over what data is appropriately identifying has a more frightening counterpart among the protocols of more literal policing. Compiling lists is a foundational practice of the national insecurity state. Whether individuals, groups, locations, phone numbers, Web addresses, or any other component of identity, the valenced list is the defining instrument of the panoptic police. A recent controversy over the legality of the provision—by EU member states—of lists of U.S.-bound air travelers to American security authorities is another reminder of a presumptive suspicion of everyone who comes here, of the ubiquity of the space of no privacy, and of the existence of numerous additional lists and algorithms to identify those who—by virtue of acts, origins, or associations—fall into some higher category of suspicion. The universality of profiling is accomplished only through the valuation of identity, and the politics of difference finds its dark side as marker of dangerous classes, inherently suspect.

The sudden enumeration of the presence of 11 million illegals in the United States—and the attendant discussion of "fool-proof" identification (now including mandatory DNA swabs)—seeks to make these targets visible by making it clear who they are. The modern national insecurity state is constantly confronted with a dramatic excess of information. Everything about us is visible but more and more incomprehensible in its "raw" form. The state builds its own unconscious via profiles and programs to mine the trillions of bits of information that pour in, searching for suspect features, keywords, repetitions, anything that can be induced to stand out—classifiable identities. In this sense, lists of the righteous, whether in the innocence of their victimhood or in the elective heroism of their deaths, sustain the validity to the act of classification, if only in establishing the magnitude of the score to be settled.

Names and numbers become more and more crucial: bureaucracies, including police organizations, rely on a culture of quantification in which lists loom large. The ethics of governmentality—which Foucault identifies as the modern medium of state sovereignty—are founded in the abstraction of numbers, in the statistical subject. Adolf Eichmann (the Nazis, aided by IBM, were pioneers of computer compilations and profiles) was all about train schedules, lists of deportees, arrivals and departures—a numerology of slaughter. Ironically, we remember the Holocaust in the names of its progenitors and the numbers of its victims, forced to acquiesce by sheer magnitude. But numbers are the medium of alienation, what makes us *numb,* the neutralized balance sheet in which the comparative weights of us and them are measured and adjusted, body counts. The relationship of naming and numbering is critical, sorting out those who are to be reduced to numbers (the Iraqi dead) and those who are to be named, whether as good or evil. This triple classification into those who are to be honored and protected, those who are to invested with malice and hunted down *for cause,* and those who—in Agamben's formulation—are reduced to a "bare life" beneath subjectivity and rendered collateral and disposable, is a functional requirement of the national insecurity state.

Ground Zero—the null site—is to be re-filled with numbers and lists: the enumerated names, the 1776-foot-tall Freedom Tower, the solar azimuth of the wedge of light, the 125 conserved column stubs, and other data intended to inscribe the site's symbolic mysteries. But there are other numbers that are, perhaps, of greater consequence and the synesthesia of these real, hard, numbers with the constant fluctuations of the symbolic or imaginary numbers of commemoration establish the numeracy of meaning that defines both place and event, a mathematics differentially equated. The prime number, the one number that would not budge—even as the casualty count and reconstruction costs rose and fell—was the 10 million square feet of "space" lost on 9/11, a number which irresistibly defined the parameters of reconstruction, Ground Zero's 10 million commandments.

Various pieties were attached to this figure which, despite some advocacy (including, briefly, that of outgoing Mayor Rudolph Giuliani and, more persistently, of many survivor groups) for the consecration of all of the site to memorialization, was never seriously challenged as the programmatic basis for reconstruction. The association of healing with economic recovery has been the mantra of the LMDC, an organization comprised almost entirely of business leaders and other toadies of big money. The insistent parallels between what was destroyed—the global symbol of "free trade" and the flow of revenues it conduced—and freedom itself have provided the twisted political and ethical underpinnings of the project of reconstruction at Ground Zero just as they did for the invasion, occupation, and reconstruction of Iraq. And questions of judgment and success are likewise numerical: boots on the ground, the price of a barrel of oil, bodies per day, and the rest of the estranging efforts to make the thing acceptably rational.

The practical and symbolic role of lease-holder Larry Silverstein in managing the numeric discourse of reconstruction was central. Silverstein has performed as a central casting embodiment of "bourgeois morality" and his oily piety and willingness to be out front in defense of property values made him an effective lightning rod for blasts from all sides, offering darkly comedic political cover for the other heavy hitters involved.

Silverstein immediately adopted the language of a sacred trust to argue his duty to reconstruct with quantitative exactitude exactly what had been there before—office space, shopping mall, hotel. The holy, inviolable, text was the lease agreement with the Port Authority, signed only weeks before 9/11 but tenaciously foregrounded by Silverstein not as the deal it was but as a civic obligation. The lease was presented as a compact virtually on a par with the Constitution, something that was not to be modified lest the fundamental basis of governance in the partnership of public and private interest be sundered by any loss-of-confidence scheme.

At his more extreme moments—including a lawsuit against his insurers that attempted to secure a double payout on the basis that the attack comprised two separate events—Silverstein's blinkered adamancy verged on the Shylockian and he became a shaman—Mammon on speed-dial—to test the commercial bearing capacity of the site. An unspoken, sub rosa, anxiety at Silverstein's unembarrassed advocacy was his unself-conscious embodiment of that particular grasping stereotype (he was called "greedy" by both the mayor and the *New York Times*) in a context in which so many of the major players—including Mayor Michael Bloomberg, master-planner Daniel Libeskind, Michael Arad, designer of the memorial, Santiago Calatrava, architect of the rail station, Alexander Garvin, head planner of the LMDC, and Frank Gehry, chosen to do the arts center—were themselves Jewish (not to mention men). The combination of stereotypes—Jews as monied, Jews as powerful, Jews as exemplary sufferers, Jews as artistic, Jews as cosmopolitan—moved in a context of a war that was increasingly defined by the national administration as a "crusade" against Islam and an attack for which its anti-Semitic perpetrators had identified the proximate cause as the existence of Israel.

The position of Jews as the faces of so many aspects of the redevelopment (including, it must be said, among the opposition) has helped both concretize the political meanings of Ground Zero and provide another list of names, one with its own iconographic import. The large Jewish presence in the work of reconstruction also stands in an inescapably dreadful relationship to the vilest canards to emerge from 9/11, the allegation that Israelis and Jews were given warning of the impending attack and were able to leave the buildings and the suggestion that the attack itself was the work of the Mossad. Although these claims are surely psychotic, they are nonetheless lodged at the outer reaches of a commutative system of abstracted signification that too freely attaches arbitrary meanings to forms and events, part of a strange and promiscuous collusion of control. It is also a continuation of national politics in which it's an open question as to the degree to which the imminence of the Apocalypse or the personal whisperings of

God are drivers of policy, the ultimate unquestionable authority and the guarantor of a securing nimbus of irrefutable irrationality that drifts over every decision.

After five years of maneuver and encryption, the numbers game is now being played in the clear, with the numbers that count—dollars—freely discussed. In 2006, as if liberated by the expiration of some formal statute, a new deal was cut between the Port Authority and Larry Silverstein in which the PA took over the Freedom Tower—widely bruited as an unleaseable white elephant that could only be made economic via massive leasing by public agencies (precisely the scenario that unfolded with the World Trade Center and has now become part of the Ground Zero deal, with city, state, and federal agencies agreeing to massive leases at unprecedented rates), with Silverstein retaining the rights over the other, more marketable, office towers (also to benefit from public subvention in the form of leases). The shift in control was itself the product of a shift in power on the site as the result of the frustrations of Mayor Bloomberg—a billionaire of vaunted fiscal acumen who vociferously alleged that Silverstein was out of his financial depth and lacked the wherewithal to complete the job—and of Governor Pataki who, nearing the end of his governorship and harboring ambitions to higher office, had increasingly identified his own legacy with the construction of the Freedom Tower.

At the same moment that the state (via the Port Authority) took over the Freedom Tower in this dubious deal, the budget for the Memorial (and the numerous supporting and ancillary elements it had accreted) passed the billion-dollar mark. Once again, the symbolic, memorial, aspect of the site had been called on to as metonymic camouflage for larger issues and another blue-ribbon committee has now proposed a series of strategies (including bringing the names up to grade) for reducing the price of the memorial by half, to a still staggering $500 million (for a work meant to find its profundity in abstract simplicity). The drama of the cost cutting accomplishes its purpose via its scale: the discourse of meaning is shifted from memory to price. The debate over the memorial, once sequestered behind the walls of art, has been commercialized, taken up in the larger rationales determining the future of the site. No longer does the ethos of "spare no expense"—still dominant in the conduct of the war itself—reign: it is now time to acknowledge practicalities.

From the first, this has been the most ethically fraught territory in the reconstruction as well as the scene of its most extravagant misdirection. It is also what makes the process so operationally exemplary. The current writ for municipal planning is that it must be a public–private partnership, which, in practice, has meant that public power and resources are to be directed to the creation of a congenial environment for the formation of private capital and profit. The public sector uses the power of condemnation to assemble a site (another twice-told tale, repeating the origin of the Trade Center itself), finances infrastructure, public space, and services, and offers an array of tax incentives, zoning bonuses, low interest financing, and other direct and indirect subsidies. The process is facilitated both by traditional public agencies but also by a variety of semi- and quasi-public institutions, like the Port Authority, the LMDC, Business Improvement Districts, and other dedicated structures that form the complex interface between capital and its public sector representatives. Although the Lower Manhattan BID was initially cut out of the action because its director was a Democrat, it was brought to the table by Mayor Bloomberg when he was able to name several new directors to the LMDC. More significant is the way in which public agencies that should have been influential—the City Planning Commission and the local Community Board—were simply cut out of the process.

Perhaps the most "successful" of these initiatives in New York has been the redevelopment of Times Square, a model for the deployment of the same package of policies and incentives at work at Ground Zero as well as crucial formal concretization of a visual ethos of place meant to make the area family and (big) business friendly. On the private side, a major driver (and beneficiary) of the deal has been the Disney Corporation (joined by other media giants including Bertelman, Reuters, Conde-Nast, and others) and Times Square has now acquired much of the feeling of a theme park with its spectacular blanket of advertising, its multinational chain stores, and its tepid cartoon-inspired musicals. Although the feeling at Ground Zero will be somewhat different, the architectural strategy is very much the same: the construction of very large corporate office towers with a carefully regulated patina of expressive iconography, the literal semiotics of giant signs at Times Square morphed into the solemn camouflage of recollection downtown, anchored by the memorial.

The energetic and effective BID that facilitated this transformation was directed by Gretchen Dkystra who went on, for thirteen months, to head the World Trade Center Memorial Foundation, a private, non-profit corporation established in 2003 to "own, construct, operate, and maintain a memorial." This meant both controlling the memorial's content and raising private money to partner the $200 million in public funds available for construction. In late May 2006, in the wake of the cost overrun debacle, Dykstra (one of the few women in positions of any leadership in the process) was obliged to take the fall and resigned her position, victim both of out-of-control costs and limited success in raising money. She was successful, however, in formalizing the logic that the memorial be built on the public–private model, that is, on the same model that was dictating the form and finance of the site as a whole. Indeed, the same model that has been operationalized in Iraq, a war in which the public (military) sector continuously provides the antecedent decimation for the reconstruction and privatized security opportunities offered to private corporations like Halliburton or Bechtel and shares military duties with an array of private security firms whose armed cadres number in the thousands.

Dykstra's removal was, like that of Larry Silverstein, a strategy of misdirection meant to suggest fiscal prudence while concealing collusive deals off center stage. One of the more egregious of these has been the "arrangement" worked out to induce Goldman Sachs to construct its new headquarters on a site across the street from Ground Zero, a move touted as critical to the revitalization of downtown. Like many corporations, Goldman Sachs—which has recently reported staggering, record, profits—had threatened to take its business elsewhere unless it received special treatment. In this case, the demands included not simply massive financial subsidy but the redesign of the memorial site itself to eliminate a proposed tunnel that would have suppressed the 10-lane boulevard that currently forms one edge of the memorial site, an extremely logical move for assuring the dignity and quiet of the place but one that Goldman Sachs felt would adversely impact the security and convenience of its own site near the opening of the tunnel.

After protracted negotiations—including a hugely successful histrionic walk away by Goldman Sachs—the authorities acceded to every demand, producing a package including $1.65 billion in low-interest, triple tax exempt "Liberty" Bonds—estimated as yielding a cool quarter billion dollar subsidy—additional tax breaks valued at $150 million, a $9 million reduction in rent for the site, and the elimination of the tunnel. It was, perhaps, no coincidence that at the time of these negotiations, the director of the LMDC was the venerable John Whitehead (who served from the agency's inception until earlier this year and who remains on the board of the Memorial Foundation). Whitehead was also the former Chairman of none other than Goldman Sachs and has been a longtime financial supporter of Governor Pataki, who appointed him to the post. Whitehead has been to Ground Zero what Dick Cheney has been to Iraq, masterfully incompetent at the nominal main agenda but smooth in assuring that the money— including the $2 billion in federal funds controlled by the LMDC—flows to the right people. The provision of interest-subsidized post-9/11 "Liberty Bonds" has included $650 million to the Durst Organization for the construction of the Bank of America Tower on 42nd Street and a smaller sum to the Barry Diller–controlled company that runs "Ticketron" for its Frank Gehry–designed headquarters on 18th Street.

Although the rebuilding of Ground Zero has been remarkable for the calculated reticence of both the municipal and national governments to intervene directly in the "process," the surrogacy of the interlocking directorate of private and quasi-private operatives who move with ease from sector to sector has assured that the mission is accomplished. This is the inevitable logic of three tiers of Republican control—president, governor (until January 2006), mayor—and the party's insistent disdain for the public sector (other than as a conduit for economic trickle-up), a self-fulfilling critique that has resulted in the fatal incompetencies of Iraq, New Orleans, and Lower Manhattan. The story of the difficulties in finding and assigning meaning at Ground Zero is precisely that of locating the seam between public and private, a seam that is not simply contested but deliberately obscured. The work of commemoration has, from the beginning, been the major instrument of this careful ambiguity.

The Libeskind masterplan was an especially useful hinge for maintaining the commercial character of the site because it simultaneously delivered a standard-issue deployment of quotidian corporate towers while slathering them and the site itself with a bathetic appliqué of coerced, univalent, meanings, an iconographic Disneyland of democracy walls, Statue-of-Liberty spires, heroes plazas, and other nominalist ready-mades intended to drape the aura of sacrality ubiquitously while having not the slightest impact on the central holy of holies, the 10 million square feet of office space that remained unchallenged by any of the chosen competitors in the LMDC sponsored competition. And Libeskind's remarkably treacly, near-parodic, self-presentation as innocent immigrant patriotic paragon only deepened the cover.

In the clash of sacred and profane values so successfully finessed in the Libeskind master plan, the potentialities of meaning on the site have devolved on mastery of the proprieties of aura: questions of how the site should mean have publicly overwhelmed questions of how the site should be. Although there have been many arguments over content and strong resistances to the course of reconstruction of the site, one of the most charged (if least heard) has been precisely over the return of business-as-usual in the form of business. The struggle over the site's representation has been so evocative because it is the expressive terrain of the subterranean psychology of the necessary passage through the stages of grief beyond the undefined but (contested) period of mourning to a new normal, the state of transformation that both resumes life and acknowledges permanent alteration. Mourning is the antidote to the permanent indefinite of melancholia, to the endless susceptibility so carefully infused into the Orwellian language of the war on terror, the war without end.

One steady theme of this auratic struggle has been criticism of the numerous individual vendors (perennial targets of BID clean-ups all over town) encamped around Ground Zero selling souvenirs, a complaint that has functioned as a useful stage in the managed succession of grief. Like the hawkers and pornographers of the old Times Square, these merchants—a motley collection of immigrants and minorities—have been deemed offensive to the tone of solemnity held apt to the place—vulgar, cheap. In many ways, though, their profusion and homely, sentimental, merchandise reflect the profusions that quickly followed the disaster itself, first the heart-breaking Xeroxes of the missing, later the tiny memorials that still cling to fences and buildings around the city. The souvenir sellers have been kept off the "actual" site by its surrounding fence while its aura is polished, sanctified, and strictured by an official interpretation and the space is readied for occupation by the more genteel commerce of big corporations and chain retailers.

The ongoing emptiness of the voided site has usefully potentiated the manipulation of its transformation. On the one hand, it has marked the nothing that has been done to fill it and served as a useful incitement to arrange and rearrange the circumstances of action, creating a measurement of failure with which to shift the rules and players in the game, to assure the right success. On the other hand, it has served as a vessel for the evaporation of memory. With every day that passes, the abstraction of emptiness has become the tragedy's most imageable residue, serving to lift the burden of particularity—and of pain—from what will eventually fill it. The task becomes more and more focused on the removal of the void (Ray Nagin was right to call it an unfilled hole in the ground), less and less on the specific significances of what its successor will evoke. We want to be rid of the awful emptiness and look for a strong man to fill the (w)hole. Like the war on terror, the facelessness of the problem authorizes any measure that will produce a result, any strategy for the creation of a tractable (and, in the case of the war, killable) identity.

In its secure authority, the figure of the footprints has played a central, almost metaphysical, part in this. The footprints cannot disappear. But, because they left virtually no trace in the cleared site, they need to be reconstructed in some fresh form. Reduced to an almost purely conceptual condition, it became necessary to instigate both their presence and their meaning in all axes. Many initially argued that they should be literally recreated, that the towers themselves should be rebuilt. Others made claims for the greater authority of the void and felt that their space should descend to bedrock and ascend to infinity, a vision movingly evoked by the "towers of light" that marked the first anniversary of the attack. But the infinitude of space above proved far more easily achieved than a grounding in the living rock below. A commuter train had run beneath one of the towers and its replacement, in its former alignment, would oblige any void above to stop at an artificial floor. And, as plans for reconstruction proceeded, greater and greater demands for logistical space quickly doomed the possibility of the sacral voids descending to the rock face.

The transit line is now up and running across the site and a temporary station has been built to serve the thousands of commuters who reach Lower Manhattan via Ground Zero. The trains—a Port Authority line to New Jersey and several lines of the New York City Subway—marked the return of the site to everyday use and their presence for over three years has acted as a ritual cleansing of the site's most horrific meanings, returning it to approachability by their repetitive passage. That they are "public" transportation and facilitators of public assembly has helped neutralize what might have been objectionable in more overtly commercial uses and the dialectic of the fenced-off commerce of the vulgar vendors at the periphery of the site and the restorative purposiveness of the trains has informed the schedule for the roll-out of Ground Zero's new meanings. At the train station's lowest level—far nearer to bedrock than most of the memorial will descend—is a single commercial facility, a commuter newsstand. It is a potent totem: the serried cover images of Britney Spears and the chilling ranks of Diet Cokes let us know that life as we're expected to know it can and will go on.

The meaning of 9/11 is being crafted to enable many meanings more: Ground Zero is the workshop where the agenda of a post-traumatic America is being tested for its limits and its public iconography fashioned under conditions of telling difficulty. These stresses are conduced by the implacable remains of the mass murder itself (fragments of bodies continue to be found), by the contesting coalitions of the variously willing and empowered participants in the process, and by the "if you can make it there" pressures of New York City and its notoriously liberal and disputative climate. The high dramas of the reconstruction have been about expression and the field of the right to it and the lurid insistence of Larry Silverstein on the right to control the form of "his" buildings is a parable of the meaning of speech akin to the sour saw about the press being free if you happen to own one. Money lubricates rights big time and the discourse of reconstruction returns again and again to the question of whose money will talk.

Hovering above this is the elastic figure of "freedom," what we are fighting for, what we are insisting on. At Ground Zero, freedom is highly fungible. One medium by which the site was to embody the message of free expression was the inclusion of a number of cultural institutions, facilities dedicated to the most freely licensed form of expression: art. It was argued that the presence of such a component would give the site a "mix" that had been lacking in the Trade Center and in downtown more generally, that such facilities would mitigate the grubby aura of the purely commercial, bridging the gap between that world and the memorial, and that the celebration of art's noninstrumental, pure, forms of self-expression would send a message to the wider world about the value we place on free forms of speech.

That particular message is unlikely to be received. The powers downtown have been tenacious in the preemption of expressions that resist reduction to party-line slogans or that exceed the tame vagaries of abstraction. Among the institutions now purged are the Drawing Center, a serious and respected gallery, and the proposed International Freedom Center. In both cases, the disqualifying affront was purely hypothetical, like Iraqi WMDs or Saddam's collusion with Osama. With scarcely a murmur of dissent, the two institutions were axed not for anything that could be named but on suspicion that they *might*—at some unspecified date in some unspecified form—display some work or act critical of the unitary "America" that 9/11 was meant to have produced. Preemptive censorship joined the Bushian repertoire of buggings, tappings, detentions, renditions, and assaults allegedly necessary to the preservation and propagation of freedom.

The one building reconstructed to date, Number Seven World Trade Center, a structure just north of the Trade Center site that also was destroyed on 9/11, is a succinct harbinger of things to come. Efficiently rebuilt by Silverstein—who had owned it before his lease deal with the Port Authority—it is a tall, sealed, minimalist tower, designed by the corporate architecture firm Skidmore, Owings, and Merrill, the author of the plans for the Freedom Tower that will rise across the street. Like it, Number Seven has a massive, blast-proof base (housing an electrical substation), veneered in reflective glass. Like it, too, Number Seven is taller than its predecessor, enabled by the fact that it occupies only a portion its earlier site, now reconfigured to allow the passage of a street that had been blocked and creating a small triangular park in the residual space.

The project includes two works of art. In the park is a Christmas-tree-ornament-red balloon dog by Jeff Koons. In the lobby—on a long wall behind the security desk—is an electronic "zipper" by Jenny Holzer and James Carpenter on which crawl giant quotations from "quality" writers–Walt Whitman, Frank O'Hara, Langston Hughes, Edna St. Vincent Millay—that evoke New York, another list of names. This is the current public art default, easily cleared by the Central Committee. There are (much easier to read) quotes about New York just down the street at Battery Park City. Koons balloons are just brand-name "plop-art," isomorphic with the standard-issue mirror glass tower opposite. Public space comes in its traditional forms—a vehicular street, a mini-park—and in its traditionally subservient relationship to private development, the tiny green plaza next to the giant office building. Art as usual.

Through this whole dreary story, architecture has been a constant. A feature of reporting on both 9/11 and the Iraq war has been the substantial absence of images of bodies, both of our own dead and of the enemy. (The corpse of Al Zarqawi, whose image we could not fail to produce, was scrupulously retouched for his close-up by military undertakers and we are spared the sight of both terrorists' and our own hangmen's beheadings.) The administration has tried to prevent the broadcast of the flag-draped coffins of our returning dead just as the media have largely air-brushed falling bodies from accounts of 9/11. What we see again and again is the collapse of buildings, an attack on architecture. These images become more and more ambiguous, too easily assimilated to the repertoire of demolishings that are a staple of the evening news and to Hollywood disaster films (Oliver Stone has already "rebuilt" the 9/11 rubble for his 9/11 film)—even the conspiracy theorists insist that buildings must have been sabotaged from within precisely because of the resemblance of their demise to a "controlled" demolition. This is surely much as al-Qa'eda prefers it too, the act stripped to the symbolic, a blow against the preeminent icons of global power, not the slaughter of thousands of men and women who had simply gone to work. If it was architecture that was attacked, it is architecture that must be repaired. And, if architecture was the site of eloquence in destruction and resurrection, then it is to architecture to which we must look for healing address.

The discourse of 9/11 has produced a deluge of architecture that has become the perfect form of neutered speech, a surrogate for meaningful plurality—branding. The culture has recognized the fundamentally performative character of architecture, the way it invariably plays a part not of its own creation, and seamlessly assimilated it to the star system. We admire the originality with which it performs its role—office building or cultural center—and are content with the shopworn formats—romantic comedy, cartoon adventure, hi-tech, decon, neo-trad—above which it seeks to rise. Ground Zero has become a vehicle for the designs of a group of architectural stars, the big names above the title, the same gambit that Hollywood plays to repackage its turkeys: Ground Zero as The Poseidon Adventure 4. How many starchitects can we get to show in the new multiplex?

The redemptive value of architectural celebrity is reinforced at Ground Zero with a light gloss of social responsibility via a pale tint of green. Larry Silverstein has advertised Seven World Trade Center as New York's "greenest" office building. The press release announcing Norman Foster's commission (by Silverstein) to design one of the site's towers describes him as a renowned "green architect." The original Libeskind proposal for the Freedom Tower included a shaft filled with miniature gardens and a subsequent version (done in the forced—and failed—collaboration with David Childs who now reigns solo and supreme) had a lattice-work top filled with windmills. The site's other notable forced marriage—between the memorial competition winner Michael Arad and landscape architect Peter Walker—modulated the hard austerity of the original scheme by surrounding it in a green grove.

This decorative environmentalism is put in sharp perspective by one of the more memorable images in Al Gore's film about global warming, "An Inconvenient Truth." A series of animations depicts the effects of the rising sea on cities around the world, including New York, where the deluge inundates Ground Zero, filling and overtopping the memorial voids. In the triad of securities that figure in the reconstruction—security from terror, economic security, and environmental security—that latter is clearly least consequential in its seriousness and effects. This green-ness is of a piece with Bush's proposal to encourage the production of ethanol from switch-grass, another little act of misdirection against the background of his real policy, to drill in the arctic, to secure Iraqi oil, to burn more coal, to reinvigorate the nuclear industry. The meaning of the new Ground Zero is not to be found in its minimal environmental innovations, which function like the single, all-redeeming, salad among the toxic offerings on the McDonald's menu.

Ground Zero will, rather, become a model for the architecture of the national insecurity state, a summary of the spatial and symbolic protocols of a global economic regime that increasingly draws its power and authority from the production and manipulation of fear, even as it endlessly proclaims its mission of freedom. Surrounded by hermetically sealed office towers (indistinguishable from their kith in Pudong, London, and Dubai), adjoined by abundant multinational shopping opportunities, permeated by omniscient and inescapable surveillance, and centered on a memory chamber to evoke the horror that makes the reconfiguration necessary and possible, Ground Zero will compactly express both what we are fighting against and what we're fighting for. It will be an object lesson in the new meaning of freedom, a place where expression is carefully curtailed, and where choice is distilled to fashion, to the spectacular pleasures of high-style architecture and shopping in the big designer mall. It also will let us know that thousands died to make this possible.

The New Emotions of Home
Fear, Insecurity, and Paranoia

SETHA M. LOW

Introduction

Home is defined as a haven in the turbulent seas of urban life (Appleyard 1970). It embodies the familiar, a place where residents are comfortable and feel at ease. Home anchors place identity by providing a locale perceived as "ours" that acts as a symbol of self (Marcus 1976; Marcus 1997). Thus, a home is not simply a place to live, but encompasses a wide variety of personal concerns such as aspirations, motivations, and values, as well as physical well-being and lifestyle choices (Hayward 1975; Feldman 1990). The emotions associated with this concept of home are predominantly positive including feelings of love, warmth, trust, and understanding combined with comfort, relaxation, and security. Home, however, is also a defended place, even a fortified castle, where residents retreat from the outside world (Ladd 1977, Fried 2000).

Thus, there are two ways in which home is emotionally rewarded and rewarding. The first is "proactive," and includes the associations of love, warmth, trust, comfort, and relaxation. The second is "reactive," associated with defensive feelings and a desire to be protected from perceived and imagined dangers. Proactive aspects are generally positive; reactive aspects also may be positive—such as security and safety—but they also remind residents of their vulnerability. A useful metaphor is a fort or castle where the interior living quarters represent safety and protection—the proactive aspects of home, whereas reactive aspects are symbolized by the high wall, the drawbridge gate, and the moat, militaristic elements built to defend the life within.

Historically, the meaning of home changes during the seventeenth and eighteenth centuries when it begins to be associated with personal and domestic circumstances rather than one's native village or birthplace. With the urbanization of northwestern Europe, the home is separated from the workplace and becomes a stronghold of family living for the upper and middle classes, whereas poorer families and lower-class women continue to labor where they live (Janeway 1971). During the eighteenth century, the house, as the architectural representation of home, emerges based on increasing middle-class wealth, and the demand for more informality and comfort by the ruling class (Holt 1966). For Walter Benjamin (1982), it becomes an interior private space of collected objects without use-value, reaffirming the fantasy of an all-consuming, modern life. Not until the late nineteenth and early twentieth centuries does home life take on the mystique of a sacred space overseen by women who protect family morality from the dangerous public realm of the street (Hayden 2002; Hayden, 2002; Wright 1981). Many of the proactive meanings of home such as "the heart and hearth of moral guidance," nurturing, emotional support, and home cooking derive from myths and idealized memories that obscure working women's hardships and the ennui of middle class women trapped in isolated living situations. Throughout this epoch, home encompasses associations and feelings dependent on an individual's experience, physical location, and social mobility.

Now, in the late twentieth and early twenty-first century, the proactive and idealized emotions of home are being encroached on by increased globalization, economic restructuring, and political instability that characterize the postindustrial, post-Cold War, and post-9/11 period. Rapid transformations in social, economic and political conditions are producing new structures of feeling and disrupting local environments in ways that influence people's experience of home (Williams 1977; Low & Smith 2005). The Bush regime's war on Iraq, terrorism, and stepped-up media reporting of violence and natural disasters have created a national ethos of paranoia and culture of fear embodied by institutions such as the Homeland Security Administration (Glassner 1999; White 2005[1]). Locally, increasing socioeconomic inequality, cultural diversity, racism, downward mobility, and social exclusion reinforce the sense something is wrong and that the moorings of the middle class are shifting, reinforcing the salience of reactive feelings and defensive strategies reflected in the everyday discourse of residents (Young 1999; Newman 1993; Low 2003). The feelings of insecurity, fear, paranoia, worry, and status anxiety contradict and overwhelm proactive aspects of home as a friendly place where a resident feels safe and comfortable. For example, gated community residents say that they are looking for the "kind of neighborhood where they grew up, where they knew everyone" as a gloss for a homogeneous, White, safe housing development, but find they rarely know their neighbors and are plagued by anxiety based on worry about crime and intruders. And even four years after 9/11, a citywide survey reported that 67 percent of New Yorkers were personally concerned about another terrorist attack in New York City, and 52 percent would not work in anything constructed on the higher floors of the World Trade Center site (*New York Times* 2005: 34). These feelings of fear and anxiety are exacerbated when people discuss their concerns of becoming victims, whereas television continues to play an unhealthy role in raising negative emotions in public life (West & Orr 2005; Ackerman & Fishkin 2005).

These fears and insecurities are reinforced, and ultimately exploited, by a variety of commercial and political interests. The security industry has expanded exponentially and advertisements for everything from safe rooms and nanny-cams to gated communities with roaming armed guards are commonplace (Katz 2005). Local governments recommend more policing, but also real-time video surveillance and face recognition technology. Politicians—at both the national and local level—manipulate this increased sense of fear and foreboding to gain support for previously unpopular civil rights intrusions giving government agents the ability to detain 'suspicious' people and encouraging racial profiling by police and immigration agents (Sorkin & Zukin 2002).

This chapter explores the increasing salience of these social and political messages on the emotions of home. Empirical evidence of insecurity, fearfulness, worry, and anxiety as dominant themes in resident interviews is drawn from two ethnographic studies of vulnerable residential populations: The first, a 10-year comparative study of gated community residents in the United States and Mexico, and the second, a longitudinal study of the emotional reactions of Battery Park City residents in downtown New York City, 10 months and 22 months after the 9/11 terrorist attack on the World Trade Center. Examples are drawn from the two ethnographic studies focusing on how residents talk about their neighborhood concerns, choosing to live in a gated community, or struggling to continue to live in Battery Park City after 9/11. The conclusion explores the commonalities in the two studies: fear of others (gated communities) or newcomers (Battery Park City), disruption of a previous home (gated communities) or current home (Battery Park City), and an emotional shift in the previous neighborhood (gated communities) or current neighborhood (Battery Park City).

The Ethnographic Study of Gated Communities

Across the United States lower-middle- , middle- , and upper-middle-class gated communities are creating new forms of exclusion and residential segregation, exacerbating social cleavages that already exist (Blakely & Synder 1997; Low 2003). Although historically secured and gated communities were built in the United States to protect family estates and to contain the leisure world of retirees, these urban and suburban developments now target a much broader market, including families with children. Based on 10 years of ethnographic research in seven gated communities in New York, Texas, and Mexico, I found that people move for safety, security, "niceness," and community—they talk about a fear of crime and other people, and echo a deep-seated sense of insecurity about the world and their everyday life.

Background

Definition of a Gated Community

A gated community is a residential development surrounded by walls, fences, or earth banks covered with bushes and shrubs, with a secured entrance. In some cases, protection is provided by inaccessible land such as a nature reserve and in a few cases, by a guarded bridge (Frantz 2000–2001). The houses, streets, sidewalks, and other amenities are physically enclosed by these barriers and entrance gates operated by a guard, key or electronic identity card. Inside the development, there is often a neighborhood watch organization or professional security personnel who patrol on foot and by automobile.

The number of people estimated to be living in gated communities in the United States has rapidly increased from four million in 1995, to eight million in 1997. By 1997, there were in excess of 20,000 gated communities with over three million housing units. Two new questions on gating and controlled access were added to the 2001 American Housing Survey, establishing that 16 million, or 6 percent of all households, currently live in gated, walled housing areas (Sanchez & Lang 2002).

A more detailed analysis of this survey in 2005 found that renters are nearly 2.5 times more likely to live in walled or fenced communities and over 3 times more likely to have controlled entries than homeowners. In fact, based on a recent demographic analysis two distinct gated resident profiles emerge: (1) White, affluent, older owners with slightly larger households and living in the suburbs, and (2) low- to middle-income renters with smaller households and lower incomes. Hispanics (both renters and owners) are more likely to live in gated communities than Whites or Blacks, whereas Black homeowners are the least likely group to live in either (owned or rented) type of gated communities, with an exceptionally low number of Black homeowners (1.6 percent) reporting living with walls and gates or a secured entrance (Sanchez & Lang 2005).

Methods

The research began with gaining entry into upper-middle- and middle-income gated subdivisions in 1994 and 1995: one in Nassau County on Long Island, and three in the northern suburbs of San Antonio, Texas. Additional gated communities were added: an upper-middle- to middle-income community in Mexico City in 1998, and a middle-income and middle- to lower-middle-income community in the New York City area in 2000 and 2005, to answer questions about class and cultural differences that arose later in the project.[2]

Utilizing family contacts and interested real estate agents to gain entry to these communities, we[3] employ a "snowballing" sampling technique using each interview respondent to lead to the next. In some cases a key informant referred others who might be willing to speak to us. It has been a slow and difficult process to recruit interviewees: a total of 50 households were interviewed over the first eight years, and another four more recently.

The two hour open-ended interview is organized around a semistructured residential history conducted in the home with the wife or single woman, husband, or husband and wife together. The majority of the interviewees are European Americans and native-born; however, four interviews to date were conducted in households in which one spouse was from Latin America, West Africa, Asia, or the Middle East. Interviewees are 18 through 75; men are mostly professionals such as doctors, lawyers, and teachers; working in industry as businessmen, managers, and foremen; or retired from these same pursuits. A majority of the women are stay-at-home mothers and wives or work part time nearby, while the husband commutes to work in the city. Of the three single, widowed or divorced women in the sample, however, two worked full time and one was retired from full-time employment.

Participant observation is ongoing in the gated communities, and in the shopping, transportation, and recreational areas near each development. The analysis of participant observation field notes focuses on identifying empirical evidence of changes in the local environment. Furthermore, it produces data on naturally occurring conversations and everyday observations that provide a test of ecological validity for the interviews. Field notes and interviews are coded by emerging themes throughout the research process. A thematic content analysis of the interviews and documents collected from the media, marketing, and sales materials provide the documentation of the range of discourse available.

Ethnographic Examples

In the following sections, I have selected examples of residents who talk about their reasons for moving to a gated community. I focus on both the characterization of the fear, insecurity, and anxiety, as well as on the rhetorical strategies used to explain these reactive feelings. By presenting these ethnographic vignettes the intensity of their reactive emotions and discursive practices surrounding their homes emerges clearly.

Fear of Crime

Most gated community residents say that they are moving because of their fear of crime, but what residents are expressing is a pervading sense of insecurity with life in the United States. Policing, video surveillance, gating, walls and guards do not work because they do not address the basis of what is an emotional reaction. An ever-growing proportion of people fear that they will be victimized. Not surprisingly, then, fear of crime has increased since the mid-1960s, even though there has been a decline in all violent crime since 1990 (Brennan & Zelinka 1997; Stone 1996; Flusty 1997).

It is not an entirely new sense of insecurity, but comes from the increasing globalization, declining economic conditions, and insecurity of capitalism that have plagued the United States from its beginning. 9/11 and Homeland Security have exacerbated it. What is new is evidence that gating does not solve residents' safety preoccupations.

For example, Cynthia was concerned about staying in her old neighborhood:

Cynthia: And then I have a lot of friends who live in [my old] neighborhood in Queens, and there's been more than forty-eight robberies there in the last year and a half. And I said to myself those are homes with security and dogs and this and that ...

Setha: And are they gated?

Cynthia: No, they're not gated. They had alarms, and they were getting robbed because they were cutting the alarms, the phone wires outside. So I'm saying to myself, all this is in my mind, and I'm saying ... I can get robbed. That's why I moved ...

Cynthia goes on to explain that she needed something more secure, but she seems unsure of the Manor House guards and still feels afraid at night:

Cynthia: ... during the day it's great with James [the guard] who you've met. But at night, it's like anything else [she worries]. I feel ok because if I had a problem I could call the guard house. I remember the first night I stayed here by myself. I said if something goes wrong, who am I going to call? I don't know what to do.

Fear of Others

Compared to most large cities, suburbs do not have many public places were strangers intermingle, and the relative isolation and homogeneity of the suburbs discourages interaction with people who are identified as the "other." M. P. Baumgartner's study of an upper middle class suburban town outside of New York City illustrates how this social isolation is transformed into moral expectation, and becomes a yardstick by which residents measure the social order and safety of their neighborhood. Those who disturb the town's "protected world offend its inhabitants by doing so" (Baumgartner 1988: 103).

Baumgartner (1988) documents how local residents in this town are upset by outsiders appearing on residential streets. Strangers by virtue of their race or unconventionality are singled out as "suspicious" even if merely walking down the street. The physical organization of the street pattern—cul-de-sacs and dead end streets—enables residents to monitor their neighborhoods and to spot outsiders who linger. Residents explain their behavior by citing their "fear of crime," by which they mean "predatory behavior by strangers." They voice concerns about poor Blacks and Hispanics entering their town and preying upon residents. Despite the low rate of crime in the area, residents are overly concerned about people who seem out of place.

Fear of crime as a rhetorical strategy thus translates into fear of poor people, the supposed perpetrators of the crime. For example, Felicia relates her fear of crime and poor people who live outside the gates very clearly:

Felicia: When I leave the area entirely and go downtown [little laugh], I feel quite threatened, just being out in normal urban areas, unrestricted urban areas. ... Please let me explain. The north central part of this city, by and large, is middle-class to upper middle-class. Period. There are very few pockets of poverty. Very few. And therefore if you go to any store, you will look around and most of the clientele will be middle-class as you are yourself. So you are somewhat insulated. But if you go downtown, which is much more mixed, where everybody goes, I feel much more threatened.

Setha: Okay.

Felicia: My daughter feels very threatened when she sees poor people.

Setha: How do you explain that?

Felicia: She hasn't had enough exposure. We were driving next to a truck with some day laborers and equipment in the back, and we were parked beside them at the light. She wanted to move because she was afraid those people were going to come and get her. They looked scary to her. I explained that they were workmen, they're the 'backbone of our country,' they're coming from work, you know, but ...

Another aspect of fear of others is how the characterization of the other is used by residents to explain why gates are an important addition to protect their home. Karen is worried about the porous boundaries of her gated community, and we talk about her concern about the workers in her neighborhood in the following exchange:

Setha: One thing you did say is that the undocumented workers concern you. Or is it that they are construction workers, or undocumented workers in general?

Karen: It's like they can slip in and slip out. Where there's no record of these guys at all. They're here today and gone tomorrow.

Setha: I was trying to get a sense about who the people are?

Karen looks at me puzzled: Mean like now? If you asked me tomorrow if I was going to move, it would be only to a gated community.

When I probed about who the workers are, she switches the conversation to her reasons for moving to the gated community. Such a digression indicates an intentional shift away from a sensitive or socially inappropriate topic. Following her lead, I ask her for clarification, and she returns to the discourse of the fear of crime.

Setha: To a gated community? Why?

Karen: I think that the security is most important; I really like knowing who's coming and going. I like knowing I'm not going to come home and find my house burglarized. Once you've been violated like that, it's really hard, I think, to continue living without one [a gate].

Racism

Gating also involves the "racialization" of space, in which the representation and definition of "other" is based on racial categories. In the past, overt racial categorization provided the ideological context for restrictive immigration laws and discriminatory deed restrictions and mortgage redlining programs. More recently, phenotypical characteristics are used to justify social prejudice and unfounded fears (Ngin 1993). Racist fears about the "threat" of a visible minority, whether it is Blacks, Latinos, Asians, or Koreans, are remarkably similar. This is because many neighborhoods in the United States are racially homogeneous, thus, the physical space of the neighborhood and its racial composition become synonymous. This racialized spatial ordering and the identification of a space with a group of people is a fundamental aspect of how suburban landscapes reinforce racial prejudice and discrimination. Helen highlights how race still plays a dominant role in eliciting fear in one's home life. She illustrates her point by telling me what happened to a friend who lives "in a lovely community" near Washington, DC:

Helen: She said this fellow came to the door, and she was very intimidated because she was White, and he was Black, and you didn't get many Blacks in her neighborhood. She only bought it [what he was selling] just to hurry and quick get him away from the door, because she was scared as hell. That's terrible to be put in that situation. I like the idea of having security.

Helen feels that there is less crime in gated developments than in San Antonio in general. She knows people living in equally nice, nongated neighborhoods who have had their homes broken into and who have been assaulted with weapons. The worst that has happened in her development is a few cars have come through and "messed things up." She thinks that it was probably kids. Only a few families have been robbed or burglarized. Helen and Ralph put on their burglar alarm every time they leave, although she thinks they may be overly cautious:

Setha: Are you concerned about crime in Sun Meadow?
Helen: No, not here, but in San Antonio.
Setha: What do you mean?
Helen: There are gangs. People are overworked, they have families, they are underpaid, the stress is out of control, and they abuse their children. The children go out because they don't like their home life. There's too much violence everywhere. It starts in the city, but then the kids get smart enough and say 'oh, gee, I need money for x, y or z, but it's really hot in the city, let's go out and get it some place else.' We're the natural target for it. So being in a secure area, I don't have to worry as much as another neighborhood that doesn't have security.

Fear of Kidnapping

All children have fears, but in the United States, younger children are experiencing more fear about being harmed by other people than ever before. Living behind gates reinforces the perception that people who live outside are dangerous or bad. Dualistic thinking is a form of social splitting used to cope with anxiety and fear. It fuses cultural definitions and social expectations that differentiate the self from the other. It is a means of dealing with contradictory and often conflicting feelings through projection from the self (Klein 1975; Silver 2002). For example, Donna's concerns focus on her child:

Donna: You know, he's always so scared. … It has made a world of difference in him since we've been out here.

Setha: Really?

Donna: A world of difference. And it is that sense of security that they don't think people are roaming the neighborhoods and the streets and that there's people out there that can hurt him.

Setha: Ah … that's incredible.

Donna: … That's what's been most important to my husband, to get the children out here where they can feel safe, and we feel safe if they could go out in the streets and not worry that someone is going to grab them … we feel so secure and maybe that's wrong too.

Setha: In what sense?

Donna: You know, we've got workers out here, and we still think "oh, they're safe out here." …In the other neighborhood I never let him get out of my sight for a minute. Of course they were a little bit younger too, but I just, would never, you know, think of letting them go to the next street over. It would have scared me to death, because you didn't know. There was so much traffic coming in and out, you never knew who was cruising the street and how fast they can grab a child. And I don't feel that way in our area at all … ever.

Status Anxiety

Residents moving to gated communities do not only talk about their insecurity and fear, but also are interested in finding a "nice" house in a "nice" community. Niceness is a way to talk about wanting to live in a neighborhood with people who have similar values and concerns, and keep their houses and gardens in a particular way. It reflects the micro-politics of class exclusion and is about distinguishing oneself from the family who used to live next door. Status anxiety about downward mobility as a result of declining male wages and family incomes, shrinking job markets, and periodic economic recessions increases their concern that their own children will not be able to sustain a middle class lifestyle (Newman 1993; Ortner 1998). Middle-class status anxiety also takes the form of symbolic separation from other families who have fallen on hard times, families who share many of the same values and aspirations, but who for some reason "did not make it."

Ted and Carol try to explain:

Ted: Our [previous neighborhood] was very, very educated. ... You know so everyone goes on to college, and it stressed the role of family, and you know, it's just a wonderful community. But it's changing, it's undergoing internal transformations.

Carol: It's ethnic changes.

Ted repeats: It's ethnic changes, that's a very good way of putting it.

Carol (nods her head): In the last, probably, seven to eight years.

Setha: What about your prior residence in Brooklyn?

Ted shrugs his shoulders and finally Carol answers. She tells me they had moved from Brooklyn to bring up their children in a better environment. The school system was changing, and they did not want their children to go to school with children from lower socioeconomic backgrounds who were being bused into their Brooklyn neighborhood.

Carol: Those kids were wild and had a different upbringing. We wanted to protect our children from exposure to those kinds of problems.

Paranoia and Its Symbolic Substitutes

Barry Glassner (1999) argues that news reporting capitalizes on our greatest fears proposing that it is easier to worry about "Mexicans" or "workers"—that is, focusing on symbolic substitutes—rather than face our moral insecurities and more systematic social problems. The bombing of the World Trade Center on September 11, 2001, adds to New York residents' concerns. Linda, a single mother who is now living in a house her mother bought in Pine Hills, Long Island expresses them well.

Linda: My mother had moved to Pine Hills because she wanted to be in a setting where there would be neighbors close by, and to have the safety of the gate. [She laughs] The security of the gate. Five dollars an hour, when they're asleep. I don't know how much security the gate is worth. Some of the guards just let you fly right in. The others have to strip search you. It really depends. I guess that has been my experience with coming in. Some of them are OK, others want your finger prints.

… A couple of years before that we had something [happen]. There were helicopters flying over. … I don't remember specifically when, but some inmate, they were looking for someone who had escaped who had a murder record. That was quite freaky. You would look out in the back yard and there would be woods out there, and you'd wonder who is out there.

Because, you know … people can come in here on foot. There's a golf course right behind us, and anyone could be wandering around on there, and decide to traipse through here. Honestly I don't know how useful the gate is.

Linda tells the following story to illustrate her point.

Linda: One time, one of my neighbor's boys, the little one was missing. And this woman, I mean, she was white as a sheet, and she was really going to have a nervous breakdown. And we couldn't find him. He was actually in another neighbor's house with his friend, playing. I had called that house to find out, not realizing they were away, and there was a workman in the house. And these boys didn't know the workman. The workman just walked in there, went into the kid's room and started working. So she wasn't at ease [because it was so easy for the workman to walk in without any adults being home, and that her boy was there with a strange workman]. You know, we are not living in very secure times now [post 9/11].

Setha: What do you mean?

Linda: This is my theory, Long Island is very prestige minded. And I think the very fact of having a guard at the gate is akin to living in Manhattan in a doorman building versus a three flight walk-up type of thing. There's a certain 'pass through the gate' type of thing, this is a private community. That actually, sadly enough, may be part of it. You know, other than the safety issue, just a kind of separating our selves from the great unwashed, shall we say.

And I think with the gate thing, there is an increasing sense of insecurity all over the place. I think people are beginning to realize they are not really safe anywhere, in middle America. We have had so much violence occurring. … That could be part of it.

Whether it is Mexicans, Black salesmen, workers, or "ethnic changes," the message is the same: residents are using walls, gates, and guards to keep perceived dangers outside of their homes and neighborhoods. Contact and neighborhood change incite fear and concern, and in response they are moving to secured residential developments where they can keep other people out. The perceived threats of crime, other people, downward mobility, a changing neighborhood, and terrorism engender a defensive emotional climate within which residents attempt to create safe and comfortable homes. But the reactive emotions of home—fear, insecurity, worry, paranoia and anxiety—dominate their conversations.

The discourse of fear and anxiety of Battery Park City residents after 9/11 is different from that of gated community residents in that it is focused on the possibility of another attack and the aftermath of living in a memorial of death and destruction. Nonetheless, some of the same reactive emotions of home appear, especially fear, anxiety, and worry, and a discourse about the negative aspects of others: in this case, young newcomers who came for cheap rents and might ruin the sense of community. The findings suggest that a potential disaster or attack also promotes reactive emotions that are supported by the media and the ongoing deterioration and disruption of a residential area.

Battery Park City Residents Post-9/11

Background

On September 11, 2001, the day of the World Trade Center terrorist attack, 6,000 of the local neighborhood residents fled for their lives, and eight residents of Battery Park City died (Bernhard, 2002). Residents of Battery Park City,[4] a planned community built along the Hudson River next to the World Trade Center, had to leave their apartments for at least a week. During the initial weeks, marital law was enforced; residents were not allowed to enter their homes or neighborhood without being accompanied by security personnel. Some residents returned to the area and weathered the difficulties of living in a disaster zone. Others suffered such trauma that they could not return.

The part of Battery Park City closest to the trade center sustained considerable damage, especially the World Financial Center and residential buildings at Gateway Plaza. September 11th was a beautiful day, and many residents had left their windows open. They returned days or weeks later to find a thick layer of dust on everything. One woman describes her experience of returning:

I work at home, and my windows face where the World Trade Center was. I was there; I heard the planes and saw it all. I think about it every day—how all those people died. I can function all right—I work, take care of my kids—but I'm sad. I don't feel depressed, but it's still heartbreaking. It was so difficult—do you know what happened to us? We were all evacuated in pickup trucks, nobody could stay here. We stayed in New Jersey for awhile. But in November, coming back here—you had to take a shuttle just to get in here, passing all those little teddy bears. There were barricades and police all over the place.

A *New York Times* survey reported an average residential vacancy rate of 45 percent in the months after the attack. The survey of 26 residential buildings containing 7,000 dwelling units within a four-block radius of the trade center site found that vacancy rates ranged from one-quarter to three-quarters of the dwelling units in any one building (Winter 2002). The buildings with the highest vacancies had leased large blocks of apartments to corporations for employee housing. At Gateway Plaza, the oldest residential development in Battery Park City, about 700 out of a total of 1,711 apartments were vacant after the complex reopened in October. However, by August 2002, vacancy rates in the survey area had dropped back to just under 5 percent overall, and many buildings were full. The surge of new residents surprised many in the real estate industry who expected the downtown residential market to remain soft much longer. The resurgence was attributed to the $300 million rental assistance program, which offered up to $12,000 in federal funds to people who moved into the area, and rent reductions of up to 25 percent and sometimes with one month free rent.

Methods

Informants were approached randomly in the numerous open spaces: the dog runs, sidewalks, pathways, parks, tot lots, supermarkets, pizza shops, and entry ways of apartment buildings and restaurants.[5] The interviewee was asked if he/she lived in Battery Park City, and if the answer was affirmative, the project was explained and permission to interview requested. An open-ended interview schedule was used and notes were taken, although in the case of community leaders, the interview was tape recorded. These notes and tape recordings were then transcribed and/or written up by research question and theme.

Because of the immediacy of the research situation, the study was designed as a three month Rapid Ethnographic Assessment Procedure (REAP) that took place the summers of 2002 and 2003 (Taplin, Low, &

Scheld 2004; Low, Taplin, & Lamb 2005). Sixty-five individual interviews, five to seven expert interviews, and two transect walks were collected each summer. Behavioral mapping, individual and expert interviews, and participant observation each provided separate bodies of data that were compared and contrasted, improving the validity and reliability from what was otherwise a relatively small sample. The qualitative analysis focused on the triangulation of the data from the various methods, and a search for common elements, patterns of behavior, and the identification of areas of conflict and differences.

The New Demographics

The post-9/11 residents interviewed were ethnically similar to the population demographics reported in the 2000 census: 73 percent were White, 15 percent Asian, 7 percent Latino (the greatest difference from the census), 3 percent African American, and 2 percent West Indian. Sixty percent of the residents interviewed were female, 40 percent male. Of the residents interviewed, 78 percent rented their apartments and 14 percent were owner-occupants. The remaining 8 percent were not residents but spent considerable time in the neighborhood. Seventy-nine percent of the interviewees intended to stay in the neighborhood, 16 percent wanted to leave, and 5 percent were undecided. During the research period, at least two families decided to leave, almost a year after the attack occurred. Forty percent of the interviewees were newcomers, 27 percent had lived in Battery Park City for up to five years, 13 percent had lived there for up to 10 years, and 19 percent had lived there for more than 10 years.

Despite the absence of a strict random procedure, the interview sample replicates the 2000 census in terms of ethnicity, language spoken, and other demographic characteristics. It therefore seems reasonable to compare the interview sample to the 2000 census to describe demographic changes after 9/11. From such a comparison we found that family households dropped from 30 to 14 percent after 9/11, married residents increased from 48 to 68 percent, and the number of singles remained relatively stable (22 percent pre-9/11 and 18 percent post-9/11). Individuals from 26 to 35 years old increased from 29 to 40 percent, yet the proportion of adults ages 26 to 45 increased much less (from 60 percent pre-9/11 to 66 percent post-9/11).

Fear of Newcomers

Some older residents were suspicious of the newcomers, in one case citing hearsay that there had been "rent problems and upkeep problems with the new folks." There was a lingering sense that the newcomers were made of lesser stuff—not quite the type of people Battery Park City should be renting to. "Our complex used to rent through a management office," a Gateway resident complained, "now they have a rental office. These people were offered tremendous incentives." The same woman suggested that new residents might even be "doubling up," creating postcollegiate households of roommates rather than families.

There was some change in the community's demographic composition. A young resident living in Battery Park City four months, interviewed while walking her dog in her pajamas and slippers, said that, "I certainly wouldn't be living here if it [rent reductions] hadn't happened." There are more college kids, remarked a resident of 10 years. Another longtime resident felt that something special had been lost:

Before September 11 we were a family, with warm, natural, sincere interactions. We knew each other, asked after each other. The new people are young. They consider it a jumping stone for the next endeavor. They don't get attached to it as a home. They don't care about the look of the place. They're so involved in their radio, three phones ringing in each pocket.

Veteran residents had the unsettling experience of watching the exodus from Battery Park City. As one respondent told us: "Day after day there were moving vans and you would think, 'why am I staying?' All the renters considered it [leaving], and fifty percent left, and owners felt trapped." Another described the situation in his building: "My building was emptied out. … On my floor I was the only one left. In the building, only the tenants with subsidized apartments remained." Another resident who was active in neighborhood organizations was concerned about what this exodus would do to neighborhood life.

We were worried that people would abandon the neighborhood. The renters had the ability to do that. Gateway Plaza was letting people out of leases with no penalty. And the others realized that they couldn't enforce penalties either. People are not fungible. A neighborhood is made up of complex relationships, built up over time. It took a long time to get Battery Park City to where it was. If you throw people out and figure in nine months you'll fill it up again, it will take years before it is a neighborhood again.

Long-term residents and community leaders also were concerned that young people who are coming in search of low rents would leave when their leases expire and the rents go up. One longtime tenant association activist worried:

The tenancy has changed. We had 600 vacancies. Old people moved out, and new people are not involved at this point. It is disillusioning. People who moved in came for the Lower Manhattan Development Corporation grant rent subsidy, not to build a community, and they are likely to leave.

Overall, residents and community leaders agree that Battery Park City has undergone a profound change in demographic character. The fear of newcomers is similar to the fear of crime in gated communities—it has little to do with the newcomers (or others) and more to do with the perceived disruptions in social life and the loss of neighbors after 9/11. Instead of discussing the residents who left, the residents who stayed are displacing their feelings of fear, anger and sadness on to the new residents (Low, Taplin, & Lamb 2005).

Change in Emotional Climate: Fear, Anger, and Sadness

When asked what the primary impact of 9/11 was on the community, a five-year resident in her fifties replied, "We feared—there was so much fear—would this end here? Was this going to stop, or was it just going to keep escalating? There was a tremendous fear of the unknown." While this particular woman used the past tense, many current residents mentioned fear as a lingering effect of the attack. They may not be as frightened as they were on September 12, 2001, but fear is a still a part of their daily lives. Considering that about half of the pre-9/11 residents had not returned to Battery Park City, these numbers are even more striking.

Even new residents feel a change in the emotional climate. When asked what the primary impact of that day was on the community, one new resident in her fifties answered quickly, "Shock. Terror. Lives disrupted. Lives rearranged. You hear stories of people who haven't left their apartments since it happened. They're just too scared." A man in his 40s who moved to Battery Park City two months ago says matter-of-factly, "I think it's less safe here. After what happened, I mean. This area is a target."

A resident of 10 years recently found out just how much he'd been affected:

My confidence was shaken," he says, "I didn't realize it so much until I was stuck in my elevator for an hour, two days ago. The lights went out and I was stuck in there and I had no idea what was going on out in the world. Just me and my dog. It was very scary.

An explosion at a local power plant during the summer of our research aroused feelings for many. A few days after the explosion a resident of 15 years commented:

It brought everything back. It was a very triggering event for those of us who were here. It brought back those feelings—helpless, vulnerable, isolated, scared. I didn't know I still had all this post-traumatic stress.

Many adults still live in fear, and it is not surprising that the events have cast a shadow over the lives of children as well. A woman in her 30s who has lived in Battery Park City for almost three years says that a deep sense of fear has been 9/11's greatest legacy:

My son is scared to go outside. He's scared of planes now, too. He'll ask me, 'Isn't that plane flying too low?' People get really nervous. On the river, when you see a lot of police boats, everybody sort of just looks at each other—scared.

Other changes include negative emotions such as anger and a lack of energy and vitality. For example, one resident comments: "People are very angry, the level of tension is high. Some people are on drugs—well, not drugs, but medications. It's definitely different than it was." Another resident said "a lot of people were depressed—now they're just pissed ... angry that we were attacked." Others say that the streets and restaurants are too quiet and dead; that there are not enough children or people in the streets like before. An older resident notes that:

There's not the energy there used to be here. There was so much activity, there were thousands of people coming through these parks, people from all over the world. ... The main issue is dealing with that ... incredibly sad void right there.

Sixteen of the original 65 residents interviewed said that the primary impact of 9/11 was a heightened sense of fear, another seven report a lingering sense of sadness and grief, and an additional four an increase in anger. By the end of our second research year (2003), 60.2 percent of the 124 interviews collected mentioned emotional changes due to 9/11 (from 108 valid cases for this item).

Other national surveys report similar or even higher incidence of negative emotional reactions to terrorism. A Brown University study in Providence, Rhode Island, found 60 percent of respondents were willing to reallocate funds to protect against terrorism, about half said that terrorism makes them angry, and 28 percent have stocked an emergency kit of food, batteries, first aid, or other supplies in case of a terrorist attack (2004 unpublished report discussed in West & Orr 2005). West and Orr (2005), building on the Providence study, found that talking about 9/11 and terrorism is linked to worry over becoming a victim and being less likely to go downtown. "The more people talked about 9/11, the more worried they became about becoming a victim" (West & Orr 2005: 99). Defensive behavior of not going downtown and staying home, encouraging increased home surveillance (Low 2002; Low 2003), and hiring professional security guards (West & Orr 2005) as well as building home-based safe rooms and keeping two weeks of supplies on hand in a safe place, have emerged as common home behaviors with negative—fearful and anxious—emotional reactions. 9/11 has had an impact on people not only in downtown areas like Battery Park City, but also along the entire Northeast corridor, and in other large cities such as Los Angeles.

Conclusion

The comparison of the fears and concerns of gated community and Battery Park City residents illustrates the different ways that the fear of others and newcomers is experienced and represented. Based on the findings, gated community residents say they moved to a gated and guarded development when their neighborhoods changed, in the case of Ted and Carol, when "ethnic others" moved in. Although I have presented only a few examples in this chapter, it is a common reaction, although the "others" may be "ethnic," "Black," "Mexicans," or "those kind of people." In each case, residents claim that the change disturbs their sense of belonging, especially when the newcomers do not conform to their ideal or desired social—race, class, or ethnic—status. The changing neighborhood composition is rhetorically accompanied by statements about increased crime—of which there is little evidence, their "fear of being robbed," and the need to live somewhere more secure. It is rare that the interviewee is able to articulate how the changing neighborhood threatens their sense of community, but the discursive elements of this translation are visible in each transcript. Even when questioned about the "others," interviewees avoid answering, but repeat that they need some place more secure, exemplified by Karen's response.

In the Battery Park City case, the attack on the World Trade Center and post-9/11 landscape produces many of the same reactions. Residents who returned after the attack are very anxious about the newcomers attracted by lower rents. They worry that the newcomers are younger, single, lack commitment, and will destroy the sense of community. Yet there is little evidence the newcomers are demographically different or less committed to staying. Instead, the fear of newcomers is rhetorically linked to their sense of loss from the death and departure of other residents, and the destruction of an image of Battery Park City as a safe, family environment.

In both studies, the residents are fearful, worried, anxious, and even paranoid about their social world and immediate environment, and their distorted perceptions are rationalized and legitimated by their fears. Thus, fear of others and an emotional shift in the local environment play significant roles in the transformation of how residents feel about their home places.

These reactive emotions, however, are not independent of the historical moment in which they occur and are sustained by a social and political context of fear and distrust. Geoffrey White (2005) refers to this context as emotive institutions that "consist of socially situated discursive practices that variously evoke, represent, and transform emotional experience" (2005: 248). Residents' fear, worry, anxiety, and paranoia are constructed out of a discourse of fear of crime and others that resonates at many scales including the local, regional, and national.

Most people want to feel loved, safe, and secure at home. But the strategies being used to accomplish this security—building higher walls and adding trained guards and security patrols to gated communities, improving home surveillance technology, adding both a private and public police presence on city streets and in neighborhood complexes, creating safe rooms, and stockpiling supplies for a terrorist attack—produce a new level of reactivity. And although many Americans want home security, most do not want to live in a police state.

The social impact of fear, anxiety and paranoia provides a paradox. The reactive emotions of home have real world consequences: they restrict participation and limit aspects of social interaction that are important to participatory democracy. Fear creates a citizenry more concerned with protecting their homes than with protecting social and political freedom. The McCarthy era and red baiting of the 1940s and 1950s documented in the film *Good Night and Good Luck,* portrays how fear and distrust of others creates a world where political freedoms are curtailed, quite similar to the ethnic profiling, political arrests, and increased surveillance sanctioned by the World Trade Center attack. We are enmeshed in a historical period when fear and anxiety are being manipulated to produce unhealthy political ends. The consequences of this social atmosphere, though, are not just political, but produce increasing fears in children and an obsession with safety and security that is claiming ground and appropriating feelings even within the ultimate retreat—home.

Notes

1. In many ways, this discussion is informed by the work of Geoffrey White on "emotive institutions," and I am indebted to him for our many discussions on this topic. This chapter, however, cannot fully address how the concept of

emotive institutions informs this analysis, but is explored in another paper on the emotions of home, "Emotive Institutions and the New Emotions of Home."

2. **Gated communities in the New York area: Manor House.** Located in Nassau County, Long Island, New York, this mostly White and wealthy development of single, detached houses is situated on an old estate with the original manor house retained as a community center. There is a security guard at the entrance who controls the gate. The individual houses are large (3,250 to 4,500 square feet), generally two-story structures, built in a variety of traditional styles, and sell for anywhere between $745,000 and $1,000,000. The development contains 141 houses, tennis courts, outdoor swimming pool, and the mansion has been renovated to accommodate an indoor pool, billiard saloon, library, conference rooms, sauna, and cigar smoking rooms.

Pine Hills. Pine Hills is a gated townhouse development of 80 units completed in 1997. There is a gatehouse and residents use electronic identity cards to raise the arm blocking the entrance. Located near the Long Island Expressway in Nassau County, Pine Hills is a middle income, mostly White community made up of long rows of similar-looking attached houses in three basic styles. The location and quality of the townhouses have kept the prices in the $400,000 to $500,000 range even though it is located in a prestigious, suburban neighborhood.

Waterview. Waterview is a gated condominium complex of 800 units located in the middle class neighborhood of Bayside, Queens. There is both a guarded entrance and a pedestrian entryway that can be opened with a key. Organized as a series of three story buildings, each with three apartments arranged around a swimming pool with health club facilities and sauna, Waterview has been successful in maintaining its prices in the $350,000 to $450,000 range. Many of the apartments are rented by their owners, so that there is a broad spectrum of residents of various income levels and greater cultural diversity including African nationals, African Americans, Korean Americans, and White workers and professionals.

Gated communities in the San Antonio area: Sun Meadow. Sun Meadow is part of the master-planned suburban development centered on a private golf and tennis club with swimming pools, restaurant, and clubhouse. The subdivision includes 120 lots, a few fronting the golf course, surrounded by a six-foot masonry wall. The main entrance is controlled by a grid design gate that swings opens electronically by a hand transmitter or by a guard who is contacted by an intercom and video camera connection. The single family detached houses are large (3,000–6,000 square feet) two-story brick colonials or stucco Scottsdale designs with a few one-story brick ranch-style houses and sell for between $275,000 and $650,00. These different models accommodate the mostly White and a few Hispanic upper-middle- and middle-income families.

The Links. The Links is a mostly White and upper-income luxury gated community with a 24-hour guarded entrance and a divided main thoroughfare filled with ponds and lush vegetation. All of the 22 lots face the golf course. The single family houses are large (4,000–6,000 square feet) designed by individual architects to look like small mansions with French, Italian, or Southwestern architectural details, and sell for between $500,000 and $750,000.

The Lakes. The Lakes is a White and Hispanic middle-income gated community in a northwestern central suburb of San Antonio. The 59 lots are organized along a series of curving roads with three cul-del-sacs. Located on a hill that looks out at the city, these lots are smaller and include three blocks of attached townhouses among the single family detached homes. The mixture of house types is unusual, and lowers the overall house prices to the $250,000–$300,000 level.

3. The research team was made up of Andy Kirby and Elena Danaila in New York City with assistance from Suzanne Scheld in the early training.

4. Battery Park City occupies a 92-acre site of reclaimed land in lower Manhattan along the Hudson River between Battery Park and Chambers Street with 35 acres of waterfront parks and 57 acres of streets and buildings. Landfill operations began in the 1960s using material excavated from the foundations of the World Trade Center. Battery Park City's residential sector is divided into two neighborhoods separated by the World Financial Center. Construction in the south neighborhood began with Gateway Plaza, between Liberty Street and Rector Place, in the late 1970s. The north neighborhood includes a new building for Stuyvesant High School, a hotel and movie theater, and a handful of completed residential buildings. Several more are planned or in construction. The office component—the World Financial Center (WFC)—consists of four towers linked by low-rise atria and retail space. The WFC was connected to the World Trade Center by bridges over West Street at Liberty Street and Vesey Street.

5. The research team included, in the first year, Mike Lamb, Dana Taplin, and Mirele Goldsmith, and, in the second year, Mara Heppen and Mike Lamb, graduate students in Environmental Psychology at the Graduate Center of the City University of New York.

Acknowledgments

Portions of this chapter are drawn from Low (2003) and Low, Taplin, and Lamb (2005). An earlier version was presented at "Doing, Thinking, Feeling Home: The Mental Geographies of Residential Environments" at the OTB Research Institute for Housing, Urban and Mobility Studies, Delft Univeristy of Technology, Delft, the Netherlands. I would like to thank the organizers of this conference, Marco van der Land and Leeke Reinders, for the opportunity to address these ideas. I also would like to thank the members of the Public Space Research Group who worked on various parts of this project: Dana Taplin, Associate Director, Mike Lamb, Mara Heppen, Andy Kirby, Suzanne Scheld, Mirele Goldsmith, and Elena Danaila, Research Assistants. Without their help this research could not have been completed. My thanks also to Grace Campagna, who edited and provided comments on the manuscript.

References

Ackerman, Bruce and James Fishkin. *Deliberation Day*. New Haven: Yale University Press, 2004.

Appleyard, Donald. "Home." *Architectural Association Quarterly* 11, no. 3 (1979): 4–19.

Baumgartner, M. P. *The Moral Order of a Suburb*. Oxford: Oxford University Press, 1988.

Benjamin, Walter. *The Arcades Project*. Cambridge, MA, and London: Belknap Press of Harvard University Press, 1999.

Bernhard, S. "Out of the Ashes." *New York* (2002).

Blakeley, Edward, and Mary Gail Synder. *Fortress America*. Washington, DC: Brookings Institute, 1997.

Brennan, D. and A. Zelinka. "Safe and Sound." *Planning* (1997): 4–10.

Dixon, John and Kevin Durrheim. "Displacing Place-Identity: a Discursive Approach to Locating Self and Other." *British Journal of Social Psychology* 39 (2000): 27–44.

Feldman, Roberta M. "Settlement-Identity: Psychology Bonds in a Mobile Society." *Environment and Behavior* 22, no. 2 (1990): 183–229.

Flusty, S. "Building Paranoia." *Architecture of Fear*. N. Ellin (ed.). New York: Princeton Architectural Press, 1997.

Frantz, Klaus. "Gated Communities in the USA: A New Trend in Urban Development." *Espace, Populations, Societes* (2000–2001): 101–13.

Fried, Marc. "Continuities and Discontinuities of Place." *Journal of Environmental Psychology* 20 (2000): 193–205.

Fried, Marc. "Grieving for a Lost Home." *Urban Condition*. ed. Len Duhl. New York: Basic Books, 1963. Notes: Also in: H. Gans' *The Urban Villagers* (New York: Free Press, 1963).

Garland, David. *The Culture of Control: Crime and Social Order in Contemporary Society*. Chicago: University of Chicago Press, 2001.

Glassner, Barry. *The Culture of Fear*. New York: Basic Books, 1999.

Hayden, Dolores. *Building Suburbia: Green Fields and Urban Growth, 1820–2000*. New York: Panetheon, 2003.

Hayden, Dolores. *Redesigning the American Dream*. New York: W.W. Norton and Company, 2002.

Hayward, D. Geoffrey. "Home As an Environmental and Psychological Concept." *Landscape* 20, no. 1 (1975): 2–9.

Holt, Elizabeth. *From the Classicists to the Impressionists: A Documentary History of Art and Architecture in the Nineteenth Century*. New York: Doubleday, 1966.

Janeway, Elizabeth. *Man's World, Women's Place*. New York: Belling Publishing Company, 1971.

Katz, Cindi. "Terrorism at Home." *The Politics of Public Space*. Setha and Neil Smith Low, New York and London: Routledge, 2005.

Klein, Melanie. "On the Sense of Loneliness." *Envy and Gratitude and Other Works, 1946–1963*, 300–313. New York: Delta, 1975.

Ladd, Florence. "Residential History: You Can Go Home Again." *Landscape* 21, no. 2 (1977): 15–20.

Laing, R. D. *The Divided Self*. New York and London: Penguin, 1960.

Low, Setha. "Anthropology As a New Technology in Landscape Planning." *Proceedings of the Regional Section of the American Society of Landscape Architecture,* ed. J. Fabos. Washington, DC: American Society of Landscape Architecture, 1981.

Low, Setha. *Behind the Gates: Life, Security and the Pursuit of Happiness in Fortress America.* New York and London: Routledge, 2003.

Low, Setha, Dana Taplin, and Mike Lamb. "Battery Park City: An Ethnographic Field Study of the Community Impact of 9/11." *Urban Affairs Review* 40, no. 5 (2005): 655–82.

Low, Setha, Dana Taplin, and Suzanne Scheld. *Rethinking Urban Park: Public Space and Cultural Diversity.* Austin: University of Texas, 2005.

Low, Setha M. and I. Altman. "Place Attachment: A Conceptual Inquiry." In *Place Attachment.* eds. I. Altman, and S. M. Low, 1–12. New York: Plenum Press, 1992.

Low, Setha and Neil Smith. *Politics of Public Space.* New York and London: Routledge, 2006.

New York Times Poll. "Four Years Later." *New York Times,* 11 September 2005, sec. Metro, col. 5&6 p. 36.

Newman, Katherine S. *Declining Fortunes: The Withering of the American Dream.* New York: Basic Books, 1993.

Ngin, ChorSwang. "A New Look at the Old "Race" Language." *Exlplorations in Ethnic Studies* 16, no. 1 (1993): 5–18.

Ortner, Sherry. "Generation X: Anthropology in a Media Saturated World." *Cultural Anthropology* 13, no. 3 (1998): 414–440.

Proshansky, H. M., A. K. Fabian, and R. Kaminoff. "Place-Identity: Physical World Socialization of the Self." *Journal of Environmental Psychology* 3 (1983): 57–83.

Rainwater, Lee. *Behind Ghetto Walls.* Harmondsworth: Penguin, 1963.

Sanchez, Thomas and Robert L. Lang. "Security Vs. Status: the Two Worlds of Gated Communities." *Census Note* 02, no. 2 (2002).

Sanchez, Thomas W. Robert E. Lang and Dawn M. Dhavale, "Security Versus Status? A First Look at the Census' Gated Community Data." *Journal of Planning Education and Research* 24, no. 3 (2005): 281–291.

Silver, Catherine. "Construction Et Deconstruction Des Identites De Genre." *Cahier De Genre* 31 (2002): 185–201.

Sorkin, Michael and Sharon Zukin. *After the Trade Center.* New York and London: Routledge, 2002.

Stone, C. "Crime in the City." *Breaking Away: the Future of Cities,* 98–103. New York: Twentieth Century Fund Press, 1996.

Taplin, Dana H., Suzanne Scheld, and Setha M. Low. "Rapid Ethnographic Assessment in Urban Parks: A Case Study of Independence National Historical Park." *Human Organization* 61, no. 1 (2002): 80–93.

Vale, Lawrence J. and Thomas J. Companella. *The Resilient City: How Modern Cities Recover From Disaster.* New York: Oxford University Press, 2005.

West, Darrell and Marion Orr. "Managing Citizen Fear: Public Attitudes Toward Urban Terrorism." *Urban Affairs Review* 41, no. 1 (2005): 93–105.

White, Geoffrey. "Emotive Institutions." *A Companion to Psychological Anthropology: Modernity and Psychocultural Change.* Conerly, C. and Edgerton R., 241–254. Malden, MA, UK: Blackwell Publishing, 2005.

Williams, Raymond. *Marxism and Literature*. Oxford: Oxford University Press, 1977.

Winter, Greg. "Exodus of 9/11 Is Thing of Past Near Tower Site." *New York Times*, 20 August 2002, p. 1.

Wright, Gwendolyn. *Building the Dream: A Social History of Housing in America*. Cambridge, MA: MIT Press, 1981.

Young, Jock. *The Exclusive Society*. London: Sage Publications, 1999.

Staged Authenticity Today

DEAN MacCANNELL

In the late 1960s while still in graduate school I noticed a quirk in the places that attracted tourists. This was before our society became shot through with replicant forms like "the new urbanism" and other "variations on a theme park." This odd bit of social engineering in tourist settings involved the pretentious revelation of "back region" procedures, even "secrets." Factories encouraged visitors to stroll along the line following the progress of product assembly; orchestras permitted paid attendance at rehearsals; farms converted to bed and breakfasts invited their guests to participate in the harvest; morgues and sewers were open for touristic visitation. The tourists, for their part, appeared to be endlessly fascinated with the deep inner workings of society. The idea of multitudes of strangers able to "see what is going on" in the private recesses of localities would be a paranoid fantasy. Except that, in the case of tourism, the putatively paranoid subject encourages and controls the tourists' perception. The prying eyes of tourists do not constitute a paranoid fantasy, or if they did, it would be minimally a weightless or harmless one. Tourist attractions, by contrast, do model themselves on paranoid structures.

Goffman, Foucault, and the Tourist Gaze

Also in the 1960s, Foucault was writing about "the gaze" as an instrument of power. I did not find his formulations helpful as tourist attractions seemed to operate according to a different, even opposing principle. The sights and spectacles I was studying were powerful not because they *possessed* the gaze but because they could *attract* the gaze. The tourist gaze lacks power to coerce, or even to resist. Tourists may behave boorishly to those who serve them, and some do arrogate to themselves an aura of wealth and power, but they look where they are told to look and they see what they are told to see. The tourist gaze is a flaccid mechanism for turning tourist desire into regional economic development. The power is not in the gaze but in the various strategies used to attract it. One might argue that the entire world is now preparing itself for, even preening for tourism and this is a manifestation of the power of the tourist gaze. But what could possibly be easier? Tourists have proven their enthusiasm for looking at anything. The *New York Times* uncritically reports that a small town in the Peruvian Andes had no tourism until a local bar owner erected 86 five-foot-high stone phalluses in a field and someone made up a back-story à la Disney that in "ancient times young women who wanted to conceive sat on top of these stones and had beer poured over them." Now tourists come from every continent to gaze on the stones and hear the story (Kummer, 2006).

The principal mechanism devised to compete for the tourist gaze is a promise to reveal parts of the society, the past, traditions, practices, or beliefs that are ordinarily kept from visitors. This promise very often involves the suggestion that the tourist will see and experience things the way locals and natives experience them, not tourists. We take this for granted today, but fifty years ago this kind of glimpse implied both a violation and a privilege.

It is difficult to reproduce the sense from 50 years ago of trespass in a "peek behind the scenes" into the authentic inner workings of a community or group. Erving Goffman had just given us the most authoritative account of our social situation at that time in his *Presentation of Self in Everyday Life* (1959). He suggested we must be able to keep secrets from one another, and be able strategically to reveal our secrets, in order to function both *socially* and as *human beings*. He did not see the social and the human as perfectly congruent. It is only by maintaining a certain degree of strategic control over our secrets that we can sort our associates into intimates, familiars, acquaintances, strangers, and enemies. What he discovered in *Presentation of Self* is a structural division running through every social interaction, every institution and establishment, separating "front" from "back."

"Personal front" includes all the more or less official, publicly known, or knowable, qualities of character, personality, and social station. "Personal back" includes the less desirable quirks and traits that we try to keep in check and are only revealed to intimates, i.e., potentially discrediting secrets, medical conditions, prison records, and the like. The "front regions" of a social establishment are those places where the routines and transactions necessary to its social functioning occur. They are the meeting grounds of host and guest, professional and client, clerk and customer, and so on. Formal norms govern appearances and behavior in the front. In the back, the local team of intimates can relax, blow off steam, engage in teasing and joking one another, and berating the customers or the neighbors. In fact, Goffman suggests, we are normatively required to dramatize more relaxed standards in the back lest we threaten the intimacy and solidarity necessary to credible team performances out front. If we take Goffman seriously, any *actual* revealing of back region secrets, of the sort tourism promises, undermines the social and the structural supports for group solidarity and for expressions of character and personality.

The idea for writing about the peculiar status of back regions in tourism came to me while I watched a salad chef in an exclusive restaurant prepare an elaborately beautiful salad on a cart in full view of the guests who were about to eat it. I had taken Introduction to Sociology from Goffman as an undergraduate at Berkeley, and read his *Presentation of Self.* As I watched the salad being prepared I thought, 'According to Goffman, that's supposed to be a back-region activity.' I was halfway through graduate school and had already decided to study tourism. I wondered if this transposition of back-to-front occurred in other tourist contexts. My initial thoughts into this matter were set off by an empirical observation, an observation of a particular kind, one that did not fit into existing relevant theory, that is, by an anomaly.

Staged Authenticity in Tourist Settings   I found examples of strategic back region revelations, and staged back region activities, where tourists gather. In a 1973 article, I introduced a new concept with some lightly ironical observations of school children's tours where they go to a farm, visit the barns, and are invited to touch a cow's udder; or, at a bank, are let into the vault and allowed to look at a big stack of money. I supplemented my observations of tourist visits to actual back regions with descriptions of places constructed to appear as back regions made especially for tourists. I did not harbor any illusion that tourists were gaining access to the actual inner workings of the places they visited. I was merely intrigued by a new kind of space I found in tourist settings: a front region decorated to appear as a "back region," or a back region, normatively and functionally revised so it could be opened to outsiders. The first name I gave to this space reflected my suspicion that it was only a stratagem for making tourists feel special by seeming to let them in on what was going on. No one wanted to think of themselves as having superficial tourist experiences, especially the tourists. I was reading Herbert Marcuse at the time (everyone was) and called my discovery the space of "inauthentic demystification."

Fortunately, before going to press, I renamed the concept "staged authenticity." The name should not be taken to suggest that there is any such thing as "real" or "actual" authenticity in social life. It means only that there are myriad behaviors and arrangements, including architecture and décor for tourists designed to imply that tourists are experiencing, or at least seeing into, the real or the actual. The dodge of the Peruvian Indians and their stone phallus attraction is ubiquitous in tourism: in the eyes of the tourist, a fictional back stage is equal to an actual back stage. "Staged authenticity" does not necessarily involve authenticity. It only involves the putative removal of barriers to perception between front and back regions. It names a structural shift authorizing the tourist to believe she can peer into everything with an enfeebled Foucaultian gaze.

I am about to suggest that staged authenticity, originally restricted to the limited domain of tourists and tourism, has replicated itself in every realm of contemporary social life. When it was only a matter of tourism I was able to shrug off my concerns, and the concerns of others, about what staged authenticity might mean for society-in-general, and for what we once quaintly called "the human." What does it mean when an entire civilization is told that it can go everywhere, see everything, experience everything, do everything, and know everything when clearly it cannot? In this paper, I argue that both Goffman and Foucault (and eventually Lacan) are needed to approach these questions. But, here at the outset, it is necessary to signal the strangeness of this undertaking by acknowledging there can be no logical synthesis of Goffman/Foucault.

Goffman's subjects present themselves and act out their regard for one another on a symbolic stage. Their interactions are framed by language and other symbolic arrangements including moral norms, which Goffman found operating on the micro-details of everyday social life. What they see in one another is shaped in advance by their society and their group, especially their mutual agreement to accept socially imposed barriers to perception, which permits everyone to maintain back-region privacy and intimate solidarities. According to Goffman, the gaze that serves to define self and other and to shape the trajectory of human interactions is fully inscribed in the symbolic order. It is noteworthy that Goffman is congruent with Lacan on this. According to Lacan, both seeing and being seen occur under terms established by the symbolic. Lacan's visual field with its screens and mirrors, and 360 degrees of vanishing points, in which the viewing subject cannot avoid becoming an object of some other's gaze, is a good fit with Goffman's sociology.

Foucault accepts something like a Goffman/Lacan version of the gaze but only long enough to set it aside in favor of a more radical definition. In *Birth of the Clinic,* he argues that the historic progress of medical science is founded on the "purity of an unprejudiced gaze" (195), a "gaze that has broken free of language to establish its own truth" (39). He is emphatically clear about the possibility of a gaze operating independent of language and every other symbolic system. "The gaze will be fulfilled in its own truth and will have access to the truth of things if it rests on them in silence" (108). Moreover, there is no place to hide. According to the logic of the gaze, the invisible is only the future visible (167). Throughout this remarkable text, Foucault emphatically insists that the gaze is nondialectizeable and rigorously protected from the equivocations of language: "Several observers never see the same fact in an identical way unless nature has really presented it to them in the same way" (102).

The differences between Goffman's gaze and Foucault's cannot be satisfactorily resolved simply by noting that Goffman has deployed his observations over the empirical domain of everyday social behavior, while Foucault is rigorously philosophical. I am about to argue the opposite: namely, that Goffman's account is philosophically superior, but Foucault now has considerable traction when it comes to *empirical* descriptions of a turn society took after these two masters wrote their last books, a turn I am suggesting we examine under the heading "the routinization of staged authenticity."

Let me suggest, contra Foucault, that "several observers never see the same fact in an identical way unless they see it as given by their deeply held belief in a singular ideology." The only way they will ever see it in the same way is if they do not actually see it, but think they are seeing it the way they have been told to see it. The history of science, no less than the history of tourism, is a vast profusion of this kind of misprision punctuated at intervals by observations that might qualify as Foucaultian, that is, pure and unprejudiced, but which very quickly give rise to new orthodoxy and misprisions of their own. The very possibility of a gaze that operates outside of language requires language for its enunciation.

No matter how many objections we might raise against Foucault's theory of the gaze, nothing eventually undermines its accuracy in accounting for our current social situation. Politics by spectacle and news leaks, show trials, surveillance in all its new manifestations, from ubiquitous closed circuit video to warrantless wire taps and cellphones with GPS so parents can determine every moment the exact geographic location of their children to within three feet; open plan house designs where even the bedrooms lack visual and aural separation; desire for fame and recognition trumping (or Trumping) all other desires; quick-time underage masturbation on the web; frontal nudity in other popular entertainments; wardrobe malfunctions and similar famous exposures and exposés; all of this and additional similar material constitute an avalanche of evidence that radical visibility is rapidly becoming the central organizing principle of contemporary social life. If the most compelling facts in this series continue to flow from the growth of tourism, now the world's largest industry, it is because tourism today operates on the principle that anyone has the right to see anything anywhere on the face of the earth. Goffman did not anticipate this. Foucault did.

Total Visibility and Paranoia

Lacan begins *Seminar III* with his observation that it is difficult to recognize paranoia because every description of it works equally well as a description of the normal (19–20). The paranoid subject is one for whom the world has begun to take on "meaning." The paranoid knows that "something is going on." This is not different from a normal subject or a scientific subject. The paranoid, according to Lacan, believes there is a real meaning hidden behind or within the everyday accepted meanings of words and things. It is his special mission to get at that truth. Again, this may be true even for normals. Meanings are layered on one another just as Saussure taught us. But normal certainty about the hidden meaning of things is always provisional. For normals, there is always a second hidden meaning behind the first hidden meaning even if we provisionally grasp the first. The difference for the paranoid is *meaning stops*. He's got it. He *sees*. He *has discovered* what's going on. This happens also to be the grounds of Foucault's gaze.

> To *discover* ... will no longer be to *read* an essential coherence beneath a state of disorder, but to push a little farther back the foamy line of language, to make it encroach upon that sandy region that is still open to the clarity of perception ... (*Clinic* 169, stress as in the original)

Paranoid structures emerge at precisely those points where there is no longer any possibility of a dialectic: known–unknown, seen–unseen, recognized–misrecognized.

Paranoia involves an identification with the other's truth, or the truth of the other, as object of undeniable desire. The fragile ego prevents itself from being eaten alive by its own primitive competition and jealousies. It accomplishes this by identifying with that which is great and desirable beyond all questioning—God, the truth, the secret of the universe. The proper field of paranoia is visibility without limits. Total visibility is the requisite condition for the free play of paranoid fantasies, permitting the ego to engage in a kind of insane bricolage, constructing a world for itself composed of weighty and important symbols: a tourist world. Lacan summarizes Freud's mad judge Schreber's final descent into insanity in the same terms one might use to describe a trip to a new destination, that is, as an "irruption in the real of something he has never known." Lacan further describes Schreber's madness as "a radical submersion of all categories [natural, sexual, social, etc.] to the point of forcing a virtual reshaping of the world." I can think of no more precise an account of the effect of the routinization of Foucault's "pure" and "unprejudiced" gaze in every domain of human life. The singular difference is, according to Lacan, that German Supreme Court appointee Schreber did not believe in the reality of his hallucinations. He knew he had not actually been chosen by God to be His lover. But he also was certain his hallucinatory sexual liaisons with God concerned him and implicated him somehow in their awful unreality. It is only so-called normal people who are privileged to believe in the reality of their fantasies. How else does a tourist from New Jersey explain paying $20 million to gaze on the earth from a Russian space ship? Not even Schreber was that insane.

The Routinization of Staged Authenticity

The following sections provide a preliminary assessment of the social impact of the systematic removal of barriers to perception from all areas of human life, not just tourist contexts. They can be read as descriptions of the replacement by paranoid structures of the serviceably functional social arrangements described by Goffman.

The Transformation of the Domestic Establishment

The houses Goffman knew, "domestic establishments," as he called them, were the teletype of his front-back paradigm. The American middle class (and above) had two *front* rooms, the living room and the parlor. The parlor, the more formal of the two, was used on occasions of weddings, funerals, birthdays, promotions, and retirements. The practice of viewing the recently deceased in the parlor is what gave the living room its name as a kind of residual formal space—for the living.

Today's homes, at least the most fashionable and desired contemporary homes, are marked by the aggressive removal of the walls, screens, barriers that once separated front and back. The simplest statement of the new design program would be, "eliminate the division between front and back region as much as possible." The new "open plan" allows for smooth traffic and visual flow from area to area. Living, family, dining, kitchen, study, are all visually accessible to one another, perfectly mirroring the ethos of the new companionate marriages they are supposed to contain and friendship based parent–child relations. Even the bedroom is only a step away.

What about bathrooms? Surely their classification as Goffmanian backregions is unambiguous and secure. Anyone believing this has not studied up-scale new construction. I visited friends who just finished building a home in the River Oaks neighborhood of Houston not far from where recently indicted "Kenny Boy" Lay lives. The first part of the house they showed me was the guest powder room. It was perhaps a bit smaller than a three-car garage, finished entirely in exotic stone with European fixtures, and controllable recessed lighting. The main room had life-sized statues of domestic animals made by a Mexican artist. In a series of radiating chapels there were bidets, saunas, hot tubs, showers, exercise equipment, and a selection of toilets with their own libraries. This was as far from being a Goffmanian back region as any place I have seen, including the Forecourt at Versailles. It was a urinary palace where one could sit, literally in the spotlight, on stage, and imagine oneself to be a celebrity, super-star, A-list defecator. It is patently evident that this so-called powder room had been built not to meet the biological needs of my hosts or their guests. It had been built to be visited, or toured (realtors and tourism researchers use the same words); to be gazed on by visitors and to elicit our responses. My friends were quick to express solidarity with their guest by enthusiastically agreeing it was excessive and disgusting, but something they had to do to insure the future saleability of a house such as theirs in this particular neighborhood of Houston.

No doubt some innocent souls celebrate the obliteration of barriers between front and back. It is easy to be seduced by the putative prospect of a more open, honest, sharing society; one that is relaxed, informal, casual, where everyone is willing to share intimacies, etc. A constructed sense of solidarity has always been part of the allure of staged authenticity even in its tourist days. Much has been written about invasions of privacy in the new surveillance society. At the level of culture, it is easy to document the many ways that invasion is being welcomed, or how we are learning to stop worrying and start loving it.

Let me be clear on this point. I am not employing the Foucault panopticon concept in precisely the way it has been used, that is, as a strategy of control by the state or other powerful agency. The cultural process I am trying to finger here is different from critical ideas about the power of the gaze. It is more akin to a kind of naïve narcissism in response to the Foucauldian gaze. It involves volunteering to become the object of the gaze of power and anything and anyone else that comes along. But especially power. Power is good. It is good to be noticed by power. It involves an eager willingness to remove barriers to perception from domestic and commercial establishments. It celebrates the disappearance of Goffmanian back regions and the emergence of new normative requirements that we live our lives as if we are sharing back-region intimacy even with near strangers, that we become tourists and tour guides even in our own homes. The institution of paranoia as a kind of quasi-social norm takes the form of the routinization and spread of staged authenticity beyond the confines of tourist settings. It is a kind of "grinning idiot" happy face return of the gaze.

It is also perverted. Any ultimate belief in this new California-style intimacy and solidarity is a fantasy of the terminally gullible. The wholesale elimination of the "barriers to perception" that once separated front from back regions in our society does not mean everything is now out in the open. The lesson learned from tourism is it means the opposite. The pretentious revelation of supposed back region secrets suggests that what remains actually hidden in postmodern society is so appalling we cannot permit it to appear even behind the scenes, or joke about it back stage. Foucault can guide us into and through what is actually happening on the cultural stage, but we still need Goffman and Lacan to articulate a critique and lead us out.

The questions that intrigue me now, the analysis that is missing from my original article on staged authenticity and all the debate and discussion it has engendered, are these: What are the human implications of the loss of an everyday dialectic of front and back? What happens when there are no longer barriers to perception between front and back? What are the human implications of supposedly opening everyday life to a pure and implacable gaze? As I ask these questions, I acknowledge that not everyone enthusiastically embraces these changes. But there is need for greater resistance than one hears in the sporadic inarticulate mumbling about warrantless wiretaps.

According to Goffman

Goffman was meticulous in explaining in detail how much of what we might have once quaintly called our humanity is hanging in the separation of front and back. Here is the reticent way that he introduced the concept of back region in *The Presentation of Self*:

> In order to appear in a steady moral light it is necessary for performers to "accentuate" some facts while suppressing others. Accentuated facts make their appearance in the front region. It should be ... clear that there may be another region—a "back region" or "back stage"—where the suppressed facts make an appearance. (111–112)

For Goffman, as for Freud, behind every revelation there is something not revealed; a secret behind everything we think we know. But for Goffman, contra Freud, society dependably provided myriad micro-settings for dealing with the dark side. His conceptual division of front and back regions is what allows us, as humans, to become spontaneously involved in the conduct of our affairs with an "effortless unawareness" (Goffman 1961: 25) of everything that must be suppressed to maintain the definition of each social situation. Every performance, every self, was presented with a mutual understanding that at any moment a discordant tone or even a discrediting revelation might make an unwanted appearance. That humans live, or once lived, their lives on both sides of the line between front and back is what gave our performances out front a tension and their distinctive colorations. Or, in Goffman's words, "It is here [in the back region] that the capacity of a performance [out front] to express something beyond itself may be painstakingly fabricated" (1959: 112).

On a psychological level, when a person's performance could "express something beyond itself," the result was what we once called personality and sometimes even character. Goffman saw social life as a framework of opportunities to exhibit "dexterity, strength, knowledge, intelligence, courage, and self-control" (1961: 68). And he saw life equally as providing the obverse, a chance to be clumsy, weak, foolish, cowardly, and sloppy. Every social occasion is an occasion to express one's thoughts and opinions or to hide behind what Goffman derisively called the "surface of agreement," or "veneer of consensus" (1959: 9). Every social role allows one to slavishly do one's duty and nothing more, or to exhibit some detachment and humanity. "If an individual is to show that he is a 'nice guy' or, by contrast, one much less nice than a human being need be then it is through his using or not using role distance that this is likely to be done" (1961: 152).

In short, social structure, roles, rituals, institutional arrangements are not merely ways of arranging and organizing people and their mutual dealings. They also provide the tools for specific expressions of humanity. Every encounter is a kind of trial in which both individual character and social standing can be won and lost. Do we exhibit poise and rise to the occasion, or do we become flustered and embarrass ourselves, or withdraw? In Goffman's own words, "personal front and social setting provide precisely the field an individual needs to cut a figure in—a figure that romps, sulks, glides, or is indifferent" (1961: 115).

I am about to argue that the routinization of staged authenticity and the institutionalization of paranoid structures is precisely deployed against the possibilities social life once provided to test character. I suspect the reason tourists were once so derided for being "personalityless" and "characterless" was because they were the first to inhabit the space of staged authenticity where the structural supports for expressions of personality and character had been removed.

Staged Authenticity and the Replacement of Character by Appearance

The kinds of people we once called personalities are now referred to as celebrities, superstars, media sensations, and A-list, nicely sidestepping the question of what they might be famous or respected for. When asked what he wants to be when he grows up, an American teen today often honestly answers, "Famous." When asked what he wants to be famous for, he may respond, "Whatever, just famous." In the new generic space of staged authenticity, in place of personality we find raw ego. Performers still accentuate some facts while suppressing others, but compared to the possibility of a return of the repressed, this is a paltry resource for the construction of character. The role of personality in social relationship formation is being taken over by physical appearances.

For some Generation Xers, sex, dating, marriage, even a conversation, can occur only when individuals, based on mutual inspection of their physical attractiveness, decide they are unlikely to find someone better looking, to "hook up" with. A Hollywood informant told me he can walk into a party and in five minutes predict with high accuracy who will leave with whom, and whom he should be "hitting on," based solely on conventional hierarchies of appearance, or cuteness. They may discover a few days, or a few years, later that the person they are in a relationship with has a putrid personality or no personality at all, but if he or she is cute enough this might be overlooked. Some of the individuals whose nuptials are announced on the Society pages of the *New York Times* have carried this ranking process to a logical extreme and only marry those who by appearance could be their twin.

Among the habitués of the space of staged authenticity the closest thing to a personality is a narcissistic ego hiding behind bland pleasantries and lightly ironic cynicism about everything and everyone it encounters. The ego-mimetic exception to this would be encounters with the very powerful or very beautiful, who, following the logic of paranoia, are admired without reservation.

The merely psychological affects of the systemic loss of back regions are small compared to the psychoanalytic implication. In another book, Goffman (1961B) describes the "underlife" of an insane asylum as a thicket of back-region opportunities to get around the institutional definition of the self of the inmate. He calls the many stratagems of inmates to construct alternative livable worlds for themselves "secondary adjustments." When there is no back region and the opportunities it provides for convivial resistance to the institutional status quo, there is no social space where the subject, even temporarily, can shake off the identity that has been handed to it. The space of staged authenticity is like an asylum without an underlife. A perfectly realized panoptic asylum where there can be only primary adjustments. This ideal, which was never achieved in the administration of penal institutions, made its first appearance in tourism and is now beginning to flourish in everyday life in postmodern societies.

The loss of back-regions and an underlife would be highly consequential in a mental institution where the official definition of the self of the inmate is that she is crazy, and the only way for her to act otherwise is by means of unofficially sanctioned secondary adjustments in the underlife.

What happens when opportunities for secondary adjustments are systematically removed from the world outside the asylum? What happens when everything that was once a societal secondary adjustment (gangster lifestyles, lost weekends, profit-skimming, exercise addiction and other obsessive compulsive distractions, extra-marital affairs, resume inflation, dope-dealing, dope taking, food fetishism, prostitution, heartless conning, slacking off and doing nothing—the list can be as long as anyone wants to make it and extended to such things as fanatical recycling and energy conservation); what happens when everything that was once a societal secondary adjustment becomes merely another suburban lifestyle choice?

What to Wear?

When Goffman published *The Presentation of Self* in 1959, there was a clear-cut distinction between formal dress, casual dress, and work clothes, and generally accepted setting-specific norms about appropriate attire. The most powerful sorting engine for these norms was the structural division of social establishments into front and back regions. In the 1950s, in our society's front regions, men decorously wore suits and ties and women coordinated their shoes and handbags. The outdoor daytime downtown areas of major American cities were public spaces then as they are now, but they functioned as a kind of giant front stage for the entire society, and had very different dress codes from today. Men wore dark suits and homburg hats from Labor Day to Easter, and light suits and Panama straws from Easter to Labor Day. Women wore dresses below the knee, nylons, heels, hats, and white gloves. Anything less would mark you as possibly being from the wrong side of the tracks. The separation of front and back was considered to be so important in bourgeois circles that a bra or panties coming in direct contact with the inside of a blouse or skirt was thought to be tasteless. Mediating layers of camisoles, slips, and girdles were marshaled against the possibility of vulgar back to front contamination. The lingerie sections of every fine department store sold a specialized item called a "breast petal" a kind of daisy-shaped padded pastie to be worn under the bra to guard against nipple-stiffening becoming an unwanted visible feature of one's personal front.

We postmodernites with our belly buttons hanging out find it almost impossible to believe our immediate forebears took *that* much trouble to maintain the separation of back from front. We have learned comfortably to inhabit the space of *staged authenticity* and dress accordingly: that is, like tourists. In virtually every contemporary setting, including the outdoor daytime downtown areas of major cities, the clothes people wear are carefully selected to *seem* to be casual. The universal uniform is the kind of clothing that can be purchased at The Gap and worn in the gap between front and back regions. The same expensive exercise outfits composed of matching sports shoes, sweat pants and shirts, bearing designer logos, are worn in public by suburban women and young inner-city gangster males.

Everyone except the homeless dress so as to appear both responsible and laid back, casual and serious. Even some among the homeless have figured out they can seem to fit in by wearing the exercise outfit. We don't take formality seriously. Instead, we are seriously casual; not exactly on stage, but always worthy of an admiring glance. Our radical liminality between the old formal–informal dichotomy makes sense only in the space of *staged authenticity*. Everywhere we turn the theme of making a show of back region informality and personal authenticity is clearly evident. Today, the lingerie departments no longer stock breast petals. In their place are bras with built-in simulated stiff nipple contours.

What to Drive?

We still have work trucks and formal limousines reflecting the persistence of a front-back division. But neither the work truck nor the limo has much symbolic cachet. A limousine is as likely to be carrying a bunch of drunken teenagers to an after-prom party as a captain of industry on her way to a power lunch. The choice today is a leather-lined, rosewood trimmed, high-centered, four-wheel drive SUV with Mark Levinson stereo, GPS, "custom" chrome magnesium wheels, low-profile tires, and a clear coat of lacquer over its metallic paint. How do we explain this fabulous symbolic object that began life as a humble military vehicle? It is perfect for highway cruising or for bouncing over stumps, off-road in the back woods. It is appropriate for trips to the opera or camping in the high Sierra. It is neither a work truck nor a luxury sedan, but a perfect amalgam of both.

Everyone can desire to drive one of these: soccer moms, macho men, gangstas, cops, liberals, CEOs and plumbers. Porsche sells one that will climb a cliff in underdrive low gear and, if you order the turbo-charged version, is also capable of making 160 miles per hour with five passengers and all of their luggage. If you get into one of these you could be going nowhere or anywhere. Other than having power, money, and a willingness to waste, its purchase signifies positive nothingness: a large investment in maintaining a zero degree of identity, no specificity or purpose, and total lack of direction. Its singular adaptation is to move quietly through the space of *staged authenticity* without disturbing its symbolic integration.

According to Bentham

The most energetic theorization of the human effects of systematic removal of barriers to perception is found in Jeremy Bentham's writings on prison reform and his general philosophical writing. Let me suggest that the routinization of staged authenticity as described in the last sections constitutes the first synthesis of Jeremy Bentham's panopticon prisons with his ideal of government as the promotion of the greatest happiness to the greatest number of citizens and harmony of public *and* private interests. What we forget about Bentham today is the infamous panopticon design he proposed for prisons, schools, asylums and factories was only a partial, and in his mind, wholly unsatisfactory realization of his social theories. (For this and other insights on Bentham I am indebted to Janet Semple's fine "Introduction" to his prison writings, 1993.)

In a move all-too-familiar in our present historical moment, Bentham drew heavily for his ideas on Evangelical Christianity and free market ideology. He was opposed to government having a role in any human affairs that might be self-regulated by market forces—especially the administration of prisons. He was infuriated that the prisons act of 1799 provided for professional staffing by state employees.

He argued that the Crown should appoint wardens to life terms compensated from profits they made by hiring out the inmates to merchants, manufacturers, and farmers. The profit motive is all that would be needed to ensure responsible custodial practices and maintain decent standards of diet, hygiene, and comfort for the inmates—this to maintain inmate fitness for maximum extraction of labor. To prevent any nonmarket irrationalities from destabilizing the system, Bentham argued, the first generation of Crown appointed warders should be able to pick their own successors on retirement. He was especially contemptuous of boards of directors or any other device that might second-guess the decisions of the warders. What he proposed did not very much resemble actual prisons, then or now. It was more like the general culture promoted by modern day corporations. And then, as now, this is where the panopticon comes in on a theoretical level.

The panoptic principle was more radically expressed by Bentham than by any of our modern interpreters of it, including Foucault. Bentham believed the new prison had to be designed so as to ensure much more than the constant visibility of the prisoners to the warders and guards. He said prisons must be designed to guarantee visibility of the whole of the prison to the whole of the outside world. Total visibility according to Bentham is both economical and progressive. The "impartial, humane, and vigilant" eyes of the public could be used to reduce the size of the custodial staff, enormously simplify prison architecture, and replace the cruelties of "iron fetters and fetid dungeons" (145). Complete openness to the public would block any tendency on the part of the prison administration to become corrupt. And it would be the most awful punishment imaginable for the inmates. He sloganized his panoptic prison design as "a mill for grinding rogues honest" (Semple 1993: 152). He went so far as to suggest the warder's toilet should have a commanding view of the inmate population ensuring that the warder "is *necessarily* obliged, as well as without trouble enabled, to give a look into the prison once a day at least, at uncertain and unexpected times" (Semple 1993: 141, Bentham's emphasis).

Foucault was attracted to Bentham's panopticon not just because his theory of the gaze is heavily indebted to it. He was also intrigued with the way the panopticon proffered a nondialectical arrangement of power. In the panopticon, every individual becomes the principle of his own subjugation. As they are constantly visible, they never know whether they are being watched or not, so they must watch themselves all the time. In the panopticon, power, conformity and production can all increase together. Older and less sophisticated structures of power based on physical containment and brute force always produce resistance that increases as force is applied. Panoptic power does not necessarily result in resistance.

Bentham promised that if his prison was built he would *personally* keep an eye on the inmates at random intervals and report them:

> I will keep an unintermitted watch upon him, I will watch until I observe a transgression. I will minute it down. I will wait for another: I will note that down too. I will lie by for a whole day. ... The next day I produce the list to him. You thought yourself undiscovered; you abused my indulgence: see how you were mistaken. ... Learn from this, all of you, that in this house transgression never can be safe. (Semple 1993: 141)

It might be remarked at this point there is a built-in assumption here that the powerful will live forever, or at least until the apocalypse. If Bentham died, who would watch the prisoners? Bentham did not insist his body be stuffed and mounted on a strategic overlook at some prison. But, perhaps because of shifting priorities, he did leave his entire estate to the University of London with the provision that his stuffed and mounted remains be present at all future meetings of the board.

The university has dutifully accommodated his wishes keeping his stuffed body and shrunken head in a cabinet in the boardroom. No back-region refuge for Bentham, not even postmortem in a grave.

Bentham was thoroughgoing in his drive to set up a "system of superintendence, universal, unchargeable [sic] and uninterrupted, the most effectual and *indestructible* of all securities ..." (Semple 1993: 143). Foucault is openly indebted to Bentham for his extension of the concept of *the gaze* in *Discipline and Punish*. Once tested in the prisons, the panoptic principle ought, according to Bentham, apply to other institutional sectors. Again, in his own words, "I take it for granted as a matter of course ... that the doors of all public establishments ought to be thrown wide open to the body of the curious at large—the great *open committee* of the tribunal of the world" (Semple 1993: 142).

These passages are interpreted by some specialists as foundational to law requiring transparency of functioning of democratic institutions. They also were sufficiently resisted that Bentham's panopticon was regarded in his lifetime as a failed project, especially by Bentham himself. As I have suggested, we had to wait until the mid-twentieth century for this entire project to take root and grow in the myriad micro-details of human life. The overall condition of social life increasingly resembles an endless series of mutually mirroring staged authenticities. As this system approaches perfection, everything and everyone at home, at work, or at play; everyone up to good or no good, clothed or naked, is bathed in the same dim moral light. Every secret is supposed to be out in the open, and every person cooperates in the fabrication of intimate "solidarities" or at least agrees we should share a "sense" of "community." In this system, entertainment is a "reality show." Presidents are elected not because they are qualified to be president, but because they appear to be "presidential." When this totalization is complete we will have witnessed the replacement of social structure by paranoid structure. Let me suggest the best index of its progress will be found in the design of what is supposed to be society's deepest back region, its prisons.

Pastel Prisons

The first thing to be noted here is the transposition of prison design after Bentham to other social realms. The first version of the panoptic prison was called the "telegraph pole" design because it had a long central hall with transecting cellblocks that in plan view looked like the cross-bars of a telegraph pole. The idea was to economize movement along the pole necessary to see into all the blocks. This arrangement is now mainly discredited for prisons, but it has been adopted as the most common interior design program for new homes in Disney's town of Celebration, Florida. It realizes better than other arrangements the contemporary requirements of openness, movement, and flow for house design.

In the better-known iconic panopticon prison design, the cellblocks radiate from the guard station like spokes from the hub of a wheel. This is precisely the design Disney adopted for the entire town of Celebration. Viewed from the air, the principal streets radiate out from the town center exactly on the plan of a panoptic prison. And lest we fail to notice the connection, in the center of town there is a device called the "Preview Center," which is a tower, the tallest structure in the town sitting at the point where all the major streets converge. It is not a guard tower, of course, but an annex of Celebration Realty. Prospective home buyers are invited to climb up, gaze upon the entire town, and "pick their neighborhood type."

The current idiom of hip new urban projects plays up a kind of industrial back region appearance. Exposed brick interior walls, industrial steel stairs, polished cement floors and counters, are de rigueur in industrial remodels and are also simulated in new infill construction. This ultra-utilitarian aesthetic is very often quite indistinguishable from stereotypical notions of what jails are like. Under the regime of staged authenticity, our homes and towns increasingly resemble prisons.

New prisons, by contrast, increasingly take pains to distance themselves from utilitarian industrial aesthetics, and certainly from their past as oppressive and "fetid dungeons," and now reach for a kind of light and airy "signature architecture," upscale look. The illustrations in the remarkable book *The Architecture of Incarceration* (Spens, 1994) are brightly beautiful and alluring.

The Federal Correction Institution in Marianna, Florida (Richard Nelson/ Hansen Lind Meyer), for example, combines elegant symmetrical geometric forms (massive squares and triangles) of gray and white stone, red steel, and reflective glass. It resembles a large version of the Robert Venturi and Denise Scott Brown Bank of Celebration, except it is a stronger and more appealing design. Similarly, the Bartholomew County Jail in Columbus, Indiana (Hisaka and Associates/Silver and Ziskind) is a larger and better version of the William Rawn–designed Celebration High School. The jail has energetic Moorish patterns of red brick framed by white stone and is topped by a giant steel mesh dome resembling the profile of a state capitol building.

It is well known that the state now spends more tax money housing felons than it does on college and university education. What is not generally known is not just the money but also the talent, libido, and progressive thinking about the design of living space are now fully invested in systems of incarceration. This is no less the case for interiors as for exteriors. We find in new jail construction in the United States pool tables with pastel felts color coordinated with interior paint, glassed in atria with white gravel floors and mature trees, paisley-shaped interior planters made of chocolate colored polished concrete with matching ceramic tiles on the walls, etc. These kinds of elements are now the norm, not the exception.

I have yet to see a recently constructed jail or prison in the United States that is not more inviting in its exterior, interior, entrances, and common areas than any of the new or renovated loft spaces in Oakland or San Francisco.

When I recently gave a talk at a university in Southern California, several students came forward and told me that the best dormitory on their campus was recently built by an important prison architect and that the university touted this fact in their outreach to new students who considered themselves to be fortunate to be housed there.

These remarks should not be taken as supportive of those who grumble about coddling prisoners. Every human being should have the best housing possible. Rather, I intend these remarks as supportive of my main point. What we have here is society's ultimate back region appearing to be not merely presentable, but well-designed, aesthetically pleasing, even chic. Certainly worthy of anyone's gaze. From the perspective of the forgoing, this can only mean one thing: our prisons are more crowded, violent, and disease-ridden than they have ever been. It is time to bring Goffman and Lacan back into the discussion. It is evident that the dialectic is operating still within our cultural complexes based on total openness and visibility. The unseen is still there, it has just receded further from view and from consciousness. The beautiful images we have of the prisons before they are occupied are masks for the unimaginable brutality and horror they will eventually contain. We have the series of images in *Architecture of Incarceration,* and we have Abu Ghraib, Guantánamo, and an archipelago of extraterritorial torture sites. In short, we have staged authenticity today.

References

Foucault, Michel. 1975. *The Birth of the Clinic: An Archaeology of Medical Perception.* New York: Vintage.

Foucault, Michel. 1975. *Discipline and Punish: The Birth of the Prison.* Alan Sheridan, Trans. New York: Vintage.

Goffman, Erving. 1961a. *The Presentation of Self in Everyday Life.* Garden City, NY: Doubleday.

Goffman, Erving. 1961b. *Asylums: Essays on the Social Situation of Mental Patients and Other Inmates.* Garden City, NY: Doubleday.

Goffman, Erving. 1963. *Encounters: Two Studies in the Sociology of Interaction.* Indianapolis: Bobbs-Merrill.

Kummer, Luke. "How Real is That Ruin? Don't Ask, the Locals Say" *The New York Times,* March 21, 2006. <http://www.nytimes.com/2006/03/21/arts/design/21inca.html?ex=1143608400&en=fd0631db5a528bbc&ei=5070&emc=etal>.

Lacan, Jacques. 1993. *The Seminar of Jacques Lacan, Book Three: The Psychoses, 1955–1956.* Russell Grigg, Trans., New York: Norton.

MacCannell, Dean. 1973. "Staged Authenticity: On Arrangements of Social Space in Tourist Settings," *The American Journal of Sociology,* 79 (3), 589–603.

MacCannell, Dean. 1999. *The Tourist: A New Theory of the Leisure Class,* reprinted with a new afterword by the author. Berkeley: University of California Press.

McReynolds, Kenneth L. 1972. *Physical Components of Correctional Goals.* Report of the Research Centre of the Solicitor General of Canada.

Semple, Janet. 1993. *Bentham's Prison: A Study of the Panopticon Penitentiary.* Oxford: Clarendon.

Spens, Iona, Ed. 1994. *The Architecture of Incarceration.* London: Academy.

Architecture Emblematic
Hardened Sites and Softened Symbols

TREVOR BODDY

Architecture can help us cope with tragedy.

There's an architecture of reassurance and an architecture of provocation.

In the case of a tragedy like this, we want architecture to reassure us,

to define who we are and our place in this moment.

Robert A. M. Stern
Quoted in the Christian Science Monitor
November 23, 2001

If you find Robert Stern's thoughts less than reassuring, read on.

The architectural symbol of George W. Bush's first term as president is not one of Stern's confections for Disney or other corporations, it is not a slickly Neo-Modern condominium penthouse owned by a beneficiary of his tax cuts, it is certainly not Daniel Libeskind's Freedom Tower, it is not even a New Urbanist town green concocted by Andres Duany for some stretch of sunbelt exurbia. No, the architectural symbol of Bush's first term in office is the New Jersey highway barrier.

When that state's highway engineers first shaped its beveled surfaces a half century ago, they had no idea that they were also shaping the first visual icon of the Homeland Security era. Jersey barriers line every freeway in the country, and were designed to deflect a fully loaded tractor trailer going 60 miles per hour. But through 2002 and 2003, New Jersey barriers also became an architectural embellishment for nearly every important building in Washington. Many key federal government edifices had a row of them planted out front, a rude and rustic visual base that reframed the New Roman architectural ambitions rising above them. Jersey barriers were strung across Pennsylvania Avenue, turning it for a time into a pedestrian precinct, while others ringed security stations improvised on parks and esplanades.

The Jersey barriers that so defined Washington in those years might be better described as the "architecture of dis-assurance." They were the visual analogue of the rhetoric of the war on terror, a concrete icon inserted into the city to sustain the "all is changed" sense of unease amongst law-makers, lobbyists and the media. To prop up support for the sweeping anti-terror powers requested by the Bush administration in the months after the September 11 attacks, Washington had cause to change its look for the cameras almost instantly, and changing the architecture of permanent buildings is difficult, expensive and slow. America's center of government framed by Jersey barriers visually emphasized that a new kind of war had begun, and the old rules, and the assurances of yore were off, gone, banished.

But there is a problem with this picture; the security justification for this mania of Jersey barriers did not stand up to scrutiny even as long as the rationale for the Iraq war, a similar weaving of fact and fantasy conceived about the same time. The sectional concrete barriers installed in Washington could have some efficacy against Oklahoma-style truck and car bomb attacks, but they would prove utterly useless against the air-born mode of attacks of September 11 itself, and equally ineffective in stopping suicide bombers with explosives wired around their middles. But there was an instant need for the symbolism of war—something needed to be seen to be done, and under pressures like these, public architecture and urban design shifts from the pragmatic into the emblematic.

Although the Jersey barriers were largely pointless as security devices, they succeeded brilliantly as emblems—visual symbols anchoring deep emotions, like flags in wartime. Emblems have exaggerated importance when national security is thought to be on the line. Although they are many other things as well, the debates over the appropriate architectural and urban forms for the World Trade Center site rebuilding turned on the nature and importance of emblems, though many other words were used in its stead. Never a particularly profound architectural proposition, the Daniel Libeskind proposal for the Freedom Tower got as far as it did almost entirely through the architect's hyperactive promotion of associated emblems—the Statue of Liberty, 1776, and so on. Emblems are vastly more important to the culture and practice of architecture than recent design theory predicts, architectural and urban writing from the past few decades lacking a vocabulary to discuss shared visual symbols.

This absence is in large part because recent discussions of the symbolism of buildings have been short-circuited by the postmodern/deconstructivist/neo-modern debates, or more accurately, nondebates. The style wars of the late twentieth century eerily echo those of the late nineteenth century, but the former conflict was a cold war, largely conducted in the lecture and crit rooms of architecture schools, and turning on the appropriateness of rarified symbolic systems (New England classicism, Russian constructivism, the possibility of reviving the forms without the substance of the Modern Movement, etc.). Compared to the nineteenth-century battle of the styles—which was intensely public, and had the self-identity of the imperial nation-state at its core—this was a struggle within the profession and within the parameters of its own recent history. The notion of emblematic architecture is not only important to understanding public space-making in the years since September 11, but also in understanding the very events of that horrific day. The symbolic and security realities of the war on terror—at home and abroad—are already changing the concepts and professional practices of architects, landscape architects and urbanists. Now we need fresh talk about what has really changed.

The Architecture of Dis-Assurance

When Robert Stern speaks of an "architecture of reassurance," it is a direct reference to an exhibition and related book of the same name produced by University of Minnesota art historian Karal Ann Marling for the Canadian Centre for Architecture in Montreal, and which toured across the United States after opening there. The exhibition and the 1997 book entitled *Designing Disney's Theme Parks: The Architecture of Reassurance*[1] argued that the success of Disneyland, Disney World, and their imitators rests in the emotional reassurance they provide Americans shell-shocked by the constant change of modernity.

> [Disney] believed instead that [his art] ought to provide comfort and refuge from that world of woes he knew at first hand. His park was built behind a berm to protect it from the evils that daily beset humankind on all sides. It aimed to give pleasure. Joy. A flash of sunny happiness. The small, sweet, ordinary, domestic emotions seldom implicit in the definition of aesthetic pleasure. The architecture of reassurance.

Marling notes that the reassurance Disney evokes in his theme parks comes at a price, and that price is manipulation of emotions, streaming of experience, and the reduction of options, in a word, control: "Reassurance and control ... are not qualities readily associated with the Modernist canon. At least not when control is placed in the service of reassurance."

Marling sees the power and popularity of theme parks residing in their enforcement of the constancy of family, church, nation and corporation, strung between an imagined Main Street past and a techno-optimist future.

> Walt Disney Imagineering—Walt's own term: imagination + engineering = "Imagineering"—has conceived a whole range of retail stores, galleries, and hotels, expressly calculated to create and sustain a mood. In the contemporary Hotel on the grounds of Walt Disney world, that mood was futuristic optimism, c. 1969.

Marling's is a Tory argument in the extreme, carried on in her subsequent books on Norman Rockwell and Grandma Moses. It should be noted that Robert Stern's own architectural works for the various Disney parks are featured prominently in Marling's exhibition and related book. No wonder that Stern remembered Marling's phraseology when interviewed by the *Christian Science Monitor,* just weeks after the New York and Washington suicide attacks.

When you take the pro-Disney rah-rah away from Marling's writing, her key insight is that the parks work by coding spaces with emotions, not ideas. The Disney parks are as manipulative of emotions as the on-screen death of Bambi's mother or an anthropomorphized Old Yeller.

> The gentle fakery of style is entertaining and Disneyland aimed, above all, to entertain. It soothes and reassures the visitor, too, in ways the designers began to understand only after the dust had settled and they could look down from their drafting tables in [Disneyland's] City Hall and watch the happy crowds streaming down Main Street toward the castle.

Architectural criticism and history both tend to emphasize ideas over emotions, and it may say much about the public discussion of buildings that these more emotional operations should lack a critical vocabulary. Critics and urbanists talk knowledgeably about the historic sources of contemporary urban forms—from the City Beautiful, Le Corbusier's Plan Voisin, Levittown—but less well about the ideological forces behind city-building, and almost never about this kind of emotional coding of urban effects. This was not always true, as the patriarch of the Anglo-Saxon tradition of architectural and urban criticism, John Ruskin, imbued his critical writings with emotional responses to what he saw, and what he saw were cityscapes conceived out of emotion. Lacking the vigor of Ruskin's moralizing prose, the only emotions to be found in most contemporary built environment criticism is celebrity love and a generic hatred of the poor and the ordinary.

The "fear theming"—or architecture of dis-assurance—deployed with those hundreds of Jersey barriers installed throughout central Washington and the Stock Exchange district of Lower Manhattan in 2002 and 2003 has a strangely inverted analogue in the "hope theming" of the Green Zone in Baghdad several years later. Within a city and country torn by insurrection, this fortified oasis of a small portion of the city's center seems less the proud home of true urban improvement, than the artificial base for media and reconstruction teams, a kind of theme park designed to advance the myth of Iraqi stabilization. And designed it was—the boundaries of the Green Zone so determined as to include not just some key hotels and government buildings, but also extensive riverside parks (hence the name) and a scenic mosque, just the right background for the filing of stories by television journalists. Thus imagistic urbanism was enlisted to support the Administration and Defense Department's selling of military policy, these zealously maintained square miles of relative tranquility being necessary to sustain those stand-up accounts by Green-Zoned reporters predicting the turning of the corner in Iraq. The Green Zone's illusion of tranquility was punctuated by the insurrectionists' rockets and suicide bombs just often enough to indicate that they knew full well what was going on.

The wish to imbue urban spaces with narrative messages—the theme in the theme parks—extends globally these days. Islamic fundamentalists promote an urban and environmental fantasy of their own, the organic reintegration of a unified faith-based society, culture, and economy that supposedly existed under the Caliphate 1,100 years ago. Accounts of the New Caliphate that would result if al-Qa'eda, Hezbollah and related groups got their way are eerily similar to the "architecture of re-assurance" of theme parks. They propose cities and countries structured by imposition of a narrative—in their case, the Koran, the Hadith, and subsequent interpretations—which will encode spaces with emotions, specifically faith and its opposite, anger against those without faith. If Marling is right in her proposition that Disneyland and other theme parks are Americans' ultimate refuge against the shocks and incomprehensibility of modernity, how different is the Islamist's fantasy of a New Caliphate from Morocco to Indonesia?

The architecture of dis-assurance of New Jersey barriers all around Washington, and subsequent public buildings constructed with very evident moats, gates and impregnable bases exploit the fears rather than the hopes of Americans, but are just as effective. By 2004, Washington's National Capital Planning Commission was publicly worrying that the use of Jersey barriers was communicating "fear and retrenchment, and undermine the basic premises of an open and democratic society," whereas the conservative *Weekly Standard* suggested that security-obsessed designs for new buildings there could be read as "unwitting memorials to Timothy McVeigh and Al Qaeda."[2]

In the inventory of human emotions that shape buildings and cities, fear often comes disguised as pride. We accept a little too easily arguments that new buildings or re-fashioned squares are manifestations solely of the superstructures of ego and identity—be they of the architect, client or nation-state—and not indicative of the substrates of darker motivations that lay stratified beneath them. In reading the messages of a courthouse, an embassy, or a condo tower, we usually remain content to regard only their public faces, and miss the more subtle messages subsumed into their body language: the realities expressed through architectural twists of spines, the folding of shoulders, the tilt of thighs.

Changing conceptions of public space in the Homeland Security era can be read through the body language of recent buildings and urban designs. This means reading constructions as emblems, certainly, but it also means reading ideas of democracy and security subsumed into their architectural body politic. Because the design and construction of public buildings is such a slow process, the architectural implications of 9/11 have only recently become apparent. Even now, we remain too close to those events to fully anticipate how permanent any shifts in conceptions of public architecture and public space will prove to be. This emblematic architecture may well prove to be a fleeting epi-phenomenon of the politics of fear, destined to fade away along with the alarmist politicians who have exploited our insecurities.

Embassies Emblematic

Architecture is inescapably a political art, and it reports faithfully for ages to come what the political values of a particular era were. Surely, ours must be openness and fearlessness in the face of those who hide in the darkness. A precaution, yes, sequester, no.

—**Senator Daniel Patrick Moynihan**
to a November 2001 security conference

There is one building type—because of prominence, vulnerability, and political associations—that has been the subject of hardening for far longer than others, and may predict where the architecture of the insecurity state is headed. The building type is, of course, American embassies—that most emblematic of all emblematic architectures. The car or truck laden with bombs and piloted by a suicidal driver has shifted design and public space considerations for American embassies for over two decades. If the rhetoric of dis-assurance continues, the design considerations of recently constructed embassies may well predict the security features that will be built into public buildings in the years to come.

In speculating on which antiterror features of embassies might migrate to mainstream design, there is no point examining one of the bunker-embassies constructed over the past two decades, such as the fortified, almost completely autonomous live-work embassy and staff quarters compound outside of Sanaa, Yemen. This design was initiated after the 1983 Beirut bombings that sparked the current tightening of embassy design standards. That year, 83 had been killed in the bombing of the American embassy in the Lebanese capital, followed by the bombing and residence building collapse there that cost the lives of 241 Marines. Situated a half-hour drive outside of the Yemeni capital, and isolated from the diplomatic, business and government life of the city, the armed fort on an isolated exurban site was not an option for the larger and more important American missions abroad.

Not that the State Department did not advocate fortification and isolation, as illustrated in the mounting security concerns that shaped the American embassy in Ottawa, officially opened by president Clinton in 1999. Americans had been well-served by the Neo-Roman swagger of Cass Gilbert's 1932 American embassy there, a white marble classical foil to the picturesque textures and Gothic arches of the Canadian Houses of Parliament, across Wellington Street. American trade, consular and diplomatic missions had long outgrown the Gilbert-designed building, and the completion of the North American Free Trade Agreement in the mid-1980s made acute the need for a much larger embassy.

The first of many security-prompted debates for the American embassy in Ottawa was one about the choice of site. The Canadians were much further along in the process of building their own Arthur Erickson–designed Chancery in Washington—in fact, Washington officials had assembled a very high-profile site, one ensuring that Canada's will remain the only foreign mission ever to be constructed along the sanctum sanctorum of Pennsylvania Avenue itself. Quid pro quo, the Canadians had assembled a similarly prominent American embassy site beside Parliament Hill—next to the Byward Market, and adjacent to Moshe Safdie's National Gallery of Canada, neatly analogous to the Canadian embassy site near I. M. Pei's East Wing of the National Gallery.

The symmetrical symbolism of friendship intended by the Parliament Hill site was disrupted by the Beirut bombings. Worried State Department staffers promoted a second, much larger site in a suburb to the east, one that would ensure that installations were well isolated from truck bombers. The final choice of site was dominated by Senator Moynihan and other politicians, not State Department staffers. Siting and architectural decisions for the American Embassy in Ottawa were deeply influenced by the success of the emblematic architecture of Arthur Erickson's Washington Chancery. *Washington Post* architecture critic Benjamin Forgey has consistently named the Erickson design amongst the best buildings of the past 25—admittedly weak—years of Washington architecture. Erickson's Washington achievement was to find a way to conform to the mandatory classical design requirements of the Fine Arts Commission and other approving agencies, while confounding the pomposity and lack of visual porosity of the Imperial PoMo that has become the city's house style. Embellished by a tempietto on the corner and a free-standing entablature in the open courtyard that conformed to the letter if not the sense of the Washington design guidelines, Erickson hollowed out the site at grade, breaking the 'heavy base with piano nobile' compositional logic for Washington buildings, and making us Canadians look oh-so-friendly, and oh-so-open for business.

Shamed by Erickson on Pennsylvania Avenue, American politicians overrode the State Department's worries and accepted the downtown Ottawa site, wedged between two busy streets. Impressed by his ability to weave through design guidelines and mandarins in Washington honed during a decade in practice there, the embassy design job went to David Childs of Skidmore Owings Merrill, knowing the project would encounter a similarly prescriptive treatment from Ottawa's National Capital Commission. This same skill for architectural power brokerage would later land Childs the commission for the World Trade Center site.

Figure 1 Perspective study of the Ottawa American Embassy by Skidmore Owings Merrill. The Byward Market is in the foreground, the Gothic spires of the Library of Parliament at top left, Douglas Cardina's Museum of Civilization near the horizon, and Moshe Safdie's National Gallery of Canada to the right of architect David Childs's design proposition.

Childs's early design propositions for Ottawa adopted an Erickson-inspired version of a 'good neighbor' urban design policy—lots of visual porosity, a centerpiece atrium, gestures to the local Neo-Gothic architecture of power. But the climate in Washington was changing, largely due to increasing support for a 1985 report to the State Department chaired by retired admiral Bobby Ray Inman.[3] Prepared in the wake of the Beirut bombings, what have since been labeled "The Inman Standards" set the agenda first for American embassies abroad in the 1990s, and in this decade, for federal buildings generally. This is the constitutional document for the public architecture of the insecurity state, even though it contains only a few design standards as such, just a broad-based call for better-managing the hardening of American installations, plus limited suggestions on the use of "blast zone" separations from streets, a 15 percent ratio of windows to exterior walls, and so on. The Inman report is constitutional for the Fortress America era, not because of the power of its prescriptions, but because it embodies the philosophy of the times—a framework of belief for living under threat, real or imagined.

The Inman report proposed spending billions of federal dollars to secure and harden most of the nearly 500 American missions and offices abroad, and much of this work has been accomplished in its wake. The truck-bombing of the Alfred P. Murrah Federal Building in Kansas City in 1995 accelerated the extension of "Inman Standards" to federal buildings across the country, both for new buildings at the planning stage, and in the retrofit of existing facilities. After the bombing of American diplomatic posts in Nairobi and Dar es Salaam, former chairman of the Joint Chiefs of Staff Admiral William Crowe produced a 1999 follow-on report urging implementation of the Inman standards, a process which accelerated after 9/11.

This darkening of attitudes complicated Childs's design development of the Ottawa embassy. Visual porosity was traded for the impermeability of a more reflective glass, the atrium was moved to a more secure location in mid-plan, and more and more, the building came to resemble the crenellated Scottish Baronial style of Revenue Canada's Late Victorian castle next door. More problematic was the proximity of the planned embassy's two main facades to essential city streets—one of them, Sussex Drive, being the Canadian equivalent of Pennsylvania Avenue, linking Parliament Hill to the Prime Minister's official residence, just as the Washington grand avenue links Capitol with White House.

In the chilling language of perimeter safety experts, the distance from the place where vehicles can be stopped to building walls is called the "standoff distance." Setbacks of a standoff distance sufficient for blast protection (the Inman report suggests one hundred feet) would reduce the site to the point of complete unbuildability, and plans were now too advanced to abandon this building plot. As stated in the Inman report, "Being on the busiest or most fashionable street or corner may have been an asset in earlier days; today it is a liability."[4] It is an interesting side speculation here that Childs' success in arguing for security perimeter control without a huge building setback in Ottawa may have led to the same strategy—spectacularly rejected in the summer of 2005—in his site plan for the World Trade Center site.

Enter the march of the bollards. Elaborate negotiations were then undertaken between SOM, the State Department and urban designers at Ottawa's National Capital Commission to literally ring the new embassy with dozens of bollards on each side along much-widened sidewalks. These are not the pleasantly low traffic separation indicators of old, but waist-high hardened steel posts, each with its own deep foundations, wrapped in a casing of dark stone, and topped with eyes of built-in lights.

After the building opened, Ottawans took to calling this permanently assembled ring of bollards "The Ewoks," after the height-challenged, berobed *Star Wars* characters. The metaphor is apt. With the Ottawa American Embassy's horizontally banded reflective windows framed by polychrome stonework, and all this capped by a jaunty "chateau chapeau" in mid-plan, the building evokes the production design look of period revival architectural nostalgia laminated onto high tech devised for the last few George Lucas space tales. There is a cinematic symmetry to this. The first of those films had its title adopted by President Reagan to legitimate his space weapons initiative, so it is appropriate that the last of them

Figure 2 Industrial Light and No Magic? As built, David Childs'/SOM's Ottawa American Embassy has view-impervious banded glass facing Parliament Hill, with a 'Chateau Chapeau' and quoined flanking wings alluding to the Canadian capital's Victoriana.

would resonate with so pompous a symbol of American empire in decline, set for all to see in the capital of its closest neighbor.

Passive-Aggressive Urban Design

Edges of empires are always the most revealing of imperial drift, and my second key example is at the northwest edge of the Lower 48, seemingly out of the main terrorist line of fire. The future of the emblematic architecture of a war on terror without end is not revealed in new embassies for some African nation—America's missions abroad will be variations on a bunker in perpetuity—but in one of its most liberal cities, in a showpiece project authored by a progressive design firm.

With the rise of its dot.com wealth through the late 1990s, Seattle started an ambitious rebuilding program for its key public institutions. There were new or vastly enlarged buildings for its main public library, federal courthouse, opera house, art gallery, justice center (county courthouse), public safety commission and city hall. These last three were combined into a three block government building campus on the south end of Seattle's downtown core.

Newly establishing a Seattle practice after a significant European career—including the design of the Princess Diana garden in London—Kathryn Gustafson's firm of Gustafson Guthrie Nichol was selected as landscape architects and public realm urban designers for the entire Downtown Civic Campus, in association with Swift and Company. This is a three-block area including the city hall plaza and it provides a continuous landscape and public space plan for the two adjacent blocks, the one uphill being the site of the Justice Center, the one downhill on this, the steepest portion of downtown Seattle, being future home to a new public safety building (as yet unbuilt). The architecture firm of Bohlin Cywinski Jackson in joint venture with Bassetti Partnership was selected to design the city hall building.

The whole endeavor was so Seattle: city hall's building design and the layout of the public spaces around it were subject to an exhaustive public consultation process; an ambitious public art program was conceived for the site; a commitment to LEED gold certification was made; and local politicians demanded and got the most transparent home to civic government possible. Bohlin Cywinski Jackson took this last demand literally, and the city council chamber pavilion and the main civic office block are almost entirely sheathed in glass. All of these concerns for the public realm are consistent with Seattle's reputation for Nordic liberality, born of the out-of-the-woods Swedes and Norwegians who first built the town in the

Figure 3 Uphill view of Bohlin Cywinski Jackson's new Seattle City Hall with the Gustafson Guthrie Nichol plaza in the foreground. (Courtesy of Gustafson Guthrie Nichol Ltd.)

1870s, and of the constant infusion of Canadian values, with ever-progressive Vancouver astride the border just two hours away.

As preliminary planning work began for the new civic spaces, the city was home to the WTO meetings and related "Battle for Seattle" in December 1999. It is hard to over-emphasize how difficult this kind of global exposure was to liberal, tolerant, inclusivist Seattle—certainly just as much a challenge to its burnished self-image as the dot-com collapse which followed soon after. Later, public safety and civic officials carefully studied security camera and network television coverage of the attacks against chain stores, restaurants, banks and other symbols of global capitalism. Of particular interest was the role played by a small plaza in the

Figure 4 Passive-aggressive security design a la Cascadia? The adjustable shallow fountain and upspouts of the new Seattle City Hall plaza may be low-key but very useful for crowd control. (Courtesy of Gustafson Guthrie Nichol Ltd.)

Westlake area of the downtown shopping district. It was soon evident to authorities that this public space—something downtown Seattle has very little of—had served as a kind of staging area for the riots, and that pavers there provided missiles, and movable street furniture was turned into shields and barriers.

According to landscape architect and Gustafson partner Jennifer Guthrie,[5] the legacy of the WTO riots shaped design requirements they were given for the new Seattle Civic Campus, including the City Hall plaza. To begin with, every item in the public domain had to be "tied down"—elaborate and often hidden tie-backs and anchoring devices so that pavers, railings, stone ledges and walls could not be pulled apart, and their components turned into hurled weapons. Public safety concerns shaped other details, their design rationale often not at first evident. For example, one of the most baffling details from Gustafson Guthrie Nichol is on the courthouse block, where what looks like a handrailing extends from the plaza level, *horizontally*, out over the top a row of dense planting. According to Guthrie, there was a continuing problem at the old courthouse: miscreants arriving for court appearances were using any available shrubbery or other niche as a temporary hiding place to stash their weapons and drugs. The horizontal railing would require bending down and reaching over in a much more obvious way, and the awkward act was sure to be more obvious to security staff positioned at viewpoints above.

More problematic is the largest public square on the three blocks, down a large ceremonial stair from the front doors of Seattle City Hall. This is the obvious spot for a demonstration at city hall, but it has an oblique visual relationship at best with the main public spaces inside City Hall looming above. The City Hall plaza is framed by brightly-colored glass fronting, what is currently called 'soft space,' a zone that will eventually become home to shops and fast food restaurants when leasing conditions are right. Somehow, "Demo at the Food Court!" just does not raise the pulse of urban insurrection, and no security plan is yet in effect for flying pieces of Kentucky Fried Chicken, though assault with stone-like day-old Dunkin' Donuts should be covered by existing laws.

What can only be described as a passive aggressive urban design strategy is apparent in the adjustable water feature covering a variable portion of this plaza. This is one of Gustafson's trademark shallow fountain-squares, similar to the linear one she designed for the Seattle Center forecourt of the city's McCaw Hall opera house. The pavement is sloped slightly to a spill edge, with water supplied in nearly two dozen vertical spouts, which can be electively turned off and on, their heights adjusted from bare dribbles to geysers taller than an antiglobalist. The presence of the shallow pond on the piazza quietly discourages public assembly, and the vertical spouts have the potential to disperse demonstrators, though Guthrie cannot imagine the mayor selectively turning these features on or off to eliminate trouble-some crowds. The point here is that it *can* be used this way, and a shallow pond at the psychic center of the only key assembly point can be read as a kind of prior censorship of protest, even in rainy Seattle.

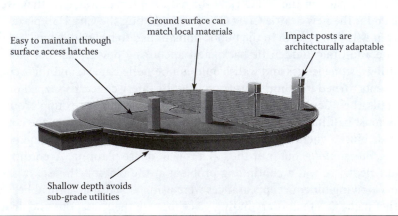

Figure 5 Designed by the Rogers Marvel spinoff firm Rock Twelve Security Architecture, the rotating table uses revolving restaurant technology to spin hardened bollards out of the way to permit entry by security-cleared vehicles. The turntable plate surface can be covered with brick, pavers, asphalt, or even living grass to match the urban context.

Figure 6 The thin concrete shell of the "Tiger Trap" permits pedestrian activity, while falling away under the weight of a vehicle, trapping potential bombers, in this design by the New York architectural firm of Rogers Marvel in association with Rock Twelve Security Architecture, published in the 2005 National Capital Planning Commission report "Designing and Testing Perimeter Safety Elements," page 6.

The square is a beautifully crafted piece of urban design, but one that cannot completely transcend the political assumptions built into its creation. As such, it represents the future of the hardening of public buildings and public space—soft on the outside, hard within, the iron hand inside the civic velvet glove. The obvious hardening of urban installations was a temporary emblem, as much a symbol of its times as color-coded terror alerts, as architecture and urbanism shaped by the Homeland Security era has got more subtle recently.

Because of the design ingenuity of Gustafson and her team, some of the most powerful antiterrorism features have been rendered all but invisible. This is in stark contrast to the all-too-evident late 1990s approach to perimeter security, evident just a few blocks away in the moat that almost entirely surrounds Seattle's new Federal Courthouse. Perimeter safety for Seattle's Downtown Civic Campus is not achieved with obvious walls or moats, but by the subtle shifts and geometries of the key landscape design features themselves. The clever disposition of plantings, sitting ledges, and exploitation of the steep grade changes across the three-block Downtown Civic Campus all combine to prevent vehicles bearing explosives from gaining access to the site.

Insecure Ingenuity

This same progression toward softer, more invisible perimeter security features, and away from the obvious hardening of Jersey barriers and

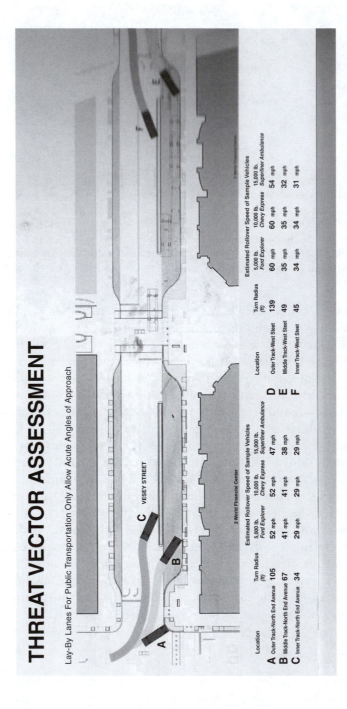

THREAT VECTOR ASSESSMENT

Lay-By Lanes For Public Transportation Only Allow Acute Angles of Approach

2 World Financial Center

Estimated Rollover Speed of Sample Vehicles

Location	Turn Radius (ft)	5,000 lb. Ford Explorer	10,000 lb. Chevy Express	15,000 lb. Superliner Ambulance
A Outer Track-North End Avenue	105	52 mph	52 mph	47 mph
B Middle Track-North End Avenue	67	41 mph	41 mph	38 mph
C Inner Track-North End Avenue	34	29 mph	29 mph	29 mph

Estimated Rollover Speed of Sample Vehicles

Location	Turn Radius (ft)	5,000 lb. Ford Explorer	10,000 lb. Chevy Express	15,000 lb. Superliner Ambulance
D Outer Track-West Steet	139	60 mph	60 mph	54 mph
E Middle Track-West Street	49	35 mph	35 mph	32 mph
F Inner Track-West Steet	45	34 mph	34 mph	31 mph

VESEY STREET

Figure 7 The Rogers Marvel "Battery Park City Streetscapes Project" is the first synthetic urban design plan of the Homeland Security era, the plan here demonstrating how the use of traffic control devices and traffic lay-bys can render more oblique the angle of attack by a hostile vehicle.

building-wrapping moats evident in Seattle also was emerging as public urban design policy in Washington. Always a security-conscious national capital, the Oklahoma attacks prompted major security studies by the National Capital Planning Commission in 1999, and a second NCPC report released in October 2001 from the Interagency Task Force,[6] although they were in preparation for years. The focus of these studies is largely the hardening of public buildings and memorials from attack by car or truck bombs.

By 2004, the National Capital Planning Commission had come to recognize the limits to the task before them, when it became apparent that many of the initial protective measures against car and truck bombs did little for chemical, biological, or suicide bomber threats:

> The Commission has grown concerned that these escalating threat assessments and potentially extreme security responses undermine its objectives for a vibrant capital city that showcases democratic ideals of openness and accessibility. In addition, the cost of ever more sophisticated security measures against an expanding array of threats is beginning to overwhelm individual agency budgets.[7]

On May 5, 2005, the NCPC had rolled out the chapter and verse of their security strategy in a policy document entitled "The National Capital Urban Design and Security Plan—Objectives and Policies." The scope and the inherent limitations of balancing security with the democratic need for vital urban spaces are apparent in the second and third of five key policies:

> To strike a balance between physical perimeter security for federal buildings and the vitality of the public realm.

> To acknowledge that acceptance of a reasonable level of risk is inherent in striking an appropriate balance between security provisions and other fiscal, planning, design and operational objectives.

In other words, the NCPC bureaucracy was acknowledging that the era of the Jersey barrier was over, and that security planning efforts were to be mainstreamed into ongoing planning policies and procedures. The plan calls for perimeter safety measures integrated with other landscape and urban design concerns such as streetscape improvement and contextualism. With the adoption of the 2005 plan, the "the architecture of dis-assurance" would no longer advance the rhetoric of the war on terror, though even today, a few Jersey barriers linger around a handful of Washington buildings, visual reminders of an era of color-coded terror warnings and a xenophobic mentality that sought perimeter safety, be it of buildings or the nation itself.

New York City had a neatly parallel experience with "the architecture of dis-assurance" in the years after 9/11. Thought to be a likely target, the streets around the New York Stock Exchange were quickly blocked with Jersey barriers, with awkward security checkpoints monitoring all traffic in and out. Corporate office towers in Lower Manhattan and Mid-Town soon developed their own, distinctly New York version of the wave of Jersey barriers flanking Washington federal departments and agencies. In New York, the Jersey barriers were almost always set curbside to line streets, in order to prevent bomb-laden vehicles crashing into lobbies or through storefronts, where explosions could cause serious damage, even building collapse.

The ring of Jersey barriers often ran right around street corners, hugely inconveniencing pedestrians and adding to the air of an armed camp set within the world's business and media capital. Smaller and historic buildings did not have barriers in front of them, and the sequencing of the barriers soon became a marker of the location of the largest and most security-conscious corporations. Since the barriers were private initiatives set up by individual building owners, the range of differently shaped or spaced barriers soon became a curbside analogue to the corporate fashion show of the architecture they flanked. In an attempt to mitigate their visual impact and emotional weight, the barriers were sometimes interspersed with flower-bedecked planters, or even had their gray concrete flanks painted lively colors. The net effect of these mitigation efforts was like wrapping wall-mounted fire extinguishers with lace, or maybe planting the Maginot Line with decorative shrubbery—decorative efforts only drawing attention to the very public safety threats they were intended to camouflage.

One New York architectural firm used a string of public security commissions to build up expertise in architecture and urban design for the Homeland Security era. The partnership of Rob Rogers and Jon Marvel began in 1992, their Lower Manhattan–based firm winning awards for their innovative academic pavilion, community gallery building and urban design work. Teaming up with "force protection engineers" and urban security expert Bob Ducibella, Rogers Marvel won a major 2002 contract to design permanent alternatives for the Jersey barriers and security checkpoints around the New York Stock Exchange. Rob Rogers calls the domination of New York streetscapes by Jersey barriers "really brutal and really dumb."[8] One of their first and still most famous security designs were brass-covered bollards like no other that they named the "NOGO barrier," and fabricated and installed in time for the 2004 Republican National Convention in New York. A series of oblique surfaces intended to deflect attacking vehicles, the geometry and metallic surfaces of Rogers Marvel's NOGO barriers were so seductive to the eye and the touch that a prototype was included in a 2004 Museum of Modern Art exhibition on design for security. There is now a NOGO installed in the lobby of their architectural offices, like a meteorite dropped from the Homeland Security universe into an otherwise conventional design firm setting.

Rogers Marvel soon joined together with security engineering experts to form a spinoff firm with the Jean Claude van Damme-worthy macho name of "Rock Twelve Security Architecture." The number in the firm's name comes from "K12," the highest design standard for perimeter security devices as established by military researchers, sufficient to stop a 15,000 pound truck traveling 50 miles per hour. Designed to that same

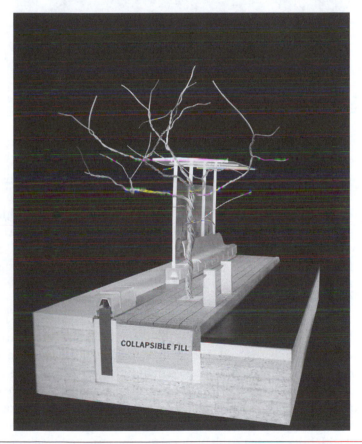

COLLAPSIBLE FILL

Figure 8 The Rogers Marvel plan for Battery Park City's streetscapes is the first *gesamtkunstwerk* of Homeland Security era urban design, with this architect's model demonstrating the smaller version of the Tiger Trap combined with steel-armatured illuminated benches and bus stop street furniture.

Figure 9 The Rogers Marvel plan for Battery Park City's streetscapes is the first *gesamtkunts-werk* of Homeland Security era urban design, with this architect's model demonstrating the smaller version of the Tiger Trap combined with steel-armatured illuminated benches and bus stop street furniture.

standard is Rock Twelve's next design for the Stock Exchange district, the "innovative operable vehicle attenuation device," another Pentagon-sounding euphemism. Replacing the awkward and breachable vehicular check stations for Lower Manhattan, this is better known as the "turntable barrier system," a kind of Lazy Susan rotating plate with a string of secure bollards on one side. Once a vehicle is security-cleared, a switch is flipped and the turntable holding secure bollards rotates 90 degrees, temporarily creating a gap large enough for entry. The design of this "operable anti-ram device" is a masterstroke of Yankee ingenuity, requiring only two feet of excavation to install the turntable, less than most other barriers or hydraulically controlled bollards, and thus saving a fortune in relocation costs for subterranean utility lines. There is a wonderful irony of spectacle being turned into invisibility here, with the turntable powered by the same Macton Corporation friction wheel drive system used in panoramic rotating restaurants all over the world, but the surface of its plate being able to be covered with bricks, stone, asphalt or even living grass to blend in with its urban surroundings. Thus Rock Twelve's rotating barrier echoes the shift from 2002's rhetorical architecture of dis-assurance, to 2005's security features mainstreamed into design-integrated invisibility.

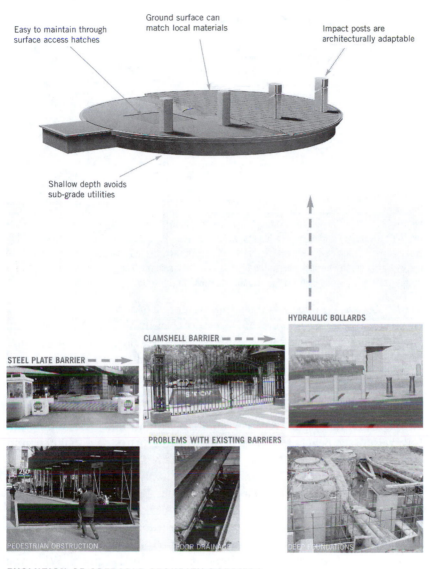

Easy to maintain through surface access hatches

Ground surface can match local materials

Impact posts are architecturally adaptable

Shallow depth avoids sub-grade utilities

HYDRAULIC BOLLARDS

CLAMSHELL BARRIER

STEEL PLATE BARRIER

PROBLEMS WITH EXISTING BARRIERS

PEDESTRIAN OBSTRUCTION

POOR DRAINAGE

DEEP FOUNDATIONS

EVOLUTION OF OPERABLE SECURITY BARRIERS

Figure 10 The thin concrete shell of the "Tiger Trap" permits pedestrian activity, while falling away under the weight of a vehicle, trapping potential bombers. (Drawings courtesy of Rogers-Marvel/ Rock Twelve Security.)

Perhaps the most brilliant of all the Rock Twelve security designs for active urban spaces is the "Tiger Trap: a patented invention designed to reduce the impact of force protection installations on public space."[9] The key technology here is a collapsible form of aerated concrete developed

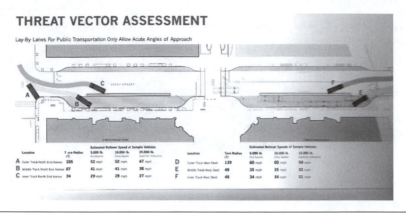

Figure 11 Rogers Marvel plan showing "threat vector analysis" for Vesey Street in Lower Manhattan, part of Battery Park City. The Rogers Marvel "Battery Park City Streetscapes Project" is the first synthetic urban design plan of the Homeland Security era, the plan here demonstrating how the use of traffic control devices and traffic lay-bys can render more oblique the angle of attack by a hostile vehicle. (Drawing courtesy Rogers-Marvel/Rock Twelve Security.)

by the Zodiac Engineered Arresting Systems Corporation (believe me, I could not make these names up) to stop aircraft overshooting runways. Under the terms of the Rock Twelve patent, the Zodiac concrete product is installed under a thin shell of concrete, sufficient to support every range of pedestrian activity, but which will shear away and collapse to form a pit when the weight of any motorized vehicle passes over it. With installations to date in Lower Manhattan, Battery Park City and the Pentagon, the vehicle-catching "Tiger Trap" is combined with an innocent looking but fully reinforced bench, proven in actual crash tests to stop a 15,000 pound truck hurtling at 50 miles per hour, as per the K12 design standard.

Rogers Marvel use most of their sister company's safety gizmos in their recently completed "Battery Park Streetscapes Project,"[10] for a large site near Ground Zero. Working for the Battery Park City Authority—one of New York's most design-sensitive and public-minded agencies—this public realm design study is a holistic streetscape improvement scheme, and the first *gesamtkunstwerk* of the Homeland Security design era. While the Tiger Trap and the smaller version called the "Pit Trap" are installed along Vesey Street, the use of these expensive installations is minimized through "threat vector assessment," a new branch of urban design that uses much cheaper lay-bys and other traffic control devices to reduce the possible maximum speed and angle of attack for any vehicle with terrorist intentions. Using lighting structures and shade devices to temper the visual environment at all times of day, the study also proposes continuous glass benches, lit from within. Typical of design sensibilities in the Homeland

Figure 12 This view of a portion of the constructed Rogers Marvel-designed public spaces at New York's Battery Park City shows landscape elements and a tiger trap in place—architecture of the Homeland Security era no longer emblematic, but part of everyday design practice, its presence unknown to the public. (Photo courtesy Rogers-Marvel, Rock Twelve Security.)

Security era, these luminously light urban embellishments secretly contain continuous steel armatures that could stop a truck, more of the velvet-over-steel-glove, passive-aggressive urban design innovation demanded by the current climate.

The Tiger Trap and other increasingly invisible perimeter safety design elements are promoted in the 2005 study "Designing and Testing of Perimeter Safety Elements," published by the National Capital Planning Commission. Much of the NCPC report demonstrates how ordinary street furniture elements can be transformed into formidable devices to thwart vehicular bombers. Beware oh ye forces of evil: that ordinary-looking *Washington Post* newspaper coin box has a steel shaft up its wazoo; hear-ye all wastrel Talibanians and dis-affected Idaho survivalists, don't dare drive your fertilizer-laden Ford 150 through that bus shelter, as its hardened base will ensure your pickup's cab separates from your box enroute. It is just a matter of time until Hollywood cottons on to the dramatic potential of patriotic street furniture—park benches and bus shelters taking on the forces of darkness. I proposed the Jersey barrier as the architectural icon of the first Bush presidency, and now suggest that the Tiger Trap is the equivalent symbol for his second term, with the unintended resonance that an image of a disabled truck full of explosives provides for the frustrated ambitions of his latter-day administration.

Conclusion: Emblems Problematic

The Tiger Trap, the Gustafson Guthrie Nichol Seattle features and the other perimeter security design innovations are gee-whiz, can-do, American Imagineering ingenuity at its finest, and demonstrate the mainstreaming of hardening considerations into the standard design process for public buildings and urban spaces. This mainstreaming of security urban design has its historic precedents in the manner in which fire safety issues were normalized into architecture and planning practice over the past century and a half, and in the way Green design features are currently being integrated into everyday professional work. Recognizing the evident design skill of firms like Rogers Marvel, there are tragic flaws with these strategies, however, at both the micro and the macro scale of terrorist activity.

The pedestrian suicide bomber confounds all of this research and design innovation aimed almost entirely to date at stopping car and truck bombs. There is no strategy for the physical design of public buildings and public spaces that can discourage, never-mind prevent, a determined suicide bomber, acting alone. Starting in the Middle East and now extending elsewhere, the suicide bomber "de-architecturalizes" terrorist threats, because effective prevention and screening cannot be accomplished through change in the physical form of buildings or the shape and appointments of public space alone. As any Tel Avivian or Bogotano knows, it is the human chain of bomb inspectors, mirror-bearing under-carriage-checkers, bomb-sniffer operators, entry point friskers and other omni-present security forces that best protect urban populations from the threat of suicide and package bombers, calling into question the fear-driven shift to physical hardening that has taken place over the past half decade. Although pathetic laggards such as the teenager-dominated fundamentalist cell discovered in Toronto in the spring of 2006 still assemble bulky bags of fertilizer for truck-borne attacks, the leading edge of terrorist strategy has shifted to neatly miniaturized package and suicide bombs on public transport, as in Madrid and London.

By comparison, integrating antivehicular-attack features is a piece of cake compared to predicting accurately whether a visitor's thickness around the middle is adipose fat or explosives, whether that rucksack or briefcase is full of briefs or bombs. The entire political and technocratic infrastructure of antiterrorism-through-design was confounded by the suicide-bombings of London Transport buses and tube trains in the summer of 2005, and the urban trains of Madrid before that. For one, the Madrid, London, and Toronto terror schemes were almost entirely planned and executed by home-grown terrorists, not imported evildoers. These facts push into question the demonization of the foreign, and the subsequent homeland security-driven national-border and even building-by-building perimeter safety obsessions of the Blair government in Britain, the Bush administration, and Canada's new right wing regime under Stephen Harper. Terrorist evil, it turns out, can grow up just down the street, and might just walk instead of drive.

At this point in the argument, the notion of the emblematic must be re-introduced. Functioning emblematically, the Jersey barrier era exemplified the architecture of dis-assurance, visual markers that things had changed, it was not business as usual, that every public building was a potential target, and that a state of war existed. The urban design equivalent to a continuous state of red-alert, this set of alarmist visuals could not be maintained, because of their clumsiness and the dulling of fear that comes with daily encounter. With the design ingenuity of firms like Gustafson Guthrie Nichol at Seattle's Downtown Civic Campus, and with public realm design standards such as those in the National Capital Planning Commission's 2005 "Designing and Testing of Perimeter Safety Elements," things switched to the more typical and comfortable mode of an architecture of reassurance. Whether faux-historical bollards that could stop a tank or vehicle-deflecting topiary and fall-away sidewalks, these innovations are emblematic of the new theme park of security that has enveloped us. The theme is fear, and it can be overt, or it can be sublimated, but it is always there.

If architectural and urban design security strategies common in the Bush/Blair era fail to deal with the solo suicide bomber, they also fail to deal with the singular act that initiated it—the piloting of an airplane into a large building. Engineers investigated, then quickly abandoned the notion of design strategies for roofs and walls that would withstand a direct hit from a Cessna loaded with Sentex, never mind an airliner loaded with fuel. There is no way to do this that will not lead to almost uninhabitable bunkers, or built structures of ludicrous expense. For example, the hyperbolic-formed concrete towers over most nuclear power installations are usually known as "cooling towers" and indeed often have small vents within them, but one of the key reasons for their peculiar shape, huge size and solidity is not just containment, but to deflect direct attacks by airplanes and small missiles. They are also so expensive that they have effectively precluded new installations for a generation. Appropriate for a culture in which the traffic engineer rules supreme, architects and urban designers have fiddled solely with scenarios of vehicular terrorism, whereas the most acute threats lie instead at the micro and macro ends of the spectrum. The solo suicide bomber who walks into a public building and the hijacker who flies into it cannot be dealt with by architectural means.

There is a final irony of architecture emblematic here. It is a story so important that few have written about it, and this absence says much about the place of architecture in American culture today, and even more about the place of culture in American politics. It has been known from just days after September 11 that lead hijacker Mohamed Atta graduated in architecture in his native Cairo, and was enrolled in a graduate program in urban design in Hamburg at the time of his death with the other 18 hijackers.

So successful has been the Bush Doctrine to date that this biographical fact has been discounted, just as the Saudi Arabian identity of 15 of them was deemphasized, for geopolitical and spin control reasons. The president, vice president, and cabinet have continually infantilized the hijackers, portraying them as rural, fanatic evildoers, and not purposeful, educated students of technology who used their intellect to further their murderous aims, as the facts indicate. There were similar interpretations placed on the choice of Minoru Yamasaki's World Trade Center as primary target—it was picked, we were told, because it was the biggest, the tallest, even because it was filled with a significant proportion of Jewish financial workers. Airborne attacks against dams, power installations, and airports might have left greater damage and death tolls, but Atta's team chose buildings in New York and Washington as targets.

To date, there has been almost no published speculation that this team led by an architect might have selected the World Trade Center and Pentagon, at least in part, for architectural reasons. The heinous murder of nearly 3,000 New Yorkers and hundreds more in Washington is the signal cultural event of our times, but, so far, culturalist readings of these acts have not been possible. Why is this so? It may be because culturalist readings are thought to diminish the horror and malice of any key tragedy, in the same manner that recognizing Adolf Hitler's early and late architectural obsessions and motivations is thought to diminish the enormity of his wrongdoing. Implicit in this interpretation is a diminution of culture in North America, implying that architecture is of insufficient importance to be read morally and politically. This diminution includes the removal of the fine arts from most public school curricula in North America, and the supplanting of what media cultural coverage there once was with celebrity accounts. These shifts are particularly cruel when it is evident that there is a cultural dimension to many of the world's current conflicts, and nearly all of its terrorist campaigns.

Like any other any cultural form, architecture can be a force for good or a force for evil, and its place in the events of 9/11 needs an airing. The thesis for a German university Mohamed Atta was working on at the time of the attack was "Modernity Versus Islam in the Urban Development of Aleppo, Syria." Security analysts have interpreted Atta's choice of this academic topic and this caravan route medium-sized city as a mere pretext for frequent travel in the region. I do not mean to minimize this motivation, but after talking to some of the architects who supervised his thesis research in Aleppo, Atta's fundamentalist religious beliefs did seem to connect with others he held about the conflict of modernity and tradition in the architecture and urbanism of the Islamic world. This debate was widespread amongst young architects who studied in the Arab world in the 1980s, intensified by the long periods of unemployment that many of them endured after graduation, intensified by seeing the success found by older brethren who had pursued the same subjects. Some of these surplus architects, engineers and other technocrats left for advanced studies in Europe or America like Atta, whereas others took low-status work in Western countries like some of his fellow hijackers, whereas still more volunteered for service with the Taliban in Afghanistan.

In the Islamic world as in the Judeo-Christian, a critique of architectural and urban Modernism crystallized in the 1970s. Architects throughout the Islamic world pursued debates about the legacy of the Modern Movement and the possibilities of the Postmodern architecture through the 1980s and into the 1990s, almost in phase with those occurring in the journals and architecture studios of the West. Circulating in Cairo at the time of Atta's first architectural studies were Arabic translations of Charles Jencks's 1977 book *The Language of Post Modern Architecture,* a book that famously dates the end of Modern architecture from the 1972 demolition of Minoru Yamasaki's Pruitt-Igoe public housing project in St. Louis. Egyptian architect Abdelwahed El Wakil started publishing a string of buildings in the 1980s that quote and transform the language of Islamic architecture in the same way Western Postmodernism of the same period was transforming the forms and memory of classical architecture.

One of the aporias of Atta's uncompleted thesis, according to his Syrian advisors, was his refusal to acknowledge modernity as a positive force for Islamic cultures, arguing instead a crude opposition of the faith-integrated Caliphate (with Aleppo having much of its medieval urbanism in tact, and hence a viable subject for such a thesis) with contemporary social and urban forms that have by definition been contaminated through contact with the West. The last gathering of the core 9/11 hijackers is known to have occurred in Las Vegas, and we will never know if they discussed the pervasive architectural theming there as a precedent for the faith-theming of buildings and cities in that most dismal of all possible theme parks, the New Caliphate. Mohamed Atta, architect of reassurance.

It is deeply disturbing to design culture's liberal and progressive self-image to raise these issues, but an act of terrorism led by an architect toward a globally significant work of architecture is not the act of malicious naivety as described in the Bush Administration's favored account. Atta and his team selected Yamasaki's World Trade Center because it was big, available, full of financial workers, but not incidentally, because of its emblematic status in the culture and history of architecture. Among many other dreadful things, the attacks were history's most extreme and terrible act of architectural criticism.

Notes

1. *Designing Disney's Theme Parks: The Architecture of Reassurance,* edited by Karal Ann Marling; New York, Flammarion, 1997.
2. Quoted in "A Capitol Offense" by Michael Z. Wise in the April 2004 issue of *Travel and Leisure* magazine.
3. Report of the Secretary of State's Advisory Panel on Overseas Security, Department of State, 1985.
4. Report of the Secretary of State's Advisory Panel on Overseas Security, Department of State, 1985.
5. Lecture by Jennifer Guthrie to the Canadian Society of Landscape Architects, Vancouver, February 14, 2006.
6. "Designing for Security in the Nation's Capital," October 2001 report of the Interagency Task Force for the National Capital Planning Commission.
7. 2004 Addendum to the 2002 report entitled 'The National Capital Urban Design and Security Plan" published by the National Capital Planning Commission, Washington.
8. Interview at Rogers Marvel studio, May 6, 2006.
9. Rock Twelve Security Architecture promotional brochure.
10. "Battery Park City Streetscapes Project" summary compiled by Rogers Marvel Architects, 2005. The study has been subsequently awarded the 2005 AIA NY Institute Honor Award for Regional and Urban Design, as well as the 2005 American Society of Landscape Architects Honor Award in Analysis and Planning.

Me and My Monkey
What's Hiding in the Security State

CINDI KATZ

In the impulse purchase section next to the cash registers of my neighbor-hood drugstore is a spindle of disposable camera packages that look a bit whimsical. Screaming "child-friendly," the cartons, on closer inspection, make a travesty of the term. Not at all the cameras for kids I imagined them to be, these were "Child Safety Camera I.D. Kits" that contained a camera for taking mug and full body shots of up to three children, includ-ing their particular birth marks or unique characteristics; three "DNA bags," otherwise known as "ziplocs," for storing a lock of hair (missing from my kit); three "personal profile sheets" for recording vital statistics such as the child's seemingly unchanging height and weight as well as their dental chart and medical conditions; and three "non-toxic ink strips" for fingerprinting. Dragnet comes home.

By what logic has surreal fear been made so banal that such a hokey kit (Figure 1) might be picked up with some Juicy Fruit® gum for your kid to take to camp? In what universe has such a commodity been pro-duced, let alone positioned as an impulse purchase? In the world of post-9/11 New York, is this the new normal? Yes and no. Yes, in the sense that the performance of security through objects, technologies, and displays is meant to stage and foreground a pervasive sense of fear; and no, in the sense that most parents aren't yet buying this form of protection though the fear-mongering strikes responsive chords associated with other domestic realms of hypervigilance, and seems to be authorizing its broad attractive-ness. In this chapter, I fuse my concerns with social reproduction, precious parenting, and what I call banal terrorism, to argue that the contemporary

Figure 1 Child safety camera kit.

security state and the reign of trumped up paranoia it engenders have not simply altered the spaces and material social practices of contemporary childhood but have fed into a burgeoning regime of surveillance in which the household mirrors the practices of the state while softening its future subjects for what the Bush spin-meisters might call "Operation Enduring Watchfulness."

The amplified fear along with the moral panics with which it is associated provide ready means of distraction from the political, economic, social, environmental, and personal problems that face families of children coming of age in the United States at present. These problems, as I have argued elsewhere, produce a pervasive sense of ontological insecurity that crosses class, race, and gender lines with differentiated effects among various groups (Katz 2005). At the heart of this insecurity are the shifts associated with the globalization of capitalist production, including an increasingly mobile and insecure employment landscape, wear and ruptures in the long-standing relationship between production and social reproduction, the precipitous rolling back of a century's worth of advances in the social wage, and new forms and arenas of militarization and policing. These changes have led to increasing economic inequality among both classes and nations, the privatization of formerly public or corporate responsibility for various elements of the social wage, and reworked geographies and temporalities of investment and disinvestment at a number of

scales. The insecurities produced by these changes are palpable, and register in a variety of material social practices from the demise of welfare such
as it was in the United States to unsure and unstable job markets worldwide. But in rerouting as anxiety the political, economic, and social problems that produce it, the experience of ontological insecurity can derail
potentially political responses as it rehearses the neoliberal tendency to
privatize social concerns. In the thrall of insecurity, individuals as much
as social formations are all the more vulnerable to fear-mongering, the
machinations of banal terrorism, and 'terror talk' (cf. Katz 2006a, 2006b).
They tend to turn inward in response.

Rescripted as insecurity, the political, economic, and social effects of
capitalist globalism are individualized. At the same time, the collective
experience of insecurity around employment prospects and pensions;
access to social services, health care, and housing; educational achievement; or social justice and self-determination—all of a piece with the
United Nations's initiatives to redefine "security" as an issue of human
health and well-being (e.g., UN Office for the Coordination of Humanitarian Affairs 2004) as much as with what I am calling ontological insecurity—is redirected, if not callously preyed on, by the paranoia purveyed
by the security state. Security in its hardened, bunkered form is built on
and made more acceptable by the widespread and differentiated effects of
insecurity of a completely different order. In another register, pervasive
social insecurity and the individualized anxiety it engenders seem to call
forth various mechanisms of securing the home and domestic environment that is played out with a particular vengeance around children. As
people feel less and less secure in the nation, its future, and the promises
of capitalist modernity, they seem to struggle even harder to control what
they can—their bodies, their domestic environment, the circumstances of
their children's everyday lives—fraught as such efforts might be. The latter
reflects, as much as it propels, the current spectacularization of children
and childhood in the United States. It is the collision of a moment in which
children have become spectacle (capital accumulation to the point where
childhood becomes image [cf. Debord 1983]) and a historical geography
that channels social and ontological insecurity into discourses of fear and
domestic vulnerability that creates ideal conditions for parental hypervigilance, among other things.

The regime of parental hypervigilance has much in common with that
of the homeland security state. They both tend toward inappropriate strategies and targets, offering at best a false sense of security through overkill
in one area and blithe disregard or ineptitude in others, and along these
lines ignore or divert attention from grave problems of a wholly different
order. The parallels in tactics, strategies, and effects between the two scales

of "domestic" security are revealing, and examining them can help expose some of the alibis that undergird both realms as well as the limits of technologies of fear. It also can show the ways that material social practices of security at these two scales feed off of and help justify one another, reconfiguring daily life and legitimating practices unthinkable even a decade ago.

The technologies of fear are witnessed as the nation enacts broad and aggressive security measures ranging from domestic wiretapping and other surveillance strategies through the war on terror to the fantasy of a completely walled southern border. In the name of fear, the public environment is monitored, bunkered, and conspicuously patrolled while the home is increasingly fortressed. But the technologies of fear are also increasingly apparent in children's everyday lives as parents, teachers, and others aspire to complete child safety if not total lockdown. In the contemporary United States and elsewhere, the market for child-protection is growing as parents of all backgrounds are drawn to a host of means intended to shield children from perceived (but still quite rare) risks, physical, social, and (increasingly) metaphysical. Some of these strategies are familiar and fairly benign, but others are as disturbing as they are bizarre.

Among the familiar are privatized play corrals, often associated with fast food restaurants, that come with fairly intense security protocols. For instance, *Chuck E. Cheese,* which bought out the free standing *Discovery Zone,* offers play equipment, entertainment, game arcades, and prizes with its pizza as it proudly touts its security measures to prevent child abduction. Greeted by the always staffed "Kid Check" booth, customers with children are stamped with a family identification number in invisible ink. On leaving, the black light in the booth ensures that "everyone who comes together, leaves together"(http://www.chuckecheese.com/html/safety2. html). I always like a little creepiness with my pizza, to say nothing of the comparable threats to American children posed by obesity and abduction. Other familiar devices include the now ubiquitous room monitors that allow parents and others to hear, and increasingly to see, their child from other parts of the house or its surrounds. Although the burgeoning number of means to ensure children's physical safety are not my focus here, it's worth noting that despite the importance and effectiveness of many of these measures such as child safety seats or bicycle helmets, there is also much excess here that is of a piece with protections in the realm of social danger. Even around physical harm, the manufacture of risk and the attraction to technological means of reducing it can get out of hand when studies have shown that parental monitoring and greater parent-child communication offer a more effective and long-lasting means of ensuring children's well-being (Hart & Iltus 1988).

The child protection industry, a thriving component of the home protection industry, offers a range of wares to parents bent on security. Visual systems figure prominently in the arsenal. Nanny cams, for instance, are an increasingly popular item as reflected both in sales and in growing attention in parent magazines and blogs. Nanny cams are concealed video cameras to view the activities of children, childcare workers, and others—including parents—either through a live feed or recording. The best ones provide high resolution color or black and white images, and work in very low light (although infrared light emitters can be added). Most nanny cams do not record sound in part because it is illegal to do so without permission in several states. Images are transmitted through wireless devices from cameras hidden in all manner of mundane objects from clocks and pencil sharpeners to bad paintings and fake plants, but in the spirit of child protection they are also in teddy bears and other innocuous toys. My favorite is a stuffed monkey wearing a black leather vest (Figure 2). Not exactly innocuous, but somehow appropriately perverse—a little biker monkey to spy on the person in whom trust should be paramount. Such ethical qualms apparently are rippling fewer and fewer parental ponds. "Ethics, schmethics," sneers Rhyder McClure, a New York peddler of the cameras (Burson 2004). And indeed those selling surveillance seem to have little. They are not averse to staging scenes supposedly picked up on nanny cams that show child minders in various acts of negligence or keeping notorious incidents in people's minds. Nanny cam sales took off in 1997 after

Figure 2 Monkey.

the British au pair Louise Woodward was accused of murdering one of the children in her care. As prices drop and the regime of paranoia grips more and more parents, sales have gotten stronger. According to technologies market analysts at Parks Associates in Dallas, the number of households with at least one child indicating interest in using a nanny cam more than doubled between 2002 and 2004 from 19 to 39 percent (Haller 2006). Although this does not translate directly as sales, of course, a number of Internet businesses have reported substantial annual sales increases for nanny cams over the last five years. This trend is sure to accelerate as the technology gets cheaper. As the writer David Brin observed several years ago, $100 nanny cams will be "utterly hopeless to resist" (Strauss 1998).

Although some of the debate on parent Web logs focuses on whether or not to get a nanny cam, with naysayers raising questions of trust or suggesting—often smugly—that a stay-at-home parent would resolve the question, much of the blogging centers on whether to reveal that the camera is there. The cameras are largely workplace surveillance tools after all, and so parents ponder how they would catch their nanny if she knew she were being watched as if the point was to catch her in the act of negligence rather than prevent it altogether. Many respondents rationalize this behavior by noting that their bosses probably spy on them. The downscaling of the indignity is somehow comforting to them. Others tout the sovereignty of the home as castle over workplace. As they accuse one another of being naive about privacy, most are adamant that in any case the nanny's rights to privacy come a distant second to ensuring their children's well-being, as if these were not connected. Having installed the cameras, parents swap news of minor annoyances—nannies using their showers (a common complaint), talking on the phone, or benignly neglecting their charges—and the occasional instance of more troubling behavior, such as napping on the job, speaking sharply, hitting or jostling the children, to justify their use of concealed cameras. These discussions, compounded by sensationalized media accounts of nanny or caregiver violence, seem to have provoked growing numbers of parents to get nanny cams and other surveillance technologies simply because they can. Not to do so starts to seem negligent as peace of mind at any price becomes the order of the day.

Fear only begins at home. Its tentacles extend from there pretty much in inverse proportion to children's exposure to risk. One aspect of this phenomenon is Webcam systems in day care centers and schools, which allow parents password-protected access to either Webcam images or streaming live videos of their children's days. Parents can log on and view the images on any computer or various hand-held devices. Purveyors of these technologies promote them as means to both ameliorate the quotidian separations of contemporary family life and ensure that the services delivered meet expectations, but underneath they tap into the anxieties traced above (cf. Katz 2001). A small but growing number of childcare centers offer these systems, and those marketing them appeal to day care operators' competitive advantage in demonstrating to consumers that they have nothing to hide. The contemporary penchant for security notwithstanding, these systems may not achieve the sort of market saturation that seems likely for nanny cams. Staff members often object to being under the watchful eyes of so many doting parents. But, more to the point, it can be costly to install and maintain the security of these systems, and childcare businesses—to say nothing of public facilities—operate with relatively tight budgets. While it is a bit different for older children, where their own behavior rather than exposure to risk seems to have led a growing number of public schools in the United States and elsewhere to install surveillance cameras, security around young children remains more privatized, focused more on the home and the child's (mobile) body than anywhere else.

In the private realm, things have intensified and become stranger at the same time as they echo the performative overreach of measures taken in the public sphere. A growing number of people are saddling their children with monitoring devices that allow parents and others to keep tabs on them using two-way radio type technology or more elaborately to locate them using GPS (geographic positioning systems). The former, which are widely available and inexpensive, consists of a transmitter encased in a child-friendly pendent or small stuffed toy worn by the child and a small receiver worn or held by the caregiver. The receiver beeps loudly when the child wanders beyond a certain distance. Thanks to 'smart' technology, the range varies according to density; in crowded situations the receiver will sound if the child goes further than about three meters, whereas in less busy conditions the child may reach 10 meters before the alarm is sounded. The transmitters are also outfitted with panic buttons so that children can alert their care givers with a 95-decibel alarm if something is awry (or if they want ice cream). Promising peace of mind and the possibility of allaying panic for all involved, those promoting these devices routinely remind parents that they cannot replace actual supervision. Of course, one needs to be already pretty panic-prone to want to be alerted every time a child strays more than three meters in a commercial venue, to say nothing of the ways these devices—beeping as they will—are panic emollients.

Panic of another order entirely underlies the use of radio frequency identification (RFID) technology in combination with GPS to identify and locate children (and others). Under the trademark, Digital Angel®, RFID microchips have been produced over the past few years offering location tracking for high-value assets such as livestock (or children) and providing medical—and potentially other—information about the wearer that is accessible remotely through Web-enabled wireless telecommunications. The chips were initially to be available for subcutaneous implantation or as a wristwatch. Privacy concerns about "chipping" children, even one's own, seem to have encouraged the manufacturers to market a subcutaneous chip for pets that can be loaded with medical and other information and an ambulatory model for children (and other wanderers, such as people with Alzheimer's disease). First used in large water parks and the like, the Digital Angel has been marketed for private use since late 2001 for about $400 and a monthly subscription fee of about $30. Some models require a special tool to remove and thus are fixed on children until their caretakers take them off. Their pastel shades and floral or goofy motifs distinguish these devices from those used on people under house arrest. But even here there is some convergence as celebrity convicts get their ankle bracelet monitors covered in colorful leather (McAndrew 2005). What else could be expected when Martha Stewart does time?

Surveillance technologies like the Digital Angel are obviously not (yet) for everybody, and have been acquired only by a minute segment of the population. But where privacy objections of all denominations—from civil liberties advocates, 'big brother' alarmists, and apocalypse-anticipating Christians who saw the implantable chip and its surrogates as the 'mark of the beast'—were raised around the development of the technology during the late 1990s and into the new century, these objections were muted in the security landscape that followed September 11, 2001. Not only did the manufacturer return to talking about implantation—a possibility they had previously seen wise to bury—but the corporation and its backers invigorated their discussion of the technology as a security tool, mentioning such things as chipping immigrants or tracking workers seen as posing a security risk in certain industries. September 11 also helped domesticate these technologies and enhanced their appeal to an already anxious public. Indeed by chance the Digital Angel came on the market just in the wake of September 11 and the manufacturer immediately noted an upsurge in demand. Peace of mind was now imagined as the possibility of a happy ending to a catastrophe (A "Digital Angel" for Troubling Times 2001). Getting a leg up on the surveillance systems and invasions of corporeal privacy that became the new normal after September 11, Digital Angel quickly stepped up its production process to meet the new demand. With its potential to transmit biological and location data through building materials with extraordinary accuracy, the Digital Angel seemed to some at least the perfect technology for horrific times.

If 9/11 provided a Trojan horse for smuggling in this quintessential tool of biopolitics to widespread acceptance, it has also proven attractive to parents who think that children can and should be protected from everything. Although Digital Angel's parent company, Applied Digital Solutions, is in the business of tagging livestock and other assets (such as art work and expensive equipment) as well as providing chips that provide location and medical information for pets and people with certain diseases, it also envisions a multibillion dollar market in security at all scales, whether in individual protection, e-commerce, parolee tracking, or border patrol. Individual protection is crucial to the industry's success. The devices have been marketed successfully, for instance, in various South American countries where the perceived threat of kidnapping is high, they have been promoted as a replacement for dog tags for military personnel, and they remain on the table for child protection. A K–8 charter school in a poor neighborhood of Buffalo, New York, for instance, pioneered the integration of RFID chips with student I.D. cards a few years ago at a cost of $25,000. The school's director expressed enthusiasm for his electronic attendance and record keeping system and was unabashed in touting its ability to track his 425 or so students throughout the day. Somewhat ominously, the tags use the same Texas Instrument chip technology that is used in various jails and by the military in Iraq (Scheeres 2003). As they cut across already blurred lines between schools, prisons, and the military, the chips also are being quickly domesticated. Various companies are developing and marketing wearable RFID tags to put into children's shoes or clothing, for instance. The technology—which remains expensive—may be sold at such popular outlets as Target, Old Navy, or the Gap (cf., e.g., http://www.smartweartechnologies.com/home.html), but thus far has been slow to catch on. Its advocates persist, however. As Matthew Cossolotto, a spokesperson at Digital Angel, put it, "We have GPS devices for our cars, why shouldn't we have similar devices for our children? Do we love our cars more than our kids?" (Marvel 2002). Cossolotto's weighing of assets contrives in its cloddish off-handedness to draw in the potentially huge parental market as it naturalizes a surveillance technology that fuses the global and corporeal in hair-raising ways. But the path to this telemetric collapse of scale was already paved by widely available and utterly domesticated cellphone technology.

If most people remain resistant to chipping their loved ones and themselves despite the appealing fantasy of complete protection, it is clear that telephones are increasingly used to provide similar kinds of information both within the family and more broadly. Telephones tether and locate loved ones as well as coworkers and others, calling forth copresence at any time of the day or night while identifying the source—if not necessarily the geographic location—of the call. As the potential for constant contact has become commonplace and the mobile phone market saturated, a growing number of wireless phones have been outfitted with GPS technology so that users can be located with pinpoint accuracy. This feature has been used to track workers as well as for law enforcement[1] and in emergency situations, but it is now being marketed as an easy way to keep tabs on family members. Indeed, child protection has been packaged as an add-on to various family calling plans. For $10 a month, services such as Verizon's "Chaperone" or Sprint's "Family Locator" enable parents to locate their child's kid-friendly wireless phone on a small map visible on their own phone or through the Web. For an additional $10, the Verizon plan allows the parent to define a geographic area from which the child cannot stray without their being alerted. When the "Child Zone" is breached the parent will receive a text message. What happens next is unclear, because as the fine print cautions, these systems are not suitable for child management and are no substitute for supervision and actual communication.

These services are supposed to offer peace of mind—the phrase is ubiquitous in the child protection industry—but if their use catches on, Big Mother will have done a lot to soften Big Brother's future subjects. Sprint, for one, takes pains to reassure that theirs is not an Orwellian operation—children must agree at the outset to have their parents check on their whereabouts. They are sent a text message each time the parent does a safety check and locates their cell phone. Of course, if the phone is off, it cannot be located, and I've already read accounts of children passing their phones to one another at least in part to foil their parents. Like so many security technologies, these devices for all their sophistication are easily thwarted. All of this begs the question of child management, and the serious issues of open communication and trust it raises. As in the larger society, the distorted focus on an ever present—but most unlikely—threat authorizes and provides an alibi for a range of invasive, inadequate, and often inappropriate measures (cf. Kelly 2003).

Chipping of an entirely different kind is a case in point. Cell phones themselves chip away at family time with much bemoaned but little addressed invasions of work and external responsibilities or distractions. These erosions of family life are surely more damaging to children overall than the conjured predators that haunt the domestic imaginary. That haunting increasingly makes life without cell phones unimaginable if not unbearable for many families, but the ghosts are usually intimate ones. It is almost always the parents—or the children—who are spectral or more aptly, antispectral; their cell phones lure their heads and hearts elsewhere while their bodies stick around. Many parents suffer under the delusion that they are "there" for their children, but their presence can be more of an absence as they take this call or put out that fire. They may occupy the same time-space as their children but they do not actually share it. If in these instances the cell phone blurs the boundaries between family and other kinds of time-space—placing family members in a kind of 'parallel play' of disconnected copresence—in other instances it enables the interpolation of family members who are physically apart.

It is by now a commonplace that families are yoked by electronic leashes through mobile phones and other devices. Much of this tethering enables children and young people to have a bit more spatial autonomy than they might as it gives parents (and children) the peace of mind that comes with ready contact, although the virtual base touching of some parents can render this freedom moot. If young people use mobile phones to stay on top of constantly evolving social situations, parents view them as a way to make sure their children negotiate their travels and schedules smoothly and safely. But just as the borders between work and home are blurred by cell phones, so, too, are the newly charted boundaries between young people and their parents, which are shaky at best. The phones may be a means of granting kids some autonomy, but the constant contact they enable can just as easily hem it in. As Rachel Pain and her colleagues suggest, mobile phones may simply "reshape" rather than reduce parental fears (Pain et al. 2005: 826). Some parents cannot rest unless they are called at every transition—on the bus, off the bus, leaving school, arriving home, whatever—and are informed of every change in plans however small. As cell phones become latter-day umbilical cords, young people's facility to make sound judgments about their social activity space and everyday engagements may be hobbled by such micromanagement as the burgeoning concern from colleges and universities about 'helicopter' parents suggests.

Just as the specter of abduction and other extremely rare crimes against children are trotted out to legitimate parental hypervigilance, so, too, the looming threat of terrorism has been added to the repertoire of rationales for a cell phone on every body. These issues were all out in force in April 2006 as the New York City public schools began to enforce their long-standing ban on cell phones. As Tim Johnson, chair of the Chancellor's Parent Advisory Council, made clear, "In the times we are living in, this is completely a safety issue for the overwhelming number of families" (Hartocollis 2006). The council filed a suit against the Department of Education within a few months to get the ban lifted. I agree that the ban is problematic (and unrealistic), but the hysteria it produced is inseparable from the paranoid regime of domestic terror that only became more apparent following 9/11. Typical was the parent of a sixth grader who fumed, "The Chancellor will have civil disobedience on his hands. No one in New York is going to let their child go to school without a cell phone" (Gootman 2006). Far from her mind in the throes of this crisis was that plenty of kids in New York City public schools go to school without breakfast, let alone a cell phone. A little civil disobedience on those grounds would be a fine thing. Of course in the private schools things are ratcheted up a notch—there it's a question of rights. But somewhat hilariously the rights in question were those of worry. In the words of Alexandra Peters, former President of the Parents League, they "feel pretty strongly that parents have a right to be concerned about their kids' safety, and that cell phones are a good way for them to make sure" (Hartocollis 2006).

Speaking of worry, the manufacturers and marketers of most of these technologies warn of their creating a false sense of security just as frequently as they offer them as means toward 'peace of mind.' But it seems that a false sense of security is what people have been reduced to—or have learned to find solace in—in the absence of anything resembling true security. Here the parallels between the state and home are direct and obvious. In several venues, I have pointed out the absurdity of desert camouflaged soldiers guarding the public environments of New York City and elsewhere. Their attire—the antithesis of camouflage—makes them readily apparent to everyone, and that seems to be the point. Although undercover police work the same environments unnoticed, the military *performs* homeland security. This display of security is no doubt meant to reassure the public, but it is a reassurance that rehearses and reinstates a sense of constant threat. And it is that everyday production of fear that gets camouflaged. The performance secures docility while the fear exacerbates and excuses all manner of hypervigilance, including parental.

Yet even as these novel strategies of child protection become the norm, the broad promises of the social wage achieved by the late twentieth century (their unevenness notwithstanding) continue to be worn away by a neoliberal state consumed by its own security and a corporate sector bent on reducing labor costs. Nothing in any of these security measures at whatever scale can redress the sorts of insecurities these shifts provoke. But these insecurities—and the deeper ontological insecurity with which they are associated—seem to be sublimated in the false sense of security on offer. The technologies of homeland (as well as home-based) security essentially respond to the symptoms and not the causes of most of the serious problems facing young people in the United States. But worse, these measures in themselves propel a state of insecurity, first by making a paranoid regime pervasive at every scale from the body to the nation, second by absorbing funds that might be spent on more constructive arenas of social reproduction, and third by drawing young people, especially those with few job prospects, into the maw of 'the war on terrorism' itself.

Beyond all of these issues, it is neither possible nor desirable to protect children from everything as much as we might like to. The practices of hypervigilance and other variants of "hyperparenting" miss this point entirely. In the flurry of overprotection, children and adolescents may not be learning to make their own sound judgments, to adjudicate various disputes, or to develop a sense of trust in themselves and others. Moreover, focusing on the insecurities bred of fear—whether of nannies, criminals, terrorists, or others—diverts attention and resources away from less dramatic but much more common problems faced by children and families. These problems—which encompass everything from the failures of public education, the inadequacies of public play environments, the lack of work- or community-based childcare centers, the dearth of affordable housing, or the number of children and families without health insurance to things like the regimentation of everyday life, the epidemic of eating disorders in the midst of hunger, and the persistence of domestic violence—actually might have a chance of being ameliorated if the energy and resources expended on troubles that almost by definition transcend resolution were redirected toward them.

Parallels with the urban, national, and global scales are clear. As in the home, so with the state. It is a fantasy that any mode of security can safeguard the public from everything. Moreover, the metastasizing security charade under which we currently live puts even greater resources at the disposal of the military, the police, the prison system, and the surveillance complex. All the while in the home as in the United States, many of the most pernicious threats to security and well-being come from within—likewise at larger scales. If what was spent on security were redirected toward the goods, services, and spaces that comprise the social wage, it might temper some of the free range insecurity—ontological and material—that pervades contemporary life in the United States. The erosive toll of revanchist globalization should be counted among the terrors of everyday life; it takes the lives of far more people—in slow seeping ways—than the horrific but exceedingly rare terrors that command so much attention. As suggested earlier, there is a great and growing divide between rich and poor households in the face of these erosions and how their toll is extracted. These shifts seem to provoke wealthier families to further fetishize their children, whereas poorer families often have to scramble just to secure the means of their children's existence. As inequality is exacerbated so, too, is the nature of childhood troubled in different ways by these circumstances. Childhood itself is compromised on the one hand by material insecurity and on the other by the fetishized enactments of fear and security as young people are denied the promise of a secure future. And as the war in Iraq continues, even the possibility of a future is tragically foreclosed for all too many.

These problems will not be solved by piecemeal private strategies that at best try to compensate for an eviscerated social system and at worst take the pervasive individualism of neoliberalism to heart. Even in the problematic realm of the conjured and too easily stoked fears around childhood, there is a difference between a campaign that hails some notion of community by asking, "Have you seen this child?" and a drive that would clamp an RFID tag on one's own child. It is time to attend to the circumstances that underlie contemporary insecurities around children, rather than fritter around the insecurities themselves. These circumstances demand a reinvigorated politics around the social wage in all its permutations. Elaborations of hypervigilance are a diversion. And not only that, it is also time to recognize the creeping neoliberalization of the security state. Not only are we witnessing the downscaling of the security state into the home, and thus the parallels I've been tracing here, but also and increasingly the technologies of the state security apparatus are being privatized (cf. Katz 2001, 2005). As more and more households avail themselves of cellular telephones that offer GPS tracking services, for instance, the more people can be tracked by law enforcement agencies or in the vague interests of homeland security. Likewise the growing number of home-based DNA and fingerprint archives, such as those produced with the "Child Safety I.D. Kits" found in my local drugstore, which most people would readily share with their local police department if asked in the interests of child safety. These are not benign bits of mom and pop data, as the overreach of the Department of Homeland Security around cell phone records should make clear, but how convenient that they are provided at your expense. Meanwhile in the interests of preventing "passport fraud" and meeting U.S. visa requirements, the European Union has reportedly been debating mandatory fingerprinting of all children six and older, with plans to store the information on a centralized database (Doward 2006). Whether through an American-style do-it-yourself impulse or a more state-centered approach as in Europe, the trend is clearly to produce massive amounts of personal data and make it available to the state. The (con)fusion of personal security and national security is breathtaking, as is the way the interests of the former can so easily be made to serve the latter. These troubling practices are only the beginning of what may come of the conjuncture between heightened individual anxiety and a strong security state. What is already clear is that home and childhood are remade in this twisted space.

As home and childhood are transformed in and by the security state so, too, is that state made and remade. There is much at stake for young people coming of age as the sprawling apparatus of security and control come home. As I have detailed here, the security project of the state has literally been taken home, and in the process has itself been domesticated. Its naturalization through well-developed discourses of domestic security has enhanced and emboldened the contemporary national security state. In the process, the home is no longer confined to the everyday material social practices of securing the future, but is framed in relation to all manner of outside threats, including terrorists. But if the ways the home has become a fortified citadel, trussed and gated against all outsiders, are by now familiar, these formations shift when it comes to children. Here—as with the national security state—the dread of perforation is paramount—the enemy can be hidden within the fortress (cf. Katz 2006b: 355). And although this recalls what lies buried in the discourses around home-based security— that the greatest threat to children and women comes from intimate others in the home environment—the fears around perforation are not rallied against these family members and friends but against those "others" such as nannies and other domestic workers who share (and help to make possible) the comforts of certain people's homes. Thus devices like nanny cams (and by extension, surveillance cameras in childcare centers and schools) rehearse the anxious monitoring of nonintimate environments—always already on the lookout for the breach from within—at the same time as they reproduce its paradoxical quality in creating a fortress that encloses its own enemies, real or imagined. Nonetheless, just as the discourse of safety enables the spread of the government's security apparatus, imagining the home as threatened creates conditions wherein the "technologies of individual empowerment become inseparable from those of surveillance" (Grewal 2006: 35). The power of both is reinforced in the process.

There are other parallels in security practices at the national, urban, and home scales. In each arena, security is framed in relation to externalized threats rather than home grown troubles, and in ways that produce flattened and demonized others—whether as terrorists, foreigners, gang members, Arabs, or illegal aliens. But also at each scale these practices come at the expense of dealing with security problems of another order entirely. This distinction might be understood as attending to the (exaggerated) concerns of security *from* at the expense of attending to the more widespread problems of social reproduction that can be framed as the security *of*. Focusing on selected dramatic—but exceedingly rare—risks diverts attention and resources from other less dramatic but more common and erosive problems such as those produced by the retreats in the social wage associated with the globalization of capitalist production and the ascendance of neoliberal public policy. Perhaps worse, as these sorts of disinvestments in social reproduction take place they are masked and rationalized by the stepped up discourse of fear and the apparatus of security that is attendant on it. Children and young people pay dearly either way. As Inderpal Grewal (2006: 37) points out, the heightened state of security displaces the violence of the family onto various racialized, classed, gendered, and otherwise flattened others, and then calls on and reinstates patriarchal authority to protect against these dangers. This dynamic works across scales, wedding the differentiated but often mutually reinforcing interests of U.S. imperialism, biopolitics, and capital accumulation. Just as patriarchal authority is called forth to 'protect' the home—smuggling in a host of material social practices that attempt to control the bodies and minds of women and children—so, too, does the security state assert its authority around the biopolitics of heteronormativity, racism, and sexism as it promulgates its "surveillant assemblage" and militarizes the spaces of everyday life (cf. Grewal 2006).

The citadel home functions in similar ways. Taking fear and distrust for granted, it remakes the state in domesticated form, offering technocratic solutions for economic and social problems such as the decline of the welfare state, the enduring inequities of the gendered division of household labor, and the attenuated geographies of everyday life wherein extended families are dispersed and the distance between home and work is stretched. In this new realm, parents try to make up for the deteriorations in the (social welfare) state but they also rehearse the state's overreach in other arenas. As they scramble to secure the means of social reproduction privately, with predictably uneven outcomes, many parents may experience the sorts of visceral insecurities—ontological and otherwise—these conditions make palpable. A growing number appear to respond to these circumstances by instating a surveillance apparatus of their own and installing themselves as community police. As I have detailed here, parents spy on workers in their homes, especially those caring for their children, and those who have contact with their children in other settings. But more and more parents—in the interests of safety—spy on their children as well. Leaving aside the technologies that I have been discussing, such as child monitors, RFID chips and GPS location services, DNA collection kits, and nanny cams and cameras in day care and school settings, a small but growing number of parents appear to be drawn to other aspects of child protection. These parents engage such surreptitious technologies as home drug testing kits, keystroke monitoring programs, and automobile speed monitors (often provided by insurance companies). As with the other technologies discussed here, the use of these devices responds to and propels the breakdown of trust within families, and makes it increasingly likely that young people coming of age now will literally embody the sense that they are always under surveillance whether in the intimate settings of the home, on their computers or telephones, in the family car, at school, or in the various public environments of their everyday lives. Apart from the serious developmental consequences of pervasive distrust and limited privacy, these practices go a long way toward producing a new generation of docile subjects. The perverse genius of these circumstances is that now even the production of governable subjects has been privatized. As the neoliberal capitalist state engenders various strains of insecurity, which are responded to in part by stepped-up parental hypervigilance, the next generation is softened for other more invasive modes of hypervigilance.

Finally, among the parallels in security operations across scale from the home to the nation is the almost lurid attention to the *performance* of security over and above the less visible acts of security that might be worth the name. I've highlighted some of the performative aspects of the security state at the urban and national scales, pointing out how they produce and reproduce a paranoid environment of fear. Although these performances surely accomplish some measure of protection, they also mask and distract attention from well recognized gaps in the security landscape such as the relative lack of oversight for containerized shipping, the inadequacies in screening of checked luggage at most U.S. airports, and the vulnerability of the public water supply to malicious contamination. These concerns are frequently covered in the literature. I mark them here to draw out the parallels between comforts offered by the performance of security on the part of the state, and the 'peace of mind' proffered by the technologies of parental hypervigilance.

In my readings, discussions, and other forays into the apparatus of home-based security, I am struck by how often the phrase "peace of mind" comes up. Apart from how pathetically the statement papers over the futility of most of these technologies in ensuring children's safety or security in any real sense, the phrase seems to embody the very retreat from the social that ushers in so much of the apparatus of security, and calls forth such widespread desire for it. Peace of mind is a privatized existential state. Elusive though it may be, its desirability marks a defeatist recognition that collective peace is virtually impossible. How can anyone achieve peace of mind in a world racked with so much violence, such rapacious environmental destruction, and such callous disregard for the well-being of others? Yet people grasp at it as a privatized oasis even as the mechanisms through which peace of mind might be attained reproduce and harden the sorts of uneven social relations that create its allure in the first place. Is this all we can hope for? Is even peace privatized now? There is of course a vigorous and growing peace movement in the United States, but its work gets almost no press coverage. When this willful inattention is compared to the sort of coverage given to the slightest blip on the terrorist frontier, to say nothing of the media attention to missing college students or children murdered a decade ago, it becomes easier to see how the horizon of aspiration might be peace of mind. Peace activism has long and venerable associations with the politics of motherhood and the domestic. The shift in these realms from peace activism to peace of mind must be framed in relation to the productions of fear and the technologies of security I have traced here. But, of course, these productions disturb even the achievement of peace of mind, because everything that invites, condones, or gives an alibi to 'banal terrorism' and the apparatus of the security state unsettles even the possibility of 'peace of mind.'

It is time to refuse the bait of fear and its erosive consequences at all scales. The strategies associated with hypervigilance as much as the performance of security cannot redress the serious problems provoked by the imperatives of capitalist globalism, violent imperialism, and neoliberal retreats from the social wage. These imperatives produce a broad range of material insecurities and for many a deep sense of ontological insecurity about the future. These insecurities help make people receptive to the promises of security in whatever precious or bunkered form it is offered, but they can only be countered by returning to notions of security rooted in social justice and focused on the broadest concerns of social reproduction and restoration of the social wage. Everything else is indefensible.

Note

1. The use of cellular technology for the live tracking of criminal suspects has faced legal hurdles in the past couple of years following several 2005 federal court decisions denying prosecutors the right to the information without showing probable cause. These decisions—which are nonbinding—suggest a higher privacy standard shaping up for live tracking than for the use of cell phone records, which are commonly turned over to the government (Richtel 2005). But these privacy standards are routinely thwarted by the government's security apparatus. As the U.S. public learned in May 2006, almost all of the wireless companies have been handing over their customers' calling records to the National Security Agency since 2001.

References

"A 'Digital Angel' for Troubling Times" 2001. M2 Communications Ltd.

Burson, Pat. 2004. "Parents Have No Qualms in Using Nanny Spy Cams." *Tulsa World,* December 27.

Chuck E. Cheese. http://www.chuckecheese.com/html/safety2.html.

Debord, Guy. 1983. *Society of the Spectacle.* Detroit: Red and Black.

Doward, Jamie. 2006. "Millions of Children to be Fingerprinted." *Observer,* June 30. (http://observer.guardian.co.uk/uk_news/story/0,,1833407,00.html)

Gootman, Elissa. 2006. "City Schools Cut Parents' Lifeline (The Cellphone)." *New York Times* A1, B5, 27 April.

Grewal, Inderpal. 2006. "'Security Moms' in the Early Twenty-first-Century United States: The Gender of Security in Neoliberalism." *WSQ: Women's Studies Quarterly,* 34, 1&2, 25–39.

Haller, Sonja. 2006. "Parents Monitor Kids, Nanny from Afar with Tiny, Increasingly Popular Cameras." Associated Press State and Local Wire, April 17.

Hart, R., & Iltus, S. 1988. Developing a Model of Families as Safety Management Systems for Children at Home, in *Safety in the Built Environment,* Jonathan D. Sime (ed.). London: E. & F.N. Spon.

Hartocollis, Anemona. 2006. "Parents to Sue Over Schools' Cellphone Ban." *New York Times,* July 13. (http://www.nytimes.com/2006/07/13/nyregion/13phones.html)

Katz, Cindi. 2001. "The State Comes Home: Social Reproduction and the Global Retreat from Social Reproduction." *Social Justice,* 28, 3, 47–56.

Katz, Cindi. 2005. The Terrors of Hypervigilance: Security and the Compromised Spaces of Contemporary Childhood, in *Studies in Modern Childhood: Society, Agency, Culture,* ed. Jens Qvortrup, pp. 99–114. New York: Palgrave Macmillan.

Katz, Cindi. 2006a. Power, Space, and Terror: Social Reproduction and the Public Environment, in *The Politics of Public Space,* Setha Low and Neil Smit (eds.), pp. 105–121. New York: Routledge.

Katz, Cindi. 2006b. Banal Terrorism: Spatial Fetishism and Everyday Insecurity, in *Violent Geographies,* Derek Gregory and Allan Pred (eds.), pp. 349–361. New York: Routledge.

Kelly, Peter. 2003. "Growing Up as Risky Business? Risks, Surveillance and the Institutionalized Mistrust of Youth." *Journal of Youth Studies,* 6, 2, 165–180.

Marvel, Bill. 2002. "It's 2002: Do You Know Where Your Kids Are?" *Dallas Morning News,* October 2. (http://www.globalpetfinder.com/article5.html)

McAndrew, Siobhan. 2005. When They've Got You By the Ankle, *Reno Gazette-Journal,* March 5. (http://www.rgj.com/news/stories/html/2005/03/05/93805.php)

Pain, Rachel, Grundy, Sue, & Gill, Sally, with Elizabeth Towner, Geoff Sparks, & Kate Hughes. 2005. "'So Long as I Take My Mobile': Mobile Phones, Urban Life and Geographies of Young People's Safety." *International Journal of Urban and Regional Research,* 29, 4, 814–830.

Richtel, Matt. 2005. Live Tracking of Mobile Phones Prompts Court Fights on Privacy, *New York Times* Section A; 1, December 10.

Scheeres, Julia. 2003. "Three R's: Reading, Writing, RFID." *Wired News,* October 24. (http://www.wired.com/news/technology/0,1282,60898,00.html)

Strauss, Gary. 1998. "Nanny Cams Ease Parental Angst." *USA Today* 1–2A, February 27.

UN Office for the Coordination of Humanitarian Affairs. 2004. http://ochaonline.un.org/DocView.asp?DocID=3293.

Thanatotactics

EYAL WEIZMAN

The fighter plane is the quintessence of modern civilization. ... It soars above good and evil, a celestial goddess with an insatiable thirst for sacrificial tribute.[1]

—**Azmi Bishara**

On September 13, 2005—the day after the day after—when the Israeli evacuation of the Gaza Strip was completed, the ground bases of the occupation were relocated to the airspace over the strip, to the territorial waters off its coastline and to the border terminals along the fences that cut it off from the rest of the world. The geography of occupation has thus completed a 90-degree turn: the imaginary "orient"—the exotic object of colonization—was no longer beyond the horizon, but now under the vertical tyranny of a Western airborne civilization that remotely managed its most sophisticated and advanced technological platforms, sensors, and munitions above.

Since the beginning of the second Intifada, limitations on its ability to maintain a permanent ground presence throughout the Palestinian territories reinforced Israel's reliance on a tactical logic that sought to disrupt Palestinian armed and political resistance through targeted assassination—extrajuridical state executions—undertaken most frequently from the air.[2] In fact, the tactical precondition for Israel's policy of territorial withdrawal was that its security services be able to maintain domination of the evacuated areas by means other than territorial control. An IDF think tank called the "Alternative Team" (as if it was a group of comics heroes) involved in rethinking Israeli security after the evacuation of Gaza admitted: "whether or not we are physically present in the territories, we should still be able to demonstrate our ability to control and affect them ..."[3] The occupation that will thus follow the Occupation—that is, the domination of Palestinians after the evacuation of the ground space of the Gaza Strip and parts of the West Bank is completed—was alternately referred to by these and other military planners as the "invisible occupation," the "airborne occupation" or "occupation in disappearance."[4]

The ability of the Israeli Air Force to maintain a constant "surveillance and strike" capability over Palestinian areas is one of the main reasons for the Sharon government's confidence, and popular support, in pursuing unilateral ground withdrawals and accordingly transforming the logic of occupation. Sharon's sacking of Chief of Staff Moshe Ya'alon and his replacement with the pilot and former Air Force commander Dan Halutz, several months before the ground evacuation of Gaza, testified to the perceived offset of military emphasis from the ground to the air, and of the Israeli government's acceptance of Halutz's mantra: "technology instead of occupation."[5] Until the result of the 2006 war in Lebanon made him realize otherwise, Halutz was known as the strongest proponent of the perception that airpower could gradually replace much of the traditional functions of ground forces. In a lecture he delivered in the military National Security College in 2001 he explained that "the capability of the Air Force today renders some traditional assumptions—that victory equals territory—anachronistic."[6]

Indeed, throughout the years of the second Intifada, a major effort was directed at the development and "perfection" of the tactics of airborne targeted assassinations. From a "rare and exceptional emergency method" it has become the Air Force's most common form of attack. According to Ephraim Segoli, a helicopter pilot and former commander of the Air Force base in Palmahim, located halfway between Tel Aviv and Gaza, from which most helicopter assassination raids have been launched and where now the largest fleets of remote controlled killer drones are located, airborne "liquidations are the central component of IDF operation and the very essence of the 'war' it is waging." Segoli, speaking in May 2006, claimed, furthermore, that "the intention to 'perfect' these operations meant that Israel's security industries have ... started concentrating [much of their effort] on the development of systems that primarily serve this operational logic."[7]

Thanatotactics reverses the traditional aims of warfare. The military does not kill enemy soldiers as a means to obtain the strategic ground they occupy, but temporarily obtains strategic ground in order to kill its enemies. Killing is not a by-product of military maneuver (remember Liddell Heart's perhaps overly optimistic claim that at its best the "indirect approach" he promoted for territorial warfare could bring victory by maneuver and positioning and without battle)[8] but its very aim. It is mainly, but not exclusively, this logic of Israeli security operations that would explain current calls for some Israeli officers traveling abroad to face a war-crime tribunal.[9]

Most states at one time or another have engaged in assassinations of their enemies' military and political leadership; Israel has used assassinations in its conflict with Palestinian and Lebanese resistance for many years.[10] However, since the beginning of the Al-Aqsa Intifada in September 2000 and increasingly since the evacuation of Gaza, targeted assassinations became the most significant and frequent form of Israeli military attack. From the beginning of the Intifada to the end of 2006, 339 Palestinians were killed in targeted assassinations. Only 210 of those were the intended targets for assassination; the rest were Palestinians whose daily lives brought them to the wrong place at the wrong time, 45 of them were children.[11] The assassinated included as well most of the political leadership of Hamas.

The policy of targeted assassinations, as this chapter seeks to show, cannot be understood according to the logic of terrorist prevention alone; rather, it has become a political tool in Israel's attempt to maintain control in the Palestinian areas from which it has territorially withdrawn, thus acquiring a territorial dimension.

Urban Killing

The movement of Israeli manhunt squads through the Palestinian urban terrain often resembles the movement of security forces—through ceilings and walls—in Terry Gilliam's 1985 classic film, *Brazil*. In a previous article, "Walking through Walls," I explained how Israeli soldiers move within Palestinian cities from house to house through holes they blast in party walls and progress across 100-meter-long "over-ground-tunnels" carved out through dense and contiguous built fabrics.[12] Within Palestinian towns and refugee camps Israeli soldiers do not use the streets, roads, alleys, or courtyards that constitute the syntax of the city, nor the external doors, internal stairwells, and windows that constitute the order of buildings but, rather, move horizontally through party walls, and vertically through holes blasted in ceilings and floors. Rather than submit to the authority of conventional spatial boundaries, movement becomes constitutive of space. This "un-walling of the wall," to borrow a term from Gordon Matta-Clark, ignores the limitation of the built fabric and allows for a three-dimensional movement through walls, ceilings and floors across the urban balk in search of its suspects.

To complement military tactics that involve physically breaking and walking through walls, new methods have been devised to allow soldiers to see and kill through them. The Israeli company *Camero* developed a hand-held imaging device that combines thermal imaging with ultra-wideband radar, which, like contemporary maternity-ward ultra-sound systems, has the ability to produce three-dimensional renderings of biological life concealed behind barriers.[13] Human bodies appear on the screen as fuzzy heat sources floating (like fetuses) within an abstract clear medium wherein everything solid—walls, furniture, objects—has melted into the background screen.[14] Weapons using the standard NATO 5.56mm round are complemented with some using the 7.62mm round, which is capable of penetrating brick, wood and adobe without much deflection of the bullet-head. Instruments of "literal transparencies" are the main components that help produce a ghost-like (or computer-game-like) military fantasy world of boundless fluidity, in which the space of the city becomes fully navigable as if it offers no barriers to movement, vision and fire.

Shimon Naveh put it to me in these terms: *"military units think like criminals ... like serial killers ... [they] are allocated an area and learn it for months, they study the persons within the enemy organization they are asked to kill, their appearance, their voice [as heard in telephone tapping], their habits ... like professional killers. When they enter the area they know where to look for these people and start killing them."*[15] In his testimony to B'tselem, Khalil 'Abd a-Rahman Barghouthi tells of the April 2004 killing of Husni and Iyad Daraghmeh near the town of Qabatiya: *"a white van appeared, pulled out of the lane in which it was traveling and stopped in the middle of the road. Two armed men in civilian clothes got out of the van. One of them shouted in Arabic at two men who were standing at the intersection: 'Stop! Stop and raise your hands!' ... the two men immediately raised their hands in the air, and one of the armed men then shot at them. One of the two young men was hit and fell down. The other remained standing, his hands raised. Immediately thereafter, one of the armed men again shot at him; he was hit and fell to the ground."*[16]

"Technology Instead of Occupation"

Perennial overoptimism regarding air power led successive generations of airmen, from the early theorist of aerial bombing, the Italian Giulio Douhet at the beginning of the twentieth century, to the present, to believe that unprecedented technological developments would allow wars to be won from the air, bombing to intimidate politicians into submission, and native populations to be managed by air power. The fantasy of a cheap aerial occupation, or "aerially enforced colonization," is thus as old as Air

Forces themselves. In the 1920s Winston Churchill, as Minister of War and Air, was fascinated with what he perceived to be the economically efficient, quick, clean, mechanical, and impersonal alternatives that air power could provide to the otherwise onerous and expensive tasks of colonial control. Emboldened by a murderous aerial attack on a tribal leader in Somaliland in 1920 that put down a rebellion, he suggested that aircraft be further adapted to the tasks of policing the empire. In 1922, Churchill persuaded the British government to invest in the Air Force and offered the RAF six million pounds to take over control of the Mesopotamia (Iraq) operation from the army, which had cost 18 million thus far.[17] The policy, called "control without occupation," saw the Royal Air Force successfully replacing large and expensive army contingents. Sir Percy Cox, the high commissioner in Baghdad, reported that by the end of 1922 "on [at least] three occasions demonstrations by aircraft [have been sufficient to bring] tribal feuds to an end. On another occasion planes ... dropped bombs on a sheik and his followers who refused to pay taxes, held up travellers and attacked a police station."[18] Arthur "Bomber" Harris (so called after his infamous bombing campaigns on German working-class districts when commander of the RAF's bomber wing during World War II), reported after a mission in Iraq in 1924: "The Arab and Kurd now know what real bombing means, in casualties and damage. They know that within 45 minutes a full-sized village can be practically wiped out and a third of its inhabitants killed or injured."[19] The methods pioneered in Somaliland were also applied by the RAF against revolutionaries in Egypt, Darfur, India, Palestine (mainly during the 1936–1939 Arab Revolt),[20] and in Afghanistan's Jalalabad and Kabul. Anticipating the logic of targeted assassinations, Harris later boasted that the latter war was won by a single strike on the king's palace.[21]

Similar belief in "aerially enforced occupation" allowed the Israeli Air Force to believe it could replace the network of lookout outposts woven through the topography of the terrain by translating categories of "depth," "stronghold," "highpoint," "closure" and "panoramas" into "air-defense in depth," "clear skies," "aerial reconnaissance," "aerially enforced closure" and "panoramic radar." With a "vacuum cleaner" approach to intelligence gathering, sensors aboard unmanned drones, aerial reconnaissance jets, attack helicopters, unmanned balloons, early warning Hawkeye planes and military satellites capture most signals out of Palestinian airspace. Since the beginning of the second Intifada, the Air Force has put in hundreds of thousands of flight hours, harvesting a stream of information through its network of airborne reconnaissance platforms, which was later put at the disposal of different intelligence agencies and command-and-control rooms.

If previously the IDF would cordon off an area with fences and earth dykes, and place checkpoints on the approach roads, the airborne occupation of Gaza enforces its closures by leafleting villages and refugee camps around the area to be shut off, declaring it off limits—and then targeting whoever tries to enter. In this very manner the evacuated settlements of the northern part of Gaza remained under closure ever since the 2005 evacuation. Following the evacuation, another procedure, code-named "a knock on the door" replaced military bulldozers with bomber jets for the purpose of house demolition. This new method involves an Air Force operator calling the house to be demolished as happened on August 24, 2006, at the A-Rahman family home in Jabalia refugee camp:

> At Thursday 23:30 24 August 2006 someone called the telephone at the house of Abed A-Rahman in Jebalia claiming to be from the IDF. The phone had been disconnected because the bill had not been paid to the Palestinian phone company, but was activated for the sake of this conversation. The wife of Abed A-Rahman, Um-Salem answered the phone ... [on the other side of the line a voice] said 'evacuate the house immediately and notify the neighbours.' She asked 'who is talking?' and was answered: the IDF. She asked again but her interlocutor had hung up. Um Salem tried to use the phone but it was disconnected again. ... the entire family left the house without having the possibility to take anything with them. At 24:00 the house was bombed by military helicopters and was completely destroyed.[22]

Operational Planning

The operational aspect of airborne targeted assassinations relies on military developments that originated in Israel's war in Lebanon during the 1980s and 1990s. In February 1992, Hezbollah Secretary General Sheikh Abbas Mussawi was the first to be killed in an airborne assassination as a group of Israeli helicopters flying inland from the Mediterranean Sea attacked his convoy, killing him and his family. The first airborne targeted assassination in Palestinian areas took place on November 9, 2000, when an Israeli Apache helicopter pilot launched a U.S.-made "Hellfire" anti-tank missile at the car of a senior member of Tanzim al-Fatah organization, Hussein Muhammad Abayit, in Beit-Sahur near Bethlehem, killing him and two women, Rahmeh Shahin and 'Aziza Muhammed Danun, who happened to be walking by the car when it exploded in the middle of their street. The IDF's spokesperson announced that the killing was part of "a new state policy."[23] In recent years, it is Gaza, however, that has become the world's largest laboratory for airborne assassinations. The U.S. administration feebly protested Israeli assassinations, diplomatically demanding that it merely "considers the results of its actions," and different branches of the U.S. security forces, themselves engaged in unacknowledged assassinations using unmanned drones in the Middle East "examine Israeli Air Force performances and results in order to draw lessons for its own wars."[24]

Ephraim Segoli explained that targeted assassinations are "a success story based upon a high degree of cooperation between the General Security Service and the Air Force."[25] Above all, the machinic operation of targeted assassinations was fed by the information and organizational powers that the GSS developed under Avi Dichter, who gained considerable popularity with the public and with Sharon as a result of their "success." The efficiency of the operations relied on the close networking between the intelligence provided by the GSS, fast-tracked political decisions and the strike capacity of the Air Force. The GSS drafts the death-lists and prioritizes targets (once included, rarely has a name been removed from them alive), provides files on each person to be liquidated (including details of their involvement in resistance and their prospective danger to Israel); a special ministerial committee gives its approval (the typical length of deliberation is 15 minutes, and there are generally no objections); and the Air Force does the killing.

Each targeted assassination is a large-scale operation that integrates hundreds of specialists from different military branches and security apparatuses. Beyond its reliance on background intelligence, targeted assassination depends on sharing real-time information between various agents, commanders, operators, and different military planes, and their ability to act on it. After a Palestinian is put on the death list he is followed, sometimes for weeks, by a "swarm" of different kinds of unmanned aerial vehicles. Often, different swarms follow different people simultaneously in different areas of the Gaza Strip. In this way, the security services establish the targeted person's daily routines and habits, and maintain continuous visual contact with him until his killing.[26] As well as being cheaper to operate, unmanned drones have an advantage over manned planes or helicopters because they can remain in the air around the clock, some for as long as thirty hours, and because their formations circulate in relatively small areas while providing a multiplicity of angles of vision. Moreover, drones are quiet and barely visible to the human eye. This is the reason that from 2004 the Air Force started to shoot its missiles from drones rather than from its more visible battle helicopters. A swarm of various types of drones, each circulating at a different altitude up to a height of 30,000 feet, is navigated by a GPS system and woven by radio communication into a single synergetic reconnaissance and killing instrument that conducts the entire assassination operation. Some drones are designed to view the terrain vertically downward in order to establish the digital coordinates of a targeted person, whereas others look diagonally, in order to distinguish facial features or identify a vehicle's license plates. Some drones are designed to intercept radio signals and mobile phones; others can carry and shoot missiles. With the development and proliferation of drone technology, there remains, as Shimon Naveh put it, "very few Israeli soldiers in the airspace over Gaza ... the air is mainly filled with Golems ... an army without soldiers." Although until 2004 military jets and helicopters carried out the assassinations, they are now largely used to divert attention from the real area of operations by flying over other parts of the strip when the assassinations take place.[27] During the second Intifada, Israel's *Armament Development Authority—Rafael,* developed the "Spike" missile to replace the U.S.-made "Hellfire" laser-guided, antitank missile for the purpose of targeted assassinations. The Spike is itself a small joystick-navigated "kamikaze" drone with an "optical eye."[28]

Targeted assassinations often rely on cooperation from the ground. The clandestine Unit 504, jointly operated by military intelligence and the GSS, is responsible for the recruitment and direction of foreign agents, and for forcing Palestinians into collaboration. From one of its bases south of Haifa—where it also maintains Facility 1391, a Guantánamo Bay–style secret prison for "administrative detainees"—Unit 504 trains groups of Palestinian commandos to mark targets, plant and detonate bombs, or "shake the tree for the Air Force."[29] In previous years, members of this Palestinian military unit of the IDF would splash ultraviolet paint on the roof of a car to identify the target for a pilot to destroy.

The planning of a targeted assassination follows the traditional principles of Air Force operational planning. The unit of "operational analysis," part of the Israeli Air Force's "operational group," is responsible for optimizing bombing missions. At the simplest level, this involves matching munitions with targets, and calculating what size and type of bomb is needed to destroy a particular target. In this role it has been criticized twice for incompetence, first in an operation on July 23, 2002, when it proposed a one-ton bomb to destroy a residential building in Gaza where the leader of Hamas' military wing, Salah Shehadeh, was spending the night, causing the building to collapse, killing Shehadeh and an additional 14 Palestinian civilians, more than half of them children.[30] The second, two years later, for allocating a quarter-ton bomb for the attack on a meeting of Hamas' leadership. The bomb failed to collapse the building, allowing the leaders to escape unharmed from the ground floor.

The unit's function extends beyond physical destruction. It attempts to predict and map out the effect that a destruction of a particular target might have on the enemy's overall system of operation. Following the principles of "system analysis,"[31] the enemy is understood as an operational network of interacting elements. Unlike state militaries, much of whose power is based on physical infrastructure and equipment, the effectiveness of the Palestinian resistance is grounded in its people: political and spiritual leaders, spokespersons, financiers, commanders, experienced fighters, bomb-makers, suicide volunteers, and recruiters. The killing of a key individual much like the destruction of a command and control center or a strategic bridge is intended to trigger a sequence of "failures" that will disrupt the enemy's system, making it more vulnerable to further Israeli military action.[32] "Killing," according to Shimon Naveh "injects energy into the enemy system, disrupting its institutional hierarchies … 'operational shock' is best achieved when the rhythms of these operations is rapid and the enemy system is not given time to recover between attacks." Although "there can be no precise prediction of the outcome of these killing," the effect, according to Naveh, is a degree of institutional and political chaos that allows Israeli security forces to sit back and see "how the cards fall."[33]

When the opportunity for an assassination arises, or when an emergency situation develops, information about the targeted person's location, direction and speed is transferred as radio and image data between the drones and the control room where members of the GSS, the General Staff and Air Force overview the operation on multiple screens. After the GSS identifies the target, and the chief of the Air Fore authorizes the operation, two missiles are simultaneously fired from two different drones. The missiles aim most often at a vehicle, but, increasingly, and because Palestinians now often take the precaution and walk, at pedestrians. Each assassination thus juxtaposes different spaces and domains: a control room in central Tel Aviv in which young soldiers remote-pilot drones and missiles as in a live computer game into the narrow dusty alleys of Gaza's refugee camps where young Palestinians end their lives. The code for "hit" is Alfa and for "kill" is 'Champagne.' Cheap Israeli versions of the latter are traditionally served by the GSS after a successful operation.

One of a hundred counterpoints to these digitized visions of "precision" killing was provided by 'Aref Daraghmeh, a witness to an August 2002 targeted assassination in the village of Tubas in the West Bank:

> The helicopter … fired a third missile towards a silver Mitsubishi, which had four people in it. The missile hit the trunk and the car spun around its axis. I saw a man stepping out of the car and running away. He ran about 25 meters and then fell on the ground and died. The three other passengers remained inside. I saw an arm and an upper part of a skull flying out of the car. The car went up in flames

and I could see three bodies burning inside it. Three minutes later, after the Israeli helicopters left, I went out to the street and began to shout. I saw people lying on the ground. Among them was six-year-old Bahira. … She was dead … I also saw Bahira's cousin, Osama. … I saw Osama's mother running towards Bahira, picking her up and heading towards the a-Shifa clinic, which is about 500 meters away. I went to the clinic and saw her screaming after seeing the body of her son, Osama.[34]

Legalizing Killing

The IDF employs the sanitizing term "focused obstruction" or "focused preemption" to describe these assassinations. Such rhetoric is repeated by most of the popular Israeli media, which conceals as far as possible the real impact of the killings, mostly avoiding to mention the names of Palestinian civilians killed in Israeli attacks and the display of the corpses, blood, and body parts—the very images on which it lingers when covering the aftermath of a Palestinian terror attack. Indeed, the Israeli media's use of selective imagery allows it to project assassination not only as necessary but also as ethical, rhetorically legalizing them by what Neve Gordon called "the discursive production of a pseudo-judicial process."[35] Clips from the "kamikaze" camera on "smart missiles" and from other airborne sensors are later broadcast in the popular media to support IDF refutations of Palestinian accusations about indiscriminate killing, and to focus political and public resolve for the further application of this tactic. The images and videos from these munitions are as much a media product as they are "operation footage." It would be unsurprising if their ability to produce "broadcast-able" images were not actually specified in the briefs of their technological development.[36]

Another factor helping maintain a high level of popular support was the daily terror alerts that Dichter's GSS routinely released. Their average during the height of the Intifada, in the years 2001 to 2003, was between 40 and 50 a day, and Israeli public support for targeted assassination stood at about 80 percent.[37]

Targeted assassinations were presented to the public by the GSS according to a *vindictive* logic that insisted that the victims had "blood on their hands." However, press releases describing a victim as the "most wanted" or senior individual in a particular Palestinian organization were issued so frequently that even the bellicose Israeli public started to question their accuracy.

Revenge is clearly not a legal argument for state killing. When challenged in the Israeli High Court of Justice (HCJ) over the killings, government representatives justified assassination with a preventive logic that described the targeted individual as an imminent danger, a "ticking bomb" about to explode in an impending terror attack, often even in a "mega terrorist attack."[38]

The legal framework for targeted assassinations developed in response to the pace of events. The most common legal basis for IDF killings conducted by ground raids in the West Bank is that the victim "violently attempted to resist arrest" (no such option even exists when killings are conducted from the air), but ground forces do not always allow militants to surrender and often try to steer them away from it. According to figures released by B'tselem, between 2004 and May 2006, Israeli security forces killed 157 persons during operations referred to as "arrest operations."[39] Immediately after the start of the second Intifada, the head of the IDF's legal branch, Colonel Daniel Reisner, stated that as a result of the heightened level and frequency of Palestinian violence, Israel could start defining its military operations in the occupied territories as an "armed conflict short of war," which laced the Intidafa in the context of international law rather than criminal law.[40] Such a definition implied that, for the purpose of their killing (but not their internment), members of militant Palestinian organizations could be seen as combatants and thus attacked at will, not only when in the process of a hostile action or while resisting arrest.[41] Given that, in international law, distinctions between "inside" and "outside" regulate the logic of security operations ("internal" operations are perceived as policing or security work; external ones as military) and that the definition of "inside" depends upon whether a state has "effective control" over the territory in question,[42] the unilateral evacuation of the Gaza Strip strengthened Israel's conviction that targeted assassinations were legal and has made their use more frequent. Politically, Israel expected that once it had evacuated settlements and retreated to the international border around Gaza, the international community would be more tolerant of these forms of military action.[43]

The Politics of Killings

Many of the people involved in the development and promotion of assassination methods, and in the tactic's extension from an exceptional emergency measure into state policy, were former members of *Sayert Matkal*, a military elite commando and assassination unit whose ex-members form Israel's military and political "elite." They included former Prime Ministers Ehud Barak and Benjamin Netanyahu, former Defence Minister and current Deputy Prime Minister Shaul Mofaz, former Chief of Staff Moshe Ya'alon and GSS chief Avi Dichter, now Minster of Internal Security. As prime minister, Ehud Barak renewed orders for targeted assassination of

Palestinian activists a month after the outbreak of the second Intifada. The policy was to gain its momentum, however, during the premiership of Barak's successor, Ariel Sharon, himself former commander of *Sayert Matkal's* precurser, Unit 101. After he assumed office, Sharon allowed this tactical operation to become the center of Israel's security services response to Palestinian terror, but he found ways to let it be used also as an alternative to negotiations with the Palestinians, and even a method of derailing diplomatic initiatives. For targeted assassinations to assume this preeminence, they had to rely upon not only the maturing of operational and technological developments, but also on legal and popular support. When all these components were put in place, less than a year after the beginning of the Intifada, targeted assassinations assumed an appetite and a life of their own, spinning beyond the ability of the military, the government, parliament, media, or judiciary to restrain it.

Given the high level of Israeli public support for it, no government minister could afford to let slip his opposition to the policy or the timing of a particular assassination, as recommended by the GSS, lest it was leaked by the media. The obsession with assassination gripped the entire Israeli security system and political leadership, so much so that in a 2002 meeting called to discuss the assassination of several Palestinian leaders, a military officer suggested conducting one killing every day as a matter of policy. The Minister of Defence thought it was "indeed an idea" and Sharon seemed excited, but the GSS recommended the idea be dropped; it was for it, not the military, to decide where and when Palestinians are to be killed (at that point, in any case, killings were already being carried out at an average rate of one every five days).[44] The Israeli government, confident of its ability to hit anybody anywhere, at any time, started publishing in advance the names of those to be killed.[45]

Israel's operational planning always saw the potential of targeted assassinations beyond a tactical response to imminent dangers, but as a component of a larger political project.[46] Military operational planning continuously (and always in vain) tried to model the possible impact assassinations may have on political developments.[47] From the very start of the Intifada, Palestinian political leaders were themselves targets of assassinations. At the end of August 2003, government authorization was given to kill the entire political leadership of Hamas in Gaza without further notice. The method was referred to as the "hunting season"—the first leader to reveal himself would be the first to be killed. The first one to be killed was Ismail Abu Shanab, a relatively moderate political leader of Hamas, who was targeted on August 21, 2003. In March 22, 2004, Israel assassinated the spiritual leader of Hamas, Sheikh Yassin. A month later, on April 17, 2004, Yassin's successor, Abd al-Aziz Rantissi was killed. Dichter and the Israeli government explained that the reason for these assassinations was to strengthen the position of Abbas and the moderates in the "Palestinian street." At the beginning of 2006, when the "moderates" were ousted by the newly elected Hamas government, Defence Minister Shaul Mofaz repeated the warning, promising that "no one will be immune," including the Palestinian Prime Minister Ismail Haniyeh.[48]

The government, however, still believed that targeted assassinations provided it with "military solutions to situations that were thought of as militarily unsolvable."[49] It was, however, security operatives that filled the political vacuum of the Intifada, dictating political developments. The way that these operatives sought to generate a political effect was in fact no different than the way Palestinian militant groups timed their terror attacks to maximize political impact. Every time a political initiative, local or international, seemed to be emerging, threatening to return the parties to the negotiation table, an assassination followed and derailed it. The list demonstrating this is long; the following are just few examples: On July 31, 2001, the Israeli Air Force bombed an apartment building in Nablus, in which a Hamas office was located, killing two Hamas leaders, Jamal Mansour and Jamal Salim, and two boys, bringing the end of a nearly two-month-long Hamas cease-fire. The January, 2002, killing of Ra'ad Karmi, a leader in Fatah's own militant group, *Tanzim*, in the preparation of which the GSS has already invested millions, could not have been stopped or postponed by anyone within the political system, although the killing was certain to bring about the collapse of a cease-fire that started in December 2001 and to bury an American diplomatic initiative. The assassination achieved this aim, leading to the spate of Palestinian suicide attacks of February and March 2002. On July 23, 2002, a day before the *Tanzim* was to announce a unilateral cease-fire, Salah Shehadeh was assassinated, foreclosing this development. A year later, at the beginning of the summer of 2003, another type of cease-fire, the *Hudna*, was declared and another American diplomatic initiative was launched. As it got formulated, on June 10, 2003, the military attempted to assassinate Abdul Aziz Rantisi with missile fire. A few weeks later, Israeli security forces targeted *Tanzim* militant Mahmoud Shawer in Qalqiliyah, derailing the initiative completely. On December 1, 2003, the same day the Geneva Initiative was launched, the IDF conducted a massive operation attempting to kill Sheikh Ibrahim Hamed, head of Hamas in Ramallah. In June 2006, just as Mahmoud Abbas was about to declare a referendum vote on a progressive political initiative of the "prisoners' document," Israel targeted Jamal Abu Samhadana, the commander of the *Popular Resistance Committees* in Gaza and the idea for the referendum was cancelled.

"Radical" Palestinian leaders could thus be assassinated to open the way for a more "pragmatic" politics. "Pragmatic" leaders could be assassinated to open the way for direct confrontation or to stave off a diplomatic initiative. Other assassinations could be undertaken in order to "restore order," others still to "create chaos"; some assassinations would be undertaken simply because they could be undertaken, because too much money was already invested in the manhunt, because security forces enjoyed the thrill, wanted to impress foreign observers, test new technological developments or to keep themselves practiced. It is the same people, members of the same organizations that train for these operations, the same agents and officers that need "successful" kills in their resume to gain promotions, that are as well those in charge of assessing their effects, and based on their own assessments, continue demanding that the government authorize more attacks. In fact, the assassinations have been supervised by none else but their executioners.

A considerable part of Israel's security logic of assassinations is grounded in the bias of Israel's intelligence agencies toward personality analysis. The Israeli sociologist Gil Eyal demonstrated that, following a long Orientalist tradition, the Israeli intelligence services have tended to seek motives for political developments, as well as for terror attacks, not in response to a history of repression or in pursuit of rational political goals, but in the personal irrationalities, idiosyncrasies, and inconsistencies of Arab leaders.[50] When undertaken, political and economical analysis generally only provided context to the work of psychological profiling.[51] The natural consequence of this logic was the belief that in killing, Israel's security services not only remove a leader but also the cause of a political or security problem.

Although so much effort has been put into modelling enemy behavior, and the security services remain confident in their methods, years of targeted assassinations did not managed to limit violence, nor did they reduce Palestinian motivation for resistance; or strengthen the hand of President Mahmoud Abbas or "reinforce the moderates in the Palestinian street"; nor yet did the killings ever manage to "sear the Palestinian consciousness" regarding the futility of resistance. On the contrary, assassinations fed the conflict by creating further motivation for violent retaliations, and dramatically increased Palestinian popular support for acts of terror.[52]

The power of targeted assassination to affect politics has been, however, most strongly felt within the Israeli political system itself. In the half year from the beginning of 2004, when the political debates regarding the evacuation of Gaza settlements began, to June 6, 2004, when the "disengagement plan" came into a vote and was authorized by the Israeli government, targeted assassinations were accelerated, leading to the death of 33

Palestinians.[53] In anticipation of the evacuation operation itself, scheduled for August 2005, the level of assassinations increased again, with July 2005 being the bloodiest of this year.[54] This bloodshed helped Sharon present himself as "tough on terror," while pursuing a policy that was understood in Israel as left leaning. In this manner, targeted assassination paradoxically increased the support for "territorial compromise."

The "Humanitarian" War

In the months following the evacuation, targeted assassinations remained almost the sole form of attack the Israeli military, now deployed around Gaza's fences and in the airspace over it, could undertake. Palestinian home-made Qassam rockets were fired at Israeli development towns. The rate of assassinations further increased, with 52 Palestinians killed during such attacks in the period to April 2006.[55]

In March 2006, the Israeli Air Force was criticized for a particularly horrific attack in which unmanned drones fired missiles at an ice cream van in order to kill two *Islamic Jihad* militants that took refuge in it. In the event, a man and two children—the brothers Ra'ad and Mahmoud Al-Batash—who were the only ones to fall for the improvised camouflage—were killed along with the militants. Responding to the widespread condemnation of the attack, the Chief of Israel's Air Force, Eliezer Shakedy, called a press conference where he claimed that the Air Force makes "super-human efforts in order to reduce the number of innocent civilian casualties in aerial strikes."[56] To prove his claims, he projected charts that numerically "demonstrated" how the Air Force had reduced the ratio between the victims of aerial raids it defined as "combatants," and those victims it was willing to concede were "non-combatants" or "uninvolved civilians." Data collected by the Israeli human rights organization B'Tselem shows that military figures were skewed—largely because the military included within the definition of "combatants" all men of combat age that happened to be in the vicinity of the assassination.[57]

Since the end of 2003, in response to ongoing international and local protests over the killing of many bystanders to targeted assassination, and significantly since the refusal of several Israeli Air Force pilots to fly on these missions,[58] the military began to employ operatives whose task was to minimize "collateral deaths." Using cameras on auxiliary drones, they observe the surrounding context of an impending attack in order to judge the "safest" moment to launch missiles. These specialists have effectively become the "trigger" of the operation, deciding to what level of danger Palestinian bystanders can be acceptably subjected. As one of these operators explained to me, they see their work not as facilitating assassinations but as saving lives; minimizing the slaughter that will have undoubtedly occurred were they not there to maintain vigilance.[59] Following this trend, in the summer of 2006, a new type of explosive started to be used within missiles shot in targeted assassinations. That new munitions were used became apparent when doctors in Gaza hospitals started receiving Palestinian victims with horrifying burn wounds, amputations, and internal burns never seen before. A former Israeli Air Force officer and head of the IDF's weapons-development program, Yitzhak Ben-Israel, explained that these are new munitions—referred to as "focused lethality munitions" or "munitions of low collateral damage"—designed to produce a blast more lethal, but also of smaller radius than traditional explosives. "This technology allows [the military] to strike very small targets ... without causing damage to bystanders or other persons ..."[60]

At the end of November 2006, again in response to local and international protests regarding the killing of civilians, the government wanted to demonstrate it was acting to further regulate targeted assassinations. It established a "legal committee" to rule about the assassinations of individuals, with the assassination of senior political leaders subjected to the opinion of the Attorney General. A few weeks later, on December 14, 2006, in response to petitions by the *Public Committee Against Torture in Israel,* and the *Palestinian Society for the Protection of Human Rights and the Environment* (known by its Arabic acronym, LAW) the Israeli High Court of Justice issued a ruling in which other regulatory directives were outlined: Assassinations could take place only when there is "well-founded, strong and persuasive information as to the identity [of the person assassinated] and his activity"; if they could help curtail terror attacks; if other more moderate use of force, such as an arrests, cannot take place without gravely endangering the lives of soldiers, and if it will not lead to a "disproportionate collateral harm to innocent civilians."[61]

Whether or not these measures will reduce the deaths of bystanders to targeted assassinations, a critical perspective must contend with the *claims* that these, and military developments in the technology, techniques and proficiency of targeted assassination will eventually bring about fewer unintended deaths, without having this possible outcome exonerate the act. Lacking another mode of critique to justify or oppose military actions, one would have to accept the Israeli terms of a *necro*-economy in which a "lesser evil" or "lesser evils," represented in a lower body count, should be measured against an imaginary or real "greater evil," represented by more suffering and death on both sides.[62]

The theoretical terms of this argument were articulated by the human-rights scholar and now leader of the Liberal Party of Canada, Michael

Ignatieff. Ignatieff claimed that in a "war on terror," democratic societies may need to breach some basic human rights and allow their security services to engage in other covert and unsavory state actions—in his eyes, a "lesser evil"—in order to fend off or minimize potential "greater evils," such as terror attacks.[63] Ignatieff is even willing to consider Israeli targeted assassination under conditions similar to those articulated by the Israeli HCJ, "qualifying within the effective moral-political framework of the lesser evil."[64]

In the terms of this *necro*-economy, targeted assassinations are to be understood as the "lesser evil" alternatives to possible greater evils that could occur to both Israelis and Palestinians. Israel, who undertakes these operations, would like Palestinians to understand that because it uses targeted assassinations it restrains more brutal measures that would affect the entire population, killing only, or mostly those "guilty." According to former Chief of Staff Ya'alon, "focused obstructions are important because they [communicated to the Palestinians that we] make a distinction between the general public and the instigator of terror."[65] From the perspective of Israelis, by allowing their state to undertake extrajuridical executions, they are simply acting to save their lives.

However, as Israeli philosopher Adi Ophir suggested, this conception of the "lesser evil" raises a problem of a different nature: a less brutal measure is a measure that may easily be naturalized, accepted, and tolerated. When normalized, this measure could be more frequently applied. Because it helps normalize the low intensity conflicts, the overall duration of this conflict could be extended, and, finally, more "lesser evils" could even be committed.[66]

The quest to make war more "humane"—written since the nineteenth century into different conventions and laws of war—may under certain conditions similarly result in making it more imaginable, more frequent. Regulating violence, the laws of war, and other moral rules that societies may voluntarily impose on themselves, may end up legitimizing it, and even prolonging it. Another analogous phenomena that can help clarify this paradox can be seen in the IDF's use of rubber-coated steel munitions. Soldiers believe that "rubber bullets" are nonlethal munitions and that their use demonstrates restraint in non-life-threatening situations. But this perception leads to their more frequent and indiscriminate use, causing the death and permanent injury of many Palestinian demonstrators, mainly children.[67]

The military belief that it can perform "controlled," "elegant," "pinhead accurate," "discriminate" killing could bring about more destruction and death than "traditional" strategies do because these methods, combined with the manipulative and euphoric rhetoric used to promulgate them, induce decision makers to authorize their frequent and extended use. The illusion of precision, here part of a rhetoric of restraint, gives the military-political apparatus the necessary justification to use explosives in civilian environments where they could not be used without injuring or killing civilians. The lower the threshold of violence a certain means is believed to possess, the more frequent its application might become.

The promoters of the instruments, techniques, and rhetoric supporting such "lesser evils" believe that by developing and perfecting them they actually exercise a restraining impact on the government and on the rest of the security forces, which would otherwise succeed in pushing for the further radicalization of violence; that targeted assassinations are the more moderate alternative to the devastating capacity for destruction that the military actually possess and would unleash in the form of a full-scale invasion or the renewal of territorial occupation, should the enemy exceed an "acceptable" level of violence or breach some unspoken agreement in the violent discourse of attacks and retaliations. Confirming this logic, Air Force chief Shakedy, arguing for targeted assassinations, explained, only a few weeks before the June 2006 invasion of Gaza, that *"the only alternative to aerial attacks is a ground operation and the reoccupation of Gaza ... [targeted assassinations] is the most precise tool we have."*[68]

The reoccupation of Gaza starting June 2002 and the Lebanon war of July–August 2006 demonstrated that more destructive alternatives are always possible, especially when the "unwritten rules" of the low intensity conflict are perceived to have been broken. Since the June 28 kidnapping of an Israeli soldier in Gaza, over 500 Palestinians have been killed, including 88 minors, and more than 2,700 injured.[69] Forty-six million dollars worth of infrastructure, including a power plant, 270 private houses and residences were destroyed. The killing of civilians, the displacement of communities, the intentional destruction of property and infrastructure including airports, power stations, and bridges in both Gaza and Lebanon, should be understood as eruptions of violence meant to sustain the threat of greater measures.

Military threats could function only if gaps are maintained between the *possible* destruction an army can inflict in the application of its full destructive capacity, and the *actual* destruction it does inflict.[70] Restraint is what allows for the possibility of further escalation. A degree of restraint is thus part of the logic of almost every conventional military operation: however bad military attacks appear to be, they could always get worse.

Naturally, I am not suggesting that "greater evils" should be preferred to lesser ones, or that war should be more brutal, rather, that we question the very terms of the economy of evils. These terms are not only part of the nature of military planning, but are integral to political "militarism"—a culture that sees violence as permanent as a rule of history and thus military contingencies as the principal alternative available to politicians. Israeli militarism accordingly always sought military solutions to political problems.[71] Locked within the limits defined by the degrees of violence, it continuously forecloses the exploration of other avenues for negotiations and participation in a genuine political process. At the beginning of 2006, Chief of Staff Dan Halutz expressed this world view when he stated that "the intifada is part of an un-resolvable ... permanent conflict between Jews and Palestinians that started in 1929." The military, according to Halutz, must therefore gear itself to operate within an environment saturated with conflict and a future of permanent violence. With this, he echoed an often-recurring claim within Israeli security discourse: In June 1977, as Foreign Minister, Moshe Dayan explained the presumption that Israel's conflict with the Palestinians could be "solved" was fundamentally flawed. "The question, was not, 'What is the solution?' but 'How do we live without a solution?'" In the absence of both options—a political solution or the possibility of a decisive military outcome—the Israeli military should merely "managing the conflict." At the beginning of 2006, Halutz still thought that the precision method of the Israeli Air Force would help keep the conflict "on a flame low enough for Israeli society to be able to live and to prosper within it."[72] This projection for an ongoing conflict has all likelihood to fulfil itself.

NOTE: A version of this chapter was published in Hollow Land: Israel's Architecture of Occupation by Eyal Wezman. Verso, 2007.

Notes

1. Azmi Bishara, "When The Skies Rain Death: The culture of the fighter plane is the culture of annihilation," *Al-Ahram*, 3–9 August 2006.
2. These attacks have been referred to as: "targeted killing," "assassinations," "targeted assassinations," "liquidations," "extrajudicial executions," and "focused prevention." The choice of terminology has implications to those arguing for or against the legality of the act. I have chosen to use the term "targeted assassination" as it combines an operational logic with the designation of an illegal act.
3. Yedidia Ya'ari and Haim Assa, *Diffused Warfare, War in the 21st Century,* Tel Aviv: Miskal—Yediot Aharonot Books and Chemed Books, 2005, pp. 9–13 [Hebrew]. The book is the summary of positions developed within the "Alternative Team" and under the influence of OTRI. Yedidya Ya'ari, the former commander of the Israeli Navy, and Haim Asa, a former member of a comparable Air Force think-tank, directed the team. Affiliated to it were Air Force pilot Dror Ben David, Brig. General Gadi Eisenkott, Brig. General Aviv Kochavi. General Benni Gantz was assigned to implement this study within the IDF. The "Alternative Team" was operating in cooperation with

the U.S. "Transformation" group under U.S. Secretary of Defense Donald Rumsfeld. In 2006 Chief of Staff Dan Halutz dismantled the "Alternative Team." There were as well a large number of parallel and smaller teams with similar aims, for example, the *Military Research Centre for the Study of the Tactical Environment*, directed by Gabrial Siboni. On the latter see: Gabrial Siboni, "The Importance of Activity," *Bamahane* [in the camp], IDF's official journal, December 31, 2004, pp. 14–18 [Hebrew].

4. The last of the terms was coined in a joint program between former commander of fighter squadron Dror Ben David and researchers at OTRI.

5. Halutz constantly defended the technology behind his airborne assassinations, even when it regularly took the lives of many bystanders. When asked for his reaction to the death of many civilians in an operation of targeted assassination, he famously retorted, " ... if you want to know what I feel when I release a bomb, I will tell you: I feel a light bump to the plane as a result of the bomb's release. A second later it's gone, and that's all. That is what I feel." See Vered Levy-Barzilai, "Halutz: The High and the Mighty," *Ha'aretz Magazine*, August 21, 2002.

6. Israel Harel, "The IDF protects itself," *Ha'aretz*, August 29, 2006. On another occasion while still chief of the Air Force, Halutz reportedly mentioned, "Why do you need to endanger infantry soldiers. ... I can resolve the entire Lebanon [situation] from the air in 3 to 5 days a week maximum." See: Amir Rapaport, "Dan Halutz is a Bluff, Interview with Shimon Naveh" *Ma'ariv*, Yom Kippur Supplement, October 1, 2006.

7. Interview with Ephraim Segoli, Tel Aviv, May 22, 2006.

8. According to Liddell Hart the essence of the indirect approach is in creating advantage by positioning, rather than by killing. See: B. H. Liddell Hart, *Strategy*, New York: Plum Books, 1991.

9. Brigadier General Aviv Kokhavi captured the attention of the media in February 2006 when the chief legal advisor to the IDF recommended that he not make a planned trip to a U.K.-based military academy for fear he could be prosecuted for war crimes in Britain; for an earlier statement implicating Kochavi in war crimes, see: Neve Gordon, "Aviv Kochavi, How Did You Become a War Criminal?" www.counterpunch.org/nevegordon1.html (April 8, 2002).

10. These assassinations have been undertaken either for revenge (as in the assassinations of those involved in the Munich Olympic massacre), in attempt to prevent attacks (such as the killing in 1996 of the main Palestinian bombmaker—Yehiya Ayash in Gaza) or to "decapitate" enemy organizations (Khalil Al-Wazir [or Abu-Jihad] PLO deputy commander was killed for this reason in Tunis in 1988), Hezbollah Secretary General Sheikh Abbas Mussawi was killed by an Israeli aerial attack in 1992, the head of the Islamic Jihad, Fathi Shakaki, was killed by Mossad agents in Malta in 1995). Yassir Arafat has reportedly escaped more than half a dozen assassination attempts.

11. *B'Tselem*: "683 people killed in the conflict in 2006" December 28, 2006, http://www.btselem.org/english/Press_Releases/20061228.asp.

12. Eyal Weizman, "Walking through Walls: Soldiers as Architects in the Israeli Palestinian Conflict," *Radical Philosophy*, March–April 2006.

13. Zuri Dar and Oded Hermoni, "Israeli Start-Up Develops Technology to See through Walls," in *Ha'aretz*, July 1, 2004. Amnon Brazilay, see also Amir Golan, "The Components of the Ability to Fight in Urban Areas," *Ma'arachot* 384 (July 2002), p. 97.

14. Contemporary methods and weapons seeking life without the destruction of property are reminiscent of the function of the 1970 neutron bomb designed to leave all equipment and buildings intact and kill all the people within them.

15. Interview with Shimon Naveh.

16. Quoted in: "Take No Prisoners: The Fatal Shooting of Palestinians by Israeli Security Forces during 'Arrest Operations,'" *B'Tselem*, May 2005, http://www.btselem.org.

17. Sven Linqvist, *A History of Bombing*, Linda Haverty Rugg (Trans.). New York: The New Press, 2000, entry 101.

18. Philip Anthony Towle, *Pilots and Rebels: The Use of Aircraft in Unconventional Warfare, 1918–1988*, London: Brassey's, Defence Publishers, 1989, p. 17; David Willard Parsons, "British Air Control: A Model for the Application of Air Power in Low-Intensity Conflict?," *Airpower Journal*, Summer 1994 at http://www.airpower.maxwell.af.mil/airchronicles/apj/apj94/parsons.html.

19. Quoted in Lt. Colonel David J. Dean, USAF, "Air Power in Small Wars: The British Air Control Experience," *Air University Review* 34, No. 5 (July–August 1985).

20. Dean, "Air Power in Small Wars"; David Omissi, *Air Power and Colonial Control: The Royal Air Force 1919–1939*, Manchester: Manchester University Press, 1990; David MacIsaac, "Voices from the Central Blue, The Air Power Theorists," in Peter Paret, *Makers of Modern Strategy, From Machiavelli to the Nuclear Age*, Oxford: Oxford University Press, 1986, pp. 624–647, especially p. 633.

21. Linqvist, *A History of Bombing*, entry 102.

22. Darryl Li, "Gaza Consultancy—Research Findings, 20 to 27 August 2006," [draft submitted to B'Tselem] 10 September 2006. Testimony number 3287. Unpublished.

23. Orna Ben-Naftali and Keren Michaeli, "'We must not make a scarecrow of the Law': A Legal Analysis of the Israeli Policy of Targeted Killings," *Cornell Int Law Jnl*, Spring 2003, 234, footnote 22.

24. The quote is from Segoli in an interview. In November 2002, a car traveling in a remote part of Yemen was destroyed by a missile fired from an unmanned Predator drone, killing six suspected members of al-Qa'eda. Although the U.S. administration did not publicly acknowledge responsibility for the attack, officials let it be known that the CIA had carried it out. The June 2006 killing of Abu Musab al-Zarqawi and the January 2006 attempt to kill Ayman al-Zawahiri were undertaken from the air. Previous strikes killed Mohammed Atef, al-Qa'eda's military chief, and Hamza Rabia, a senior operative in Pakistan. Currently the U.S. military plans to double the number of Predator and Global Hawk drones used for surveillance and targeting. See: Anthony Dworkin, "The Yemen Strike: The War on Terrorism Goes Global," Crimes of War Project, November 14, 2002, available at

http://www.crimesofwar.org/onnews/news-yemen.html; Chris Downes, "'Targeted Killing' in an Age of Terror: The Legality of the Yemen Strike," *Journal of Conflict and Security Law* (2004), Vol. 9, No. 2, pp. 277–279.

25. Segoli, in interview.

26. Aharon Yoffe, "Focus Preemption, Chances and Dangers," *Nativ*, 109 (2), March 2006 [Hebrew]. See as well Ya'ari, *Diffused Warfare*, p. 37.

27. Interview with an Israel Air Force pilot, April 10, 2006.

28. David A. Fulghum and Robert Wall, "Israel Starts Reexamining Military Missions and Technology," *Aviation Week*, August 20, 2006.

29. Interview with former member of unit 504, May 2006.

30. Ariel Meyerstein, "Case Study: The Israeli Strike Against Hamas Leader Salah Shehadeh," Crimes of War Project, http://www.crimesofwar.org/onnews/news-shehadeh.html, September 19, 2002.

31. Ludwig von Bertalanffy defines a system as a complex of interacting elements. Thus a system's problems, according to Bertalanffy, are problems of the interrelations of a great number of variables, which occur in the field of politics, economics, industry, commerce and military conduct. See Ludwig von Bertalanffy, *General System Theory: Foundations, Development, Applications*, New York: George Braziller, 1976.

32. This logic was reflected in a March 2006 presentation to U.S. security personnel at the Washington, DC, Brookings Institute by Avi Dichter, the former chief of Israel's General Security Service (GSS). Dichter, the driving force behind the tactical success and frequent application of targeted assassinations, observed that "By eliminating ... generators of terror through arrests (the preferred method) or by targeted killings (if absolutely necessary), a state can greatly disrupt the operations of terrorist organizations." See: Avi Dichter and Daniel Byman, Israel's Lessons for Fighting Terrorists And Their Implications For The United States (Analysis Paper Number 8), March 2006, the Saban Center for Middle East Policy at the Brookings Institute, Washington, DC.

33. Interviews with Shimon Naveh were conducted on September 15, 2005 (telephone), March 7, 2006 (telephone), April 11, 2006, and May 22–23, 2006 (at an Intelligence military base in Glilot, near Tel Aviv). All transcripts and translations to English of the interviews were sent to Naveh for confirmation of content. All future references to the interview refer to those above unless mentioned otherwise.

34. *B'tselem*, "IDF helicopter missile-fire kills four Palestinian civilians and wounds dozens," August 2002. http://www.btselem.org/English/Testimonies/20020831_Tubas_Killing_Witness_Aref_Daraghmeh.asp.

35. Neve Gordon, "Rationalizing Extra-Judicial Executions: The Israeli Press and the Legitimization of Abuse," *International Journal of Human Rights*, Vol. 8, No. 3, Autumn 2004, p. 305. *Ha'aretz*, Israel's liberal daily, started in 2005 to publish, as a matter of policy, the names of Palestinians killed.

36. Indeed, during the 1991 Gulf War, the public was fed images of "kamikaze bombs," as proof of the technological superiority and surgical skills of the U.S. military. Harun Farocki, *War From a Distance*, lecture delivered at the Academy of Fine Arts, Vienna, on January 13, 2005.

37. *Ma'ariv* Gallup poll of August 10, 2001 revealed that 76 percent of the public polled supported assassinations. In later years and in particular as a result of the killing of many bystanders, public support considerably dropped. In June 2003, at the start of the campaign to assassinate the leadership of Hamas, an opinion poll by the daily newspaper *Yedioth Ahronoth* found that 58 percent of Israelis polled said the military should at least temporarily discontinue targeted killings. See: Raviv Druker and Ofer Shelah, *Boomerang,* Jerusalem: Keter Press, 2005, p. 216.

38. This argument was introduced after Siham Thabet, the wife of the assassinated Secretary of Fatah Movement in Tulkarm, Thabet Thabet, filed in January 2001 the first of several petitions to the HCJ, asking the court to outlaw the use of extra-judicial executions. Thabet Thabet was killed by Israeli snipers on the last day of the year 2000. See: Orna Ben-Naftali and Keren Michaeli, "'We Must Not Make a Scarecrow of the Law': A Legal Analysis of the Israeli Policy of Targeted Killings," *Cornell Interational Law Journal,* Spring 2003.

39. "Take No Prisoners: The Fatal Shooting of Palestinians by Israeli Security Forces during 'Arrest Operations,'" *B'tselem,* May 2005, http://www.btselem.org. AL-HAQ, Indiscriminate and Excessive Use of Force: Four Palestinians Killed During Arrest Raid, May 24, 2006, http://asp.alhaq.org.

40. David Kretzmer, "Targeted Killing of Suspected Terrorists: Extra-Judicial Executions or Legitimate Means of Defense?" *The European Journal of International Law,* Vol. 16, No. 2, pp. 196, 207.

41. Press briefing by Colonel Daniel Reisner—director of the International Law department of the IDF Legal Division, Israeli Ministry of Foreign Affairs, http://www.mfa.gov.il, November 15, 2000.

42. The Israeli legal scholar Eyal Benvenisti claimed that the proper measure to judge whether Israel continues to be bound by the obligations of an occupying power are facts on the ground: "If there were areas under Palestinian control, they were not subject to Israeli occupation." Eyal Benvenisti, "Israel and the Palestinians: What Laws Were Broken," Crimes of War Project, http://www.crimesofwar.org/expert/me-intro.html. Charles Shamas, a Ramallah-based legal expert, claims that because Israel still exercises effective control over movement between localities, over supply of goods and over access to natural resources, it has in effect authority over the enactment of Palestinian legislation, and therefore continues to be bound by the duties of an occupying power.

43. Indeed, since the evacuation of Gaza, the IDF became even more willing to employ violence against the Palestinians. In 2006 alone, Israeli forces killed 405 Palestinians in Gaza, half of them civilians, including 88 minors. *B'tselem:* " 683 People Killed in the Conflict in 2006." In June 2006, Israel bombed the electric grid in Gaza, cutting off 700,000 people from electricity. During 2006, Israel killed 22 Palestinians in targeted assassinations.

44. Druker and Shelah, *Boomerang,* p. 161.

45. *Ha'aretz:* "The IDF Published a List of Seven 'Assassination Candidates,'" July 6, 2001.

46. In his article "Necropolitics," Achilles Mbembe follows Michel Foucault and argues that the sovereignty of political power is not only located within the institutions of the geographically defined nation-state, nor as postmodern

thinkers suggest, within the operational networks of supranational institutions, but in the capacity of power to make decisions regarding life and death (even if this may take place outside of the traditional boundaries of the state's jurisdiction). According to Michel Foucault, the other side of politics that engages with the management of life (biopolitics) is the administration of death (thanato-politics). Michel Foucault, *Society Must Be Defended: Lectures at the College De France, 1975–1976*, New York: Picador, 2003, p. 25. Achille Mbembe, "Necropolitics," *Public Culture*, Vol. 15, No. 1, Winter 2003, pp. 11–40.

47. In this context, IDF operational planners draw on the principles of game theory—a branch of applied mathematics conceived to provide the tools to model environments in which various rational players interact. Game theory was developed after World War II as a strategic logic by Thomas Schelling and others at the U.S. Air Force think-tank RAND Corporation in order to evaluate alternative nuclear strategies, and later used to "manage" the Vietnam War. John von Neumann and Oskar Morgenstern, *Theory of Games and Economic Behavior* (Commemorative Edition), Princeton: Princeton University Press, 2004 (1944). Thomas Schelling, *The Strategy of Conflict*, Cambridge, MA: Harvard University Press, 2006 (1960). In the context of the low-intensity environment "game theory" is sometimes used for modelling the behavior of guerrilla and terror organizations, of the governments that support them, as well as of the international community. Its influence on Israel military strategy stems from the fact that since the 1960s, the Math faculty at Jerusalem's Hebrew University has become one of game theory's leading centers worldwide. Robert Aumann was awarded the 2005 Nobel Prize in Economic Sciences together with Thomas Schelling for his contribution to "game theory."

48. Quoted in Amos Harel and Arnon Regular, "IAF Probe: Civilians Spotted Too Late to Divert Missiles in Gaza Strike," *Ha'aretz*, March 7, 2006. See as well: Soha Abdelaty, "Intifada Timeline," September 30–October 6, 2004, Al-Ahram, http://weekly.ahram.org.eg/2004/710/f05.htm; Vincent Cannistraro, "Assassination is Wrong—and Dumb," *Washington Post*, August 30, 2001.

49. Ya'ari, *Diffused Warfare*, p. 147. According to a June 2003 statement by then Chief of Staff Ya'alon targeted assassinations have altogether replaced politics. "Liquidations," he claimed "gave the political levels a tool to create a change of direction." In Druker and Shelah, *Boomerang*, p. 162 and note 96.

50. For many years, Yassir Arafat remained at the top of Israel's most wanted list. The *dibbuk* haunting Israeli security services, Arafat's "irrational character" was blamed for almost every political stalemate or outbreak of violence. Chief of Military Intelligence Amos Gilead, who developed a personal obsession with him, described Arafat as "in the best psychological condition in a state of conflict, flames suffering and blood." Only an explicit promise extracted from Sharon by Bush prevented the IDF from doing what it really wanted to do. Gil Eyal, *The Disenchantment of the Orient: Expertise in Arab Affairs And the Israeli State*, Palo Alto, CA: Stanford University Press, 2006, p. 189.

51. Gil Eyal, *The Disenchantment of the Orient*, p. 183.

52. A few examples: The July 31, 2001 assassination in Nablus lead to the August 9 Hamas suicide bombing in a Jerusalem pizzeria. The suicide bombing on August 4 was a response to the July 23, 2002, Israeli assassination of Salah Shehada. On June 10, 2003, Israel's attempted assassination of the senior Hamas political leader in Gaza, Abdel-Aziz Rantisi, which wounded him and killed four Palestinian civilians, lead to the bus bombing in Jerusalem on June 11, which killed 16 Israelis.
53. *B'tselem*: "Palestinians Killed by the Israeli Security Forces during the Course of an Assassination;" http://www.btselem.org/English/Statistics/ Palestinians_killed_during_the_course_of_an_assasination.asp.
54. Eight people were killed in July 2005 in the context of assassination, six of them the intended targets of assassinations. In the 10 months before the evacuation of the Gaza Strip in August 2005, Israeli forces killed 563 Palestinians there, while during the previous 10-month period, 264 were killed. *B'tselem*: "Palestinians Killed by the Israeli Security Forces during the Course of an Assassination."
55. *B'tselem*: "Palestinians Killed by the Israeli Security Forces during the Course of an Assassination."
56. Amos Harel and Arnon Regular, "IAF Probe: Civilians Spotted Too Late to Divert Missiles in Gaza Strike," *Ha'aretz*, March 7, 2006.
57. Harel, "Nothing 'surgical.'" *B'Tselem* figures are on http://www.btselem. org/English/Statistics/Casualties.asp.
58. Chris McGreal, "We're Air Force pilots, not mafia. We don't take revenge," *Guardian*, December 3, 2003.
59. Interview with an Israeli Air Force operator of unmanned drones, April 2005,
60. Quoted in: Meron Rapoport, "Italian TV: Israel Used New Weapon Prototype in Gaza Strip," *Ha'aretz*, October 12, 2006. All signs lead an independent Italian investigative team to believe that these munitions were *Dense Inert Metal Explosive* or DIME. These comprise a carbon-fiber casing filled with tungsten powder—a metal capable of conducting very high temperatures. On detonation, the tungsten particles are propelled outward in a relatively small (about four meters) but very deadly cloud, causing severe burns, amputated limbs and internal burns. Air Force Research Laboratory: 2005 accomplishment, http:// www.afrl.af.mil/accomprpt/may05/accompmay05.asp.
61. HCJ 769/02 *The Public Committee against Torture in Israel v. The Government of Israel*. Previous petitioned to the High Court of Justice against targeted assassinations (for example, HCJ 5872/2002, M.K. Muhammed Barake vs. Prime Minister and Minister of Defense) were dismissed.
62. "Evil" in this context is best understood following Adi Ophir as a category displaced from the realm of the divine or diabolical, and relocated in a social order in which suffering and pain could have been, but was not, prevented. See: Adi Ophir, *The Order of Evils: Toward an Ontology of Morals*, Rela Mazali and Havi Care (trans.), New York: Zone Books, 2005, chapter 7.100. *"Evils can only be justified by appealing to more grave hypothetical evils that could have been caused if the prevention or disengagement actions would have taken place (3.432). The justification displaces the discussion from one order of exchange, in which the one harmed tries to create a link between damage*

or suffering and compensation, to another order of exchange, in which the defendant tries to create a link between evils that occurred to possible evils that might have occurred."

63. Michael Ignatieff, *The Lesser Evil: Political Ethics in an Age of Terror,* Princeton: Princeton University Press, 2004.

64. These conditions include they are *"applied to the smallest number of people, used as a last resort, and kept under the adversarial scrutiny of an open democratic system ..."* Furthermore *"assassination can be justified only if ... less violent alternatives, like arrest and capture, endanger ... personnel or civilians ... [are not possible, and] where all reasonable precautions are taken to minimize collateral damage and civilian harm."* Ignatieff, *The Lesser Evil,* pp. 8, 129–133.

65. Quoted in Amos Harel and Avi Isacharoff, *The Seventh War,* Tel Aviv: Miskal—Yedioth Aharonoth Books and Chemed Books, 2004, p. 343.

66. Adi Ophir, *The Order of Evils,* chapter 7.100.

67. *B'Tselem,* "A Death Foretold: Firing of 'Rubber' Bullets to Disperse Demonstrations in the Occupied Territories," November 1998. http://www.btselem. org/english/publications/summaries/199805_a_death_foretold.asp.

68. Harel, "Nothing 'Surgical.'"

69. *B'Tselem*: 683 People Killed in the Conflict in 2006, http://www.btselem.org December 27, 2006.

70. At the moment, this gap between the *possible* and the *actual* application of force closes, war is no longer a language, violence is stripped of semiotics and simply aims to make the enemy disappear as a subject. "Total wars"—marking the other limit of the conceptual spectrum—beyond their meaning in the total mobilization of society—are those wars that allow no longer any communication to take place. Colonial wars have often been total wars, because the "natives" were not perceived to share the same "humanity" as the colonizers and thus could not be considered a party capable of rational behavior and discourse. Terror is "total" as well, because, most often, it places no legal or moral limits to violence, no distinction between innocence and guilt. Moreover, it acts to attack the very possibility of discourse. Degree and distinctions are precisely what makes war less then total.

71. On Israeli militarism, see Uri Ben-Eliezer, "Post-Modern Armies and the Question of Peace and War: The Israeli Defense Forces in the 'New Times,'" *International Journal of Middle East Studies,* 36 (2004), pp. 49–70, p. 50; see as well Ben-Eliezer, *Making of Israeli Militarism,* Bloomington: Indiana University Press, 1998 pp. 1–18; Baruch Kimmerling, *Invention and Decline of Israeliness: Society, Culture and the Military,* Berkeley: University of California Press, 2001, p. 209. Further on the concept of militarism, see Michael Mann, "The Roots and Contradictions of Modern Militarism," in *New Left Review* I-162, 1987.

72. Halutz quotes are from Amir Oren, "The Tenth Round," *Ha'aretz* weekend supplement 14 January 2006; Dayan's quote is from: Foundation for Middle East Peace: Sharon's Enduring Agenda: Consolidate Territorial Control, Manage the Conflict, Settlement Report Vol. 14, No. 1, January-February 2004, http://www.fmep.org/reports/v0114/n01/01-sharons_enduring_agenda.html.

'The Poor Man's Airforce'

A Brief History of the Car Bomb

MIKE DAVIS

Buda's Wagon (1920)

You have shown no pity to us! We will do likewise.
We will dynamite you!

Anarchist warning (1919)

On a warm September day in 1920, a few months after the arrest of his comrades Sacco and Vanzetti, a vengeful Italian anarchist named Mario Buda parked his horse-drawn wagon near the corner of Wall and Broad Streets, directly across from J. P. Morgan Company. He nonchalantly climbed down and disappeared unnoticed into the lunchtime crowd. A few blocks away, a startled postal worker found strange leaflets warning: "Free the Political Prisoners or it will be Sure Death for All of You!" They were signed: "American Anarchist Fighters." The bells of nearby Trinity Church began to toll noon. When they stopped, the wagon—packed with dynamite and iron slugs—exploded in a fireball of shrapnel.

"The horse and wagon were blown to bits," writes Paul Avrich, the celebrated historian of American anarchism who uncovered the true story. "Glass showered down from office windows, and awnings 12 stories above the street burst into flames. People fled in terror as a great cloud of dust enveloped the area. In Morgan's offices Thomas Joyce of the securities department fell dead on his desk amid a rubble of plaster and walls. Outside, scores of bodies littered the streets."

Buda was undoubtedly disappointed when he learned that J. P. Morgan himself was not among the 40 dead and more than 200 wounded—the great robber baron was away in Scotland at his hunting lodge. Nonetheless, a poor immigrant with some stolen dynamite, a pile of scrap metal and an old horse had managed to bring unprecedented terror to the inner sanctum of American capitalism.

His Wall Street bomb was the culmination of a half-century of anarchist fantasies about avenging angels made of dynamite; but it was also an invention, like Charles Babbage's Difference Engine, far ahead of the imagination of its time. Only after the barbarism of strategic bombing had become commonplace, and when air forces routinely pursued insurgents into the labyrinths of poor cities, would the truly radical potential of Buda's 'infernal machine' be fully realized.

Buda's wagon, in essence, was the prototype car bomb: the first use of an inconspicuous vehicle, anonymous in almost any urban setting, to transport large quantities of high explosive into precise range of a high-value target. It was not replicated, as far as I have been able to determine, until January 12, 1947, when the Stern Gang drove a truckload of explosives into a British police station in Haifa, killing 4 and injuring 140. The Stern Gang (a proto-fascist splinter group of the Irgun) would soon use truck and car bombs to kill Palestinians as well: a creative atrocity immediately reciprocated by British deserters fighting on the side of Palestinian nationalists.

Vehicle bombs thereafter were used sporadically—producing notable massacres in Saigon (1952), Algiers (1962) and Palermo (1963)—but the gates of hell were only truly opened in 1972 when the Provisional IRA accidentally, so the legend goes, improvised their first ammonium nitrate-fuel oil (ANFO) car bomb. These new-generation bombs (first pioneered by the four student radicals who blew up the Army Math building at the University of Wisconsin in Madison in 1970), requiring only ordinary industrial ingredients and synthetic fertilizer, were cheap to fabricate and astonishingly powerful: they elevated urban terrorism from the artisan to the industrial level, and made possible sustained blitzes against entire city centers as well as the complete destruction of ferro-concrete skyscrapers and residential blocks.

The car bomb, in other words, suddenly became a semi-strategic weapon that under certain circumstances was comparable to airpower in its ability to knock out critical urban nodes and headquarters as well as terrorize populations of entire cities. Indeed, the suicide truck bombs that devastated the U.S. embassy and Marine barracks in Beirut in 1983 prevailed—at least in a geopolitical sense—over the combined firepower of the fighter-bombers and battleships of the U.S. Sixth Fleet and forced the Reagan administration to retreat from Lebanon.

Hezbollah's ruthless and brilliant use of car bombs in Lebanon in the 1980s to counter the advanced military technology of the United States, France and Israel soon emboldened a dozen other groups to bring their insurgencies and *jihads* home to the metropolis. Some of the new-generation car bombers were graduates of the terrorism schools set up by the CIA and Pakistani intelligence (the ISI), with Saudi financing, in the mid-1980s to train *mujahedin* to terrorize the Russians in Kabul. Between 1992 and 1998, 16 major vehicle bomb attacks in 13 different cities killed 1050 people and wounded nearly 12,000. More important from a geopolitical standpoint, IRA and Gama'a al-Islamiyya inflicted billions of dollars of damage on the two leading control-centers of the world economy—the City of London (1992, 1993 and 1996) and lower Manhattan (1993), respectively—and forced a reorganization of the global reinsurance industry.

In the new millennium, 85 years after that first massacre on Wall Street, car bombs have become almost as generically global as iPods and HIV-AIDS, cratering the streets of cities from Bogota to Bali. Suicide truck bombs, once the distinctive signature of Hezbollah, have been franchised to Sri Lanka, Chechnya/Russia, Turkey, Egypt, Kuwait, and Indonesia. On any graph of urban terrorism, the curve representing car bombs is rising steeply, almost exponentially. U.S.-occupied Iraq, of course, is a relentless inferno with more than 9,000 casualties—mainly civilian—attributed to vehicle bombs in the two-year period between July 2003 and June 2005. Since then, the frequency of car-bomb attacks has dramatically increased: 140 per month in fall 2005 and 13 in Baghdad on New Years Day 2006 alone. If roadside bombs are the most effective device against American armored vehicles, car bombs are the weapon of choice for slaughtering Shiite civilians in front of mosques and markets and instigating an apocalyptic sectarian war.

Under siege from weapons indistinguishable from ordinary traffic, the apparatuses of administration and finance are retreating inside 'rings of steel' and 'green zones,' but the larger challenge of the car bomb seems intractable. Stolen nukes, Sarin and anthrax may be the "sum of our fears," but car bombs are the quotidian workhorses of urban terrorism. Before considering its genealogy, however, it may be helpful to summarize those characteristics that make Buda's wagon such a formidable and likely permanent source of urban insecurity.

First, vehicle bombs are stealth weapons of surprising power and destructive efficiency. Trucks, vans, or even SUVs can easily transport the equivalent of several conventional 1000-pound bombs to the doorstep of a prime target. Moreover, their destructive power is still evolving, thanks to the constant tinkering of ingenious bomb-makers, and we have yet to face the full horror of semitrailer-size explosions with a lethal blast range of 200 yards or dirty bombs sheathed in enough nuclear waste to render mid-Manhattan radioactive for generations.

Second, they are extraordinarily cheap: 40 or 50 people can be massacred with a stolen car and maybe $400 of fertilizer and bootlegged electronics. Ramzi Yousef, the mastermind of the 1993 attack on the World Trade Center, bragged that his most expensive outlay was long-distance phone calls: the explosive itself (one half ton of urea) cost $3615 plus the $59 per day rental for a 10-foot-long Ryder van. In contrast, the cruise missiles that have become the classical American riposte to overseas terrorist attacks cost $1.1 million each.

Third, car bombings are operationally simple to organize. Although some still refuse to believe that the pair didn't have secret assistance from some government or dark entity, two men in the proverbial phone booth—that is to say, Timothy McVeigh, a security guard, and, Terry Nichols, a farmer—successfully planned and executed the horrendous Oklahoma City bombing with instructional books and information acquired from the gun show circuit.

Four, like even the "smartest" of aerial bombs, car bombs are inherently indiscriminate: collateral damage is virtually inevitable. If the logic of an attack is to slaughter innocents and sow panic in the widest circle, to operate a strategy of tension or just demoralize a society, car bombs are ideal. But they are equally effective at destroying the moral credibility of a cause and alienating its mass base of support, as both the IRA and ETA have independently discovered. The car bomb is an inherently fascist weapon.

Five, car bombs are highly anonymous and leave minimal forensic evidence. Buda quietly went home to Italy, leaving William Burns, J. Edgar Hoover, and the Bureau of Investigation (later, the FBI) to make fools of themselves as they chased one false lead after another for a decade. Most of Buda's descendants have also escaped identification and arrest. Anonymity, in addition, greatly recommends car bombs to those who like to disguise their handiwork, including the CIA, the Israeli Mossad, the Syrian GSD, the Iranian Pasdaran, and the Pakistani ISI—all of whom have caused unspeakable carnage with such devices.

Preliminary Detonations (1948–1963)

> "Reds' Time Bombs Rip Saigon Center"
>
> **New York Times** *headline (January 10, 1952)*

The Stern Gang (a breakaway from the Irgun led by Avraham Stern) was made up of ardent students of violence, self-declared Jewish admirers of Mussolini who steeped themselves in the terrorist traditions of the pre-1917 Russian Socialist-Revolutionary Party, the Macedonian IMRO, and the Italian Blackshirts. As the most extreme wing of the Zionist movement in Palestine—"fascists" to the Haganah and "terrorists" to the British—they were morally and tactically unfettered by considerations of diplomacy or world opinion. They had had a fierce and well-deserved reputation for the originality of their operations and the unexpectedness of their attacks. On January 12, 1947, as part of their campaign to prevent any compromise between mainstream Zionism and the British Labor government, they exploded a powerful truck bomb in the central police station in Haifa with 144 casualties. Three months later, they repeated the tactic in Tel Aviv, blowing up the Sarona police barracks (five dead) with a stolen postal truck filled with dynamite.

In December 1947, following the UN vote to partition Palestine, full-scale fighting broke out between the Jewish and Arab communities from Haifa to Gaza. The Stern Gang, which rejected anything less than restoration of a biblical Israel, now debuted the truck bomb as a weapon of mass terror. On January 4, 1948, two men in Arab dress drove a truck ostensibly loaded with oranges into the center of Jaffa and parked it next to the New Seray Building, which housed the Palestinian municipal government as well as a soup-kitchen for poor children. They coolly lingered for coffee in a nearby café before leaving a few minutes before the detonation.

"A thunderous explosion," writes Adam LeBor in his history of Jaffa, "then shook the city. Broken glass and shattered masonry blew out across Clock Tower Square. The New Seray's centre and side walls collapsed in a pile of rubble and twisted beams. Only the neo-classical façade survived. After a moment of silence, the screams began, 26 were killed, hundreds injured. Most were civilians, including many children eating at the charity kitchen." The bomb missed the local Palestinian leadership who had moved to another building, but the atrocity was highly successful in terrifying residents and setting the stage for their eventual flight.

It also provoked the Palestinians to cruel repayment in kind. The Arab High Committee had its own secret weapon—blond-haired British deserters, fighting on the side of the Palestinians. Nine days after the Jaffa bombing, some of these deserters, led by Eddie Brown, a former police corporal whose brother had been murdered by the Irgun, commandeered a postal delivery truck which they packed with explosives and detonated in the center of Haifa's Jewish quarter, injuring 50 people. Two weeks later, Brown, driving a stolen car and followed by a five-ton truck driven by a Palestinian in a police uniform, successfully passed through British and Haganah checkpoints and entered Jerusalem's New City. The driver parked in front of the *Palestine Post*, lit the fuse, and then escaped with Brown in his car. The newspaper headquarters was devastated, with 1 dead and 20 wounded.

According to a chronicler of the episode, Abdel Kader el-Husseini, the military leader of the Arab Higher Committee, was so impressed by the success of these operations—inadvertently inspired by the Stern Gang—that he authorized an ambitious sequel employing six British deserters. "This time three trucks were used, escorted by a stolen British armored car with a young blond man in police uniform standing in the turret." Again, the convoy easily passed through checkpoints and drove to the Atlantic Hotel on Ben Yehuda Street. A curious nightwatchman was murdered when he confronted the gang, who then drove off in the armored car after setting charges in the three trucks. The explosion was huge and the toll, accordingly grim: 46 dead and 130 wounded.

The window of opportunity for such attacks—the possibility of passing from one zone to another—was rapidly closing as Palestinians and Jews braced for all-out warfare, but a final attack prefigured the car bomb's brilliant future as a tool of assassination. On March 11, the official limousine of the American consul-general, flying the stars and stripes and driven by the usual chauffeur, was admitted to the courtyard of the heavily guarded Jewish Agency compound. The driver, a Christian Palestinian named Abu Yussef, hoped to kill Ben Gurion, but the limousine was moved just before it exploded; nonetheless, 13 officials of the Jewish Foundation Fund died and 40 were injured.

This brief, but furious, exchange of car bombs between Arabs and Jews would enter into the collective memory of their conflict, but would not be resumed on a large scale until Israel and its Phalangist allies began to terrorize West Beirut with bombings in 1981: a provocation that would awake a Shiite sleeping dragon. Meanwhile, the real sequel was played out in Saigon: a series of car and motorcycle bomb atrocities in 1952–1953 that Graham Greene incorporated into the plot of *The Quiet American* and that he portrayed as secretly orchestrated by the CIA operative Alden Pyle, who is conspiring to substitute a pro-American party for both the Viet-Minh (on whom the bombings were blamed) and the French (who are unable to guarantee public safety).

The real-life Quiet American was the counterinsurgency expert Colonel Edward Lansdale (fresh from victories against peasant Communists in the Philippines), and the actual leader of the 'Third Force' was his protégé, General Trinh Minh The of the Cao Dai religious sect. There is no doubt, writes The's biographer, that the general "instigated many terrorist outrages in Saigon, using clockwork plastic charges loaded into vehicles, or hidden inside bicycle frames with charges. Notably, the Li An Minh [The's army] blew up cars in front of the Opera House in Saigon in 1952. These 'time-bombs' were reportedly made of 50-kg ordnance, used by the French air force, unexploded and collected by the Li An Minh."

Lansdale was dispatched to Saigon by Alan Dulles of the CIA some months after the Opera atrocity (hideously immortalized in a *Life* photographer's image of the upright corpse of a rickshaw driver with both legs blown off), which was officially blamed on Ho Chi Minh. Although Lansdale was well aware of General The's authorship of these sophisticated attacks (the explosives were hidden in false compartments next to the cars' gas tanks), he nonetheless championed the Cao Dai warlord as a patriot in the mold of Washington and Jefferson. After either French agents or Vietminh cadre assassinated The, Landsdale eulogized him to a journalist as "a good man. He was moderate, he was a pretty good general, he was on our side, and he cost twenty-five thousand dollars."

Whether by emulation or reinvention, car bombs showed up next in Algiers during the last days of the *pied noirs.* Some of the embittered French officers in Saigon in 1952–1953 had become cadre of the Organisation de l'Arme Secrete, led by General Raoul Salan. After the failure of its anti-De Gaulle uprising in April 1961, the OAS turned to terrorism—a veritable *festival de plastique*—with all the formidable experience of its veteran paratroopers and legionnaires. Its declared enemies included De Gaulle himself, the security forces, Communists, peace activists (including Jean-Paul Sartre), and, especially, Algerian civilians. The most deadly of their car bombs killed 62 Moslem stevedores shaping up for work at the Algiers docks in May 1962, but succeeded only in bolstering the Algerian resolve to drive all the *pied-noirs* into the sea.

The next destination was Palermo. Angelo La Barbera, the Mafia *capo* of Palermo-Centre, undoubtedly paid careful attention to the Algerian bombings and may even have borrowed some OAS expertise when he launched his devastating attack on his Mafia rival, 'Little Bird' Greco, in February 1963. Greco's bastion was the town of Ciaculli outside Palermo where he was protected by an army of henchmen. La Barbera surmounted this obstacle with the aid of the Alfa Romeo Giulietta. "This dainty four-door family saloon," writes John Dickie in his history of the Cosa Nostra, "was one of the symbols of Italy's economic miracle—'svelte, practical, comfortable, safe and convenient,' as the adverts proclaimed." The first explosive-packed Giulietta destroyed Greco's house; the second, a few weeks later, killed one of his key allies. Greco gunmen retaliated, wounding La Barbera in Milan in May; in response, La Barbera's ambitious lieutenants, Pietro Torreta and Tommaso Buscetta (later to become the most famous of all Mafia *pentiti*), unleashed more deadly Giuliettas.

On June 30, 1963, "the umpteenth Giulietta stuffed with TNT" was left in one of the tangerine groves that surround Ciaculli. A tank of butane with a fuse was clearly visible in the back seat. A Giulietta had already exploded that morning in a nearby town, killing two people, so the *carabinieri* were cautious and summoned army engineers for assistance. "Two hours later, two bomb disposal experts arrived, cut the fuse, and pronounced the vehicle safe to approach. But when Lt. Mario Malausa made to inspect the contents of the boot, he detonated the huge quantity of TNT it contained. He and six other men were blown to pieces by an explosion that scorched and stripped the tangerine trees for hundreds of metres around." (The site is today marked by one of the several monuments to bomb victims in the Palermo region.)

Before this "First Mafia War" ended in 1964, the Sicilian population had learned to tremble at the very sight of a Giulietta and car bombings had become a permanent part of the Mafia repertoire. They were employed again during the even bloodier second Mafia war or *Matanza* in 1981–1983, then turned against the Italian public in the early 1990s after the conviction of Cosa Nostra leaders in a series of sensational 'maxi-trials.' The most notorious of these blind-rage car bombings—presumably organized by 'Tractor' Provenzano and his notorious Corleonese gang—was the explosion in May 1993 that damaged the world-famous Uffizi Gallery in the heart of Florence and killed 5 pedestrians and injured 40 others.

"The Black Stuff"

We could feel the rattle where we stood. Then we knew we were onto something, and it took off from there.

IRA veteran talking about first ANFO car bomb

The first-generation car bombs—Jaffa-Jerusalem, Saigon, Algiers, and Palermo—were deadly enough (with a maximum yield usually equal to several hundred pounds of TNT), but required access to stolen industrial or military explosives. Journeymen bomb-makers, however, were aware of a homemade alternative—notoriously dangerous to concoct, but offering low-cost and almost unlimited vistas of destruction. Ammonium nitrate is a universally available synthetic fertilizer and industrial ingredient with extraordinary explosive properties, as witnessed by such accidental cataclysms as the Oppau, Germany, explosion in 1921 (the shock waves were felt 150 miles away and only a vast crater remained of the chemical plant) and the Texas City disaster in 1947 (600 dead and 90 percent of the town structurally damaged). Ammonium nitrate is sold in half-ton quantities affordable by even the most cash-strapped terrorist, but the process of mixing it with fuel oil to create an ANFO explosive is more than a little tricky as the Provisional IRA found out in late 1971.

"The car bomb was [re]discovered entirely by accident," explains journalist Ed Maloney in his *The Secret History of the IRA*, "but its deployment by the Belfast IRA was not. The chain of events began in late December 1971 when the IRA's quartermaster general, Jack McCabe, was fatally injured in an explosion caused when an experimental fertilizer-based homemade mix known as the 'black stuff' exploded as he was blending it with a shovel in his garage on the northern outskirts of Dublin. GHQ warned that the mix was too dangerous to handle, but Belfast had already received a consignment, and someone had the idea of disposing of it by dumping it in a car with a fuse and a timer and leaving it somewhere in downtown Belfast." The resulting explosion made a big impression on the Belfast leadership.

The "black stuff"—which the IRA soon learned how to handle safely— freed the underground army from supply-side constraints: the car bomb enhanced destructive capacity yet reduced the likelihood of Volunteers being arrested or accidentally blown up. The ANFO–car bomb combination, in other words, was an unexpected military revolution, but one fraught with the potential for political and moral disaster. "The sheer size of the devices," emphasizes Moloney, "greatly increased the risk of civilian deaths in careless or bungled operations."

The IRA Army Council led by Sean MacStiofain, however, was too seduced by the new weapon's awesome capabilities to worry about how its grisly consequences might backfire against them. Indeed, car bombs reinforced the illusion, shared by most of the top leadership in 1972, that the IRA was one final military offensive away from victory over the English government. Accordingly, in March 1972, two car bombs were sent into the Belfast city center followed by garbled phone warnings that led police to inadvertently evacuate people in the direction of one of the explosions: five civilians were killed along with two members of the security forces. Despite the public outcry as well as the immediate traffic closure of the Royal Avenue shopping precinct, the Belfast Brigade's enthusiasm for the new weapon remained undiminished and the leadership plotted a huge attack designed to bring normal commercial life in Northern Ireland to an abrupt halt. MacStiofain boasted of an offensive of "the utmost ferocity and ruthlessness" that would wreck the "colonial infrastructure."

On Friday, July 21, IRA Volunteers left 20 car bombs or concealed charges on the periphery of the now gated city center, with detonations timed to follow one another at approximately five-minute intervals. The first car bomb (2:40 pm) exploded in front of the Ulster Bank in north Belfast and blew both legs off a Catholic passerby; successive explosions damaged two railroad stations, the Ulsterbus depot on Oxford Street, various railway junctions, and a mixed Catholic-Protestant residential area on Cavehill Road. "At the height of the bombing, the center of Belfast resembled a city under artillery fire; clouds of suffocating smoke enveloped buildings as one explosion followed another, almost drowning out the hysterical screams of panicked shoppers." A series of telephoned IRA warnings only created more chaos, as civilians fled from one explosion only to be driven back by another. Seven civilians and two soldiers were killed and more than 130 people were seriously wounded.

Although not an economic knockout punch, 'Bloody Friday' was the beginning of a 'no business as usual' bombing campaign that quickly inflicted significant damage on the Northern Ireland economy, particularly its ability to attract private and foreign investment. The terror of that day also compelled authorities to tighten their anti-car-bomb 'ring of steel' around the Belfast city center, making it the prototype for other fortified enclaves and future 'green zones.' In the tradition of their ancestors, the Fenians, who had originated dynamite terrorism in the 1870s, Irish Republicans had again added new pages to the textbook of urban guerrilla warfare. Foreign *aficionados,* particularly in the Middle East, undoubtedly paid close attention to the twin innovations of the ANFO car bomb and its employment in a protracted bombing campaign against an entire urban-regional economy.

What was less well understood outside of Ireland, however, was the enormity of the wound that the IRA's car bombs inflicted on the Republican movement itself. Bloody Friday destroyed much of the IRA's heroic-underdog popular image, produced deep revulsion amongst ordinary Catholics, and gave the British government an unexpected reprieve from the worldwide condemnation it had earned for the Bloody Sunday massacre in Derry and internment without trial. Moreover it gave the Army the perfect pretext to launch massive Operation Motorman: 13,000 troops led by Centurion tanks entered the 'no-go' areas of Derry and Belfast and reclaimed control of the streets from the Republican movement. The same day a bloody, bungled car bomb attack on the village of Claudy in County Londonderry killed eight people. (Loyalist paramilitary groups—who never bothered with warnings and deliberately targeted civilians on the other side—would claim Bloody Friday and Claudy as sanctions for their triple car bomb attack on Dublin during afternoon rush hour on May 17, 1974, which left 33 dead, the highest one-day toll in the course of the 'Troubles.')

The Belfast debacle led to a major turnover in IRA leadership, but failed to dispel their almost cargo-cult-like belief in the capacity of car bombs to turn the tide of battle. Forced on the defensive by Motorman and the backlash to Bloody Friday, they decided to strike at the very heart of British power. The Belfast Brigade planned to send ten car bombs to London via the Dublin-Liverpool ferry using fresh volunteers with clean records, including two young sisters, Marion and Dolours Price. Snags arose and only four cars arrived in London; one of these was detonated in front of the

Old Bailey, another in the center of Whitehall, close to Number 10. One hundred eighty Londoners were injured and one was killed. Although the eight IRA bombers were quickly caught, they were acclaimed in the West Belfast ghettos and the operation became a template for future Provisional bombing campaigns in London, culminating in the huge explosions that shattered the City of London and unnerved the world insurance industry in 1992 and 1993.

Hell's Kitchen (1980s)

> We are soldiers of God and we crave death. We are ready to turn Lebanon into another Vietnam.
>
> *Hezbollah*

Never in history has a single city been the battlefield for so many contesting ideologies, sectarian allegiances, local vendettas, and foreign conspiracies and interventions as Beirut in the early 1980s. Belfast's triangular conflicts—three armed camps (Republican, Loyalist, and British) and their splinter groups—seemed straightforward compared to the fractal, Russian-doll-like complexity of Lebanon's civil wars (Shiite vs. Palestinian, for example) within civil wars (Maronite vs. Moslem and Druze) within regional conflicts (Israel vs. Syria) and surrogate wars (Iran vs. the United States) within, ultimately, the Cold War. In the fall of 1971, for example, there were 58 different armed groups in West Beirut alone. With so many people trying to kill each other for so many different reasons, Beirut became to the technology of urban violence what a tropical rainforest is to the evolution of plants.

Car bombs began to regularly terrorize Moslem West Beirut in the fall of 1981, apparently as part of an Israeli strategy to evict the PLO from Lebanon. The Mossad had previously employed car bombs in Beirut to assassinate Palestinian leaders (the novelist Ghassan Kanfani in July 1972, for example), so no one was especially surprised when evidence emerged that Israel was sponsoring the carnage. According to Rashid Khalidi "a sequence of public confessions by captured drivers made clear these [car bombings] were being utilized by the Israelis and their Phalangist allies to increase the pressure on the PLO to leave."

Robert Fisk was in Beirut when an "enormous [car] bomb blew a 45-foot-crater in the road and brought down an entire block of apartments. The building collapsed like a concertina, crushing more than 50 of its occupants to death, most of them Shia refugees from southern Lebanon." Several of the car bombers were captured and confessed that the bombs had been rigged by the Shin Bet, the Israeli equivalent of the FBI or Special

Branch. But if such atrocities were designed to drive a wedge of terror between the PLO and Lebanese Moslems, they had the inadvertent result (as did the Israeli air force's later, indiscriminate cluster bombing of civilians) of turning the Shias from informal Israeli allies into shrewd and resolute enemies.

The new face of Shiite militancy was Hezbollah, formed in mid-1982 out of an amalgamation of Islamic Amal with other pro-Khomeini groupuscules. Trained and advised by the Iranian Pasdaran in the Bekaa Valley, Hezbollah was both an indigenous resistance movement with deep roots in the Shiite slums of southern Beirut and at the same time, the long arm of Iran's theocratic revolution. Although some experts espouse alternative theories, Islamic Amal/Hezbollah is usually seen as the author, with Iranian and Syrian assistance, of the devastating attacks on American and French forces in Beirut during 1983. Hezbollah's diabolic innovation was to marry the IRA's ANFO car bombs to the *kamikaze*: using suicide drivers to crash truckloads of explosives into the lobbies of embassies and barracks in Beirut, and later into Israeli checkpoints and patrols in southern Lebanon.

The United States and France became targets of Hezbollah and its Syrian and Iranian patrons after the Multinational Force in Beirut, which was supposedly landed to allow safe evacuation of the PLO, evolved into the informal, then open ally of the Maronite government in its civil war against the Moslem-Druze majority. The first retaliation against President Reagan's policy occurred on April 18, 1983, when a pickup truck carrying 2000 pounds of ANFO explosive suddenly swerved across traffic into the driveway of the oceanfront U.S. embassy in Beirut. The driver gunned the truck past a startled guard and crashed through the lobby door. "Even by Beirut standards," writes former CIA agent Robert Baer, "it was an enormous blast, shattering windows. The USS *Guadalcanal*, anchored five miles off the coast, shuddered from the tremors. At ground zero, the center of the seven-story embassy lifted up hundreds of feet into the air, remained suspended for what seemed an eternity, and then collapsed in a cloud of dust, people, splintered furniture, and paper."

Whether as a result of superb intelligence or sheer luck, the bombing coincided with a visit to the embassy of Robert Ames, the CIA's national intelligence officer for the Near East. It killed him ("his hand was found floating a mile offshore, the wedding ring still on his finger") and all six members of the Beirut CIA station. "Never before had the CIA lost so many officers in a single attack. It was a tragedy from which the agency would never recover." It also left the Americans blind in Beirut, forcing them to scrounge for intelligence scraps from the French embassy or the British listening station offshore on Cyprus. (A year later, Hezbollah completed their massacre of the CIA in Beirut when they kidnapped and executed the replacement station chief, William Buckley.) As a result, they never foresaw the coming of the mother of all vehicle bomb attacks.

Over the protests of Colonel Gerahty, the commander of the U.S. Marines onshore in Beirut, Reagan's National Security Advisor, Robert McFarlane, ordered the Sixth Fleet in September to open fire on Druze militia who were storming Lebanese Forces' positions in the hills above Beirut—bringing the United States into the conflict brazenly on the side of the reactionary Amin Gemayel government. A month later, a five-ton Mercedes dump truck hurled past sandbagged Marine sentries and smashed through a guardhouse into the ground floor of the 'Beirut Hilton,' the U.S. military barracks in a former PLO headquarters next to the international airport. The truck's payload was an incredible 12,000 pounds of high explosives. "It is said to have been the largest non-nuclear blast ever [deliberately] detonated on the face of the earth." "The force of the explosion," continues Eric Hammel in his history of the Marine landing force, "initially lifted the entire four-story structure, shearing the bases of the concrete support columns, each measuring fifteen feet in circumference and reinforced by numerous one and three quarter inch steel rods. The airborne building then fell in upon itself. A massive shock wave and ball of flaming gas was hurled in all directions." The Marine (and Navy) death toll of 241 was the Corps' highest single-day loss since Iwo Jima in 1945.

Meanwhile, another Hezbollah kamikaze had crashed his explosive-laden van into the French barracks in West Beirut, toppling the eight-story structure and killing 58 soldiers. If the airport bomb repaid the Americans for saving Gemayal, this second explosion was probably a response to the French decision to supply Sadaam Hussein with Super-Etendard jets and Exocet missiles to attack Iran. The hazy distinction between local Shiite grievances and the interests of Tehran was blurred further when two members of Hezbollah joined with 18 Iraqi Shiias to truck-bomb the U.S. embassy in Kuwait in mid-December. The French embassy, the control tower at the airport, the main oil refinery and an expatriate residential compound also were targeted in what was clearly a stern warning to Iran's enemies.

Following another truck bombing against the French in Beirut as well as deadly attacks on Marine outposts, the Multinational Force began to withdraw from Lebanon in February 1984. It was Reagan's most stunning geopolitical defeat. In the impolite phrase of Bob Woodward, "essentially we turned tail and ran and left Lebanon." American power in Lebanon, added Thomas Friedman, was neutralized by "just 12,000 pounds of dynamite and a stolen truck."

The CIA's Car Bomb University (1980s)

The CIA officers that Yousef worked with closely impressed upon him one rule: never use the terms *sabotage* or *assassination* when speaking with visiting congressmen.

Gunboat diplomacy had been defeated by car bombs in Lebanon, but the Reagan administration, and, above all, CIA boss William Casey, were left thirsting for revenge against Hezbollah. "Finally in 1985," according to Bob Woodward, "[Casey] worked out with the Saudis a plan to use a car bomb to kill [Hezbollah leader] Sheikh Fadlallah who they determined was one of the people behind, not only the Marine barracks, but was involved in the taking of American hostages in Beirut. ... It was Casey on his own, saying, 'I'm going to solve the big problem by essentially getting tougher or as tough as the terrorists in using their weapon—the car bomb.'"

In the event, the CIA's own operatives proved incapable of carrying out the bombing, so Casey subcontracted the operation to Lebanese agents led by a former British SAS officer and financed by Saudi Ambassador Prince Bandar. In March 1984, a large car bomb was detonated about 50 yards from Sheikh Fadlallah's house in Bir El-Abed, a crowded Shiite neighborhood in southern Beirut. The sheikh wasn't harmed, but 80 innocent neighbors and passersby were killed and 200 wounded. Fadlallah immediately had a huge "MADE IN USA" banner hung across the shattered street, while Hezbollah returned tit for tat in September when a suicide truck driver managed to break through the supposedly impregnable perimeter defenses of the new U.S. embassy in eastern (Christian) Beirut, killing 23 employees and visitors.

Despite the Fadlallah fiasco, Casey remained enthusiastic about using urban terrorism to advance American goals, especially against the Soviets and their allies in Afghanistan. A year after the Bir El-Abed massacre, Casey won President Reagan's approval for NSDD-166, a secret directive that inaugurated (according to Steve Coll in *Ghost Wars*) a "new era of direct infusions of advanced U.S. military technology into Afghanistan, intensified training of Islamist guerrillas in explosives and sabotage techniques, and targeted attacks on Soviet military officers." U.S. Special Forces experts provided high-tech explosives and taught state-of-art sabotage techniques, including the fabrication of ANFO car bombs, to Pakistani ISI officers under the command of Brigadier Mohammed Yousaf who, in turn, tutored thousands of Afghan and foreign *mujahedin*, including the future cadre of al-Qa'eda, in scores of training camps financed by the Saudis. "Under ISI direction," Coll writes, "the mujahedin received malleable explosives to mount car bomb and even Camel bomb attacks in Soviet-occupied cities, usually designed to kill Soviet soldiers and commanders. Casey endorsed these despite the qualms of some CIA career officiers."

The mujahedin car bombers, working with teams of snipers and assassins, not only terrorized uniformed Soviet forces in a series of devastating attacks but also massacred Kabul's left-wing intelligentsia. "Yousef and the Afghan car-bombing squads he trained," writes Coll, "regarded Kabul University professors as fair game," as well as cinemas and cultural events. Although some members of the National Security Council reportedly denounced the bombings and assassinations as "outright terrorism," Casey was delighted with the results. Meanwhile, "by the late 1980s, the ISI had effectively eliminated all the secular, leftist, and royalist political parties that had first formed when Afghan refugees fled communist rule." As a result, most of the billions of dollars that Riyadh and Washington pumped into Afghanistan ended up in the hands of the radical Islamist groups sponsored by the ISI. They also were the chief recipients of huge quantities of CIA-supplied plastic explosives as well as thousands of advanced E-cell delay detonators.

It was the greatest technology transfer of terrorist technique in history. There was no need for angry Islamists to take car bomb extension courses from Hezbollah when they could matriculate in a CIA-supported urban sabotage graduate program in Pakistan's frontier provinces. "Ten years later," Coll observes, "the vast training infrastructure that Yousaf and his colleagues build with the enormous budgets endorsed by NSDD-166—the specialized camps, the sabotage training manuals, the electronic bomb detonators, and so on—would be referred to routinely in America as 'terrorist infrastructure.'" Moreover, the alumni of the ISI training camps—like Ramzi Yousef who plotted the first World Trade Center attack or his uncle Khalid Sheikh Mohammed who allegedly designed the second—would soon be applying their expertise on every continent.

Cities Under Siege (1990s)

The hour of dynamite, terror without limit, has arrived.

Gustavo Gorritti

From the hindsight of the twenty-first century, it is clear that the defeat of the U.S. intervention in Lebanon in 1983–1984, followed by the CIA's dirty war in Afghanistan, have had larger and more potent geopolitical repercussions than the loss of Saigon in 1975. The Vietnam War, of course, was a more epic struggle whose imprint on domestic American politics remains profound, but it belonged to the era of the Cold War and bipolar superpower rivalry. Hezbollah's war in Beirut and south Lebanon, by contrast, prefigured (and even inspired) the 'asymmetric' conflicts that characterize the millennium. Moreover, unlike peoples' war on the scale sustained by the NLF and the DRV for a generation, car-bombing and suicide terrorism are easily franchised and gruesomely applicable in a variety of scenarios. Although rural guerrillas survive in rugged redoubts such as Kashmir, Khyber Pass, and the Andes, the center of gravity of global insurgency has moved back to the cities and their slum peripheries. In this post–Cold War urban context, the Hezbollah bombing of the Marine barracks has constituted the gold standard of terrorism; the 9/11 attacks, it can be argued, were only an inevitable scaling-up of the suicide truck bomb tactic.

Washington, however, was loathe to recognize the new military leverage that powerful vehicle bombs offered to its enemies. After the 1983 Beirut bombings, the Sandia National Laboratory in New Mexico began an intensive investigation into the physics of truck bombs. Researchers were shocked by what they discovered. In addition to the deadly air blast, the truck bombs also produced unexpectedly huge ground waves.

"The lateral accelerations propagated through the ground from a truck bomb far exceed those produced during the peak magnitude of an earthquake." Indeed, Sandia came to the conclusion that even an offsite detonation near a nuclear power plant might "cause enough damage to lead to a deadly release of radiation or even a meltdown." Yet the Nuclear Regulatory Commission in 1986 refused to authorize vehicle barriers to protect nuclear power installations or to alter an obsolete security plan designed to thwart a few terrorists infiltrating on foot.

Washington, indeed, seemed unwilling to learn any of the obvious lessons of either its Beirut defeat or its secret successes in Kabul. The Reagan and Bush administrations appeared to regard the Hezbollah bombings as flukes, rather than as a powerful new threat that would replicate rapidly in the "blow-back" of imperial misadventure. Although it was inevitable that other insurgent groups would soon try to emulate Hezbollah, American planners—although partially responsible—largely failed to foresee the extraordinary 'globalization' of car bombing in the 1990s or the rise of sophisticated new strategies of urban destabilization. Yet by the mid-1990s, more cities were under siege from bomb attacks than at any time since the end of World War II, and urban guerrillas were using car and truck bombs to score direct hits on some of the world's most powerful financial institutions (see Table 1). Each success, moreover, emboldened new attacks and recruited more groups to launch their own "poor man's air force."

Table 1 The 1990s Blitz

m/y		Dead	Wounded
4–92	City of London	2	44
7–92	Lima	39	150
2–93	New York	6	1000
3–93	Buenos Aires	30	242
3–93	Bombay	257	1400
4–93	City of London	1	30
7–94	Buenos Aires	96	200
1–95	Algiers	42	280
4–95	Israel	7	52
"	Oklahoma City	168	800
1–96	Colombo	55	1200
6–96	Khobar	19	372
10–97	Colombo	18	100
3–98	Colombo	38	250
8–98	Nairobi/Dar-es-Salaam	300	5000
"	Omagh	28	300

Beginning in April 1992, for example, the occult Maoists of Sendero Luminoso came down from the *altiplano* to spread terror throughout Lima and Callao with increasingly more powerful *coche-bombas*. "Large supplies of explosives," the magazine *Caretas* pointed out, are "freely available in a mining nation," and the *senderistas* were generous in their gifts of dynamite: bombing television stations and various foreign embassies as well as a dozen police stations and military camps. Their campaign eerily recapitulated the car bomb's phylogeny as it progressed from modest detonations to more powerful attacks on the American embassy, then to Bloody Friday-type public massacres using 16 vehicles at a time. The climax (and Sendero's chief contribution to genre) was the attempt to blow up an entire neighborhood of class enemies: a huge ANFO explosion in the elite Miraflores district on the evening of July 16, which killed 22, wounded 120, and destroyed or damaged 183 homes, 400 businesses and 63 parked cars. The local press described Miraflores as looking "as if an aerial bombardment had flattened the area."

If one of the virtues of an air force is the ability to reach halfway around the world to surprise enemies in their beds, the car bomb truly grew wings during 1993 as Middle Eastern groups struck at targets in the Western Hemisphere for the first time. The World Trade Center (WTC) attack on February 26 was organized by master al-Qa'eda bomb-maker

Ramzi Yousef working with a Kuwaiti engineer named Nidal Ayyad and immigrant members of the Egyptian group Gama'a al-Islamiyya headed by Sheikh Omar Abdul Rahman (whose U.S. visa was reputedly arranged by the CIA).[1] Their extraordinary ambition was to kill tens of thousands of New Yorkers with a powerful lateral blast that would crack the foundations of one WTC tower and topple it over against its twin. Yousef's weapon was a Ryder van packed with an ingenious upgrade of the classic IRA and Hezbollah ANFO explosive.

"The bomb itself," writes Peter Lance, "consisted of four cardboard boxes filled with a slurry of urea nitrate and fuel oil, with waste paper as a binder. The boxes were surrounded by 4-foot tanks of compressed hydrogen. They were connected by four 20-foot-long slow-burning fuses of smokeless powder wrapped in fabric. Yousef balanced on his lap four vials of nitroglycerine." The conspirators had no difficulty parking the van next to the load-bearing south wall of the North Tower, but the massive explosive was still too small: excavating a four-story deep crater in the basement, killing 6 and injuring 1,000 people, but it failed to bring the tower down. "Our calculations were not very accurate this time," wrote Ayyad in a letter. "However we promise you that next time it will be very precise and the Trade Center will be one of our targets."

Two weeks after the WTC attack, a car bomb almost as powerful exploded in the underground parking garage of the Bombay Stock Exchange, severely damaging the 28-story skyscraper and killing 50 office workers. Twelve other car or motorcycle bombs soon detonated at other prestige targets, killing an additional 207 people and injuring 1,400. The bombings were revenge for the sectarian riots a few months earlier that had killed hundreds of Moslems and were reputedly organized from Dubai by exiled Bombay underworld king Dawood Ibrahim at the behest of Pakistani intelligence. According to one account, Dawood sent three boats from Dubai to Karachi where they were loaded with military explosives; Indian customs officials were then bribed to look the other way while the 'black soup' was smuggled into Bombay.

Corrupt officials were also rumored to have facilitated the car bombing of the Israeli embassy in Buenos Aires on March 17, which killed 30 and injured 242. The next year, a second 'martyr,' later identified as a 29-year-old Hezbollah militant from southern Lebanon, leveled the seven-story Argentine-Israel Mutual Association, slaughtering 85 and wounding more than 300. Both bombers carefully followed the Beirut template; as did the Islamist militant who drove his car into the central police headquarters in Algiers in January 1995, killing 42 and injuring over 280.

But the supreme acolytes of Hezbollah were the Tamil Tigers, the only non-Moslem group that has practiced suicide car bombings on a large scale. Indeed, their leader Prabhakaran had "made a strategic decision to adopt the method of suicide attack after observing its lethal effectiveness in the 1983 suicide bombings of the U.S. and French barracks in Beirut." Since their first such operation in 1987 (to 2000), they have been responsible for twice as many suicide attacks of all kinds as Hezbollah and Hamas combined. Although they have integrated car bombs into regular military tactics (for example, using kamikazes in trucks to open attacks on Sri Lankan army camps), their obsession and "most prized theater of operation" has been Colombo which they first car-bombed in 1987 in a grisly attack on the main bus terminal, burning scores of passengers to death inside crowded buses.

In January 1996, a Black Tiger—as the suicide elite is called—drove a truck containing 440 pounds of military high explosives into the front of the Central Bank Building, resulting in nearly 1400 casualties. Twenty months later (October 1997) in a more complex operation, Tigers attacked the twin towers of the Colombo World Trade Center at 7 am. They managed to maneuver through barricades to set off a car bomb in front of the Center, then battled the police with automatics and grenades. The following March, a suicide mini-bus with shrapnel-filled bombs affixed to its side boards was detonated outside the main train station in the midst of a huge traffic jam. The 38 dead included a dozen kids in a school bus.

The Tamil Tigers, of course, are a mass nationalist movement with 'liberated territory,' a full-scale army and even a tiny navy; moreover, 20,000 Tiger cadre received secret paramilitary training in Tamil Nadu from 1983 to 1987, courtesy of Indira Gandhi and India's CIA, the Research and Analysis Wing (RAW). But such sponsorship literally blew up in India's face when Indira's son and successor Rajiv was killed by a female Tiger suicide bomber in 1993. Indeed, the all-too-frequent pattern of surrogate terrorism, whether sponsored by the CIA, RAW or the KGB, has been 'return to sender'—most notoriously in the cases of those former CIA 'assets,' blind Sheik Rahman and Osama bin Laden.

The Oklahoma City bombing in April 1995 was a different and startling species of blow-back: organized by two angry U.S. veterans of the Gulf War rather than by Iraq or any Islamist group. Although conspiracy theorists have made much of a strange coincidence that put Terry Nichols and Ramzi Yousef near each other in Cebu City, Philippines in November 1994, the design of the attack seems to have been inspired by Timothy McVeigh's obsession with that devil's cookbook, *The Turner Diaries*. Written in 1978, after Bloody Friday but before Beirut, William Pierce's novel describes with pornographic relish how white supremacists destroy the FBI headquarters in Washington, DC, with an ANFO truck bomb, then later crash a plane carrying a hijacked nuke into the Pentagon. McVeigh carefully followed

Pierce's simple recipe (several tons of ammonium nitrate in a parked truck) rather than Yousef's more complicated WTC formula, although he did substitute nitro racing fuel and diesel oil for ordinary heating oil. Nonetheless, the explosion that slaughtered 168 people in the Alfred Murrah Federal Building on April 19, 1995, was three times more powerful than any of the truck bomb detonations that the ATF and other federal agencies had been studying at their test range in New Mexico. Experts were amazed at the radius of destruction: "equivalent to 4100 pounds of dynamite, the blast damaged 312 buildings, cracked glass as far as two miles away and inflicted 80 percent of its injuries on people outside the building up to a half-mile away." Distant seismographs recorded it as a 6.0 earthquake on the Richter scale.

But McVeigh's good ole boy bomb, with its diabolical demonstration of Heartland DIY ingenuity, was scarcely the last word in destructive power; indeed it was probably inevitable that the dark Olympics of urban carnage would be won by a home team from the Middle East. Although the casualty list (20 dead, 372 wounded) wasn't as long as Oklahoma City's, the huge truck bomb that alleged Hezbollah militants in June 1996 left outside Dhahran's Khobar Towers—a high-rise dormitory used by the U.S. Air Force personnel in Saudi Arabia—broke all records in explosive yield, equivalent perhaps to 20 1,000-pound bombs. Moreover, the death toll might have been as large as the Marine barracks in 1993 save for the alert Air Force sentries who began an evacuation shortly before the explosion. Still, the blast (military-grade plastic explosive) left an incredible crater 85 feet wide and 35 feet deep.

Two years later, 7 August 1998, al-Qa'eda claimed championship in mass murder when it crashed suicide truck bombs into the U.S. embassies in Nairobi and Dar-es-Salaam in a replay of the simultaneous 1983 attacks on the Marines and the French in Beirut. Located near two of the busiest streets in the city without adequate setback or protective *glacis*, the Nairobi embassy was especially vulnerable, as Ambassador Prudence Bushnell had fruitlessly warned the State Department. In the event, ordinary Kenyans—burnt alive in their vehicles, lacerated by flying glass, or buried in smoldering debris—were the principal victims of the huge explosion, which killed several hundred and wounded more than 5,000. Another dozen people died and almost 100 were injured in Dar-es-Salaam where conspirators had managed to conceal explosives in a water truck owned by the embassy.

Sublime indifference to the collateral carnage caused by its devices, including innocent Moslems, remains a hallmark of operations organized by the al-Qa'eda network. Like his forerunners Hermann Goering and Curtis LeMay, Osama bin Laden seems to exult in the sheer statistics of bomb damage—the competitive race to ever greater explosive yields and killing ranges. One of the most lucrative of his recent franchises (in addition to air travel, skyscrapers, and public transport) has been the car bomb attacks on Western tourists in primarily Moslem countries, although the October 2002 attack on a Bali nightclub (202 dead) and the July 2005 bombing of Sharm el-Sheikh hotels (88 dead) almost certainly killed as many local workers as erstwhile 'crusaders.'

Form Follows Fear (1990s)

The car bomb is the nuclear weapon of guerrilla warfare.

Charles Krauthammer

A "billion-pound explosion"? One meaning, of course, is the TNT yield of three or four Hiroshima-size atomic weapons (which is to say, only a smidgen of the explosive power of a single H-bomb). Alternately, one billion pounds ($1.45 billion) is what the IRA cost the City of London in April 1993 when a blue dump-truck containing a ton of ANFO exploded on Bishopsgate Road across from the NatWest Tower in the heart of the world's second major financial center. Although one bystander was killed and more than 30 injured by the immense explosion, which also demolished a mediaeval church and wrecked the Liverpool Street station, the human toll was incidental to the economic damage that was the true goal. Whereas the other truck bomb campaigns of the 1990s—Lima, Bombay, Colombo, and so forth—had followed Hezbollah's playbook almost to the letter, the Bishopsgate bomb, which Moloney describes as "the most successful military tactic since the start of the Troubles," was part of a novel IRA campaign that waged war on financial centers in order to extract British concessions during the difficult peace negotiations that lasted through most of the 1990s.

Bishopsgate, in fact, was the second and most costly of three blockbuster explosions carried out by the elite (and more or less autonomous) South Armagh IRA under the leadership of the legendary 'Slab' Murphy. Almost exactly a year earlier, they had set off a truck bomb at the Baltic Exchange in St. Mary Axe that rained a million pounds of glass and debris on surrounding streets, killing 3 and wounding almost 100 people. The damage, although less than Bishopsgate, was still astonishing: about 800 million pounds or more than the total damage inflicted over 22 years of bombing in Northern Ireland (approximately 600 million). Then in 1996, with peace talks stalled and the IRA Army Council in revolt against the latest cease-fire, the South Armagh Brigade smuggled into England a third huge car bomb that they set off in the underground garage of one of the postmodern office buildings near Canary Wharf Tower in the gentrified London Docklands, killing two and causing nearly $150 million dollars in damage. Total damage from the three explosions was at least $3 billion.

As Jon Coaffee points out, if the IRA—like Tamil Tigers or al-Qa'eda— had simply wanted to sow terror or bring life in London to a halt, they would have set off the explosions at rush-hour on a business day (instead, they "were detonated at a time when the City was virtually deserted") and/or attacked the heart of the transport infrastructure, as did the Islamist suicide bombers who blew up buses and subways in July 2005. Instead, Slab Murphy and his comrades concentrated on what they perceived to be the financial weak link: the faltering British and European insurance industry. To the horror of their enemies, they were spectacularly successful: "The huge payouts by insurance companies," commented the BBC shortly after Bishopsgate, "contributed to a crisis in the industry, including the near-collapse of the world's leading [re]insurance market, Lloyds of London." German and Japanese investors threatened to boycott the City unless physical security was improved and the government agreed to subsidize insurance costs.

Despite a long history of London bombings by the Irish going back to the Fenians and Queen Victoria, neither Downing Street nor the City of London Police had foreseen this scale of accurately targeted physical and financial damage. (Indeed, Slab Murphy himself might have been surprised: like the original ANFO bombs, these super-bombs were probably a wee bit of serendipity for the IRA.) The City's response was a more sophisticated version of the 'ring of steel' (concrete barriers, high iron fences and impregnable gates) that had been built around Belfast's city center after Bloody Friday in 1972. Following Bishopsgate, the financial press clamored for similar protection: "the City should be turned into a medieval-style walled enclave to prevent terrorist attacks." What was actually implemented in the City and later in the Docklands was a technologically more advanced network of traffic restrictions and cordons, CCTV cameras, including "24-hour Automated Number Plate Recording (ANPR) cameras, linked to police databases," and intensified public and private policing. "In the space of a decade," writes Coaffee, "the City of London was transformed into the most surveilled space in the UK and perhaps the world with over 1500 surveillance cameras operating, many of which are linked to the ANPR system."

Since 9/11, this antiterrorist surveillance system has been extended throughout London's core in the benign guise of Mayor Ken Livingstone's celebrated 'congestion pricing' scheme to liberate the city from gridlock. According to one of Britain's major Sunday papers:

The Observer has discovered that MI5, Special Branch and the Metropolitan Police began secretly developing the system in the wake of the September 11 attacks. In effect, the controversial charging scheme will create one of the most daunting defence systems protecting a major world city when it goes live a week tomorrow. It is understood that the system also utilizes facial recognition software which automatically identifies suspects or known criminals who enter the eight-square-mile zone. Their precise movements will be tracked by camera from the point of entry. ... However, civil liberty campaigners yesterday claimed that millions had been misled over the dual function of the scheme, promoted primarily as a means of reducing congestion in central London.

The addition in 2003 of this new Panoptican traffic scan to London's already extensive system of video surveillance ensures that the average citizen is "caught on CCTV cameras 300 times a day," and it may make it easier for the police to apprehend nonsuicidal terrorists, but it does little to protect the city from well-planned and competently disguised vehicle bomb attacks. Blair's 'Third Way' has been a fast lane for the adoption of Orwellian surveillance and the usurpation of civil liberties, but until some miracle technology emerges (and none is in sight) that allows authorities from a distance to 'sniff' a molecule or two of explosive in a stream of rush-hour traffic, the car bombers will continue to commute to work.

The 'King' of Iraq (2000s)

Insurgents exploded 13 car bombs across Iraq on Sunday, including eight in Baghdad within a three-hour span.

news report

Almost daily for three years, car bombs driven or left by sectarian *jihadists* have slaughtered Iraqi Shiites in front of their homes, mosques, police stations, and markets: 125 dead in Hilla (February 28, 2005); 98 in Mussayib (July 16); 114 in Baghdad (September 14); 102 in Blad (September 29); 50 in Abu Sayda (November 19); and so on.

Some of the devices have been gigantic, like the stolen fuel truck bomb that devastated Mussayib, but what is most extraordinary has been their sheer frequency—in one 48-hour-period in July 2005 at least 15 suicide car bombs exploded in or around Baghdad. The sinister figure supposedly behind the worst of these massacres is Abu Musab al-Zarqawi, the Jordanian arch-terrorist who reportedly criticized Osama bin Laden for insufficient zeal in attacking domestic enemies like the 'infidel Shias.'

Al-Zarqawi, it is claimed, is pursuing an essentially eschatological rather than political goal: a cleansing of enemies without end until earth is ruled by a single, righteous caliphate.

Toward this end, he seems to have access to an almost limitless supply of bomb vehicles (some of them apparently stolen in California and Texas, then shipped to the Middle East) as well as Saudi volunteers eager to martyr themselves in flame and molten metal for the sake of taking a few Shiite school kids or market vendors with them. Indeed, the supply of suicidal *madrassa* graduates seems to far exceed what the logic of suicide bombing (as perfected by Hezbollah and the Tamil Tigers) actually demands: many of the explosions could just as easily be detonated by remote control. But the car bomb—at least in Al-Zarqawi's relentless vision—is a stairway to heaven as well as the chosen weapon of genocide.

But Al Zarqawi did not originate car bomb terrorism along the banks of the Tigris and Euphrates; that dark honor belongs rather to the CIA and its favorite son, Iyad Allawi. As the *New York Times* revealed in June 2004:

> Iyad Allawi, now the designated prime minister of Iraq, ran an exile organization intent on deposing Saddam Hussein that sent agents into Baghdad in the early 1990s to plant bombs and sabotage government facilities under the direction of the CIA, several former intelligence officials say. Dr. Allawi's group, the Iraqi National Accord, used car bombs and other explosives devices smuggled into Baghdad from northern Iraq. … One former Central Intelligence Agency officer who was based in the region, Robert Baer, recalled that a bombing during that period "blew up a school bus; schoolchildren were killed."

According to one of the *Times'* informants, the bombing campaign, dead school kids and all, "was a test more than anything else, to demonstrate capability," allowing the CIA to portray Allawi and his suspect group of ex-Baathists as a serious opposition to Sadaam and an alternative to the coterie (so favored by Washington neo-conservatives) around Ahmad Chalabi. "No one had any problem with sabotage in Baghdad back then," another CIA veteran reflected. "I don't think anyone could have known how things would turn out today."

Today, of course, car bombs rule Iraq. In a June 2005 article titled "Why the Car Bomb Is King in Iraq," James Dunnigan warned that the car bomb was supplanting the roadside bomb (which "are more frequently discovered, or defeated with electronic devices") as the "most effective weapon" of Sunni insurgents as well as of Al Zarqawi, and thus "the terrorists are building as many as they can." The recent "explosive growth" in car ownership in Iraq, he added, had made it "easier for the car bombs to just get lost in traffic." Some 500 car bombs (a total that includes duds and vehicles intercepted by authorities) had killed or wounded more than 9,000 people, with 143 car bomb attacks in May 2005 alone.

In this kingdom of the car bomb, the occupiers have withdrawn almost completely into their own forbidden city, the 'Green Zone.' This is not the high-tech City of London with sensors taking the place of snipers, but a totally mediaevalized enclave surrounded by concrete walls and defended by M1 Abrams tanks and helicopter gunships as well as an exotic corps of corporate mercenaries (including Gurkhas, ex-Rhodesian commandoes, former British SAS, and amnestied Colombian paramilitaries). Once the Xanadu of the Baathist ruling class, the 10-square-kilometer Green Zone, as described by Scott Johnson, is now a surreal theme park of the American way of life:

> Women in shorts and T-shirts jog down broad avenues and the Pizza Inn does a brisk business from the parking lot of the heavily fortified U.S. Embassy. Near the Green Zone Bazaar, Iraqi kids hawk pornographic DVDs to soldiers. Sheik Fuad Rashid, the U.S.-appointed iman of the local mosque, dresses like a nun, dyes his hair platinum blond and claims that Mary Mother of Jesus appeared to him in a vision (hence the getup). On any given night, residents can listen to karaoke, play badminton or frequent one of several rowdy bars, including an invitation-only speakeasy run by the CIA.

Outside the Green Zone, of course, is the 'Red Zone,' where ordinary Iraqis can be randomly and unexpectedly blown to bits by car bombers or strafed by American helicopters. Not surprisingly, wealthy Iraqis and members of the new government are clamoring for admission into the security of the Green Zone, but U.S. officials told *Newsweek* last year that "plans to move the Americans out are 'fantasy.'" Billions have been invested in the Green Zone and a dozen other American enclaves officially known as 'Enduring Camps,' and even prominent Iraqis have been left to forage for their own security outside the blast walls of these exclusive bubble Americas. A population that has endured Sadaam's secret police, UN sanctions, and American cruise missiles now steels itself to survive the car bombers who prowl poor Shiite neighborhoods looking for grisly martyrdom. For the most selfish reasons, let us hope that Baghdad is not a metaphor for our collective future.

Contributors

Trevor Boddy

Vancouver-based critic and curator Trevor Boddy currently writes a column on architecture and cities for the *Globe* and *Mail*, and previously for *The Vancouver Sun, Seattle Times* and *Ottawa Citizen*. He is a regular contributor to the *Canadian Architect, Architectural Review* and *Architectural Record*, plus international design magazines published in German, French, Spanish, Portuguese, Japanese, and Arabic. He has taught architecture design studio, history, and urbanism at universities across North America, and lectures globally on contemporary design and city-building. Trevor Boddy's independent critical monograph *The Architecture of Douglas Cardinal* was named "Alberta Book of the Year" and short-listed for the International Union of Architects prize for best book of architectural criticism published worldwide, and he was an essayist in Sorkin's previous collection *Variations on a Theme Park: The New American City and the End of Public Space*. A contributing editor to Seattle's *Arcade* and Toronto's *Canadian Architect* magazines, his architectural criticism has earned the 2001 Western Magazine Award for arts writing, and Boddy was named co-winner of the 2003 Jack Webster Journalism Award for civic reporting. His exhibition "Telling Details: The Architecture of Clifford Wiens" is currently touring nationally, and he recently curated the exhibition-as-event "A Dialogue of Cities," a global gathering of architecture critics.

M. Christine Boyer

M. Christine Boyer is the William R. Kenan Jr. Professor of Architecture and Urbanism at the School of Architecture, Princeton University. She is the author of *CyberCities: Visual Perception in the Age of Electronic Communication* (Princeton Architectural Press, 1996), *The City of Collective Memory: Its Historical Imagery and Architectural Entertainments* (MIT Press, 1994), *Dreaming the Rational City: The Myth of City Planning 1890–1945* (MIT Press, 1983), and *Manhattan Manners: Architecture and Style 1850–1890* (Rizzoli, 1985). In addition, she has written many articles and lectured widely on the topic of urbanism in the nineteenth and twentieth centuries. She is currently writing a book on Le Corbusier's writings entitled *Le Corbusier: Homme de Lettre;* a series of collected essays entitled *Twice-Told Stories: City and Cinema;* and a series of essays on contemporary urbanism entitled *Back to the Future: The City of To-tomorrow.*

M. Christine Boyer received her Ph.D. and Master's in City Planning from the Massachusetts Institute of Technology. She also holds a Master of Science in Computer and Information Science from the University of Pennsylvania, The Moore School of Electrical Engineering.

Teddy Cruz

Teddy Cruz's work dwells at the border between San Diego, California, and Tijuana, Mexico, where he has been developing a practice and pedagogy that emerge out of the particularities of this bicultural territory and the integration of theoretical research and design production. Teddy Cruz has been recognized internationally in collaboration with community-based nonprofit organizations such as Casa Familiar for its work on housing and its relationship to an urban policy more inclusive of social and cultural programs for the city. He obtained a Master's in Design Studies from Harvard University and the Rome Prize in Architecture from the American Academy in Rome. He has recently received the 2004–2005 James Stirling Memorial Lecture On The City Prize and is currently an associate professor in public culture and urbanism in the Visual Arts Department at UCSD in San Diego.

Mike Davis

Mike Davis tends his children in San Diego and writes books—most recently, *Planet of Slums* (Verso, 2006) and *Evil Paradists* (The New Press, 2007), edited with Daniel Monk. He is a longtime member of the editorial collective of the *New Left Review.*

Steven Flusty

Steven Flusty is an assistant professor of geography at York University in Toronto, Canada. His focal interest is the everyday practices of global formation, a topic he has interrogated most ruthlessly in *De-Coca-Colonization: Making the Globe from the Inside Out* (Routledge, 2004). His work has appeared in assorted electronic media and a selection of academic, professional and popular journals of varying degrees of repute. Dr. Flusty also practices as an architectural and urban design consultant, in which capacity he has visited his own sensibilities upon the unsuspecting cities of three continents.

Mark L. Gillem

Mark L. Gillem, PhD, AIA, AICP, is an Assistant Professor in the Departments of Architecture and Landscape Architecture at the University of Oregon and principal of The Urban Collaborative. He has prepared award-winning master plans and architectural designs for clients worldwide. He is also the author of *America Town: Building the Outposts of Empire* (2007).

Ruth Wilson Gilmore

Ruth Wilson Gilmore chairs the American Studies & Ethnicity Department at the University of Southern California. Her recent publications include *Golden Gulag: Prisons, Surplus, Crisis, and Opposition in Globalizing California* (University of California Press) and "In the Shadow of the Shadow State" (Incite! eds., *The Revolution Will Not Be Funded*). She is a founding member of the California Prison Moratorium Project, Critical Resistance, and the Central California Environmental Justice Network.

Craig Gilmore

Craig Gilmore has recently published essays in *Globalize Liberation* (City Lights) and *Radical History Review*. He is coauthor of the Real Cost of Prisons comic book *Prison Town* (download free at http://realcostofprisons. org/comics.html).

Stephen Graham

Stephen Graham is Professor of Human Geography at Durham University in the United Kingdom. He has a background in urbanism, planning, and the sociology of technology. His research addresses the complex intersections between urban places, mobilities, technology, war, surveillance, and geopolitics. His books include *Telecommunications and the City, Splintering Urbanism, The Cybercities Reader,* and *Cities, War and Terrorism*. He is currently writing a book on military urbanism.

Kathi Holt-Damant

Dr. Kathi Holt-Damant is a researcher, teacher, and practitioner of architecture and urban design at the University of Queensland. Specializing in constructs of space in architecture and cinema, Holt-Damant has lectured and taught at the University of Melbourne, Deakin University, RMIT University and been an invited studio critic at Columbia University (NY) and SciArc (LA). Current research includes the Emerging Futures Project funded by the Australian Research Council and industry partners: Queensland Rail and Queensland Transport. This collaborative project focuses on the complex spatial relationships between public transportation, transit-oriented development, environmental sustainability, security, and open space systems. Multimedia applications and cinematic editing are employed to offer new insights into working with existing urban conditions. Similar techniques were first explored in a theoretical studio project with Thomas Leeser (Columbia University, NY) entitled: '*the architecture of navigation II & III,*' later exhibited as a trilogy of installations at the Melbourne Festival in 1998 and published under their editorship by RMIT Publishers in 2001.

Cindi Katz

Cindi Katz, a geographer, teaches at the Graduate Center of The City University of New York. Her work concerns social reproduction and the production of space, place and nature; children and the environment; and the consequences of global economic restructuring for everyday life. She has published widely on these themes as well as on social theory and the politics of knowledge in edited collections and in journals such as *Society and Space, Social Text, Signs, Feminist Studies, Annals of the Association of American Geographers, Transactions of the Institute of British Geographers, Social Justice,* and *Antipode*. She is the editor (with Nancy K. Miller) of *WSQ (Women's Studies Quarterly)*. Katz is the editor (with Janice Monk) of *Full Circles: Geographies of Gender over the Life Course* (Routledge, 1993) and of *Life's Work: Geographies of Social Reproduction* (with Sallie Marston and Katharyne Mitchell) (Blackwell, 2004). Her 2004 book, *Growing up Global: Economic Restructuring and Children's Everyday Lives* (University of Minnesota Press), received the Meridian Award for outstanding scholarly work in geography from the Association of American Geographers. In 2003–2004, Katz was a fellow at the Radcliffe Institute for Advanced Study at Harvard University where she began her current project concerning the shifting geographies of late-twentieth-century U.S. childhood.

Laura Y. Liu

Laura Y. Liu is Assistant Professor of Urban Studies at Eugene Lang College of The New School. Her research interests include community organizing and urban social justice; migration and work; and race, gender, and labor politics. She is writing a book tentatively called *Sweatshop City* which looks at identity, space, and political strategy in community organizing within Chinatown and other immigrant communities in the New York City area. She has published in *Gender, Place and Culture; Social and Cultural Geography;* and *Urban Geography.*

Setha M. Low

Setha Low received her Ph.D. in Cultural Anthropology from the University of California, Berkeley. She started her career as an Assistant and Associate Professor of Landscape Architecture and Regional Planning, City and Regional Planning, and Anthropology at the University of Pennsylvania. Dr. Low is currently Professor of Environmental Psychology and Anthropology, and Director of the Public Space Research Group at The Graduate Center, City University of New York, where she teaches courses and trains Ph.D. students in the anthropology of space and place, urban anthropology, landscapes of fear, and cultural values in historic preservation. She has been awarded a Getty Fellowship, a NEH fellowship, and a Guggenheim for her work on values and the cultural landscape, and was elected president of the American Anthropological Association for 2007–2009. She is widely published and lectures internationally on these issues. Her most recent books include: *Rethinking Urban Parks: Public Space and Cultural Diversity* (2005, University of Texas Press), *Politics of Public Space* (2005, Routledge, edited with Neil Smith), *Behind the Gates: Life, Security and the Pursuit of Happiness in Fortress America* (2003, Routledge), *On the Plaza: The Politics of Public Space* (2000, University of Texas), *Theorizing the City* (1999, Rutgers University Press), *The Anthropology of Space and Place: Locating Culture* (2003, Blackwell, edited with Denise Zuniga), and *Place Attachment* (1992, Plenum, edited with Erve Chambers).

Dean MacCannell

Dean MacCannell is Professor of Environmental Design and Landscape Architecture at the University of California, Davis. He is author of *The Tourist: A New Theory of the Leisure Class* (1976/1999), *Empty Meeting Grounds* (1992), and over 80 articles and monographs on cultural analysis and criticism. His work on tourism is featured in the BBC miniseries *The Tourist*, 1996. His current book projects are *The Ethics of Tourism* and *Design's Diaspora*.

AbdouMaliq Simone

AbdouMaliq Simone is an urbanist with particular interest in emerging forms of social and economic intersection across diverse trajectories of change for cities in the Global South. Simone is presently Professor of Sociology at Goldsmiths College, University of London and Visiting Professor of Urban Studies at the Wits Institute for Social and Economic Research, University of Witwatersrand. His work attempts to generate new theoretical understandings based on a wide range of urban practices generated by cities in Africa, the Middle East and Southeast Asia, as well as efforts to integrate these understandings in concrete policy and governance frameworks. Key publications include *In Whose Image: Political Islam and Urban Practices in Sudan* (University of Chicago Press, 1994) and *For the City Yet to Come: Urban Change in Four African Cities* (Duke University Press, 2004).

Michael Sorkin

Michael Sorkin is founding President of Terreform, a non-profit organization dedicated to research and intervention in issues of urban morphology, environment, equity, architectural design, and community planning. His current work includes a project to examine the limits of self-sufficiency within New York City, a study of sustainable urban transport systems, and planning and design projects in China, Anguilla, India, Turkey and the United States. As principal of the Michael Sorkin Studio (now merged with Terreform) for over 25 years, Sorkin has authored numerous architectural and urban projects around the world.

Sorkin is Professor of Architecture and the Director of the Graduate Urban Design Program at the City College of New York. His books include *Variations on a Theme Park*, *Exquisite Corpse*, *Local Code*, *Giving Ground* (edited with Joan Copjec), *Wiggle* (a monograph of design work), *Some Assembly Required*, *Other Plans*, *The Next Jerusalem*, *After The Trade*

Center (edited with Sharon Zukin), *Starting from Zero, Analyzing Ambasz,* and *Against the Wall.* Forthcoming are *Twenty Minutes in Manhattan, Eutopia,* and *All over the Map.*

Eyal Weizman

Eyal Weizman is an architect and director of the Centre for Research Architecture at Goldsmiths College, University of London. His recent book *Hollow Land* was published by Verso Press in 2007.

Index